THE UNRAVELING HEART

The Unraveling Heart

WOMEN'S ORAL POETICS AND LITERARY VERNACULARIZATION IN MARATHI

Madhuri Deshmukh

Columbia University Press
New York

Columbia University Press
Publishers Since 1893
New York Chichester, West Sussex

Library of Congress Cataloging-in-Publication Data
Names: Deshmukh, Madhuri author
Title: The unraveling heart : Women's Oral Poetics and Literary Vernacularization in Marathi / Madhuri Deshmukh.
Description: New York : Columbia University Press, 2026. |
Includes bibliographical references and index.
Identifiers: LCCN 2025021596 (print) | LCCN 2025021597 (ebook) |
ISBN 9780231217934 hardback | ISBN 9780231217927 trade paperback |
ISBN 9780231561976 ebook
Subjects: LCSH: Devotional poetry, Marathi—History and criticism |
Marathi poetry—Women authors—History and criticism | Oral tradition in literature |
Oral tradition—India—History | LCGFT: Literary criticism
Classification: LCC PK2410 .D398 2026 (print) | LCC PK2410 (ebook)

Cover design: Noah Arlow
Cover image: Grind mill belonging to Janabai Thorat. Photo by author.

GPSR Authorized Representative: Easy Access System Europe, Mustamäe tee 50, 10621 Tallinn, Estonia, gpsr.requests@easproject.com

For Baba
Hanumant G. Deshmukh (1942–2004)
In remembrance

पाहा पां मातें तुम्हां सांगडें । माहेर तेणें सुरवाडें ।
ग्रंथाचें आळियाडें । सिद्धी गेलें ॥
—*Jnaneshvar*

Contents

Acknowledgments ix
Note on Transliteration xv

Introduction and Underview: In the Footsteps of Janabai 1

1 The Unraveling Heart: A Poetics of the Grind Mill 39

2 Colloquial Turns: Unraveling Vernacular Beginnings 88

3 The *Ovī*: A Poetics of Work in the Work of Poetics 121

4 *Bhakti* as Poiesis: A Dialogue in Verse 157

5 Women and Vernacularization: The Founding Poetics of Mahadaise and Janabai 200

Postscript: Contra Conclusions 244

Notes 255
Bibliography 305
Index 323

Acknowledgments

The Unraveling Heart went through numerous iterations before publication; in the process of research and writing it I gathered sustenance from so many scholars, authors, poets, singers, artists, teachers, friends, colleagues, and students that I could not possibly acknowledge them all here. I want to begin with profuse thanks to Wendy Lochner, editor at Columbia University Press, for her encouragement and guidance in finally bringing this book to completion. I am also grateful for the feedback of the peer reviewers and the CUP editorial board, which made the book better than when I first proposed it. My thanks also go to the talented design and copyediting staff at CUP.

I have been teaching over the duration of this long-simmering project at Oakton College, which supported me with the travel funds, sabbaticals, and leaves of absence that made it possible to do research, present at conferences, and to write. I am grateful for two American Institute of Indian Studies (AIIS) grants, a Junior Fellowship during 2005 and 2006 and a Senior NEH-funded Fellowship in 2023, which bookend the time it took for this book to move from dim aspiration to reality. The seeds were planted even earlier in an AIIS summer Marathi course in Pune in 2003. I had learned to read Marathi from my mother as a child, but I lost much of it over the years of my American schooling. Reading with Varada Khaladkar and Manjiri Bhalerao at AIIS Pune introduced me to a new world of Marathi literature. When I returned to Chicago, Philip Engblom, then teaching Marathi at the University of Chicago, generously met with me two days a week to read Marathi literature. Philip introduced me to a new way of reading poetry with a deep attentiveness to detail and specificity. Thank you, Philip, for teaching me about Marathi poetics and for your feedback on drafts of this book. Later, in India, I was fortunate to read and learn Marathi with Sucheta Paranjape, whose profound knowledge brought numerous literary works to life for me.

It was during the precious summer months in the AIIS language program that I met Lee Schlesinger, Lisa Klopfer, Anne Feldhaus, and Christian Novetzke, all of whom would remain important interlocutors over the years. Lee is no longer with us, but his uncompromising intellectual integrity lives as a voice in my mind. Lee, how I wish you were here to see this book published! Christian was working on his first book on Namdev that summer, and I was beginning my study of Janabai. Our interests have overlapped ever since. Christian, your exceptional scholarship, warmth, and generous feedback over the years, and especially on this book, have been invaluable.

That same summer, during a ride back from Deccan College to the city, Anne Feldhaus raised the question of where the word *ovī* might come from. A lively discussion ensued among the group in her car. It was the first time I had heard the question, and it stuck with me; I have spent the better part of two decades and this book trying to answer it. Anne's extraordinary command of Old Marathi and Marathi grammar, and the integrity of her research in India, are an inspiration. I would not have embarked on my own research in India without her scholarly example and could not have completed this book without her friendship and her generous comments on drafts at various stages. During Covid, Lee brought Anne, Philip, and me together to read and translate the *Jñāneśvarī* weekly over Zoom. Sadly, we lost Lee along the way, but working through this text with these scholars has been a remarkable and generative learning experience that undergirded the writing of the book.

I want to thank the larger community of scholars in the Maharashtra Studies Group. I have presented aspects of this book at several conferences of this group. The conference topics and the intense, serious discussions there sparked many insights that found their way into this book.

Accessing texts was always a bit of a challenge for me at a community college, and I must acknowledge the Oakton library staff, especially

Gretchen Schneider, Ruth Whitney, and Nicolas Klein, for helping me procure all kinds of texts. Lee Schlesinger retrieved several important texts when the Hathi Trust opened up its archives during Covid. Thank you to Jon Keune, Polly O'Hanlon, and Anne Feldhaus for sharing texts along the way. My thanks go to Digvijay Patil, who helped me catalogue and find many works of Marathi folk scholarship, and to Mohan Babhulgavkar for helping me find Mahanubhava texts, and for sharing his insights into the Mahanubhava textual and folk traditions. He introduced me to Mangala Pathade, who graciously shared her thesis on Mahanubhava women's grind mill songs and discussed them with me. I must acknowledge Dr. Deenanath Phulwadkar, who shared the publications of the Janabai Educational Foundation when I visited Gangakhed. V. L. Manjul has been very helpful over the years, and I am grateful for his insights and help in finding manuscripts and books and for introducing me to the eminent R. C. Dhere, whose advice early in my research on Janabai was pivotal.

I thank Prem Kandwal for scanning at his own expense the images of the postcards and paintings of M. V. Dhurandhar (1867–1944) (figures 1.1–1.9 and figure 5.1) from his collection at Amar Prem Lithos. Saurabh Dusane helped me track down the artist, Raghuvir Mulgaonkar (1918–1976), who painted the famous and widely circulated painting of Janabai included in the introduction (figure i.2). I also thank my colleague Erick Rohn, graphic arts professor, for the digital re-creation of an image from M. T. Patwardhan's 1937 book *Chandoracanā* included in chapter 1. Parts of chapter 5 were published in an earlier form in "Janabai's Hariścandra Ākhyāna in Marathi Literature" in Arzuman Ara and Surajit Sen, eds., *Indian Narrative Traditions: Text, Performance and Interpretation: Essays in Honour of Professor Kailash C. Baral* (New Delhi: Pencraft International, 2021), 25-47. I thank the editors for permission to use and develop further some of the material presented in it.

I reached out to numerous scholars by email, and I want to thank the following people for their willingness to engage my questions about texts that were not in Marathi, though all the final decisions (and any errors) in translation and interpretation are my own: Kamalakar Bhatt, Charles Hallisey, Gil Ben Herut, Keshavchaitanya Kunte, Andrew Ollett, Hemant Rajopadhaye, Ajay Rao, Adheesh Sathaye, T. S. Satyanath, and Sunil Sharma. Manan Ahmed Asif's encouragement over the years and his help in the final stages has meant the world to me. Sujata Mahajan, thank you for reading parts of Narendra's *Rukmiṇī Svayaṃvar* with me. Thank you to Paul Jay and Holly Graff for your feedback on drafts of chapters in this book. Holly, thank you for your moral support when I had to make hard choices to make time to write. I thank Jack Hawley and Shraddha Kumbhojkar for their warm encouragement and their comments on the final draft.

I am indebted to The Grindmill Songs Project (GSP), now under the auspices of the People's Archive of Rural India (PARI), for digitizing and translating the foundational corpus of songs collected by Hema Rairkar, Guy Poitevin, Bernard Bel, and others affiliated with the Center for Cooperative Research in the Social Sciences. Long before I learned of the GSP project, I was recording songs myself, but it was this massive digital collection that helped me to gain perspective on the songs *as an archive*, and that, too, with a searchable database. My special thanks go to Namita Waikar, managing editor of PARI, for all her help and insight into the songs and for her moving articles on the grind mill singers.

I have deep gratitude and admiration for Tara Bhavalkar, who spoke to me at length over the phone and whose knowledge of and scholarship on women's grind mill songs is unsurpassed and integral to my own project. My thanks also go to Rajaram Zagade for transcribing hundreds of grind mill songs that I collected in the first years of my research.

There is no substitute for listening to the songs sung by women themselves at their grind mills, which I had the good fortune to experience because of tireless help from my maternal uncle, Ravishankar Deshpande. He took me, sometimes by motorcycle, sometimes by rented car, to more than a dozen villages throughout the Parbhani, Hingoli, and Nanded districts and did everything he could to ensure I had what I needed. My aunts, Vidya Mami and Jayanti Maushi, helped me to communicate when my Marathi failed me. My cousins Sunetra, Ashwini, Kalyani, and Malhar, accompanied me to many destinations, taking notes, videos, and photos as we scoured the area in search of women singers. My cousin Ruturaj has helped me in countless ways, from discussing poetry to all the minute logistics of being in India. My other maternal uncle and aunt, Sadanand and Urmila Deshpande, as well as the staff at AIIS Pune, in particular Anil Inamdar, provided important support for my stays in Pune.

My deepest gratitude is reserved for the women who shared their songs with me. I found a warmth and generosity in them that is becoming ever rarer in our increasingly transactional world. I am particularly grateful to the women of Waghi, Marsul, Kathoda Tanda, Gawaliwadi, Golegaon, and Shirad Shahapur. I wish I could acknowledge by name all the many dozens of women who shared their songs over the years, but I must at least mention Janabai Thorat, Chandrakalabai Jogdand, and Lakshmibai Gavale for what they taught me.

The work of this book was always in my father's memory. Each stage of it brought me closer to understanding, sadly belatedly, his love of Marathi poetry and his reverence for Marathi folk culture. After I returned from the AIIS language program, I read Marathi daily with him; I did not know that these would be the last six months I had with him before his passing. He never tired of sitting with me as I stumbled over words until I finally gained a modicum of fluency. The last book we read together, Sane Guruji's *Śyāmcī Āī* (*Shyam's Mother*), was formative for this project. It is my own *āī*, Madhumati Deshmukh, I must credit for teaching me Marathi in the first place. Without her support I could not have found the time, between parenting and working, to write, read, and think. Finally, a word for my son Dhruv: your birth gave me new eyes on all the material I had been collecting for years. Your love of life, your curiosity, your questions, and your many new discoveries taught me just how complex, philosophical, poetic, and enchanting "everyday life" can be, something the singers at the grind mill knew well and shared with us in their songs.

Note on Transliteration

I have mostly followed the style guidelines on transliteration provided by Columbia University Press. I do not use diacritics or italics for proper names or for words that have a familiar anglicized form, such as "dharma." I have rendered the Marathi *c* as *ch*, as in **Ch**akradhar, and *ś* as *sh*, as in Mukte**sh**var, except when both consonants are together as in Hari**sch**andra. In transliterated titles and words, however, *ch* corresponds to the छ character, as used for example in the word *chanda*. The *Jña* (ज्ञ) character (pronounced *dnya* in English) is rendered simply as Jn in Jnaneshvar but with diacritics for the title *Jñāneśvarī*. All titles of works and single Marathi words are romanized with diacritics following the conventions for transliteration of *devanāgarī*. I have, however, omitted the final silent *a* in keeping with Marathi pronunciation, except when the *a* is not actually silent. I have also mostly omitted the *a* in the middle of names when it is not pronounced: for example, Namdev not Namadev, Nagdev not Nagadeva. In addition, I use the nasal character that corresponds to the consonant that follows it in Marathi words where a nasal inflection is indicated by an *anusvār* (a dot) over the consonant. To render non-nasal (or lightly nasal) *anusvārs*, common in Marathi orthography, I use *ṃ*. In quoted passages, I retain the diacritics of the original sources, even if they follow older styles. In transliterating songs, I use colloquial and regional words and spellings as they appear in my own or in written transcriptions from various sources.

THE UNRAVELING HEART

Introduction and Underview

In the Footsteps of Janabai

> The absent and the invisible have to be taken as parties in the construction of the literary cultures in South Asia.
>
> —D. R. NAGARAJ, "CRITICAL TENSIONS IN THE HISTORY OF KANNADA LITERARY CULTURE"

The Unraveling Heart began as a project on one poet-figure named Janabai, believed to have lived as a poor, orphaned *dāsī* (servant or slave) in the late thirteenth and early fourteenth centuries. Motivated in part by my personal connection to the region of Janabai's purported birth, this study was meant to address the dearth of English-language scholarship on women poets between the thirteenth and seventeenth centuries in what is now the modern state of Maharashtra.[1] In time, however, it became clear that Janabai had other plans for me. In raising the kinds of questions she did, she led the project away from its exclusive focus on her. The first nudge came from her name. While *bāī* is a common respectful form of address for a woman, *Janā* means something like "the people" or "the born." As a "woman of the people," she is meant to be a poetic figure of the many, not the one rising above all others to be placed in a literary pantheon of the select few. Her very name, the poems attributed to her, and her life story suggest that, though significant, Janabai's poetic voice may not have been all that "rare" or "extraordinary" or "superordinate," qualities often associated with the ideas of "poetry" and the "literary." More importantly, none of this diminished her importance but instead made it more poignant.

The more I searched for all things related to Janabai, the more she brought into view a wider poetic world to which she was, figured as a kinless and casteless domestic worker and poet, always both exile and participant. By "wider poetic world" I do not mean merely the context in which her poems were composed, or the historical background, or her place among other poets. Rather I mean that Janabai—and as she makes clear, other poets, too—are deeply embedded in a vast and often subterranean poetic intertext, an ongoing conversation in verse going back centuries that is at once both oral and written. Janabai brings into textual focus the poetic significance of one of the oldest, longest continuing oral traditions on the subcontinent: the grind mill song tradition. To extract her from this conversation, I realized at some point, would be like removing a tree from an old growth forest.

Many readers might not be familiar with the grind mill, a stone hand mill with a stationary stone base and a rotating top base (see figure i.1). Wheat, millet, rice, or lentils are poured through an opening at the top so that they fall between the two stones. A handle, usually made of wood, needs to be rotated by hand so that the heavy top stone grates against the base to pulverize the grains between the two parts. Flour spills out from the sides, and it is collected at the end of a grinding session. Archeological evidence shows that grinding, either on a rotating stone mill like the one I describe here, or using mortar and pestle or other kinds of household querns, was a daily, compulsory, household labor on the subcontinent for millennia.[2] It has, for the most part and as far as we know, been women who did this work, sometimes alone and sometimes in pairs or groups, passing the wooden handle from one to the other. As they made flour for daily bread, they also created what may very well be the oldest continuous song tradition on the subcontinent. These are the songs of the grind mill, sometimes also called pestle songs depending on the grinding instrument. There is no reason to doubt that the song tradition is as old as the labor itself. Such songs exist in numerous languages throughout the subcontinent, indeed throughout the world. In Marathi, the primary language spoken in the region that forms the modern state of Maharashtra, the songs are called *ovīs*.

Grinding is an ancient household labor attested in literature as early as the Vedas (ca. 1500–1000 BCE).[3] But in India it was a labor that continued as a fact of women's everyday lives until the last decades of the twentieth century, when the electric flour mill replaced the household hand mill. That the daily labor of the stone mill, and the song tradition that arose from it, continued well into the twentieth century means that we have a substantial oral archive collected by folklorists, anthropologists, and poets.

Figure i.1 Grind mill belonging to Janabai Thorat of Bhendegaon Village in the Hingoli district of Maharashtra.
Photo by author

Surprisingly, the arrival of the electric mill is itself the subject of the songs of the grind mill. While the electric mill was introduced in the early to mid-twentieth century, it would be decades before it reached into the interior rural areas, and the changes it wrought are captured in the song archive itself. Here is one verse, out of many on the various technological innovations of the twentieth century, like tractors and electricity:

Mother-in-law, Auntie,
You died grinding and grinding
In the society of our times,
Flour mills with buttons have arrived!

sāsu ātyābāī tumhī daḷu daḷu melyā
āmacyā rājyāmandī giraṇyā baṭancyā ālyā[4]

Whereas the older generation was burdened with the hard labor of the grind mill, the new generation touts the machine that does the work at the touch of a button. This *ovī* is addressed to the women who would have been oppressors in household power dynamics, the mother-in-law and the paternal aunt (*ātyābāī*) who can no longer lord their power over the daughters-in-law. This verse, a tongue-in-cheek banter between women, is one of a number of humorous and ironic songs that depict the mother-in-law hard at work, while the daughter-in-law, freed from the grind mill, sits back leisurely preparing her chewing tobacco.[5] Variations of this verse circulated widely enough to have been collected from twenty different villages across several districts in Maharashtra. The verses show a deep awareness of history and change inflected by humor and irony and should put to rest both the dismissal and the romanticized idealization of the songs as "timeless" expressions of a premodern "folk."

Janabai is often described as singing *ovīs* at a grind mill, and many of her poems, both in their formal features and in their motifs, themes, tones, and imagery, evoke these songs. One of the most iconic, popular images of Janabai features her grinding at a stone mill with her beloved god Vitthal to help her in her lonely task. The image is revered in Maharashtra even today, where grind mill songs are still well known. Many women of the older generations, especially those living in the villages, remember singing them on a daily basis, or they remember their mothers or grandmothers singing them. Janabai is thus connected to all these unknown millions of women who toiled at the stone mill, composing and singing their remarkable *ovīs* in the early dawn hours, women considered by various elite regimes of writing and literarity that developed over millennia to be far and different from the sequestered heights of poetry. That I ended up in the villages with these women recording their songs was not part of a well-thought-out research plan. All that I had intended to do was study how the poet Janabai was remembered and understood by a tradition with which she is so closely associated. In retrospect, it seems obvious that Janabai herself, true to her name, led me to these women.

Looking for Janabai

Janabai is believed to have been part of the first generation of *bhakti* poets to gather around the complex and beloved god Vitthal, whose temple in the city of Pandharpur in western Maharashtra is still the destination of a famous biannual pilgrimage of millions. This pilgrimage is known as a *vāri*, and the term Varkari likely arose from it to describe the sect of Vitthal devotees. Loosely defined, *bhakti* signifies an experience of intense belonging to a divine figure or an elevated mortal being. In this study I show that *bhakti* is not merely a feeling, experience, or even ontological condition; it is a way of making, a poiesis, hence the staggering volumes of song and poetry, much of it centered on analogies of labor and generated to articulate and create experiences of belonging in everyday life. The deity Vitthal is the singular focus of a profuse corpus of *bhakti* poetry composed in Maharashtra between the late thirteenth and seventeenth centuries by poets of every class, caste, and gender, worshipped even today as moral exemplars, or *sants*.

As with the names of other *bhakti* poets all over the subcontinent, Janabai's name does not refer to only one historically situated, individual poet. Just this fact alone widens the concept of both poetry and poet to include orality. Many scholars have written brilliantly about the unique conceptions of authorship at work in *bhakti* poetry, the way that an author is never a singular historical individual but is "corporate" or "composite" or "anamnetic."[6] There were likely many poets who used the signature line of Janabai, just as there were likely several who used the name Namdev. Yet I prefer the term figural poet to "composite" or "collective" because the poet is, in all instances, understood to be a singular figure, not really a

Figure i.2 Famous painting by Raghuvir Mulgaonkar (1918–1976), likely created for a 1950s Diwali issue of a Marathi periodical. The model for Janabai appears to be the actress Hansa Wadkar, who played the title role in the 1949 Prabhat Talkies film, *Sant Janābāī*. This painting was used as a model for the Janabai image in the Janabai temple in Gangakhed, Maharashtra, according to retired professor Dr. Deenanath Phulwadkar, chair of the Sant Janabai Literary Society. When I visited the Gangakhed temple in the early 2000s, a painted replica hung in the temple. I would like to thank Dr. Phulwadkar for sharing this image with me.

composite of many. Each poem or *abhaṅga* attributed to an author invokes the poet as a figure *within the poem itself* in the signature line, and the songs and performances transform the historical author into a figure. This is why I have spoken and will continue to speak of Janabai in the singular throughout this book. Indeed, there is something of this figurative sense of authorship inscribed, as I noted earlier, in Janabai's very name: *Janā* derives, it is likely, from *jana*, a word used in many languages to refer to "the common people," the citizens or polity, whether of a kingdom in the past or a democracy today. A Sanskrit and Marathi inscription dated 1277 CE, located at the Vitthal temple in Pandharpur, uses the term *bhakta**jana*** to refer to the "people of devotion." The reference, Christian Lee Novetzke believes, is possibly the first use of the term *bhakta* in inscriptions in the region, and he reads *bhaktajana* as one of the first signs of a *bhakti* "public."[7] Who were these people of devotion, this public? It is not entirely clear from the inscriptions, but these are the people, the public, to whom Janabai is linked by name. The influential Sanskrit compendium on music, the *Saṅgīta Ratnākara* (Ocean of music) written by Sharangadeva during the reign of the most powerful of the Yadava rulers, King Singhana (r. 1200–1245), also describes the *ovī*—the verse form of women's labor songs—as ***jana**manohara*, or "pleasing to the people," in other words, popular.[8] Janabai is also linked by name to this popular and pleasing form of verse, the *ovī*.

We might think of her name, Janabai, as a *nomen loquens*, a "speaking name" based on a person's primary characteristic. Janabai's very name connects her to the *jana*; it becomes a speaking name also in the compositions of countless grind mill songs *about* Janabai. Gregory Nagy connects the idea of the speaking name to performance practices of ancient Greece in which many speak in the name of a poet or figure, reenacting the poet's primary characteristic. Sappho, he argues, is a *nomen loquens* meaning "sister," not because Sappho was a historical figure who happened to have a name that means sister, and not because her writing constructs her poetic persona as sister, but because "her identity [as "sister"] was reenacted and kept on being reenacted by way of singing and dancing performed on festive occasions by the girls and women on the island of Lesbos."[9] There is, he argues, a distinction between a synchronic Sappho, a poet figured in historical time about whom so little is known, and a diachronic Sappho, a poet who emerges and evolves through performative and textual traditions over time.

Similarly, Janabai is figured synchronically as a poet who lived as a *dāsī* in a particular historical time, yet almost everything we know or think about

Janabai emerges in verse "reenactments" in which many, the *jana*, speak and compose using her speaking name. The grind mill songs about Janabai and other poet-figures are, in a very direct sense, a kind of "reenactment"—admittedly less festive than the ancient choral mimesis Nagy describes—of the names of the poets, especially Janabai's. When women sing *about* Janabai, often using her signature line "Says Jani" in their own compositions, they are reenacting her identity as a figure who lives a life not unlike their own, with its crushing labor and hardships, its solitude and dependency, its search for refuge and belonging in the god Vitthal. In these songs, we find an ongoing verse reenactment of her name and identity as a figure of the excluded and marginalized, a *dāsī*, by the so-called people, the *jana*, who see themselves in her. Not only do women sing about her, they also do so as they grind, in songs so integrated with their labor that the word "reenactment" is, in a real sense, of the body as well as speech and song.

Many of the names of the poets of Marathi *bhakti* can be seen as examples of *nomen loquens* in this sense, each figure associated with a primary characteristic that is then reenacted in performance and textuality. Indeed, the two purported founders of the Vitthal *bhakti* literary traditions in Maharashtra, Jnaneshvar and Namdev, have such names. Jnaneshvar is the revered author of the extraordinary and foundational work called the *Jñāneśvarī* (ca. 1290), an ornately poetic rendering of the Bhagavad Gītā and one of the very first poetic works written in Marathi. Namdev is the unlettered tailor-poet credited with inventing *kīrtan*, an important oral-performance tradition that combines storytelling, textual recitation, and song. As a learned Brahmin and scholar-poet, Jnaneshvar's speaking name ties him to the elevated philosophical and written side (*jñāna*) of *bhakti*, while Namdev's speaking name invokes the more popular oral practice of singing and reciting the name (*nāma*) of the divine. The two respectively exemplify and—through their purported friendship, as portrayed in the *Tīrthāvaḷī*, a foundational text of Vitthal *bhakti*—connect the written and the oral-performative modalities of *bhakti* poetry. Novetzke argues that this "story of friendship between a Brahmin Sanskrit philosopher and an illiterate Shimpi or Shudra tailor is also a metaphor for the elision of social difference," signaling a "turn to an inclusive social ethics."[10] Yet Namdev's *dāsī* Jani is ever a reminder of the limits of this apparent social ethics of inclusion. Not only, it is believed, did Janabai live in the same period as these two renowned founders, but she worked in the house of Namdev as a *dāsī*, a term variously translated as servant or slave. Her poetry, like all song-poems called *abhangas*, often ends with a signature line, "Says Jani, the servant (or slave) of Namdev."

It is not uncommon in South Asian religious and literary traditions for a disciple to refer to themselves as a "servant" or "slave" (*dāsa* or *dāsī*), one "given" or "surrendered" to a teacher or a god, a devotee. Indeed, while the terms *dāsa* and *dāsī* have been attested to mean "slave" in Sanskrit texts, they also carry a long history of usage to signify the loyalty and submission of moral exemplars.[11] In his study of historical documents on slavery in eighteenth-century Maharashtra, Sumit Guha found that there were more common Marathi terms in use for a slave woman in Marathi, such as *batik* and *kunbini*, but *dāsī* was also used in in this sense.[12] Still, the symbolic registers of both colloquial and classical terms for slave often obfuscated the status and conditions of those in servile positions by invoking kinship terms. Janabai's self-named identity as *dāsī* has never been understood to be only a euphemism for "devotee." It was, or at some point became, a hagiographical marker of her condition of abject servitude and social isolation in Namdev's household. "It was," Guha observes, "the mature, destitute, and effectively kinless woman within a household who gave the image of the 'female slave' its particular and subtle shades."[13] This is a strikingly accurate description of Janabai as she appears in her poems and in grind mill songs and hagiographies.

Yet the distinctions between slave and nonslave servant, between caste and other forms of forced servitude and dependency, especially the gendered servitude endemic to caste patriarchy, are more complex in the South Asian context than in the starkly dualistic system of Atlantic slavery with which we generally associate the word "slave."[14] In his landmark book *Slavery*, the non-Brahmin thinker Jotirao Phule draws a parallel between the struggles of the enslaved and those of the non-Brahmin toiling masses, but the enslavement (*gulāmgiri*, *dāsatva*) he writes about encompasses a wide spectrum of servitude and exclusion based on caste and class. Poems published in 1854 and attributed to Savitribai Phule refer to *gulāmgiri* or slavery almost twenty years before Jotirao Phule's book was published.[15] In a more recent study, Shailaja Paik uses the term "caste slavery" to describe the "sex-gender-caste complex—the sexual and gendered arrangements of the caste system as they operated to oppress Dalit Tamasha women."[16] Yet there were also forms of enslavement not tied to caste: war captives, women and girls of all castes gifted and sold, and enslaved Africans and others brought to India through the Indian Ocean slave trade. Because of the long and varied history of its forms and practices in South Asia, Richard Eaton writes that slavery on the subcontinent is better defined more broadly as "the condition of uprooted outsiders, impoverished insiders—or the descendants of either—serving persons or institutions on which they are wholly dependent."[17]

Accordingly, Janabai's figuration as *dāsī* maintains a certain plasticity and capaciousness. As a figure without caste or kin, she speaks to and for manifold experiences of exclusion, dependency, destitution, and hard labor experienced by the many as they sing about and in her "speaking name." There have been numerous efforts to "elevate" Janabai, to argue that her self-description as *dāsī* marks her as a disciple who "surrendered herself" to Vitthal and Namdev, not as a slave or a servant. But her own poems, the songs of the grind mill, and the hagiographical tradition they influenced, have never allowed the complete excision of one sense of the term *dāsī* from the other. Indrani Chatterjee sums up the complications well: "If normative codes of conduct required deflection and indirection when slaves were described by non-slaves, and the latter appropriated to their own personas the servility, loyalty, and devotion that they valued in their slaves, it must surely be asked whether slaves themselves could have developed a distinctive discursive 'voice' within such cultures of representation."[18] Janabai carries both aspects of *dāsī* in her figuration, and this is perhaps what makes hers "a distinctive discursive 'voice'" of the complex and varied experiences of enslavement and servitude in Maharashtra. The stories of her life as a laboring and lowly figure in Namdev's household continually unravel her elevated status as a revered poet, devotee, and *sant*, keeping the unforgiving systems of dependency and exclusion, of caste slavery and other forms of familial servitude that structure the lives of the many within the purview of *bhakti* poetics. As such, Janabai remains ever a figure of the unlikely poet, standing at the margins of the literary, an outsider looking in—at least if we take poetry to be, as it is understood by many literary scholars, a written and elevated artifact of language at a far remove from the everyday, the demotic, the *verna*.

This insistent marginalization, the thematics of exile predominant in her figuration and poetry, is what initially moved me to focus on her. Whatever the historical complications, could her figuration as *dāsī* serve a heuristic function, I wondered? For instance, could it help restore to the concept of the "vernacular"—a word widely used in South Asian scholarship for the regional, spoken languages of India as distinct from the cosmopolitan literary languages of Sanskrit, Prakrit, and Apabhramsha—the term's sometimes willfully severed connection to the expressive traditions of those absented and made invisible by the elite textual traditions? The Latin *vernāculus* pertains both to the domestic sphere and to the house-born or native slave, whose language would come to stand as demotic contrast to the learned, the cosmopolitan, and the literary. "The 'vernacular' in relation to human beings," writes the literary scholar Houston A. Baker, "signals 'a slave born on a master's estate,'" but, "in expressive terms, vernacular indicates arts native or peculiar to a particular country or locale."[19] Although the latter sense has prevailed in South Asian scholarship, Janabai raises the possibility of connecting the first meaning to the second, just as she bridges the dual signification of *dāsī*. As a figure of the marginalized and excluded, the *verna* understood in the capacious South Asian sense, Janabai is an important though unacknowledged third founder of *bhakti* literarity, one who brings into view the poetics of work in the work of vernacular poetics.

In US literary studies, the term "vernacular" is used most often for African American language and cultural expression emerging out of the historical experience of enslavement, for what Baker calls the "ancestral matrix that has produced a forceful and indigenous American creativity," a bridging of the two meanings.[20] Black expressivity, actively denied access to literacy by the systems of slavery and racial segregation, flourished in oral poetry and music, which have, in turn, contributed in hidden and still unrecognized ways to American literary traditions. The literary turn to the Black vernacular in the nineteenth century, by eminent Black writers like Paul Laurence Dunbar and by white writers like Mark Twain, changed the course of American literature, which became ever more attuned and responsive to the colloquial, the distinct Americanisms within English. Similarly, Black music—like the "sorrow songs" of the enslaved, the blues, jazz, work songs, hip-hop, and rap—has shaped American poetic aesthetics in immeasurable ways.[21] In South Asia, the unique longevity and continuity of the grind mill song tradition are also the inadvertent fruits of a stark gender and caste segregation inherent to literary regimes of writing. "In India, as everywhere else," Sheldon Pollock observes, "writing has been a social resource kept deliberately scarce, subject to control or hoarding, a privilege that may be granted or denied."[22] The boundary separating the written and the oral, as well as the apparatus of caste patriarchy that elevates one above the other, is precisely what Janabai calls into question. As a figure of the outsider or the impoverished insider, as *dāsī*, she shows us the limits of the written literary archive, the gaps and absences in it, but as a *poet* she also brings to our attention the generative and abundant intertext of orality and writing that undergirds it. To draw on Anjali Arondekar's formulation, there is not only archival absence, paucity, or loss, but also "abundance" when we expand what counts as archives.[23]

Janabai's poetic signature line, whether it be "Says Jani" or "Says Nama's *dāsī* Jani," ends every composition attributed to her, but the same signature is used narratively, as a *nomen loquens*, by the women who sing about her at the grind mill. It is in the ongoing conversation between the *abhaṅga* and the *ovī* that the figure of Janabai emerges. The figural poet's authority and authorship depend on the connection between an actual historical author and the life story (the figuration) of the author "reenacted" in oral forms like the grind mill songs, as well as in the written traditions. I explore this with greater detail in chapter 4, but here it is sufficient to note one of the many consequences of this conception of authorship, the way it generously distributes the authority to compose and perform poetry to those, the *jana*, who would otherwise have been excluded from poetry-making by the long-established cosmopolitan literary traditions sequestered in royal courts and elite gatherings of literati. Disavowing such gatekeepers, the concept of authorship inherent to *bhakti* poetics allows many to compose and perform under the name of one or another of the poets in arenas far from the royal courts. One way to begin to understand the author-function in *bhakti* poetry is to see it as an unlocked portal rather than a locked gate, inviting, though sometimes hesitantly or haltingly, even a household slave or servant to enter. A portal is, we sometimes forget, a two-way conduit. Just as it opens the way *into* the literary sphere, it also opens a road for the literary poet—and the scholar trailing behind her—to travel *beyond* the written text.

Beyond the Written Text

Beginning in 2006, and following Janabai's lead, I began to record women's *ovīs* in the villages around her purported birthplace, Gangakhed, in the Godavari River Valley. It did not take long, once I started, to see that Janabai was a constant and ever-present subject of the songs. Around this time, I also visited Hema Rairkar at her home in Pune. Working with the

Center for Cooperative Research, Rairkar, Guy Poitevin, Bernard Bel, and others had tirelessly recorded and transcribed more than a hundred thousand songs of the grind mill. Rairkar and Poitevin organized all of these songs using an elaborate "semantic classification" system, which has provided the basic structure for the digitization of the collection by The Grindmill Songs Project (grindmill.org), currently under the aegis of the People's Archive of Rural India (PARI). When I set out to visit Rairkar, I read the book she had cowritten with Guy Poitevin, *Stonemill and Bhakti: From the Devotion of Peasant Women to the Philosophy of Swamis*. It was groundbreaking in its scope and attention to the grind mill tradition and the first—and to my knowledge, the only—English-language book to give serious consideration to the relationship of these grind mill songs to the archive of *bhakti* poetry, with special focus on Janabai. Even so, Poitevin and Rairkar maintained a stark dichotomy between the written tradition, which they gendered as male, and the grind mill songs of "peasant" women.[24] The analysis seemed to perpetuate the very polarities I had begun to question, between the written and the oral, between poetry and song. It was not, in any case, what I was observing in my own fieldwork. From what I could see, women of all castes had no compunctions about drawing from all kinds of texts and practices to which they might have access in public performances and recitations. And poets and writers, though they often did not acknowledge it, seemed deeply indebted to the poetics of the grind mill.

Although Janabai was clearly the single most important poetic figure in the songs of the grind mill that I was recording in Marathwada, I soon realized—and The Grindmill Songs collection confirmed—that she was not the only poet women sang about. In fact, women singers often found it difficult to sing only about Janabai, to isolate and extricate her from the old growth forest, as I would sometimes request them to do. I had, after all, set out to research Janabai, and with all the impatience of the urban scholar I would ask them for songs only about her. Inevitably, during the recordings, their songs would veer from Janabai to songs about the family, about daily labors and difficulties, about gods and goddesses, above all Lord Vitthal, his wife Rukmini, the city of Pandharpur, and to all the other poets of the Vitthal *bhakti* literary corpus. I also recorded numerous songs that retell the foundational epic *Rāmāyaṇa* from the perspective of Sita, Rama's wife, a collection of verses known as the *Sitāyan*.[25] In the village of a once nomadic Banjara tribe, I recorded a song and dance performance of the story of Janabai in the Banjari language. They had learned the story through a low-budget film that they watched on a video compact disc, the kind circulating widely throughout the rural areas in the 1990s and early aughts. They were not the passive cinematic audience reviled by members of the Frankfurt School. They took the story they watched on screen and composed their *own* songs and dances based on it. I collected songs from Dalit women, Maratha women, Muslim women, Adivasi women, fieldworkers of various laboring castes, and Brahmin housewives. The fieldwork took me in many different directions because the songs are so vast and comprehensive in their outlook, subject matter, and even language. In just two districts, the Hingoli district (figures i.3 and i.4) and the Parbhani district, I found songs in numerous languages. It took some time to come to terms with them as an archive.

A sizeable corpus of grind mill verses featuring the gods, texts, figures, poets, stories, practices, rituals, and images associated with *bhakti* in its broadest sense eventually began to take shape, an actual archive of oral *bhakti* poetry. The songs support a broader understanding of *bhakti*. There

Figure i.3 Women of the Banjara community from Kathoda Tanda in the Hingoli district, 2007. Sarubai Rathod (center) and Dhurpatabai Jadhav (far right) were the main singers. Photo by author

Figure i.4 Women gathered to sing for a recording session at the home of Prayagbai Chavan (center) in Waghi village in the Hingoli district in 2023.
Photo by author

are songs about many deities, on village goddesses, on regionally prominent goddesses, on the popular god Khandoba, on Shiva, and so on. These help us to understand that the love for one god is, at least in the case of the devotees of Vitthal, always embedded in a more complex constellation of reverence, worship, and storytelling. As so many scholars have reminded us, there has never been one kind of *bhakti* or one *bhakti* movement, but a multiplicity and that, too, with sometimes conflicting ideological orientations. There is a basic living messiness to *bhakti* that the songs help us to keep in mind. Still, there is no way to deny the fact that Vitthal towers above almost all other deities in the grind mill songs, perhaps because he embodies, as R. C. Dhere has analyzed, a great confluence of the many competing worship traditions in Maharashtra.[26] In one tiny village where I had gone to record songs, an elderly woman wisely whispered to her companion that I should be researching Vitthal, not Janabai. It took some time for me to realize that she was right, that I had begun with a too narrow understanding of Janabai. In the process of looking for Janabai, I found a tremendous and much neglected *bhakti* archive in the songs of the grind mill, a deeply embedded, and generally unrecognized, complex intertext, not only of Janabai's poems, or even of *bhakti* poetry, but also of Marathi poetry in its broadest sense.

Return to the Texts

If Janabai took me to these grind mill songs, it was the grind mill songs that led me back to the texts, the poets, and even the literary traditions, with a more expansive lens; there were entanglements and overlaps, engagements and responsive critiques in the songs indicating that the oral and the written, the "high" and the "low," the ordinary and the superordinate, the literary and the so-called demotic were in constant and intimate touch. The grind mill and numerous motifs derived from the songs of the grind mill appear frequently in *bhakti* poetry, but also in other texts and traditions that came to constitute literarity as an idea in Marathi. The earliest written articulations of *bhakti* in Maharashtra come, not from the devotees of Vitthal, but more copiously, from a parallel and quite separate *bhakti* tradition, the Mahanubhava sect, founded in the thirteenth century by a wandering philosopher-ascetic named Chakradhar, whom the Mahanubhavas believe to be one of five incarnations of one Supreme God (*parameśvara*). The Mahanubhavas were a literarily prolific ascetic movement that emerged in thirteenth-century Maharashtra, though sometime in the late fourteenth century they began to keep their writings locked behind coded scripts. Only in the twentieth century did their copious and extraordinary texts come to be known by the larger public.

In some ways, this radically secretive sect was the mirror opposite of the highly public and open Varkari sect to which Janabai belonged. But there are distinct overlaps that I explore in this book. There was, for one thing, a long-standing grind mill song tradition among the Mahanubhavas, and similar *bhakti* motifs are shared between the songs and poetry of Mahanubhavas and those composed by Vitthal devotees.[27] In principle the Mahanubhavas rejected caste, gender, and class hierarchies. Women were not only accepted as equal initiates, but women were the focal audience of their early literature, the very first written texts in the Marathi language. It is in the *Līḷācaritra* (ca. 1278), the innovative prose biography of Chakradhar, considered by many scholars to be the first written text in Marathi, where we find the oldest written transcriptions of grind mill songs in Marathi. Some of these were the songs of Mahadaise, the woman who would go on to write the first extant work of narrative poetry in Marathi that drew on a poetics of the grind mill. Though Janabai is associated with the Varkaris, and she was likely from a later historical period, she nevertheless leads us to Mahadaise via routes that were burrowed through the ages and across sectarian boundaries by the grind mill songs.

In other words, there is a kind of net or web, an intertext, being woven and unraveled and rewoven by an ongoing conversation between the songs and the poems, orality and writing. Weaving and unraveling are metaphors of poetic composition that come out of the song tradition itself, as I explain in chapter 1. In fact, the most widely known and accepted etymology of the word *ovī* traces it to the verb *ovaṇeṃ*, meaning to stitch, thread, knit, or weave; in the songs, however, women describe their own singing, almost in intended contradistinction, as an "unraveling of the heart" (*huruda ukala*). Thus in Marathi poetics, the labors of grinding and weaving become the metaphoric vehicles for poetic composition. Unraveling, like grinding, is the labor of removing and reducing, while weaving, stitching, threading are labors of joining together. This language of making and unmaking, of poiesis, comes not from the venerable superposed literatures in Sanskrit and Prakrit, but from the *ovī*, the predominant poetic form of both oral and written Marathi poetry from the thirteenth century onward.

It soon became clear to me that a project to recuperate an individual woman writer for a written tradition that had excluded her was insufficient for the way poetics—especially *bhakti* poetics—works in the South Asian context. A new way of thinking about "the literary" that takes into account the complex and often subterranean routes of circulation and communication between oral and written expressive articulations was needed, a method, to use Linda Hess's words, "in which fieldwork and textwork inform and change each other."[28] In addition to the royal court and the Brahmin ecumene, I propose the stone mill as an important, originary, and continuous site of poetic composition.[29] The songs generated by women at the stone mill have been a continuous witness to and interlocutor of the written traditions, especially, though not only, in the Marathi-speaking regions of the subcontinent. The grind mill songs, I show, are a unique form of *bhakti* versification, a neglected genre of oral *bhakti* poetry, central to the making of a written vernacular poetics in Marathi. The numerous entanglements between the *ovī* of women's songs and the eponymous literary *ovī* and the *abhaṅga* open a new space of inquiry, what Hess calls an "ecoregion" into the dynamics of oral and written poetics, each the audience of the other and bound together in a centuries-old dialogue, a vast old growth forest of "intricate interdependencies and rivalries" in "the ecology" of languages and literary communities.[30]

Ecological metaphors are abundant in literary studies, but the ecological sciences have come a long way in the last few decades, revealing more intricate interdependencies than rivalries in complex and dynamic forest systems. It turns out the proverbial forest and the tree are connected through a vast mycorrhizal network that links trees and plants to each other in nonhierarchical relations of interspecies mutualism and symbiosis. What if we were to look at the literary landscape as a forest undergirded by a subterranean network of connections, shared resources, life-sustaining symbiotic assemblages between languages, poetic forms, genres, modalities, texts, authors, performers and scribes? Bringing the grind mill song tradition into focus alongside a study of textualized literature will allow us to address anew important questions about *bhakti*, about poetry, and about what constitutes "the literary." What does the song archive of the grind mill tell us about *bhakti*? What do the shared poetic resources between song and poetry say about authorship? What do the "intricate interdependencies" between the oral and the written suggest about literature and the literary? What does the history of the *ovī*—the name of both the grind mill verse form and the dominant poetic meter of premodern Marathi literature—tell us about the emergence of written Marathi poetry in the thirteenth and fourteenth centuries and women's participation in its making? The figure of Janabai lives in—and points us toward—the confluence of seemingly disparate traditions, revealing the interconnections between the literary world and the "everyday creativity" of women.[31]

Travels of the *Ovī*

In Marathi, there is a well-known adage that "songs come to you when you sit at the stone mill." Indeed, the grind mill songs are so connected to the work of grinding that women often cannot remember or recall verses unless they sit at the grind mill or imagine themselves doing so. As Smita Tiwari Jassal notes in her book on North Indian grind mill songs, called *jatsār*: "In Atara village, a Rajput (Thakur) woman confided to me that she regretted forgetting whole stanzas of many of the *jāta* songs she had once known as she now no longer engages in grinding activity. However,

Figure i.5 Chandrakalabai Jogdand in Shirad Shahapur in the Hingoli district in 2006. She knew hundreds of grind mill songs that she shared with me, but as a regular participant in the annual pilgrimage to Pandharpur, she also sang *abhaṅgas* and *bhāruds* and other types of songs. She cannot read but learns songs from songbooks by enlisting the help of literate women relatives.
Photo by author

by mimicking the semicircular motion of the hands across the grinding stone (*jāta*), the woman was able to remember the words of some of these songs from her youth."[32] I have also witnessed women recall songs through a similar kind of reenactment of grinding. This correspondence between the work of the body and song-making, a "poetics of work," defines the grind mill songs as an embedded and embodied oral genre. Whereas other oral forms are sung by traveling performers, the grind mill songs were composed and sung by women sitting in their homes, thus evoking images of a static, timeless, and unchanging "folk culture," imprisoned by their situational context.

Yet there is no question that the songs traveled. In the course of recording songs in the rural districts of Parbhani and Hingoli in south central Maharashtra, I met a remarkable Dalit woman, self-identified as being of the Mahar caste, named Janabai Thorat. Janabai is not a rare name by any count, but I still took meeting her as a serendipitous gift intended by the literary Janabai. Janabai Thorat lives in a village called Bhendegaon in the Hingoli district. Although now she lives in a house in the Dalit quarters of the village itself, in 2006 she was still living in a modest thatched dwelling on the few acres of land that she owned and farmed alongside a busy highway. I came to know of her through a family acquaintance who regularly overheard her songs as he traveled on that highway. Her songs filled the aural space well beyond her own home, which was open, not walled off from the outside world, an important architectural reminder that "public" and "private" are permeable in village life, even today. This does not mean, of course, that there were no personal and interior spaces created in and by the songs. The songs are often intensely personal, but interiority is a shared poetic space, a mark of the lyric form of the *ovī* as I discuss further in chapter 1. Janabai sang alone; no one I met from her household knew any of the songs. Because her husband preferred the taste of stone ground flour, she still used her grind mill frequently in 2006. By 2023, when I went to visit her, her lung problems prevented both the work and the songs, but for many years prior her songs pervaded the shared, aural space of home, field, and roadside. Many women of various castes that I talked to in the surrounding villages knew of her and suggested I go to visit her. She was locally renowned, rightly so as I found, for her immense knowledge of these songs.

The songs moved between households, between women of disparate castes, from one village and region to another, and even from one language to another. One of the many surprising aspects of this research has been finding that *ovīs* I recorded in the 2000s had been transcribed and published in the 1940s or 1950s or on the grindmill.org website. They were sung by women of different castes and in very distant regions, suggesting deeply embedded routes of circulation, ones that move over and through caste and regional and even linguistic borders. Mary Fuller, one of the early English scholars to collect and write about the songs, had marveled at this in the 1940s. "Often one finds the same *ovīs* with slight variations, in places hundreds of miles apart," she wrote, "even though there have been no printed collections."[33] Although it is common to counterpoise the global reach of cosmopolitan languages and literatures—indeed, that is what makes them cosmopolitan—to the provinciality of the local, the regional, and the vernacular, the songs suggest that there are other, more granular routes of transregional, translocal, and translinguistic circulation. These travels within and between vernacular expressive traditions destabilize the presumed foundational binary between cosmopolitan and vernacular. In the

Figure i.6 Janabai Thorat in 2023. She is no longer able to sing because of a lung condition, but she mouthed the words when she heard the recording of her songs from 2006.

Figure i.7 Janabai Thorat grinding chiles in a mortar and pestle, 2007. Photo by author

more polyglot realities of South Asia, movements and influences between languages, dialects, and expressive forms are quite commonplace. The songs of Sita are sung in North Indian *jatsār* and in South Indian pestle songs with clear overlaps and influences.[34] This is no mere coincidence.

The songs are also not rooted in or restricted by any specific caste or community of women, though they are linguistically marked by regional and caste distinctions. Songs by women of the lower and middle laboring castes, many self-identified as Maratha, as well as women of Dalit castes, still referred to and often treated as "untouchable," form a great majority of the archive at The Grindmill Songs Project, though there are songs by Brahmin women as well. I collected a number of songs from women of diverse castes, including several communities who identified themselves simply as *adivasi*, which after some digging, I was able to identify as the Andh tribal communities, some of the oldest inhabitants of the Godavari River Valley and especially populous in the Hingoli and Parbhani districts. Guy Poitevin suggests that a "homogenous conceptual and ideological horizon" runs through the songs of women from very different castes and regions, creating a "consistency with regard to content, vocabulary, and images."[35] For example, grind mill songs on Janabai have been collected by Hema Rairkar from far-flung regions throughout Maharashtra. There are lexical, linguistic, and even metrical variations of caste and region, but there is a consistent focus across caste and region on specific oral-formulaic phrases, episodes, scenes, themes, motifs, tropes, words, and images. This means that the songs traveled not only between women of a given family or caste or region but also among women in a more general way, beyond all of the refracting categories that would otherwise destabilize gender. Although the idea of a "women's tradition" has been roundly dismantled in feminist scholarship over the last decades, the song archive seems, in some ways, to resurrect the idea as a central organizing principle of how the songs circulated. Guy Poitevin calls the songs, "the authoritative text of an exclusively feminine tradition that surges from a common soul every morning before dawn."[36]

But the *ovīs* were hardly restricted to women exclusively, though they might be understood as "feminine" in the more gender-performative sense. In the very act of singing, to draw on Richard Bauman and Charles Briggs's foundational essay on poetics and performance, women made their verses "extractable." Even in the lonely, early dawn hours, singing the verses "lifts [them] to a degree from [their] interactional setting and opens [them] to scrutiny by an audience." Performance is already the beginning of an "entextualization" that "potentiates decontextualization."[37] And, indeed, the songs were decontextualized and recontextualized as they traveled among women, but also as they traveled into other performance arenas and texts. They were sometimes sung by men, and in literature they became a vehicle through which the gendered voice could become more gender-fluid. This entire book addresses the travels of the *ovī* between and through multiple genres, but a few examples should suffice here as introduction, one oral and the other written.

An important oral tradition in Maharashtra centers on a devotee of the goddess called the *potarāj*. This oral performer makes the rounds of a village or urban neighborhood to collect alms, wearing a long-haired wig and a sari. The verses sung by the *potarāj* are called *vahī*. *Ovī* is often pronounced colloquially as *vavī* or *vaī*, and in Old Marathi texts, it is often spelled *vovi/ī*. Scholars who have studied and collected *vahīs* describe them as versions of women's *ovīs*. Prabhakar Mande, the eminent scholar of Marathi folk traditions, describes the *potarāj* "begging for alms in town in the name of the goddess. With castanets he makes a beat to which he dances, and while he dances, he sings songs like the grind mill *ovīs*. These are known as *vahīs*."[38] The *potarāj*'s itinerant performance is one specific and discrete example of the way the grind mill *ovī* was "decontextualized" from one domestic oral genre and "recontextualized" by another more "public" performance genre.

There are, in fact, two kinds of *vahīs*, according to Mande, the short (*sphuṭ*) *ovī* of the *potarāj* and the narrative (*kathātmak*) *ovī*. Although the latter *vahīs* are also oral, they are woven together to form longer narratives, and thus, according to Mande, indistinguishable from the literary *ovī*.[39] Another important narrative oral *ovī* is the *dhangar ovī*, a performance tradition of nomadic shepherding communities called *dhangars*. The *dhangar ovīs* include both storytelling and song, and the song verses are also called *ovīs*. With the narrative drive predominant, the verses in the *dhangar ovīs* are not as complex as grind mill *ovīs* in poetic structure, rhyme schemes, or figurative elements. Such narrative *ovī* traditions might not directly invoke women's *ovīs* like the short *ovīs* of the itinerant *potarāj*, but they often show an ongoing engagement with women's song traditions in motif, poetic themes, and structures. For example, Anne Feldhaus notes the centrality and complexity of gender themes in *dhangar ovīs*.[40] Indeed, this kind "recontextualization" of women's songs and speech is hardly unique. "Feminine performativity" by all genders is widespread in the oral institutions of South Asia, in particular in worship practices around goddess figures in which, as Joyce B. Flueckiger writes, "ultimate reality is imagined as female, women share the nature of the goddess, and men are transformed to be in her presence."[41]

We also see the gender fluidity of the *ovī* in written traditions such as the Dakani-language *cakkī-nāmā* (grind mill) and *carkhā-nāmā* (weaving) song-poems composed by seventeenth- and eighteenth-century male Sufi poets who likely belonged to the Bijapur Sufis of the Chishti order.[42] These are preserved in manuscript form, some signed by male poets, and others anonymously authored. According to Eaton, "The Marathi poems that village women of Maharashtra sing today while grinding meal are functionally identical to the *chakki-namas* of the Sufis." These poets adapted "Sufi doctrine to the already existing vehicles of folk poetry" and substituted "vernacular Dakhni for vernacular Marathi or Kannada."[43] Muslim women themselves sing grind mill songs, sometimes in mixed Marathi-Urdu or Dakani, as I discovered during my fieldwork in the Hingoli district. Unfortunately, Muslim women's songs have not been collected in a sustained way in Maharashtra, perhaps a legacy of the struggle for "linguist statehood" at mid-century, which narrowed the ethnographic lens on folk cultures. However, there have been a few recent efforts.[44] The *cakkī-nāmā* poems, like *bhakti* poetry, are clearly influenced by the songs of women. Eaton notes that in them, the teachings of the Sufis, such as the *zikrs*, or specialized practices on the path to God, are "largely divested of their mystical content" and become more straightforwardly devotional.[45] The *zikrs* are described analogically through a description of the grind mill in ways reminiscent of the symbolic use of the grind mill in grind mill songs and in *bhakti* poetry. Though the poems are often seen as tools of proselytization written for an audience of women, they also likely reflect the actual devotional practices of women and their own songs of labor. Furthermore, the "aesthetics of the female voice, a poetic device in which the speaker is female," is a common and ubiquitous trope in Sufi poetry and in the South Asian musical tradition of *sufiānā kalām*, as well as in the ghazal and *rekhti* poetic traditions.[46] The *cakkī-nāmā* poems fit within this literary lineage, but they bring to light the ways that female envoicement may, in fact, carry the imprint of women's songs on written poetry.

I want to emphasize that the "voice" of women in oral and literary traditions is not simply imitation or mimicry of some essential, preliterate, ontological "womanhood" or femininity. Rather the "female voice" is conveyed through poetic structures that pervade women's oral poetries, especially the songs of grinding and pounding, but also many other song genres like lullabies, wedding songs, and songs of lament. This literary female voice is, in other words, already a poetic voice in the oral poetry of women, drawing our attention to the role of these songs in literary making. In fact, the generative confluence of women's songs and *bhakti* poetry might just be one reason, not only for the "extraordinary number of women [poets] who sang their devotional songs in Marathi,"[47] but also for the extraordinary number of men who sang their songs and wrote their texts in the voices, idioms, motifs, poetic structures, and speech genres of women's songs.

Thus, while there is some truth to the popular saying in Marathi that "songs only come when you sit at the grind mill," both oral and literary travels of women's songs show that they moved beyond their compositional contexts and functional relevance. The *potarāj* heard the songs, and he sang them during his own peregrinations, as did other folk performers and poets. The songs—entextualized and extracted, as Bauman and Briggs propose—circulated in the sphere of cultural production; their influence crossed boundaries and entered new contexts and texts. There is, in fact, no reason to doubt that every poet of the Deccan heard and knew these songs; so pervasive was the practice of grinding in every household that it would have taken a major act of willfulness to resist their reach and influence. The manuscripts of *cakkī-nāmā* poems give us clear evidence of the literary travels and wide influence of the songs of the grind mill in the seventeenth and eighteenth centuries, but the earliest Mahanubhava works and the *Jñāneśvarī*, written in the thirteenth and fourteenth centuries, as well as the *abhaṅga* poetry of Vitthal devotees written between the fourteenth and seventeenth centuries, show that engagements with the songs of women at the grind mill were not rare but centrally formative to making "literature" in Marathi—even when literature tried to distance itself from, indeed to define itself in opposition to, the "everyday creativity" of women.

The Separability Principle

In India in 1929, Justin E. Abbott, the famous English translator of the most important hagiographies of the Marathi *bhakti* poets, published a translation of poetry by a woman *bhakti* poet named Bahinabai (1628–1700). That same year Virginia Woolf's classic feminist literary manifesto *A Room of One's Own* was published in England, and the book went on to galvanize numerous and important "projects of recovery" in feminist literary criticism in the West. Bahinabai, a near contemporary of Shakespeare, penned an anguished autobiography-in-verse depicting her struggles to become a poet as a woman in an orthodox Brahmin household whose patriarchal values she both resisted and internalized. The violent beatings by her husband, about which she openly and subversively writes in her poems, neither drive her from her household nor from what she calls her "gift of poetry" (*varadāna kavitvāce*).[48] Bahinabai's name means "sister," and I can't help but compare her to Judith Shakespeare, the fictional sister Woolf created in *A Room of One's Own* to illustrate the barriers a woman would have faced in becoming a writer in Shakespeare's time. Many of Bahinabai's struggles to be a poet mirror the fictionalized struggles of Judith, a young woman with the same talent as her famous brother. Yet even if Woolf had known of Bahinabai's poems, it is unlikely that she would have characterized them as "literature." Woolf's efforts, important as they were to feminist literary criticism, also advanced a literary model based on the "incandescence" of a Shakespeare or a Milton, achieved only by maintaining distance from the everyday struggles a woman writer might face because of her gender. Woolf's fictionalized ideal woman writer "wrote as a woman, but as a woman who has forgotten she is a woman."[49]

Abbott's introduction to Bahinabai's poems takes a rather more generous approach to the question of literature. After citing the names of many "poet-saints . . . who were women of literary ability, wise in philosophy and godly in character," including Janabai, Abbott writes:

> But poetry is natural to Indian women. As in the early morning they grind the flour for the day's meals, they sing aloud, often composing words to fit the metres they enjoy. The subjects of their song may be philosophy, religion, personal sad or happy experiences, a prayer, or words that have little sense, but please the ear. All through the centuries the women have sung at their handmills, before the sun has risen, and while their men folk were fast asleep. They were too modest to record their own verses, the men folk too indifferent to do so, but all the same all through the centuries Indian women have composed verses and sung them down to the present day.[50]

Abbott situates Bahinabai's inarguably written compositions in the context of this oral verse tradition, which he expansively calls "poetry." He not only talks about women's active and intentional crafting of their oral verses—"composing words to fit the metres"—but also raises the question of why these verses had not been written down by women, whom I think he rightly recognized as "too modest," or by the men, who were "too indifferent." Though grind mill songs are the oldest attested verse tradition in the Marathi language, the first full-length book of transcribed grind mill songs did not appear until the twentieth century. Since then, there have been numerous collections of transcribed verses from every region, community, and caste of Maharashtra, published and analyzed by formidable scholars as examples of *lokasāhitya* (folk literature) and *lokagīta* (folk-song) in the burgeoning field of folk studies scholarship. Yet the idea that literature, by definition, is a text-artifact that rises above the muck of the everyday, free from purpose and relevance, persists in the division of the "folk" from the "literary."

In the West, the term "literature," Raymond Williams reminds us, replaced the more generalized category of poetry or *poesy* to refer to "imaginative composition" in the eighteenth century. Poetry, with its roots in the Greek *poiēsis* (a making, or creation), was replaced by the word "literature," with roots in the Latin *littera* (letters of the alphabet), and thus was associated with capacities of reading, rather than the skills of making. "Literature," Williams writes, "was never primarily the active composition—the 'making'—which poetry had described."[51] Literature became a category of "use and condition," an object of consumption rather than production—evaluated first by "learning" and then by "taste and sensibility," markers of class distinction (48). "Poetry" was subsequently narrowed to refer to a specific kind of metrical composition, and then even further to *written* metrical composition (47). What had once been an activity or practice of making became a "specialization . . . made in terms of social class" (47). What should or could be included as "literature" was not, he argues, determined by any "substantial difficulty" inherent to this or that genre or work, but rather by the "the practical limits of the category" of literature itself, the specific and historical social conditions of its development as a concept (48). Could drama be considered literature? What of Shakespeare? The fact that these had to be texts before they could be considered "literature" had to do, not with the intrinsic "literarity" of Shakespeare, but with the historical formation and narrowing of the idea of the literary. Literature came to be thought of more as an object, a "work of art," separated from the processes of making or doing.

Western classical music, according to Lydia Goehr, similarly moved in the 1800s from being thought of in terms of performance, something requiring skill and artistry in doing, to being thought of as "a work." This "work-concept," Goehr writes, arose when music began to borrow concepts from the plastic and productive arts, arts that produced things and objects, like painting and sculpture. In these productive arts, a schism between "fine art" and "craft" had already separated "works of art" from objects useful to the everyday. Goehr calls this "the separability principle," whereby art is "emancipated" from the skills of making and from everyday relevance.[52] All that was made for everyday use by individuals and society was "craft," while those objects answering to no extrinsic purpose or function became "art." This was a change from an earlier, more expansive understanding of "art." Goehr writes:

> When theorists spoke of art with reference less to concrete products than to skills in making, doing, and thinking, the application of the term "art" became wider than that of "work of art." For by referring to skill, the term "art" could designate both skills that resulted in a product and those that did not. Hence the performance "upon an instrument" and the composing of music could be referred to as skills—as arts—even though they resulted in "ephemeral" events rather than concrete or lasting products.[53]

The separation of art-as-object and art as an activity of making coincided with the separation of art from its long connection to function and relevance, even to the sphere of religion. Yet music, though it aspired to the enduring materiality of the plastic arts, was not an object like painting or sculpture; it did not endure beyond the performance. The score—music as text—was incomplete without performance, while the performance was ephemeral. Music came to be defined, not as performance, but as the product of individual, artistic genius, a "work" that would endure beyond each performance through what Goehr calls the "separability principle." The "separability principle" severed the connection between aesthetics and the "the transient, contingent world of mere mortals," so that "it became the custom to speak of the arts as separated completely from the world of the ordinary, mundane, and everyday" (157). Because of this influential separability principle "a rigid conceptual and evaluative distance is imposed between creative activity, the product of that activity, and the function of that activity, such that we find no difficulty in distinguishing the three aspects" (149).

In India, Pollock argues, literature, *kāvya*, had already declared emancipation from religious-liturgical and occasional-performative purpose a millennium before the birth of aesthetics as an autonomous sphere in the eighteenth-century West.[54] *Kāvya*, a courtly literary genre dominated by erotic poetry, helped transform Sanskrit from a liturgical language to the preeminent literary language on the subcontinent and beyond.[55] Yet, the Marathi vernacular turn exactly targeted for rejection the "separability" of *kāvya*. In place of *kāvya*, Jnaneshvar, the most influential of the early poets, offers *kavitva*:

> In speech, the art of composing poetry (*kavitva*) is most beautiful
> In poetry, *rasatva* is most beautiful
> In *rasatva* it is as if you touch
> Other-worldly existence

> *vāce baraveṃ kavitva*
> *kavitvīṃ baraveṃ rasikatva*
> *rasikatvīṃ paratatva*
> *sparśu jaisā*[56]

In invoking the concept of *rasa*, Jnaneshvar seems here to reach for the models of *kāvya*. *Rasa* is a notoriously difficult concept to translate; it gets at something like the emotional-aesthetic "flavor" of a literary work. It is the most important and influential of the many aesthetic-literary concepts in South Asian literary theory, but for Jnaneshvar—and for the many poets who followed his lead—*rasa* is also the best conduit for divine experience (*paratatva*). Jnaneshvar singles out poetry, *kavitva*, as the vehicle of this experience. *Kavitva* refers more to the skill of the poet than to the object, the literary artifact. In Marathi, it means "the art of composing poetry."[57] *Kavitva*, distinct from the object noun *kāvya* or even the now common modern Marathi *kavitā*—puts the focus on the activity of composing poetry, rather than on the poem as a text-artifact, forging thereby a central distinction between a vernacular conception of the literary and the superposed tradition of *kāvya*. And, for Jnaneshvar, having purpose does not lessen the importance of the literary and aesthetic. Rather, it is its greatest aesthetic quality, its *rasa*, that makes poetry the ideal vehicle of divine experience, illustrating what we might call an "inseparability principle" inherent to Marathi vernacular poetics.

This "inseparability principle" is evident in all of the founding texts of Marathi literature. Neither the Varkari nor the Mahanubhava sects was "religious" without being literary, nor literary without being "religious." This means that *bhakti*, especially in Maharashtra, is the very field in which all things literary grew. To the earliest Marathi writers the literary remained tied to purpose in the everyday. A "quotidian" focus—a "valorization of the ordinary"—was a prominent feature of Marathi vernacularization, according to Novetzke. Marathi literature emerged, he points out, in "nonelite" terrains, mainly "religious" ones centered a public of "women, *śudras*, and others."[58] But why did religion—*bhakti*—take form in poetry and literature if the main focus were indeed mainly theological? Was it the Brahmin ecumene that put the literary at the center of the vernacular project, as Novetze contends (56–57)? Or was there also a poetic and aesthetic impulse within the everyday that propelled the literary turn? If the "quotidian" is "the space in which elite and nonelite meet," as he puts it (9), then what exactly do the nonelite bring to the meeting?

We might begin to address the complexities inherent in the founding literary texts, their contexts, and their influence by recognizing that the intended audience of Marathi's first texts, "women, *śudras*, and others," were active contributors in literary making. The ordinary and the quotidian were suffused with forms of expressivity, immanent forms of aesthetic awareness. The world of the everyday in which Marathi literature first emerged was a sonorous and polyglot arena of multilingual—and multireligious—recitations, songs of devotion, traveling performers, women's songs, field songs, and oral poetries of all varieties. In the thirteenth century, written works of literature in Marathi did emerge as something new, it is true, but before, alongside, and even after these written works appeared, women were known to be accomplished versifiers in their songs of the grind mill, the first verse form to go by the name of *ovī*. Yet women's songs continue to be seen as entirely separate from the "literary," of interest to folklorists and anthropologists, not literary scholars. Though the compositions of *bhakti* poets were also sung, they attained written form much earlier, in manuscripts, notebooks, and finally in printed anthologies. They came to be recognized as *kavitva*. The *abhaṅga* is, however, a close metrical relative of the grind mill *ovī*, which makes the literary elevation of one and the relegation of the other to an entirely separate and even counterpoised category of "folksong" (*lokagīta*) more suspect. In Maharashtra, as in premodern South Asia generally, the poetic intertext was complex and interconnected. There was commerce between oral and written, "high" and "low," songs and texts.

Dhere points out that the *loka* in *lokasāhitya* or *lokagīta*—Marathi translations of "folk literature" and "folk song" respectively—does not (always) carry the same connotations in Marathi as the word "folk."[59] *Loka*, a borrowing from Sanskrit, has a wider range of meanings than "folk." It often means something like "common people" but not necessarily narrowed to "peasant" as the word "folk" has been in European contexts.[60] It also means the worldly in contrast to the liturgical, the earthly in contrast to the transcendent. In Marathi, *loka* also means outsiders in contrast to one's own people, and it is often used in this sense in grind mill songs.[61] The adjectival form *laukika* is used by contemporary scholars to mean "popular," but it also connotes oral forms with worldly purpose. For example, when the Sanskrit encyclopedic compendium, the *Mānasollāsa* (1131 CE), categorizes various regional song meters—including the first written description of the grind mill *ovī*—as *laukika prabandha* or worldly compositions, it does not mean that these song forms should be understood as "folk" forms of an idealized "peasant" people, but rather as forms used to mark purposeful events and occasions, like marriages, festivals, and daily labor.[62] Marathi folk studies scholars distinguish *laukikagīta*, popular song, from *lokagīta*, folksong. The first refers to songs that may have been composed in writing by known authors but have become popular with "the people," while the latter are songs composed orally by unknown or "collective" authors.[63] Kedar Kulkarni writes about the importance of *laukiktā* or "worldliness" in reconceptualizing the literary in nineteenth-century Maharashtra.[64] Looking at the multiple resonances of the word *loka* and *laukika* it becomes evident that they resist the binaries of "high" and "low" and of "written" and "oral," as inherent to the word "folk."

As many scholars have shown, far more fluidity and exchange between the textual and the oral has prevailed for centuries in South Asia.[65] The words for "literature"—*kāvya/kavitva* (from *kavi*, seer), *vāṅmaya* (from *vāc*, speech), *sāhitya* (rhetoric/poetics) do not have the same associations with writing as the word "literature" has to its roots in *littera*.[66] "In the Indian situation historically viewed," H. C. Bhayani writes, "The currently understood oppositions between literary and nonliterary, literality and orality, and creative literature and noncreative literature cannot always hold, at least not to the same degree."[67] Nevertheless, even in this wider recognition of the oral-textual fluidity of the literary in South Asia, women's orality has largely remained invisible, considered far and sequestered from the public performance arena no less than the written. In the Marathi literary turn, however, I show that the songs of the grind mill take on a newly visible and constitutive role in the development of literary form, style, content, and voice.

Yet we must acknowledge that the very concept of the literary, of *kāvya*, came out of a long and influential written tradition. The elite, mostly Brahminical hoarding of writing has given it an aspirational aura and has contributed to the elevation of "literature" in both concept and practice. "Thanks to a long-standing aesthetic prejudice," Paul Zumthor writes, "all artistic language production is identified with writing: whence the difficulty we have in recognizing the validity of that which is not written."[68] Conferring literary stature to oral poetry might arise out of comparative evaluations between written and oral with the written providing the model and ideal, so that a conclusion like "this oral poem is as good as this written one" can be reached. Given that aesthetic theories and ideals, indeed the entire critical apparatus of literary analysis, are mostly the fruits of a rigorous engagement with written works of literature, it is to some extent unavoidable that we turn to these concepts when discussing the aesthetics of orality. Yet there are also numerous aesthetic attributes in writing that come out of orality; and this is perhaps especially true of poetry, and even more true, as I later discuss, of lyric poetry. There is a different perspective to be gained by drawing out the *shared* elements, devices, and characteristics of oral and written poetries. I want to heed Kirin Narayan's argument for the importance of "oral literary criticism" but not only for interpreting and analyzing the oral. What if we also interpret and analyze the written through the "metafolkloristics" inherent in women's oral tradition, as well as analyze the oral through the theories of the written-literary?[69]

Though in much of the book I focus on the early centuries of the vernacular era and the early *bhakti* corpus, I begin in chapter 1 with the twentieth century when grind mill *ovīs* were first collected, researched, and theorized by scholars and poets. Although we cannot equate the contemporary archive with songs of earlier periods, they do provide us with a good sense of the poetic characteristics of the grind mill *ovī*. The first chapter develops a poetics of the grind mill by analyzing the structures and schemas of the *ovī* as a lyric form. Women describe their songs, in their own songs, as a poetry of intimacy and self-revelation, an "unraveling heart" (*huruda ukala*); they likewise sing about the texts and poems of *bhakti* figures, which they describe using analogies of sewing, threading, or weaving. These metaphors for poetic composition—for the sung and the written—seem like opposites, but they are two sides of the same loom, so to speak. The metaphor of weaving has a long history in literary cultures across the globe, right down to the word "text," with roots in the Greek *texo* and Latin *texere*, meaning "to weave." These labors—weaving and unraveling—are not opposites, I argue, but an intimately engaged, interdependent "poetics of work" that show literature as a process of making, in fact, of making together rather than as fixed and finished and frozen text-artifacts.

With this poetics of the grind mill as an interpretive frame, I go back to the era of vernacular beginnings in chapter 2. I argue that what Sheldon Pollock identifies as "literarization," the work of weaving, sewing, and threading the "literariness" of a spoken language in writing, is almost always accompanied by a counter-dynamic: the *colloquialization* of the literary, an unraveling of the written to create openings for the scope, reach, and aesthetics of orality. Where literarization is driven by "the separability principle" to build up the literary as separate from the everyday, colloquialization—a process described as inherent to the linguistic dynamics of Sanskrit, Prakrit, and Apabhramsha by H. C. Bhayani—turns the literary toward the expressive forms and lexicon of the everyday.[70] Students of literature will recognize the valorizing of the oral in the Romantic poetry of the eighteenth and nineteenth centuries. There was also a turn to the "vernacular"—Black expressivity in particular—in the United States in the nineteenth century in repudiation of the "separability principle." But the dialectic between literarization and colloquialization is much older on the subcontinent. It goes back to the multilingual dynamics inherent to the exclusive languages of literature before the vernacular turn. Marathi vernacular beginnings lie in the colloquial turn of the extraordinary first texts of the Mahanubhavas, in particular the *Līḷācaritra* (ca. 1278), in which appear the very first attested Marathi transcriptions of grind mill *ovīs*. I look at how the aesthetics of the *ovī* shape the structures of expressivity in an entirely new literary form, the *līḷā*, introduced in this work. In this chapter I examine the grind mill songs of Mahadaise, the first woman—and likely the first extant poet—to compose a written poetic work in Marathi.

In chapter 3 I focus on the *ovī*, the name not only of the grind mill verse form but of the dominant poetic form of Marathi literature from the thirteenth to the eighteenth centuries. Is there significance to this nominal concurrence? I follow the complicated story of the *ovī* by reviewing its prosodic history. Two distinct literary styles can be discerned in Marathi literature through the *ovī*: the paratactic, compressed style of the oral *ovī* and the hypotactic ornamentation of the written *ovī*, not as a foundational dualism of the oral and the literary, but as a dialectic of weaving and unraveling, literarization and colloquialization. I also examine more closely Jnaneshvar's conceptualization of the *ovī* in his high-poetic Marathi rendering of the Bhagavad Gītā in the *Jñāneśvarī* (ca. 1290).

I look at women's *ovīs* as an archive of oral *bhakti* poetry in chapter 4. By drawing a comparative parallel to the "sorrow songs" of the enslaved in the United States, I show the deep vernacular structures of *bhakti* poetics as a form of everyday poiesis of the most marginalized and excluded. By reviewing the prosodic history of the *abhaṅga*, I show its metrical connections to women's *ovīs* of the grind mill to highlight the ways that women's songs, the poetry of elevated exemplars, and written hagiographies form an inseparable intertext. I also look at the ways the manuscript cultures of the seventeenth and eighteenth centuries that canonized *bhakti* poetry acknowledged but concealed women's songs.

In the final chapter I return with a more focused lens to Janabai and Mahadaise. Both are intimately associated with the grind mill song tradition, and both are the attributed authors of significant and inaugural written works of narrative poetry. Their place in the literary tradition marks that point of confluence between the oral and the literary. I explore what it would mean to look at Janabai and Mahadaise as equally important "founders," not only of the respective *bhakti* traditions in which they took part, but of Marathi literarity. In what ways do these poets help us reconceptualize the literary?

The Underview

This book is not an argument that "folk song" or "women's songs" are the root of the literary or, to be more specific, that the literary *ovī* grew out of the oral *ovī*. The oral poetic is no less a product of aesthetic labor, even when it is conjoined to manual labor, than is the written text artifact. The labor of grinding may have been forced, coerced, or obligatory, but the songs were not; they are the product of self-directed labors of composition. An aesthetics of the grind mill has shaped and influenced poetic making, just as poetic texts have shaped the songs. The oral poetic is not, in other words, a root, but itself a tree in a forest of trees connected through a vast mycorrhizal network—a poetic interweb—of shared resources. As the brilliant scientist Suzanne Simard discovered, the modest paper birch tree, once deemed a weed by loggers and foresters, shares its photosynthetic carbon with the towering Douglas fir, highly valued by the logging industry. When paper birch trees were weeded out by foresters on the assumption that they stole soil resources from the Douglas fir, the Douglas fir saplings deteriorated and eventually died. The Douglas fir and the paper birch were not competitors, Simard discovered, but symbiotically connected, not only to each other but to diverse species of fungi and other plants. Though one tree is more highly valued by humans for its majestic height and the quality of lumber, the two trees together, connected through innumerable mycorrhizal fungi, are needed for each to survive and thrive.[71] "The roots didn't thrive when they grew alone," Simard writes, "the trees needed one another."[72] Too often we conceptualize cultural production—the making of poetry and literature in particular—as a zero-sum game of winners and losers, prized trees versus weeds, in which only the few and the fittest survive the veritable "slaughterhouse of literature."[73] If it were true that only the game of survival was important, then, too, the grind mill songs would give any written text serious competition. But what if it were not a competition?

To be sure, focus and specificity on texts, modalities, traditions, authors—even the reductive method of scientific inquiry—are needed for rigorous scholarship. But what if, taking our cue from the new ecological sciences, we balance what we glean by studying texts, authors, and traditions in isolation with methodologies that highlight the symbiotic interconnections and ecologies that sustain them? There's no doubt that for a good part of the long literary history of the subcontinent, even literature that was composed in writing was experienced by its audience aurally, through recitation and performance. As Wendy Doniger points out, this "oral tradition has made it possible for millions of Indian villagers to be richly, deeply familiar with their own classics."[74] But the story does not end there—in the aural delivery of texts. The audience of oral performances or recitations, especially in South Asia, has never been merely passive, never only a consumer. They, too, composed poetry and song, responses and reenactments. In his famous essay, "Three Hundred *Rāmāyaṇas*: Five Examples and Three Thoughts on Translation," A. K. Ramanujan tells the story of an "uncultured" villager whose highly "cultured" wife forces him to attend a nightly performance of the *Rāmāyaṇa* by a traveling performer. The husband goes reluctantly but promptly falls asleep until the night his wife makes him sit in the very first row. That night he finally listens. The performer has reached the part where Hanuman, traveling to Lanka to give Ram's ring to Sita, drops the ring into the ocean. Now listening intently, the usually sleepy husband leaps up and jumps into the ocean conjured before him and retrieves the ring for Hanuman. This, Ramanujan says, is "what happens when you really listen to a story."[75] Listening, in other words, is not passive consumption but active participation. In the act of listening, the man in the audience makes himself part of the story told. To put it another way, the listener becomes an "interlocutor-participant" of storytelling, an active partner in its making.[76]

Perhaps not surprisingly, the "cultured" wife, the one who had insisted on her husband's attendance in the first place, disappears in Ramanujan's story. What about *her* participation, like that of the countless women who, so reliably, are the audience of such performances? A large oral archive of women's grind mill songs on Sita, known widely as the *Sītāyan* (*Songs of Sita*), is evidence of women's responsive engagements and participation, not only as a passive audience, but as poets and storytellers. Many of the famous verses of the *Sītāyan* tell of Sita's forest exile after Ram banishes her in the final section of the *Rāmāyaṇa.* These verses describe her loneliness and solitude in the forest with no one to listen to her but the trees:

In this vast forest
Who is speaking? Listen!
Sita has no one
But jujube and acacia tree-women

yevaḍhyā vanāmandī
kona bolata āīkā
sītālā nāhī koṇī
borī bābhaḷī bāīkā[77]

The trees are personified as women (*bāīkā*), and the verse itself asks us to listen to Sita's story as it is told in the verses of the women of the grind mill; through them, Sita's words travel the interconnected forest, ensuring that they are heard, that we listen. The trees are not isolated or separate, after all, but part of an expansive "ecoregion" of exchange.

Instead of seeing the oral and the written, song and poetry, as separate and competing modalities—a Douglas fir versus a birch, one more prized than the other—what if we take the underview to draw out the subterranean engagements and entanglements that make both possible? One need not cancel out the other; in fact, in many important ways, each is the audience of the other and thus locked in a centuries-long conversation in verse. Drawing on the evolutionary biologist Lynn Margulis's pathbreaking work on symbiogenesis—the theory that new cells, tissues, organs, and even species evolved through intricate symbiotic convergences, not only Darwinian cancellations—Donna Haraway argues for a new way of thinking about and doing the work of culture-making as *sympoiesis.* Sympoiesis means "making with," rather than making against. It is a way of "worlding-with," in company, rather than competing against. The practice of sympoiesis is hardly new, as Haraway herself acknowledges in her discussion of Indigenous cultural forms, but the concept helps us find a new way of approaching the history of the literary. Shantanu Phukan suggested something of this direction in his advice "to cease thinking exclusively of this or that text" or this or that language, "to think instead in terms of an entire literary area with its multiple literary voices and the manner in which these *interacted with each other.*"[78] It is not only written texts that engaged exclusively in this conversation, but oral *and* written. Sympoiesis is evident both in individual and collective ways of making poetry, in oral and written forms, and it is especially relevant for the figural forms of authorship that connect the texts and songs of *bhakti.* The term works as a description of the diverse and often interdependent ways of making poetry within "complex, dynamic, responsive, situated, historical systems."[79] Rather than weeding out or clear-cutting oral traditions to cultivate our focus on the written, or vice versa as in the Romantic elevation of the "folk," what if we situate poetic works, composers, authors, and traditions within the complex oral-textual, old-growth forest in which they have grown? Such, at least, is what I attempt in this book.

CHAPTER I

The Unraveling Heart

A Poetics of the Grind Mill

Poetry is the way we help give name to the nameless so it can be thought. The farthest external horizons of our hopes and fears are cobbled by our poems, carved from the rock experiences of our daily lives.

—AUDRE LORD, *POETRY IS NOT A LUXURY*

As the stone mill turns
I sing *ovīs* of the deepest self
To my mother stone mill
I unravel my heart

—GRIND MILL SONG, INDIRA SANT, COMP., *MĀLANAGĀTHĀ*

The Marathi writer Anand Yadav, known for his vivid depictions of rural life on the Konkan coast, paints a striking scene of his mother singing at the grind mill in his autobiography, *Ploughing*. The scene takes place the morning after he tells his mother of his plans to move to the city for a job. She was troubled by the news, Yadav writes, but quiet and withdrawn, staring off beyond the doorway. No more was said between them before they settled down for the night. At the earliest dawn of the next day, she set an oil lamp on a stand and began her daily grinding. The rhythmical drone and rattle of the mill filled every corner of the house, and all the things in it began to vibrate and quiver until he also felt the reverberations in his own body. He saw his mother bent over the stone mill, as if willing the vibrations to enter her body:

> My mother leaned in with eyes closed, pulling the stone mill the way a man awaiting possession by a deity sits before his god freshly bathed, head bent, and hands folded. . . . After a while, the whirring began to break into words. Her thin, high-pitched voice only emerged when she sat to grind. That's why she seemed so different at the stone mill. In a soft tempo, she began to sing to the rhythm of the turning mill:

O Lord Mill, how much can I tell you my mind?
Between your rough stones the kernel of my heart is ground
O Lord Mill, how much more can I tell you?
In the white of your flour lies the dust of my life

jātyā īsvarā, saṅgū tulā kitī mana
tujhyā peḍāta bharaḍatī majhyā huradīcaṃ dāṇaṃ
jātyā īsvarā saṅgūn sāṅgū kitī
tujhyā piṭhāt pāṇḍharī majhyā jalmācī raṃ mātī[1]

These verses were her usual opening invocation, Yadav says, and she sang them over and over in different notes. She began each grinding session with them. They were a kind of prayer, calling forth the stone mill as divine witness and confidant. "The stone mill was her god," Yadav writes, and "the mill listened to her intently."[2] All that she thought and felt when learning of Yadav's decision to move could only be expressed here, in verse at the stone mill. His mother always said that "you should tell your happiness to your husband and your sorrow to your stone mill."[3] These opening verses were soon followed by songs about a son leaving his village for the city, songs so moving that Yadav was overcome and lay weeping in his bed. These particular verses, meticulously transcribed by Yadav, belong to a well-attested category of songs about sons leaving rural villages to work in the Bombay textile mills.[4] Here, verses in wide circulation, composed for a different historical reality, are given a new specificity, a new resonance. Yadav was not leaving for the textile mills as so many men did in the mid-twentieth century but for further education, yet the mother draws on and inhabits the lyric intensity of this oral poetry to put into words her own impending loss, worry, love.

A much earlier literary depiction of women's songs of grinding, possibly one of the first in literature according to R. C. Dhere, comes in a sixth- or seventh-century Prakrit verse attributed to the Jain writer Sanghadas.[5] Sanghadas is the attributed author of a commentary on a major canonical text of instructions for monks of the Shvetambara Jain order, the *Bṛhatkalpasūtra*. Monks are generally prohibited from staying in spaces like the verandas or courtyards of a house, presumably where they might encounter women and overhear their songs. Sanghadas's *gāthā* comes in a section of the text recounting "restraints" prescribed for monks who are unable to avoid such places.[6] As we have seen in Yadav's description, these songs of labor have great reach throughout the household; their emotive power is likewise indirectly attested in this poem composed more than a thousand years earlier:

If women who grind grain
Are singing out of tune
Weary from their pestles
Why are you grieved
Heart-struck one,
By their piteous prattle?

Jai kuṭṭaṇīu gāyanti vissaraṃ sāiyāu musalehi
Vilavantīsu sakaluṇaṃ hayahiyaya! kimākulībhavasi[7]

The figure addressed in this poem, the "heart-struck one" (*hayahiyaya*), is deeply saddened (*ākulī*) by women's grinding songs, not unlike Anand Yadav who lay weeping in his bed as he listened to his mother's verses. Both Yadav's account of his mother's singing and this *gāthā*, separated by over a millennium, depict the affecting power of the songs to strike at the heart of the listener. In both accounts, the mournful words full of pathos (*sakaluṇaṃ*) affect the listener. But the verse, written in the high literary language of Prakrit, in an elevated *gāthā* meter, questions the listener's response to the song. Is the singing really worthy of his reaction? The woman's singing is denigrated as "out of tune" and the word for her song, *vilavantīsu*, which can be translated as "lament" or "weeping," connotes, in the context of the commentarial tradition of the *Bṛhatkalpasūtra*, the sense of "prattle," which makes it unworthy of the monk's attention.[8]

There is deep suspicion of songs here but also of the women who sing them. Eroticized images of women grinding flour are among the earliest depictions of grinding in literature. They appear in the foundational text of Prakrit—and also Sanskrit—literarity, the *Sattasaī* (Seven centuries), an anthology of *gāthās* depicting everyday village life in the Godavari River Valley compiled by the Satavahana king Hala around the first or second century CE. Here is one poem with an explicit reference to the labor of grinding and pounding flour:

Look at her breasts
Powdered with the flour
She grinds for the festival,
Like two white geese sitting in the shade
Of the lotus of her face.[9]

The woman at work at her mill is depicted here as the object of an erotic gaze. The songs of grinding are not explicitly mentioned in the highly erotic *Sattasaī*, but their trace has been intuited.[10] Sanghadas's *gāthā* is, perhaps, a warning to Jain monks against the charms of just such grinding women, though it does so by denigrating women's songs. It is a perspective not unknown to one of the founding works of Marathi literature, the *Jñāneśvarī*, which warns exactly against the kind of sensual men who populate the *Sattasaī*:

They would listen to whatever women are singing
Gaze at the figures of women
And use all their senses
To embrace women[11]

Here listening to, presumably enjoying, women's songs is seen as a sign of sensual excess, of lust. Indeed, the erotic depictions of women at the grind mill inaugurated by the *Sattasaī* seem to have persisted up to the twentieth century, as the postcards and paintings of M. V. Dhurandhar (1867–1944) show (see figures 1.1–1.9). By the end of the twentieth century, however, as grinding receded from everyday life, the labor came to be more associated with elderly women, often the mothers and grandmothers of writers like Yadav, who depicted their songs with deep feelings of nostalgia.

Yadav's novel and Sanghadas's *gāthā*, from the late twentieth century and the sixth or seventh century, respectively, approach the grinding songs from opposite poles and for different purposes. They bookend a spectrum of attitudes to orality, especially women's orality, in a literary history spanning two millennia. Whereas Yadav transcribes his mother's verses, granting them a poetic presence in his text, the *gāthā* enacts a "Great Divide" between song and poem, orality and writing, one that Sheldon Pollock's sweeping history of literary composition in South Asia, the landmark study titled *The Language of the Gods in the World of Men*, argues is foundational to literary making in South Asia. In Sanghadas's *gāthā*, the grinding songs of women

Figures 1.1 to 1.9 Postcard series by the artist M. V. Dhurandhar (1867–1944). From the Collection of Prem Kandwal, printed with permission by Prem Kandwal (amarpremlithos@gmail.com)

2 At First Sight.

૨ પ્રથમદર્શન

२ प्रथमदर्शन

3 How Sweet you are!
આલિંગન.
३ आलिंगन.

4 Hush! My wife! My wife!

૪ ચુપ. મ્હારી સ્ત્રી! મ્હારી સ્ત્રી !　४ चुप बायको ! बायको.

6 What is this

૬ એ શું?

६ हें काय?

5 Wife enraged.

૫ પત્નીપ્રકોપ.

५ पत्नीप्रकोप.

8 Dismissed.

૮ કાઢી મુકી.

८ रजा दिली.

9 Reconciliation at last.

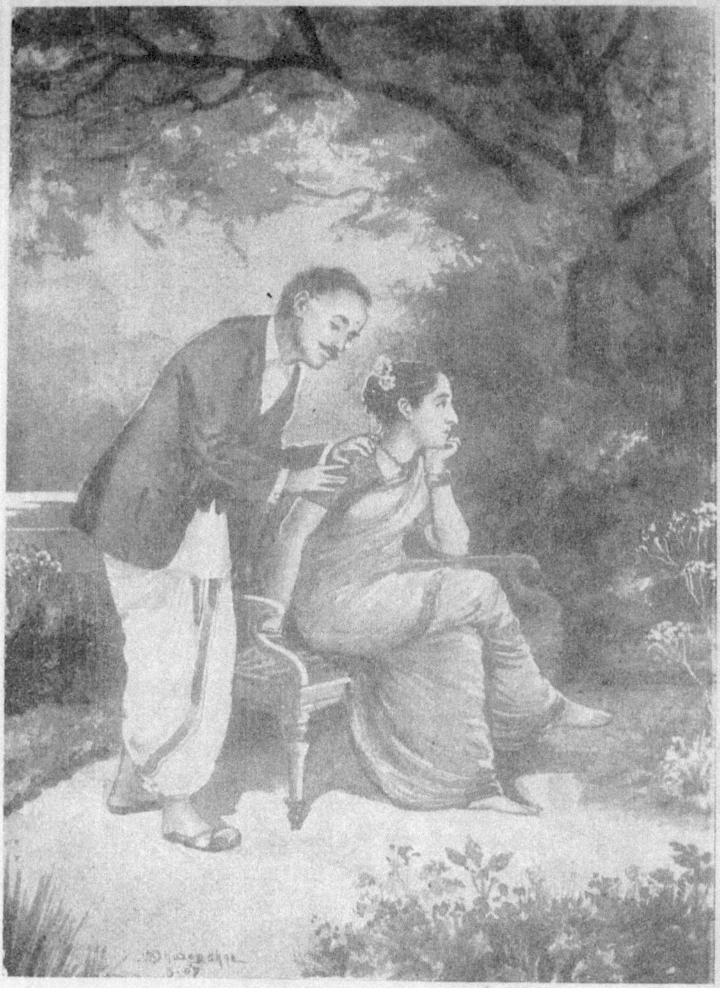

૯ મનામણું.

९ मनधरणी.

10 New maid-servant.

१० नवी दासी.　　१० नवी दासी.

are, indeed, Other, an orality hovering just out of reach of the literary (exclusively written) language of Prakrit poetry. The poem is written for the listener of the songs, who is addressed directly in the verse, while the singers are unnamed and the songs themselves unrecorded in writing. In writing a *gāthā*, its poet enacts a distinction between his verse as poetry and the songs of women. Grind mill songs are the quintessential bearers of the oral, the sung, the popular, the folk, in other words, the discourse of the everyday, the very opposite of all things literary. The songs are mere "prattle," distinct from the refined poetics of the *gāthā*. Yet, interestingly, the monk is not in danger of being heart-struck by the *gāthā*, perhaps a subtle admission of the poetic power of women's songs.

We do not know the language of the song heard by the heart-struck listener, but it was most certainly a language of the everyday, a "vernacular" at a far remove, or so it is asserted, from the Prakrit of the written verse. If the songs are ordinary and demotic, the literary *gāthā* is superordinate and rarified. Indeed, distance from the everyday, in other words rarification, is often posited as a precondition of "literarity." Given this binary schema of the oral and the written entrenched in the very concept of literarity as it developed over the course of South Asia's long and impressive textual-literary history, can we justify using the word "poetry" to describe the grind mill songs at all, even if qualified as oral poetry? To what extent is Yadav's description of his mother's poetic intensity shaped by the poetic ideas and ideals of the twentieth century, a result of democratic and modernist leveling? And, perhaps more importantly, would calling the songs of the grind mill "oral poetry" throw on them an external label that obscures their inherent craft and purpose?

The Twentieth Century

In Yadav's *Ploughing*, his second biography (published in 1990), he picks up the story where his first book left off, with his young adult years in the 1950s and 1960s. This was in fact the very period that saw the rise of a new interest in Marathi folk traditions. There had been efforts to collect Marathi folksongs during the colonial era, but it was in the mid-twentieth century, inspired by the nationalist movement, that women's songs gained a new stature and visibility through the painstaking work of folklorists and scholars who collected, transcribed, and published numerous collections, reflections, and analyses.[12] Of the several books and articles on *ovīs* published in this early period, the largest and most influential collection, the book that shaped how later generations of Marathi-speaking people would approach the songs, was Sane Guruji's 1940 *Strījīvan* (The life of women).[13] Born Sadashiv Pandurang Sane, he became widely known as Sane Guruji, a Gandhian anticolonial activist and author of the popular 1935 book *Śāmcī Āī* (Sham's mother), based on his childhood in a Konkan village. *Śāmcī Āī* was made into a feature film in 1953 by P. K. Atre, the famous playwright, political orator, filmmaker, and editor of *The Maratha*. The film went on to win the very first National Film Award of the newly independent nation that same year. *Śāmcī Āī* centers and celebrates the everyday wisdom of an unlettered mother, a eulogy of sorts for Sane Guruji's own late mother, and serves as a companion volume to *Strījīvan*, which presented 2,500 *ovīs* that he had gathered from his own relatives and neighbors.

It was the largest collection yet to be published. In these *ovīs*, he declares in the preface to *Strījīvan*, "women have a beautiful and refined literature all their own, created by themselves" (*sundar abhijāt vāṅmaya*).[14] Because they were collected from his closest kin and acquaintances, they are limited to the songs of Brahmin women. But in the preface, Sane Guruji notes this limitation and urges the collection of *ovīs* from all castes, regions, and religions, citing the considerable and beautiful songs of Muslim women he overheard during his travels. He was a great admirer of "feminine" virtues and highly sentimental about the role of mothers in everyday life. In these, he saw support for the nonviolent perspectives of Gandhi, which no doubt influenced which *ovīs* he collected and published, as Dhere himself notes in the preface. There are, for example, no *ovīs* expressing negative emotions like jealousy or sexually explicit or transgressive *ovīs* in *Strījīvan*. If the literary depictions of grinding women began with erotic imagery, the twentieth century ensured the near eradication of the erotic from the collected songs of women.

It bears pointing out one more important book in this period, though it did not have the wide influence of Sane Guruji's book. In 1948, Kamalabai Deshpande, a retired professor of Sanskrit, published the unusually titled *Divine Literature, In Other Words, Women's Songs* (*apaurūṣeya vāṅmaya arthāt strīgīteṃ*). The word *apaurūṣeya* usually refers to the Vedas, sacred texts of unknown and divine origins, but Deshpande is playing on the double meaning of *a-paurūṣeya*, which also can be read to mean "without men." Like the word "man" in English, the word *puruṣa* is used as a universal for "mankind," but the songs, she writes, actually do not involve men; they are "composed by women themselves and from the perspective of women."[15] Also, since it is impossible to trace back to an original composer of an *ovī*, its origins remain unknown, thus *apaurūṣeya*. Notice that both Sane Guruji and Kamalabai Deshpande use the word *vāṅmaya* (literature) to describe the songs without the moniker of "folk" or *loka*. The word *lokagīta* was current by the mid-twentieth century, but neither Sane Guruji nor Deshpande resort to it, though they do delimit the song tradition to a feminine sphere, separate from the world of texts dominated by men.

A major catalyst for collecting Marathi oral performance traditions after independence was the struggle for linguistic statehood, culminating in the formation of a presumptively Marathi-speaking state of Maharashtra in 1961. The Maharashtra Rajya Lokasahitya Samiti, established in 1956 to highlight Marathi-speaking folk culture—hereafter referred to as the Maharashtra Government Council on Folk Literature—published two-dozen volumes of collected oral literature and scholarship between 1957 and 1980 under the leadership of C. G. Karve and then of Sarojini Babar. Under Babar's thirty-two-year tenure, this group maintained a special focus on women's song forms.[16] Many books of collected *ovīs* from specific regions of Maharashtra that have unique linguistic features and song archives have been published since then, along with abundant academic research in a burgeoning field of folk studies.[17] The archive of the Center for Cooperative Research, led by Guy Poitevin, Bernard Bel, and Hema Rairkar, in contrast to much of the published materials, is cross-regional and remains the largest collection of songs, now available globally through the website grindmill.org. While over the course of the twentieth century grind mill songs came to be collected and published and studied as folk songs or *lokagīte*, this growing written archive also set the stage for their elevation to the literary.

One of the most salient examples of the sung *ovī* elevated to the level of "literature" in the twentieth century comes in 1953 with the landmark publication of *Bahiṇāīcī Gāṇī* (Songs of Bahinabai), a collection of verses composed by the rural and unlettered Bahinabai Chaudhari (1880–1950) in 1953. This Bahinabai is not to be confused with the seventeenth-century literate *bhakti* poet Bahinabai (1628–1700), a disciple of Tukaram, discussed in the introduction. Bahinabai Chaudhari was a widow who raised her children in a small village in the Jalgaon district and is said to have composed her songs during her household and field labors. It was her son, Sopan Dev, also a well-regarded poet of the time, who transcribed, edited, and then published her poems after her death at the behest of his mentor, P. K. Atre, the same writer and filmmaker who was, at that same time, working on the film version of *Śāmcī Āī*. Atre wrote an impassioned preface to the first and second editions of *Songs of Bahinabai* in which he extolled Bahinabai Chaudhari's earthy wisdom and wit, describing her as equal to the great poets of the classical tradition (*mahākavī*), as well as to the modern poets then in vogue. He describes her poems this way:

> From the perspective of composition and language, Bahinai's poetry (*kāvya*) is extremely modern. Every poem contains a complete event or thought. She has her eye on ensuring the dramatic effect of its beginning and end. She is especially focused on how to convey an emotion in as brief and intense a way as possible, without inflating her words or thought too much. From this angle, one must call her command over the Marathi language masterful. . . . From the perspective of *rasa* and implicature (*dhvanī*), she has used simple and beautiful words with such skill as to avoid any sense of contrivance or dryness.[18]

Atre calls her compositions *kāvya* and draws on classical literary concepts of *rasa* and *dhvanī* to evaluate them. Whether *rasa* was a quality inherent to the poet, the work itself, or something felt by the audience was the subject of several centuries of debate in the first millennium, as was the pinpointing of specific *rasas* and the best vehicles for them.[19] *Dhvanī* or implicature—indirect and suggestive speech—is the best vehicle of *rasa*, according to Anandavardhana, the influential ninth-century author of *Dhvanyaloka* (Light on implicature) (ca. 875). *Dhvanī* is what makes poetry poetic, according to a major school of literary aesthetics. Note that Atre uses these concepts without any qualms or qualifications to describe the oral compositions of a rural woman without any formal education. It is striking that on the one hand, literarity continues to be defined by classical models inherited from Sanskrit, and on the other hand, the very idea of the literary was colloquialized in the twentieth century to such an extent as to include working women's oral compositions. Atre's description of Bahinabai's poems as intense, dramatic, concise, and independent is actually applicable to women's *ovīs* as a genre. Grind mill songs are short and independent verses rife with indirection and implicature, concentrated articulations of intensely felt emotions. For Atre, however, all this was testament mostly to Bahinabai's unique and admittedly considerable poetic verve and skill as an individual poet, but it did not extend beyond that to the genre of oral poetry itself.

Sopan Dev had edited and lineated Bahinabai's poems such that they would look like poems to a modern audience. His lineation was different from the style of transcription used by Sane Guruji and other early transcribers, who present grind mill *ovīs* as couplets, tercets, or quatrains, divided into hemistiches using a space at the caesura. Usually, in *ovī* collections, the verses are arranged in a long list, sometimes categorized by subject. On the website of The Grindmill Songs Project, the verses are presented as couplets with dozens of variations for each verse. The variations are sometimes not all that different from one another, but seeing the enumerations shows all the places the verse was sung and by whom, and this maps its circulation within and across regions and castes. Sopan Dev, in contrast, presents each of Bahinabai's songs as an independent and unique poem, separated and arranged into lines and stanzas, each poem headed by a memorable title. Here's a stanza from her famous poem "Grind Mill:"

> O, grind mill, grind mill
>   The flour falls from inside you
> That's how from stomach to lips
>   My song moves

> *are gharoṭā gharoṭā*
>   *tujhyātūn pade pīṭhī*
> *tasaṃ tasaṃ mājaṃ gānaṃ*
>   *poṭātūn yetaṃ vhoṭī*[20]

Most of the stanzas in this fifteen-stanza poem begin with an apostrophe to the grind mill common to the *ovī* but here addressed as *gharoṭā* rather than the more widely used term for grind mill, *jāta*.[21] The concurrence of singing and grinding, which produces both song and flour, is a common theme in the songs of the grind mill, as we saw above in Yadav's mother's verses. The stanzas of this poem, however, are separated by double spacing, and each alternate line is indented. The spacing compensates—or is meant to compensate—for the considerable loss of affect and effect that happens when the words of a song are stripped away from the musical and performance context. Here it is the spacing, not a change in meter, that moves the words away from song to written poem. The spacing compensates for musical loss by creating time and silence in the poem, slowing it down for a more introspective effect. Before the luxury of blank space afforded by moveable type, poetry was handwritten across every inch of a page. Marathi scribes used symbols and numbers to mark line endings, but this was in aid of oral performance, not an element of a poem's visual aesthetics. It was print technology that reconfigured poetry to the aesthetics of space in a new way, moving it more decisively away from the performative and the oral toward the written, toward becoming a "text-artifact" that is read. The considerable sound tropes of Bahinabai's originally oral poetry are maintained on the printed page, but through Sopan Dev's editorial intervention, they are now supplemented, perhaps in some sense supplanted, by a new aesthetics of sight.

In contrast to the singular elevation of Bahinabai through such literary interventions, the poet Indira Sant (1914–2000) sought to present the grind mill *ovī* as oral poetry in a two-volume book set titled *Mālanagāthā* (Songs of the beautiful woman) published in 1993, just a few years after Anand Yadav's *Ploughing*.[22] Sant was greatly inspired by Bahinabai and herself committed to a certain colloquial register in her own poetry. For the title of her book, Sant draws on the word *mālan*, meaning "beautiful woman," a term of address used in the songs for mothers, sisters, daughters, and friends. *Mālan* is also sometimes a general feminine figure, a sort of everywoman, in the songs. Sant makes a strong case for the aesthetic merits of these songs without recourse to individual authorship, relying instead on the figural poetics of women. Using the lineation style introduced by Sane Guruji in *Strījīvan*, instead of the modernized lineation used by Sopan Dev, Sant showcases the verses as poetry while striving to maintain a semblance of their orality, their embeddedness in the everyday. She writes about the way the songs arise with the movement of the woman's body in labor, her fingers on the handle of the stone mill, the tilt of her hips as she leans into the work, the muscles flexing in her arms as she turns the mill.[23] In Sant's introduction, she writes about her realization that these familiar and everyday songs known to her since childhood were, in fact, a kind of poetry (*kavitā*).

Sant was home from college without any direction about her future, she recalls. As she sat one afternoon while her sister was on the swing, a domestic servant of the Gurav caste named (of course) Jana, was grinding in their house. Jana sang a verse:

On a silver plate
A red hibiscus flower
O my royal brother
Bring me a blouse just that color

cāndīcyā tāṭāmandī
phūla dāśāḷācaṃ lāla
tyāc raṅgācī coḷī
dhāḍa bandhū rāyā[24]

When Sant heard this verse, she thought about all the poetry she had studied in college. The metaphors, figures of speech, indirect poetry (*dhvanikāvya*), and the great Sanskrit poems she had been taught came to her mind. This *ovī* struck her as something unique. "This," it came to her then, "was actually a little poem!"[25] She got up and went to the prayer room and saw a silver plate there. She put a red hibiscus flower on it, and the beauty of it in the light of the oil lamp startled her. It dawned on her that the singer was subtly suggesting—through implicature, *dhvanī*—that a red blouse would look as beautiful on her body as the red flower looked on the shimmering silver plate. Here, the aesthetic and emotional *rasa* of erotic beauty, *sṛṅgārarasa*, is only implied, the erotic deferred or displaced by the direct address to a brother, not a lover. The flower in a plate is a religious emblem whose beauty is transferred to the blouse (*coḷī*). The *coḷī*, as I explain in more detail below, is an everyday object with deep personal, aesthetic, and erotic significance in the grind mill *ovīs*.

The first time Sant realized the poetic beauty of these songs, their engagement with the aesthetics of everyday life, she sat down with pen and paper to write them down. After decades of transcribing and collecting verses on random pieces of paper and in notebooks, she eventually gathered, organized, and published them as *gāthās*. In Marathi, *gāthā* is what the collected anthologies of the poems of the *bhakti* poets are called. Although *gāthā* means song, it is a literary word, not a musical one. Like the word "lyric," *gāthā* gestures toward musical origins but holds that history in abeyance. *Gāthā* is a Prakrit verse form, as we have seen in Sanghadas's verse, an independent couplet also collected, first, in anthologies as early as the second century. Yet to Sant a *gāthā* is a sequence of *ovīs*. It's not clear whether these are actual sequences that she recorded from women, or whether she exercised editorial license in their arrangements, but she seems to present verses that together give the sense of a longer song. One of the distinguishing features between the oral and the literary *ovī* is that the latter is woven into a larger narrative or philosophical whole, while the former remains a free-standing and independent verse form, even when sung in sequences. By calling the songs of the grind mill *gāthā*, Sant gives them literary stature; by writing them down, choosing the order of their presentation on the page, she turns them into something an audience would recognize as poetry but without the elevation of any one author. Between Sanghadas's *gāthā* and Sant's, it's as if a whole new idea of the literary has taken form. Like Sopan Dev before her, Sant presents these songs as "little poems." Do the poetics of the *ovī* depend on such editorial intervention? Is sung verse only poetry once it is written, or is there a poetics to the oral form that writing simply helps us to see better and analyze?

Poetics of the Everyday

The gap between the spoken and the written, the oral and the literary, no longer holds the same importance in defining "literarity" as it once did, especially as the concept of literature developed—or rather was deconstructed—over the course of the twentieth century. Long before this theoretical dismantling, processes of literary colloquialization, intensifying and then waning, often gave rise to literary movements and writers who sought to bridge the gaps between writing and orality, between poetry and everyday speech. This is as true of literature in the South Asian languages as it is of literatures in English. In the West, a clear trajectory of colloquial aspirations is traceable at least to Wordsworth's purported goal of writing in "a selection of language really spoken by men" to Mark Twain's *The Adventures of Huckleberry Finn* to the diversity of poetic forms today. Central to the "vernacular turn" in American literature was the influence of Black expressive forms like the "sorrow songs" of the enslaved, the work songs of Black laborers, and the blues. The nineteenth and twentieth centuries in Maharashtra likewise saw a distinct literary turn away from a standardized, Brahminical register to caste-inflected and regional Marathis. Jotirao Phule's adoption of a decidedly non-Brahmin idiom and the poetry attributed to Savitribai Phule seem to have paved the way for the colloquial turns of the twentieth century, from Bahinabai Chaudhari's rustic Khandeshi to the Dalit Renaissance of the 1970s. Anand Yadav's own writings and poetry are a case in point: he writes in a markedly rural register, far from the standardized language of the Pune-based grammars. There is not much theoretical scholarship on such trajectories of colloquialization in literature, but they seem to have been a harbinger of the twentieth-century theoretical dismantling of the distinctions between literary and nonliterary language, between poetic and ordinary language influenced in large part by ordinary language philosophy.[26]

Critics of literary exceptionalism point out that whereas the literary is differentiated by period, author, style, genre, linguistic register, meter, and so on, the discourse of the "everyday" is often left an untheorized blank space, a mere foil for the written and literary.[27] When it is invoked as an "idea" or a "topos," the "everyday" is rarely posited as anything more than a prereflexive space of habit and repetition, a contrast to the literary, the superordinate, and the aesthetic and theoretical.[28] There is something of this sense of the everyday, for example, in Poitevin and Rairkar's insistence on a rigid and "permanent" dichotomy between women's *ovīs* as "spontaneous" oral expressions of "commonsense" embedded in "the domestic sphere and repetitive biological time" in contrast to the abstract, urban, male world of normative written texts that impose historical time.[29] Such an interpretive schema leaves little room to acknowledge the compositional creativity of orality, the poiesis and sympoiesis immanent to everyday life, the permeability between the ordinary and the extraordinary. In a real sense, there is no more an "ordinary" language than a purely literary language, especially if both are understood to be mere opposites of one another. Even in the realm of the ordinary and the everyday, there are complex and multifarious ways that "individuals and groups construct and reconstruct the configurations through which they reflexively make sense of their lives . . . given the material and cultural resources available to them."[30]

The grind mill songs themselves—and Yadav's compelling description of his mother's verses—present a rather complex picture of the everyday for our consideration. Recall how Yadav describes the seated posture of his mother as that of a person about to be possessed by an otherworldly force, to be taken far outside the parameters of the mundane world. The sound of the grind mill creates a droning backdrop to the singing, Yadav suggests, like a *tamborā*, a string instrument used as a drone by both folk and classical singers to set and guide the note scale of a song.[31] Even the voice she uses in her songs is unusual, higher and more piercing than her everyday voice. In this description, Yadav lifts the scene of grinding out of the ordinary and the everyday.[32] While singing is an ordinary and everyday practice, it is distinct from all other ways his mother engages the world. Her songs escape the limits of their normal conversation, putting into words the experiences that she can only express in verse while she is at the stone mill. It is a solitary endeavor, this conversation in verse with a stone god, in which her deepest interiority takes verbal and sung form. When she sings, however, her verses enter the larger world; they spread like a tide over the whole household, the world of the everyday; all things vibrate with the mill, and there is no escape from her song. When Yadav hears his mother's verses indirectly speaking to his decision to leave his village, this is how he describes their effect on him: "I shivered under the covers when I heard my mother's unexpected verses. As her singing circled and repeated the verses, I wept quietly under the covers. The scene from the previous night came before me in a completely unusual form. I was beginning to realize how profound was her care for me, how it emerged out of her deepest self."[33] His mother had not said much when he told her of his decision to leave the night before, but here were all her thoughts and feelings now condensed and concentrated into the "completely unusual form" (*vegaḷac rūpa*) of the *ovī*. Although Yadav's transcriptions of his mother's songs reproduce the regional and caste-specific colloquialisms of everyday speech, her verses are described as distinct and different from any other form of everyday communication. The songs of the grind mill, he suggests, are extraordinary utterances embedded within the ordinary. He does not collapse her poetic utterance into "everyday speech," but rather recognizes the moments in which a certain kind of orality distinguishes itself as poetic within the everyday.

What exactly is "poetic" about it? When language is chosen for sound *and* sense, for the figural no less than the factual, organized and structured by patterns and arrangements of language, and when such an utterance cannot be reduced to a documentary or pragmatic function, it approaches something we recognize as "poetic" and—dare I use the term—as "literary," even when we accept that the boundaries between "literary" and "nonliterary" are more porous and permeable than fixed. The oral *ovī*, as Yadav describes it, is a verbal form within but also distinct from the flux of everyday conversation. His mother's verses at the stone mill cannot be articulated in any other way, in any other place, yet this space of the grind mill is also not a realm of autonomous aesthetics emancipated from the life of the laboring body. Yadav's mother's opening verses themselves announce this embeddedness of song and labor: the heart (*hūrūda*) and the inner self (*man*) are the kernels that will be ground between the stone plates of the mill into both song and flour. The verse describes singing as a *telling* of the heart, an expression of an inner self (*man*), a confession in words—in short what we would, today at least, recognize to be poetic utterance. This need not result in a collapse of the literary into everyday language, with the assertion as theorists like Mary Louise Pratt would have it, that there is therefore no such thing as literary language. Rather, it means only that the poetic and the literary are not the exclusive province of the written, the superordinate.

In the songs, we find a deep, ongoing, and personal engagement with the sacred, with the poetic, the symbolic, the aesthetic, the historical, and the textual, all as immanent to the "the everyday." One grind mill verse about Janabai that I recorded from Janabai Thorat, and then subsequently heard from many other women, plays repeatedly in my head:

Around Pandharpur
Jana gathers up the dung
She finds there a treasure
The pages of a book

Paṇḍharapur bhavatāla
Janā vecatiye śena
Tilā sāpaḍala dhana
Pothī pusturecem̐ pāna[34]

Janabai, the *bhakti* poet, is depicted here in one of her usual domestic labors. She is out in the area around Pandharpur, gathering dung to make dung patties to be used for kindling or for smoothing out mud walls and floors, still a common, everyday labor for women in rural India (see figure 1.10). Cow dung is an object of utmost practicality, the thing most ordinary, most functional, most earthly. In this verse, the dung (*śen*) operates as a metonym of "the everyday." Janabai finds in it the pages of a text, a *pothī*. A *pothī* is not just any text, but often a sacred book, an elevated text. When

Janabai Thorat sang this verse, she repeated the last line about the book, musically extending and dwelling on the image. The *pothī*, too, is a metonym, but for all that supersedes "the everyday," that is, for all that is considered beyond the ken of working women like Janabai.

Both the book and the dung are vivid in their earthly materiality, and in the *ovī* they are brilliantly combined, the conceptual opposition between them destabilized. What does it mean that Janabai finds this emblem of the high-textual in the dung? Were the pages of this book lost or discarded? How did they end up in the dung, in the muck of everyday life? However they ended up there, they were certainly not "intended" for Janabai. She comes upon them through the labor of gathering dung. The word I translated as "gathering" in this verse, *vecatiye* from the verb *vecaṇeṃ*, connotes picking through something. It is a cognate of the word *vivecana*, as noted by Molesworth in his definition of *vecaṇeṃ*, which means analysis, thoughtful consideration, scholarly discussion.[35] The fact that Janabai finds this

Figure 1.10 Image of Janabai making dung patties with Vitthal painted on the wall of the Janabai temple in Gopalpur in Maharashtra, 2006.
Photo by author

pothī in Pandharpur stages her discovery as *bhakti*, illustrating the way that Vitthal makes accessible what was once considered outside the purview of "women, *śūdras*, and others." It is, in another way, an allegory about Janabai's process of becoming a poet, about the field of *bhakti* poetry itself.

The *ovī* depicts *bhakti* as poiesis, but it is also itself an artifact of just such poiesis, composed and sung by women in their everyday labors at the grind mill. It is not only the depiction of Janabai the poet that implodes the binary between the ordinary and the extraordinary, the sacred and the everyday, the oral and the literary, but the very verse itself and its performance. The *ovī* is a concise and well-crafted poetic universe generated within and by the routines of everyday life. There is metonymic play, a figurative universe, and a deeply allusive poetics in this concise oral poem. It has four lines of eight syllables with an end-rhyme in the last three lines, quite similar to one variety of the *abhaṅga*. Yet only the latter is taken to be "poetry," while the *ovī* is seen as "folksong." These songs are much more than useful mirrors into women's sociological realities; they are expressive and artful articulations of complex "structures of feeling"—thoughtful emotions, emotional thoughts—*within* that social reality. As everyday compositions, they are not literal, not simply practical or functional, and not outside the world of texts. This particular verse was part of a sequence of *ovīs* that Janabai Thorat sang about the beauty and wonder of the city of Pandharpur. The verb tense used in the poem is the present continuous: Jana "is gathering" (*vecatiye*), which conjures an image of Janabai continuously collecting dung in Pandharpur in the ever-present now. With lyric intensity, the verse brings the figure of Janabai into everyday life, as poet and as *dāsī*, thereby granting her authorial name its authority. The name Janabai, which invokes the *jana*—the people of the everyday—is a *nomen loquens*, a speaking name not only the of poet but of the singer of this verse, Janabai Thorat, connecting the past and present in ways that conjoin the *abhaṅga* and the grind mill *ovī* in a continuum of verse-making, an ongoing verse dialogue.

There are different modes of engagement, what Mikhail Bakhtin calls an "extreme heterogeneity of speech genres" within the discourse of everyday life. In Bakhtinian terms, the grind mill songs would be a "secondary speech genre," a "comparatively highly developed and organized cultural communication (primarily written) that is artistic, scientific, sociopolitical, and so on."[36] Although Bakhtin does not address the issue of oral poetries specifically and had a rather limited (to my mind, incorrect) view of poetry as monological, he does point out the continuous dialogue between primary and secondary genres in utterances at every level. Paul Zumthor, drawing on the work of Jacque Dournes, makes a similar distinction between the spoken and the oral. Whereas the spoken is any utterance coming from the mouth, the oral is "an utterance *formalized* in a specific manner."[37] Indeed, oral poetry "is distinguished by the intensity of its features: it is rigorously formalized, replete with the markings of a very evident structuration."[38] Such distinctions between the spoken and oral, between different speech genres, need not take us back to the dualisms of poetic and ordinary language or between literature and nonliterature. A distinction need not be a dichotomy, need not fall into the fatal either/or flaw that characterizes so much thinking on this subject. The fact that such a poetics inheres in the ordinary need not be used to deny the existence of the literary or poetic altogether, only the dichotomy that assumes their mutual exclusivity.

Can Song Be Poetry?

In Marathi verse-making the oral and the sung have never been considered completely outside the purview of the literary, though this does not mean that song, music, writing, and orality are to be collapsed without distinction. There are discrete modes of communication, different aesthetics in each form and modality. There are distinctions, but not necessarily defining oppositions between traditions of song and poetry. There has never been a sustained or influential theoretical argument in the Marathi literary tradition to divide song as such from written poetry. In fact, we are more likely to find the very opposite, even from the earliest beginnings of Marathi literature, as I explain in the next chapter. In the foundational 1937 metrical handbook *Chandoracanā* (The composition of meters), the famous poet and prosodist Madhav T. Patwardhan, better known as Madhav Julian, illustrates a spectrum of poetic possibilities between the purely sung and the purely written (see figure 1.11). At one end, he places the Hindustani classical musical form of *tarānā*, a way of singing in "the sound-syllables of the rhythmic or string instruments" rather than in words.[39] At the other end of the spectrum, capping the extreme end of written

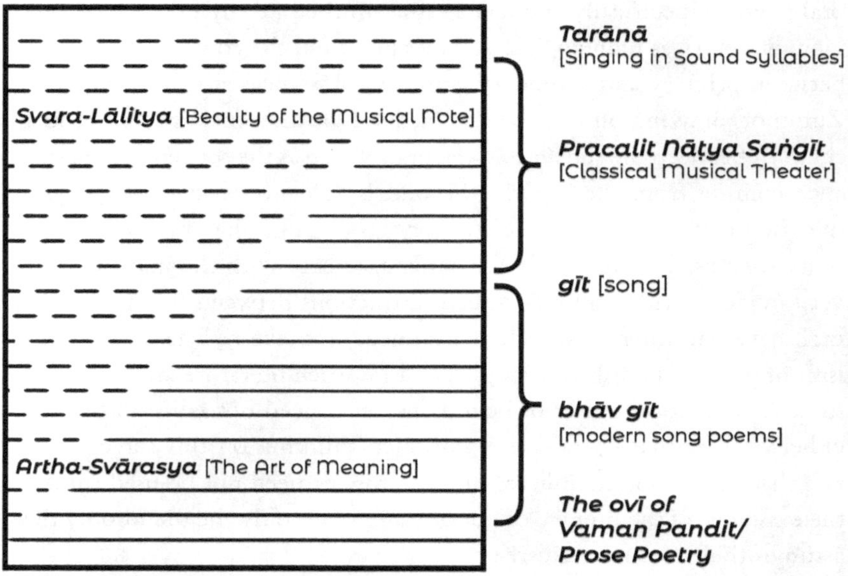

Figure 1.11 Digital re-creation of Patwardhan's hand-drawn graphic from his 1937 *Chandoracanā* showing the spectrum of verbal-artistic possibilities between the purely musical (*tarāna*) to the purely written (prose poetry).
Erick Rohn, graphic arts professor, Oakton College

literature, he places the literary *ovī* of the poet Vaman Pandit (1608–1695), known for his long, prose-like lines. He also puts prose poetry (*gadya kāvya*) at this end. He does not say where he might put something like the *ovī* of Jnaneshvar, or women's *ovīs*, but his graph gives us the option to weigh both musical and poetic attributes. The recognition that some poetry has more musical elements than other poetry gives us a good way to escape the binary trap that posits song and poetry as opposites.[40]

It is important to think both about the connections and divergences of sung verse—what we today would call song lyrics—and written poetry. Is there something like literary quality or poetic self-reflexivity that makes a song more "poetic?" Bob Dylan famously brought what might seem an arcane question for scholars into public debate when he was awarded the Nobel Prize in Literature in 2016. His lyrics have been deemed "poetry" by many admirers over the decades, though this did not mitigate the controversy that erupted when the award was announced. Dylan's lyrics had already attained written form in numerous songbooks, but the prestigious, nearly one-thousand-page compilation *The Lyrics: 1961–2012*, established the literarity of his song lyrics in a more definitive way.[41] Dylan himself concluded his Nobel Laureate speech, delivered via video with music in the background, by saying: "But songs are unlike literature. They're meant to be sung, not read. The words in Shakespeare's plays were meant to be acted on the stage. Just as lyrics in songs are meant to be sung, not read on a page. And I hope some of you get the chance to listen to these lyrics the way they were intended to be heard, in concert or on record or however people are listening to songs these days. I return once again to Homer, who says, 'Sing in me, oh Muse, and through me tell the story.' "[42] It was a thoughtful challenge to the gatekeepers of the literary sphere. Dylan places himself in good company with Shakespeare and Homer, global icons of literarity, but he also calls into question the primacy and elevation of the written as the best modality for poetry. I don't think anyone would disagree that Dylan's lyrics do more and better when heard in song than when read silently on the page. "The language of [song] lyric," Adam Bradley points out, "does not need to work as hard, and, in fact, is often better served by doing less than the language of page-born-poetry."[43] Song lyrics can "outsource" the "emotive work" of the words to the music or the vocal modulations of the singer.[44] Nevertheless, there are moments when the song lyric "incites a revolution against the tyranny of music, where it commands attention . . . primarily as language."[45]

What about the grind mill *ovī* as a song form? There is no musical accompaniment to singing at the stone mill other than the harsh discordant sound of two rough-cut stones grating against each other. The rotations of a grind mill rarely have a steady rhythm, and the songs, too, can vary by rhythm. In a brief overview of grinding and pounding songs around the world, from Burkina Faso to Belize, Ted Gioia notes the "ingenuity and variety of this music" that "deserves our appreciation."[46] The *ovī*, too, is known for its variety and flexibility as a poetic form. It is not bound by a set rhythm (*tāla*), according to Ashok D. Ranade, one of the pioneers of ethnomusicology in India. He argues that a consistent rhythm is "contrary to the very nature of the *ovī*," which is an "extremely malleable" (*atiśaya lavacik*) form. Even when certain *ovī* forms, like the *dhangar ovī*, are sung rhythmically, Ranade writes, the rhythm is intermittent, with long stretches in between, which "goes against the very nature of rhythm."[47] Yadav had likened the sound of his mother's mill, as I mentioned earlier, to the *tamborā* or drone, a stringed instrument, one of the three main accompaniments to classical Hindustani singing, the other two being rhythm and melody.[48] The drone is also widely used in folk music. A drone "provides a continuous fundamental . . . pitch-base on which a musician constructs his selected scale upward and downward."[49] Whereas rhythm and melody are variable, the accompaniment supplied by the drone "is the more constant" sound, one that is more an "atmospheric agent than a mere supply of one basic note."[50] In light of this description, Yadav's use of the analogy of the drone appears to make good sense; the grind mill, too, provides a sort of "continuous fundamental . . . pitch base" that provides a structure to women's singing but with room for improvisation, variability.

Tara Bhavalkar, the preeminent scholar of grind mill songs in Maharashtra, suggests that both the tempo (*laya*) and the musical scale of singing at the grind mill change depending on what women are grinding and how heavy the labor required. She gives the example of turmeric, a thick tuber that must be ground into a fine powder. It is hard to grind, and at such times, women describe the work as a "heavy grind mill" (*jaḍa jāta*), one that is hard to pull. The *ovī* occasioned by the heavy grind mill would be sung in a lower scale and slower tempo, perhaps in more plaintive melodies. When grinding lighter grains like rice or legumes, women sing in a higher scale, she says, and in a faster tempo. A woman might sing the exact same *ovī* to different melodies depending on the specific kind of grain she is grinding. She might, Bhavalkar suggests, even sing the exact same *ovī* as a lullaby but now following a steady beat matching the gentle tapping of a child's shoulder or head.[51] In other words, the light (*halka*) or heavy (*jaḍa*) grind mill is, like the drone, an "atmospheric agent" providing the "continuous fundamental . . . pitch base," a whirring thrum in the background of the *ovīs* sung by the singer.

It is important to keep in mind, however, that while the work influences the performance of the *ovī*, it does not exhaust its poetics. This is to say, the conditions of labor are important to consider but not the whole story. A common functionalist explanation of work songs is that they were sung to assuage hard physical labor, but this is a highly reductive view. The songs serve both "function and fancy," dialectically weaving "between physical and mental orientations," serving not only to ease labor but to lift spirits, transform the everyday.[52] They are often a form of play, of creating community, of "everyday creativity" beyond necessity.[53] Anand Yadav's mother chooses songs not based on what she is grinding but on what she is feeling and thinking after learning of her son's plans to leave home. The specific words and images in the *ovīs*, even the melody, can be chosen to express an inner state or to address social realities, to respond to things heard and learned and felt and experienced, to "unravel the heart." The huge repertoire of grind mill songs about *bhakti* figures like Janabai and Sita, about historical figures like Ambedkar, about family life, and so on cannot be reduced simply to the functional needs of the laboring process.

As far back as Sanghadas's *gāthā*, the musicality of the grind mill songs has been questioned. His *gāthā* instead highlights the power of the affecting words (*sakulaṇam*), and there is, indeed, something to be said about the verbal weight of the *ovī* if put on a scale with its musical context. This is not to diminish the affecting power of its orality, its performance. There is a world of difference in reading women's *ovīs* in a book or on the grindmill.org website and sitting among women while they sing. I have often been moved by specific melodies, the clear voices of some of the singers I have encountered, but even when sung, the words themselves carry a great deal of semantic and emotive weight. When a group of women would gather for a recording, they did not defer to those with musical talent or a good voice (*gaḷā*), but to the elderly among them, the ones who had knowledge of older songs, those with the widest recollection of songs.[54] In these sessions, the men in the family would also gather and encourage women to sing this or that verse they remembered, the focus always on the verses, the words. On Patwardhan's spectrum, the grind mill *ovī* would be past the midpoint between the pure musicality of the *tarānā* and the literariness of the written *ovī*, moving toward the latter though still a song form. To be sure, it is only scholarship that requires this kind of surgical division of music and words, this parsing of the verbal and the sung, both of which work together so well to generate the emotive and poetic power to which even a determined Jain ascetic might fall prey.

Some poetic elements do come into better view, however, when we make such surgical incisions, in other words, write the verses down. Writing allows us to dwell on each verse, to consider the poetic elements with rigor, keeping in mind that a certain sonorous experience—as happens in the analysis of any kind of poetry—is thereby lost. What emerges on closer analysis are the poetic hallmarks of the grind mill *ovī*. First, I have already noted that each grind mill *ovī* is an independent, complete poem, even when *ovīs* are strung together in sequence. *Ovī* sequences are often created through the repetition of an oral-formulaic opening refrain. Six other features are similarly structural: (1) conciseness and compactness; (2) dyadic structure and parallelism; (3) prominent sound patterns like end-rhymes, alliteration, and assonance; (4) parataxis; (5) abundant lyrical apostrophes (to the grind mill above all, but also to gods, *bhakti* poets, other figures and objects); and (6), perhaps the most recognizable, the ubiquitous feminine structures of address to mothers, sisters, girlfriends, aunts, and so on. These features organize and structure the words, thoughts, and feelings into a poetics specific to this song form. Some of these exact elements are also identifiable features of the *abhaṅga* and the literary *ovī*. Indeed, grind mill *ovīs* also abound in poetic devices and motifs common to all poetry: ample use of figures of speech, such as metaphor, metonymy, personification (though rarely similes); indirection, irony, implicature; and allusions to texts, stories, poems, historical figures, and traditions. By taking all these poetic aspects into consideration we see that the *ovī* is not only oral poetry but also recalls a specific genre of poetry found in both oral and written form and is often the bridge between the two: the lyric.

Grind Mill *Ovīs* as Lyric Poetry

It is hardly surprising that the oral *ovī*, as a short song form, shares many of the structures and features of what we would call the lyric. In ancient Greece, the lyric began as a genre of verse sung to the accompaniment of an instrument, most famously the lyre, from whence it got its name, but it went on to become a major genre of written poetry in the West. Though the term arose out of a specific cultural milieu, it has proven to be an invaluable and necessary term for similar poetries all over the world. Lyric poetry is most recognizable for the way it conveys intensely experienced thoughts and emotions in all their complexity and presentness in "short, nonnarrative, highly rhythmical productions, often stanzaic, whose aural dimension is crucial."[55] That the lyric is not an elite form but popular and widespread becomes even more apparent, Jahan Ramazani notes, in poetries outside the West where the oral and the textual, the sung and written engage in politically and socially consequential commerce.[56] In South Asian poetics, the term lyric has been used to describe everything from independent (*muktaka*), nonnarrative poetic forms like the Prakrit *gāthā* to longer strings of verses like the *stotra* and the ghazal. I am less interested, however, in arguing about whether the *ovī* can be categorized as lyric poetry, than in a comparative analysis with genres of lyric poetry that would generate serious consideration of the poetics of the oral *ovī*.

The "universality of the lyric," Boris Maslov has argued, can be demonstrated in a rigorous way in poetic structures both specific to languages but also shared across cultures. One structure of poetic utterance that bridges oral and written lyric poetry is parallelism.[57] Parallelism can include all kinds of recurrent sound patterns, but the thick sense of it as a layered poetic unit of juxtaposed statements, propositions, or images is exemplified in the grind mill *ovī*, which is, more often than not, structured as a dyad. This dyadic parallel scaffolding is reinforced by other kinds of parallelism, such as the repetition of words or clauses and end-rhymes. The correspondence between the two propositions of the *ovī* dyad is sometimes a restatement of a single experience or idea in two ways, and sometimes a contrast between images or experiences. In the Janabai *ovī* cited above, the first two lines bring us the image of Janabai gathering dung in Pandharpur; the final two lines create a scene of her discovery of the textual treasure. A kind of oppositional friction in the image of picking through dung and finding a textual treasure generates the sense of wondrous discovery. Another clear example of parallelism can be seen in an *ovī* singled out on The Grindmill Song Project homepage:

The crow built a nest
In the crotch of an acacia tree
Women are a crazy lot,
It's not like men love [them]

kāvaḷyānī kela koṭa
bābhaḷīcyā khoḍī
asturī yeḍī jāta
māyā puruṣālā thoḍī[58]

The syllabic pattern of this concise *ovī* is 8-6-6-8 with an *abab* rhyme scheme. Under the four lines is a dyadic scaffold. The crow building her nest in the first two lines works as metaphor for the ways of men and women in the last two, a parallelism reinforced by the phonological parallelism of the rhyming pair of words in lines 1 and 3, *koṭa / jāta*, that connect the mother crow and the women, just as the rhyming pair of *khoḍī* and *thoḍī* in lines 2 and 4 reinforce the parallel comparison of men to the acacia tree. The acacia tree makes a frequent appearance in the songs of the grind mill, usually as an emblem of hardship. The imagery suggests a stark contrast between the vulnerability and fragility of the nest and the stark and unfriendly thorniness of the tree, an ironic metaphor for women's lives in the company of men. In this *ovī*, words, phrases, and whole lines are deliberately placed side by side such that the parallelism is *implied*, leaving gaps that must be filled by the listener of the verse. This *ovī*, as the *ovī* about Janabai, does not explicitly connect the two images; even words are stripped of their connective grammar; for example in the line "women are a crazy lot," I filled in the gap and supplied a verb. The Marathi line, "*asturī* [woman] *yeḍī* [crazy] *jāta* [lot or group]," is highly paratactical.

Parataxis is another central feature of the poetics of the grind mill *ovī*. The *Princeton Encyclopedia of Poetry and Poetics* describes paratactic style as one in which "a language's ordinary resources for joining propositions are deliberately underused."[59] I quote this, not as definition, but to highlight the intentionality of parataxis. Parataxis should not be confused with nonstandard grammar or demotic language. In actuality, words that would normally be used in spoken communication are often removed for metrical or other poetic effects in the *ovī*. The paratactic style is an intentional method of compression, part of the aesthetics of the grind mill impelled by the process of reduction, removal, and concentration inherent to the labor of grinding itself. In the aesthetics of the grind mill, the story, experience, idea, or emotion is ground down to its most concise, concentrated articulation, the very quality that Atre praised as high poetry in Bahinabai Chaudhari's poems. The songs always attempt to say a great deal in the shortest and least verbose ways. Here is one example, almost ideogrammatic, from many variations on the topic of Sita's birth:

Says Mother Sita, what father do I have?
In the fields of King Janaka
I was born in a chest.

bolatī sitā māya malā kuṭhalā pitā
janaka rājyācyā rānāmadhī
janma peṭīta hotā[60]

This *ovī* tells the story of Sita's birth from Sita's perspective. She was not born but found by King Janaka in a chest in the furrow of a field. In the *ovī*, however, Sita questions the fatherhood of King Janaka, suggesting that he is not a real father, only the man who happened to find her. The dyadic structure of the *ovī*, the paratactic juxtaposition of question and answer, is apparent; Sita's question is answered in the lonely image of her birth in a chest, but the connection between the question and the image is left up to the listener/reader to make. The space between the question and the answer is teeming with the unsaid, both the well-known story of the epic and with Sita's own emotional turmoil, which remains unspoken yet is palpable. The *ovī* is less interested in the narrative details of Sita's birth than in Sita's interior experience of abandonment and loneliness. Her birth story also recalls her abandonment by Ram in the latter part of the *Rāmāyaṇa*, when he sends her away because of the gossip about her time in captivity with Ravan, a frequent focus of the songs. Both singer and listener—and researcher and reader—enter a shared interior space of Sita's sorrow. There is no temporal or causal sequencing, only an ever-present now. This is what Maslov calls the panchronic time of the lyric.[61]

Since the Romantic era when the lyrical "I" was narrowed to the individual subject, the lyric has been most widely understood as a poetry of "subjective" expression. But Jonathan Culler draws on the Greek foundations of lyric poetry as event and ritual to revise this Romantic inheritance. The expressive elements of lyric come, Culler argues, not only from the individual author, nor from a fictionalized speaker in the poem, but rather from the way the listener or reader of the lyric comes to inhabit, or cohabit, the lyric "I" when singing, reciting, or reading the poem. This is because the lyric is essentially a poetic text composed for "*re*performance," making it an event, not a representation of an event, one that draws the reader or listener into its modes of expression.[62] This is akin to grind mill *ovīs* and *bhakti* poetry alike, both forms created for reperformance of a type more literal than the later lyric poetry of the West, though perhaps not dissimilar to that of the ancient world. Both the *ovī* and the *abhaṅga* are sung and reperformed, without need to distinguish the composer of the verse from the one singing it. Still, though the structures of expression are shared, when a verse is sung or performed, it is the singer's experiences and emotions being expressed. The one singing the grind mill *ovī* exercises full license to revise the verse, to make it her own, put it in her own idiom to fit her own life situation, and in this the oral form departs from the written lyric. This tension between the stable parts of a verse and the innovations introduced by individual singers was observed by Albert Lord in his study of Latvian *dainas* and Serbo-Croatian women's songs, genres Lord characterizes as "oral traditional lyric poetry."[63] Each time a verse is sung, it is inhabited by the one who enters the song as the "I," as shown earlier when Yadav's mother sang verses composed in response to men leaving for Bombay mills to express her own feelings at Yadav's plans to leave his village for education.

Tara Bhavalkar calls *ovīs* a woman's *svagata*, a Sanskrit word meaning "belonging to oneself" or "passing to one's own mind, spoken to oneself, apart."[64] She says: "A woman's *ovī* is her *svagata*. Up to present times, we have been told what the *purāṇas*, the Vedas, the *Mahābhārata* have to say about women. No one ever asked a woman, 'What do *you* think?' My woman tells us in her *ovī*."[65] Notice that Bhavalkar situates *svagata* as a space in which women convey their own intensely personal responses to the texts and traditions around them. *Svagata* is a space of interiority created by and in the song, but interiority itself need not be seen only as the space of an isolated individual. I think we can all attest to experiences in which some kind work of the hands opened up a personal space of intense reflection, though mechanization has left less of this space, which is perhaps one reason why mechanized labors under industrial capitalism have not generated the same kinds of song traditions. Howard Thurman, the great Black theologian, described "the spirituals," the work song tradition that developed among the enslaved in the United States, as similarly "made for detachment from the environment so that they [the enslaved] could live in the midst of the traffic of their situation with the independence of solitude."[66] Here is an *ovī* about just this "solitude," sung by a Dalit woman named Tulasa Kamble:

O woman I grind the grain
In the still silence of the dawn
I've told my sorrows
To the mouth of the stone mill

mī ga bāī daḷaṇa daḷīte
pahāṭecyā sumāsama
mājha duḥkha sāṅgitale
jātyācyā pāḷusa[67]

In this *ovī*, it is the still silence of the morning, not the noise and rattle of the mill, that she emphasizes, conveying a space of solitude with only the stone mill to hear her sorrows. The fact that the mouth, technically called the "eye" of the mill in English, is where her sorrows are directed, suggests that she is putting her words into the mill with the grain to be pulverized through the act of grinding, an enactment of the simultaneity of singing and grinding. The "solitude," the *svagata,* is the lyric space that Yadav also describes in his mother's songs. "She must have seen her grind mill as an intimate companion of the heart [*jīvābhāvācā sobtī*]," Yadav wrote after his mother refused to share more of her *ovīs* with him so that he could write them down. "Who else did she have to tell her sorrows?"[68] Yet, in singing the songs that have traveled from one to another woman, she is also engaged in deep dialogue across time and household in the shared space of the lyric.

Against the common view of lyric as a purely subjective poetry, Culler argues that the lyric is inherently *dialogical.*[69] The many feminine structures of address, another consistent feature of the *ovī*, indeed of women's songs across genres and languages throughout South Asia, shows the dialogical basis of the song tradition. They are markers of what Bakhtin calls "intimate and familiar speech." In the grind mill *ovī*, the most ubiquitous address is to *bāī* as seen in oral-formulaic refrains like "I tell you, woman" (*saṅgate bāī tula*). *Bāī* is both the object noun for "woman" but also a respectful term of address for a woman, something more like "lady" but without the aristocratic and formal associations. *Bāī* is added as an honorific at the end of women's names regardless of class or caste, as, for example, for Jana*bai*. But in the oral-formulaic refrain "I tell you, woman" (*saṅgate bāī tulā*), the "you" is in the familiar form (*tulā*), rather than the honorific (*tumhālā*). Here at least, it invokes intimacy between women, as do other affectionate, feminine terms of address in the songs like *sakhi*, *sājaṇī*, *saī* (girlfriend) or *gavḷan* (dairy maid) or *mālan* (beautiful woman). There many songs addressed to daughters, mothers, sisters, and aunts. Another important feminine address is the simple interjection *ga*, for which there is no adequate English translation. It is a feminine interjection addressing the interlocutor, one that assumes and generates sympathy and intimacy. Such feminine structures of address are adopted in poetic works all over South Asia, especially by *bhakti* and *sufi* poetries, especially in the lyric mode. Feminine structures of address may very well be the phantom trace of women's song traditions in written poetry, a signpost of literary sympoiesis of oral and written. The traces of women's songs—lullabies, laments, festival songs, work songs—in written works often serve a specific poetic purpose: to create structures of intimacy, to invoke the familiar, the vernacular, the everyday. This is not to assert any sort of essentialism about the "feminine" or "women." It is a poetic gesture adopted by poets of all genders, and the marker of engagement, I argue, with women's own poetic compositions.

Some lyric poems are conversations with the self or an enigmatic "you." I am reminded of another particularly poignant grind mill verse about Janabai that I heard from Janabai Thorat:

In this Pandharpur,
Jana grinds all alone
How does she sing in two voices?

hyāta paṇḍharpurāta
janā ekalī daḷītī
dona gaḷe kashī gātī[70]

Although Janabai is depicted as working alone, two voices are heard, actually overheard, at the grind mill. This is a verse describing a certain lyrical interiority and solitude, not as monologue but dialogue, one that is then overheard by a third listener. The verse presents both voices as Janabai's own, though the presence of Vitthal is intimated by the listener, the third participant in the verse. There is a poem, an *abhaṅga*, attributed to Janabai with this same motif. Whether it is based on the grind mill song or vice versa is hard to say:

You sing alone but around you
Is the trace of some other's words

Who is that with you there
Singing without pause?

Panduranga is my father
Rukmini became my mother

Says Jani, I am fortunate
That I came to such a house.[71]

Here, too, the iconic image of Vitthal grinding with Jani is merely suggested. The "you" in the first verse is the invoked addressee, Janabai herself, though it is also possible to read the first two lines as the voice of someone overhearing the song sung in the last two verses. Although it doesn't come through in the translation, the language of the *abhaṅga* attributed to Janabai is less colloquial than the language of the grind mill *ovī*. Yet both the *ovī* and the *abhaṅga* depict a solitary singer whose song is overheard as dialogue. The "overhearing" illustrates the "triangulated address" of the lyric, the way that the poem speaks to one addressee directly in the poem but is heard or overheard by another implicit audience in a shared, intimate space. Yadav and the "heart struck one" in Sanghadas's *gāthā* also overhear the verses of women, while in the *ovīs* Yadav transcribes, the mother directly invokes—through apostrophe—the grind mill as her addressee.

This brings us to another defining feature of both the lyric and the grind mill songs: the ubiquitous use of apostrophe, an address to an inanimate object or a nonliving or transcendent being. When women speak to the grind mill, they treat it as a responsive being; in fact their poetic utterance wills the stone mill into a responsive being. Andromache Karanika, in a fascinating study of women's work song traditions in ancient Greek literature, suggests that apostrophes in work songs are the antecedents of apostrophes in Greek lyric poetry. In work songs apostrophes function like ritual spells, she argues, because they call on an object to move, a performative concurrence of word and action.[72] Karanika cites what may be the earliest written transcription of a grind mill song in Plutarch's *Dinner-Party of the Seven Wise Men*:

> "When I was in Eresus," he said, "I used to hear my hostess singing to her handmill:
>
> Grind, mill, grind:
> For Pittacus used to grind
> While ruling great Mytilene."[73]

The singer, though addressing the grind mill, is also speaking about and to the larger political situation of the times, a surprising similarity to Marathi grind mill songs across culture and time. Here, grinding is used as analogy for the oppressive, sexual exploits of General Pittacus (640–568 BCE). But Karanika argues that the apostrophe to the grind mill serves also a different purpose. It functions as a spell meant to move the instrument of labor into action, a common feature of work songs. Karanika then goes on to trace this verbal pattern of calling objects like the lyre or the wheel into action through apostrophes in the poetry of Sappho, Bacchylides, and Theocritus.[74] Lyric poetry has long been associated with spells and with ritual, but Karanika suggests work songs to be the source of this lyric feature.

We find a similar apostrophic invocation of the mortar and pestle for ritual purposes in the Vedas. In a famous hymn about the pressing of soma juice in the Ṛgveda (1.28), for example, there is a direct incantatory apostrophe to mortar and pestle:

> 5. For even though you are hitched up in house after house, little mortar,
> here speak most brilliantly, like the drum of victors.
> 6. And, o lord of the wood [=pestle?], the wind blows through your top.
> So then, press the soma for Indra to drink, o mortar.[75]

Throughout this hymn, the depiction of the mortar and pestle, the work of grinding, and the woman doing the work are conveyed in highly suggestive imagery, which has been the focus of much Indological scholarship.[76] The hymn has been interpreted as depicting a domestic scene of the ritual pressing of soma juice. Stephanie Jamison points out the juxtaposition of the domestic mortar (*ulū́khala*) with the high-ritual grinding stone (*grā́van*), which, along with the central participation of the woman in the ritual, suggests "a new ritual model incorporating the Sacrificer's Wife by presenting the solemn soma-pressing as if it were a domestic procedure, utilizing tools to be found in every kitchen, the proper domain of the wife."[77] If this is so, the connection between this hymn and women's pestle songs might indeed be even more warranted. The apostrophe to mortar and the pestle in this hymn is quite evocative of similar apostrophes in women's grinding songs, though we are, admittedly, comparing ancient verse to modern works songs. Yet if twentieth-century south Slavic songs of oral bards can illuminate the ancient compositional modes of the ancient Greek Homer, then why not look to contemporary oral archives of women's songs to help "ferret out traces . . . that women have left in the literature, . . . moments when women's own voices get into texts?"[78] Is it, for example, mere coincidence that the mortar and pestle make an appearance in the first poems attributed to women on the subcontinent, the *Therīgāthā: Poems of the First Buddhist Women*, composed between the sixth and third centuries BCE? Here women celebrate their freedom from the yoke of mortar and pestle in poems that also share features with women's songs of grinding.[79]

Pestle songs predate the songs of the rotary mill because the mortar and pestle itself is much older, but the invocation of the pestle as "lord of the wood," the suggestive double entendre notwithstanding, recalls the invocation of the grind mill as Lord Mill (*jātyā iśvarā*) common in the *ovī* tradition. Considering how far women, especially of the lower and Dalit castes, were from ritual Vedic contexts, I suggest it would be fair to say that the apostrophe to the grind mill did not serve a religious ritual function. This kind of apostrophe—whether to pestle, rose, wind, idea, lyre, hammer, or grind mill—marks an utterance as special, unusual, poetic speech within the everyday. Apostrophe finds little use in other kinds of speech or discourse, and works, according to Culler, as a "mark of poetic vocation."[80] Who needs address the stone instrument to which one is yoked in hard labor as a personified being for merely functional purposes? In women's *ovīs*, the apostrophe to the grind mill is an appeal to an intimate confidante, an absent mother, a much-needed sage or guide, a beloved god—not in order to cast a spell on the mill but to "unravel the heart" of the woman turning it, to establish her as a poet, singer, composer, and to transform the stone mill into her intimate listener.

A Metapoetics of the Grind Mill

Do the women who sing these *ovīs* have self-awareness about their compositions as a form of verbal art? Is there a theory of composition inherent in the practice of the song tradition? It is true that women who have sung these songs for centuries would not conceive of their own compositions as worthy of anything as rarified as literarity. But the song archive shows what Alan Dundes might call a "metafolkoristics," that is, songs about songs, a commentary on the practice of singing, as well as an aesthetic awareness of the written tradition.[81] On the grindmill.org site, over twelve hundred verses of various sorts are classified as songs about singing while grinding.[82] The very fact that women composed *ovīs* about composing *ovīs* shows a self-awareness that belies their purported spontaneity. There are also hundreds of verses about written texts like the *Jñāneśvarī* and on the poetry of the *bhakti* tradition. In fact, we can draw language and categories for a poetics of the *ovī* from within the tradition's metapoetics, which will help us out of the structural binaries that posit the literary and the oral as opposites.

A widely known collection of songs within this archive describes the act of composing and singing verses at the grind mill as "unraveling the heart." We have already seen a couple of poems from this archive in Yadav's recollection of his mother's songs. There, he presents them as an opening invocation, a depiction supported by other sources. Indira Sant opens her collection of *ovīs*, *Songs of a Beautiful Woman*, with just these songs:

As the stone mill spins, dear
I sing *ovīs* of deepest feeling
I unravel my heart
To mother stone mill

jātyācyā ga pherī
jivābhāvācyā vovyā gāte
jatyā māvalīcyā pāśī
mājaṃ hūrūda ukalīte[83]

The singer describes her act of singing as an act of unraveling (*ukalīte*) the heart. *Ukalīte* comes from the verb *ukalaṇeṃ*, which means to unravel, unwind, unbraid; *hūrūda* (or *huruda* or *hurada*) is the colloquial form of the Sanskrit and high Marathi *hṛdaya*, meaning heart. In the metaphor of the "unraveling heart" lies a grind mill poetics. The song is a kind of confessional revelation, an expression of subjective and personal experience within the poetic structure of intimate address. I translated *ga* in the first line of the Marathi verse as "dear." *Ga* is an affectionate feminine interjection, and it signals the expectation of being heard by a sympathetic feminine audience. Although the song says the grind mill is the confidante, the song also has a feminine interlocuter. Guy Poitevin calls these songs about the unraveling heart "an exercise in self-expression" motivated by an "introspective intention"—both hallmarks of what most would recognize as lyric poetry, what Bhavalkar calls *svagata*.[84]

The unraveling heart, exposed, vulnerable, and naked, stands in stark contrast to the hardness of the stone mill, grinding and pulverizing it into verses. There is a kind of ironic friction in the combination of these images. Yet the grind mill is invoked as a mother, a god, a sage:

You are no stone-mill
My sage from the north
I unraveled a heart
Of joys and sorrows to you

jāta hī navha mājhā purabīcā ṛṣī
sukhā dukhāca hurada ukala tujhyāpāśī[85]

You are no mill but a God,
O Sage from the mountain,
I unravel my heart to you
As if you were a mother

jātyā nā isavarā ḍoṅgarīcā ṛṣī
māvalīcyā vāṇī hurada ukalī tujhyāpāśī[86]

The *ovīs* address the stone mill as an ancient sage, a *ṛṣī* from the north, or as a god who is like a mother. The stone mill might be referred to as a *ṛṣī* or sage from the mountain because the stone or corundum used to make the mill is brought down from the mountains. This figuration of the stone mill sheds light on the complex figuration of Vitthal in *bhakti* poetry. Vitthal is also addressed as a stone figure, a king (*viṭṭhurāyā*), a father (*viṭṭhobā*), and a mother (*viṭṭhāī*, *viṭṭhumaulī*). The singer uses the familiar, rather than formal, dative pronoun *tujhyāpāśī*—to you—taking elevated figures out of the social hierarchy into a space of intimacy. In the first verse the sage is even more intimately invoked as "my sage from the north" (*mājhā purabīcā ṛṣī*). *Ṛṣīs* are "seers," the original *kavis* or poets of the Vedic heritage. Indeed the figuration recalls the apostrophe to mortar and pestle in the Vedas, almost as if there is an ancient intertextual dialogue, though it is unlikely that women, and the castes to which most belong, would have had access to the Vedas. When the women "unravel their hearts," they are, nevertheless, speaking to a larger cosmic order. Even in this most intimate and confessional imagery, we see the way that grind mill songs engage the complex religious-poetic and multilingual intertext.

This image of unraveling or *ukalaṇeṃ* is a direct reversal of *ovaṇeṃ*—weaving, threading, sewing—often considered the etymological root of the word *ovī*. At first glance, this reversal suggests the songs to be artless, spontaneous, and instinctive, not a making but an unmaking, and thus the very opposite of poetry. Poitevin himself describes them this way: "The *ovīs* spontaneously borrow their vocabulary from everyday life. Their similes and metaphors spring from the daily routines of their natural and social world, and especially from the various family relations."[87] Ruth Finnegan would describe this as a " 'vegetable' theory of poetic genesis," one that relegates oral poetry like the grind mill songs to "nature" not culture.[88] We should heed Finnegan's caution against such Romantic presumptions of artlessness and spontaneity. Unraveling and undoing are not, in fact, spontaneous. The agentive statement "I unravel my heart" (*hūrūda ukalīte*). suggests it to be a purposive act, a labor, a choice. The image of unraveling, undoing, derives from the specificity of the labor of grinding and pounding grain, of removing, undoing, unwinding, and crushing the grain. This is a description both of making flour and making song, as we saw earlier in the song of Anand Yadav's mother. The unraveling of the heart is not a spontaneous and thoughtless overflow but an act of labor. It is, in short, poiesis. In fact, the metaphor of unraveling and unwinding describes a method of poetic compression through processes of editing and removal until only the very concentrated expression is left. The very aesthetics of the grind mill are in this activity of compression, an editing to the shortest, most concise, most intensely heartfelt expression.

While the grind mill singers describe their own compositions as an unraveling heart, they also sing about the written compositions of poets like Jnaneshvar, Eknath, Namdev, Tukaram, and Janabai. The songs describe the poetic text as a blouse (*coḷī*) worn by women with a sari, embellished with stitchwork and embroidery, recalling the popular understanding of *ovī* as stitching or threading. Two very important motifs come together here, stitching and embroidering as a metaphor for writing, and the *coḷī* (blouse) as a metaphor of the text. The texts are written (*lihīlī*) or sometimes drawn (*kāḍhalī*) or placed (*lāvalī*) through stitchwork and embroidery on these blouses. Thus the *coḷī* is a very important and ubiquitous motif in the grind mill songs. A database subject search on the grindmill .org site yields close to eighteen hundred songs that feature this everyday object, but I am certain there are many more. There are hundreds of grind mill songs about women receiving blouses from their mothers, fathers, brothers, husbands, and also about giving blouses to their daughters to mark important life transitions like menstruation. The blouse is both a material object that signals well-being and an emblem of physical and erotic beauty. It is a deeply personal object, valued by women as an intimate gift, a thing for her body alone. That these literary works are experienced by women in a deeply pleasurable and aesthetic way is evident in this imagery. I've culled just a few examples out of hundreds to give a sense of this motif and how widespread it is. Here are a few common variations on a verse:

In the town of Pandharpur
My father buys a blouse
O Eknath, make a stitch with
a needle and thread of gold

gāva paṇḍharīta
coḷī gheto mājhā bāp
sonyācā suī dorā
ṭipa ṭāka ekanāth[89]

In Pandharpur,
My mother buys a blouse
Janabai makes a stitch with
a needle and thread of gold

paṇḍharapurāmandī
coḷī ghetī mājhī āī
sonyācyā suīdorā
ṭīpa ghālī janābāī[90]

Namdev sews the blouse
Rukmini goes to look
The side and back with pearls
Both sleeves studded with jewels

nāmadeva śivī coḷī
rukhamīṇa gelī pāhyā

pāṭha paṅkhe motīyāce
donhī jaḍītācyā bāhyā[91]

In the first two *ovīs*, marvels of poetic compression, the blouse is a gift from a member of a woman's natal family, making it especially valuable, connected to the singer's deepest attachments. The gift is also from Pandharpur, the geographic heart of *bhakti*, figured in the *bhakti* tradition as the natal home or *māher* of Vitthal devotees, who are then implicitly envoiced as daughters regardless of gender. The verb used for stitching is *ṭīpa tākaṇe*, which refers to stitchwork or embroidery on a finished piece of clothing. The poetic compositions are presented thus as an embellishment, as ornamentation, especially in the last verse above, invoking—whether intentionally or not—the Sanskrit literary tradition in which figures of speech and poetic devices are also called ornaments (*alaṅkāra*).

Poetry is depicted as aesthetic work, as ornamentation, on an article of clothing already associated with beauty and sensuality, again highlighting aesthetic pleasure. Notably, the poets are always imagined as engaged in the work of poetic composition—poiesis—making, sewing, embroidering, writing. There are some *ovīs* that mention the texts rather than the poet at work; yet even then the texts are described in the process of composition, sewing, or putting, or drawing, or writing onto the blouses. The "author" is the one who creates the experience of the text, which is ever being re-created; it is always in the process of being sewn. There is, even in this imagery of sewing, a nominal reenactment—the invocation of the *nomen loquens* of the poets. It is in the very lyric structure of this verse form to create such "effects of presence," to be an event rather than a narration of an event.

The *coḷī* is the quintessential everyday object, but it also reconfigures our understanding of the everyday. Just like the text in the dung, it reveals the everyday as a complex space of poiesis, in which the aesthetic, the poetic, the erotic, and the divine inhere. Conversely, the *coḷī* also ties the literary and the aesthetic to the daily needs and aspirations of women, thus recuperating the "work of art" from any sort of "separability principle." Poetry is embedded in the social and affective lives of women, but these works are no less aesthetically resonant for that. In the songs, texts are presented as a "work" made by skilled "artisans" like tailors. In many songs, the artisans are none other than Vitthal or Rukmini, who are described as making or embroidering these blouses. There are hundreds of songs about the *coḷī* worn by Vitthal's wife Rukmini, describing its beauty and ornamentation. Here is a striking *ovī* about *abhaṅgas* etched all over Rukmini's blouse:

Rukmini's blouse
Is filled with *abhaṅgas*
The God Vitthal has put on
The *Jñāneśvarī*

rukmīṇīcī coḷī
abhaṅgānī bharalī sārī
devā viṭṭhalāne
lāvalī jñāneśvarī[92]

I first heard a version of this verse when I recorded songs in a village named Gawalewadi in the Hingoli district in 2006. Later I found variations of it from villages all over Maharashtra on the grindmill.org website. The more variations of a particular *ovī*, the more evidence of its wide circulation. There are two ways to interpret the verb *lāvalī* in the *ovī*. It can mean, as I've translated it, "to put on" or "to place," or it can mean—in a more colloquial usage—"to begin a reading of" or to "to perform" as one might put on a show. The *ovī* implies both meanings, or rather it does not choose one meaning. It is not Jnaneshvar who is putting on the *Jñāneśvarī*, hence writing, reciting, or performing it, but Vitthal. In some variations, it is not Vitthal but Namdev or Tukaram doing so. In place of the word *lāvalī*, some verses use the word *kāḍhalī* from the verb *kāḍhaṇe* meaning "to draw," making the act of writing more explicit. In some songs, the *Jñāneśvarī* is replaced by the *Haripāṭh*, a work of twenty-eight *abhaṅgas*, attributed to Jnaneshvar and commonly memorized and recited by Varkaris.

There are also variations with Vitthal or Rukmini sewing the blouses or drawing the texts:

Vitthal sews the whole blouse
With *abhaṅgas*
On top he drew *Jñāneśvarī*

Viṭṭhala coḷī śivī
abhaṅgācī sārāsārī
vara kāḍhalī jñāneśvarī[93]

Pandharpur is my mother's home,
My dear friend
Rukmini sews a blouse
With the cotton silk of Hari's name

paṇḍharapūra māhera
mājha āhe ga sajaṇī
rukhamiṇa śivī coḷī
harī nāmācī gajaṇī[94]

In the first *ovī*, Vitthal is actually making a blouse out of *abhaṅgas*, while in the second Rukmini is doing so with a special cloth, a cotton and silk blend woven with the divine name. This is striking imagery that recalls the pervasive metaphors of weaving as poiesis. If the written poetry is embroidery—decoration, embellishment—on external clothing that is meant to conceal, the songs of the grind mill are an unraveling, an opening, a revelation at the very center of the body. Lest we think of sewing and unraveling as opposites, we should remember that the clothing—the *coḷī*—on which the literary works are sewn is the most intimate apparel, a most treasured object, worn right over the unraveling heart. The figure of Penelope comes to mind, unraveling by night all that she has woven by day, the two activities together an enactment of the continuity of composition, of poiesis, a ceaseless deferral of completion.

Just as the literary concept of the lyric gives us insight into the poetics of the oral *ovī*, the metaphors of weaving and unraveling drawn from the song tradition provide an analytical schema with which to understand vernacular conceptions of literarity that emerged in Marathi as the first Marathi texts appeared in writing in the late thirteenth century. The songs of women point us toward deeper deposits of the "vernacular" as the language not only of a region but of the household, and not only of the household, but of the women in that household, and not only of women, but of "lifeworlds" entrenched in varying structures of servitude, from patriarchal relations of kinship to enslavement. Yet this poetry-making at the grind mill was never in a wholly separate world from the literary making of Marathi's first writers. "In each epoch," Bakhtin wrote, "certain speech genres set the tone for the development of literary language."[95] Women's songs, a poetics of the grind mill, in a very substantial sense, as I show in this book, set the tone for the development of literary language in Marathi. What comes to the fore when we look at the literary through the categories of the oral and vice versa is poetry as a continuous *making*, a poiesis, indeed a sympoiesis, one that rejects the "separability principle" for the ongoing conversation coursing through the underview.

CHAPTER II

Colloquial Turns

Unraveling Vernacular Beginnings

> Orality insinuates itself, like one of the threads of which it is composed, into the network—an endless tapestry—of the scriptural economy.
>
> —MICHEL DE CERTEAU, *THE PRACTICE OF EVERYDAY LIFE*

In a now-classic study of an archaeological site in the central Maharashtrian town of Nevasa, the renowned archeologist H. D. Sankalia and his team write about the excavation of an early type of rotating hand mill from houses dating to the second or first century BCE. Quite distinct from the saddle querns and mortar and pestle found in Chalcolithic and even earlier deposits, these rotary querns appear to be a precursor to the flatter rotating stone mill that came to be used in Maharashtra up to current times. The archeological evidence, they write, indicates that milling remained primarily a household activity in India until the electric flour mill slowly made its way into the villages in the latter twentieth century:

> In one sense only this machine did not follow its development or use in the West. A rotary quern has never been used commercially. Since its introduction in India about 2nd or 1st century B.C., though we have some very large late specimens belonging to institutions, mass grinding of grain has been unknown in India. Until the introduction of power mills in cities and villages, every household, however small or big, had its own rotary quern or querns. These were worked by the women folk, usually in very early hours of the morning. This practice has given rise to some sweet and significant folk songs.[1]

In Greece and England, where similar rotary querns from roughly the same time period had been excavated, large-scale commercial grinding operations supplanted the hand mill.[2] Recall the Miller from Chaucer's fourteenth-century work, *The Canterbury Tales*. He was one (very ribald) character among others of various social rank and profession. There is no miller in the South Asian caste hierarchy comparable to the gardener (*māḷī*) or the potter (*kumbhār*) or the barber (*nhāvī*). There are *bhakti* poets representing the gardener caste (Savata Mali). the potter caste (Gora Kumbhar), and the barber caste (Sena Nhavi), but Janabai at the grind mill has no identifiable caste. Until the twentieth century, women of every household and caste worked the grind mill, though the stories about Janabai—and the postcards of Dhurandhar (figures 1.1–1.9)—show us that in wealthy households, the labor was reserved for women in various conditions of household servitude.[3] Sankalia proffers "the caste-system," with its rules against intercaste commensality, to be the main reason why flour production remained a practice of the household in India, though it is curious why the same concerns wouldn't consign other kinds of food

Figure 2.1 Early twentieth-century photograph of women grinding taken by Clifton and Company Photographic Studio of Bombay, established by Harry Clifton Soundy in 1897.
Courtesy of The Mills Archive Trust repository (www.millsarchive.org)

processing to the household.[4] Whatever the exact historical reasons, the continued relegation of this compulsory, gendered labor to "every household, however small or big" no doubt created a historically specific context for the robust and continuous development of a grind mill song tradition unique to the subcontinent in its longevity.

Though milling songs are found in cultures across the globe, including the most ancient civilizations, the continuity of the songs alongside the development of the prodigious textual traditions of South Asia is particularly noteworthy. For at least two millennia, the songs of grinding and pounding coexisted with the literary traditions of the subcontinent; they were witnesses to, and often invisible interlocutors of, the profound transformations in their making. Where there were songs, there were texts, and where there were texts, there were songs, and these did not remain in sequestered and separate spheres. It is true that direct references to the songs are rare in the elite textual traditions of the first millennium, but women's songs of grinding, I show in this chapter, were a formative presence in the vernacular era when Marathi first became a "language of literature." Though Marathi oral poetry is older than written, the advent of written Marathi in the thirteenth and fourteenth centuries gives us a novel degree of insight into it. The very fact of their orality means that women's songs move with the language as it takes shape, indeed as it comes to know itself as a literary language. This makes the vernacular era when Marathi took written form in its inaugural texts important for understanding not only written but also oral poetics and the "intricate interdependencies" between them. Indeed, the first written attestations of grind mill songs are found in the *Līḷācaritra*, the highly unique prose biography of the founder of the Mahanubhavas, Chakradhar. This text, considered by many scholars to be the first extant text written in Marathi, was also the first to give written form to colloquial Marathi. And it did so, I show here, by drawing on the poetics of the grind mill.

When Marathi took written form in the thirteenth and fourteenth centuries, it did augur a new awareness of Marathi as a literary language, but the concept and aesthetics of literarity were the outcome of complex exchanges in the early archive between the cosmopolitan and the colloquial, the written and the oral, and the writer and the audience. In this chapter, I look closely at the early texts, in particular the *Līḷācaritra*, to show that writing literarily in Marathi not only required what Sheldon Pollock called the "literarization" of a spoken language through the adoption of superposed literary models of Sanskrit, but also what H. C. Bhayani, the late scholar of Apabhramsha, identified as a countervailing "colloquialization" inherent to the practices of literary making. We might see this as an ongoing dialectic between the literary labors of sewing, threading, weaving, an aesthetics drawn (*kaḍhalī, lāvalī*) onto a spoken language to make it more artful and literary; and the labors of unraveling and breaking open the literary sphere to the gifts of the spoken and the oral. These countervailing labors of weaving and grinding, a "poetics of work," are ever in dialectical tension in the new practices of Marathi writing, and perhaps in varying degrees in all literary writing.

Oral Poetics and Vernacularization

Vernacularization is, according to Pollock, its most sustained theorist, a long historical process that unfolds in various regions of the subcontinent from the end of the first through the second millennium. Before the vernacular era, not only was literature restricted to languages deemed "literary"—the three main ones being Sanskrit, Prakrit, and Apabhramsa—but these languages themselves were restricted to literature, to writing. They operated in a closed and rarified circuit—each language formed, figured, and defined, according to Andrew Ollett, in relations of "co-figuration" with the others. With various regional culture-power realignments in the second millennium, the spoken, regional languages once considered unworthy of script entered the literary through writing, according to Pollock. Yet the very "vernacularity" of vernacular literature resides in the fact that it is written in a language also spoken and sung in the world of everyday life. Pollock deems these oralities irrelevant to the formation of a vernacular literature, however. "A world of local oral poetry of course existed long before and continued to exist long after the vernacular revolution," he concedes, "but it was now separated both in sociological and aesthetic terms from the world of vernacularity (it was retroactively constituted as a world of "song," not of literature)."[5]

D. R. Nagaraj offers a more complicated picture of orality in the vernacular literary turn. The *deśī* or the regional, Nagaraj reminds us, refers not only to language but to "a cluster of metrical forms and poetic structures."[6] Indeed, *deśī* or regional song forms (*prabandhas*) are thoroughly catalogued and described in Sanskrit compendia, sometimes, as in the case of the *ovī*, well before the advent of written vernacular literature. In the Kannada vernacular project, Nagaraj writes, early poetic treatises like the ninth-century *Kavirājamārga* (Royal path of poets) did seek "to represent the vernacular in the image of the Sanskrit cosmopolitan," creating thereby vernacular "literariness" through an "imperial redefinition of poetics." But doing so required the "disappearing" or concealing of local oral forms, especially those of the lower castes and communities, "denying them their right to exist in the space of the new literary culture." But, he writes, "Kannada poetry yielded and obeyed its theorists only partially." In the vernacular, "'folk' structures, of which Sanskrit was almost entirely devoid, also came into the field of literature, thus imposing a limit and a framework for negotiation and exchange with the cosmopolitan formation."[7] Many oral poetic forms were folded into the cosmopolitan vernacular through a process Nagaraj calls "reformulation," that is, the reconceptualization of oral forms using the categories of Prakrit poetics.[8] Some oral poetic forms like the *ragaḷe* thus "survived in disguise," whereas the "disarming simplicity" of others, such as the *vacanas* of the twelfth-century Vira-shaivas, resisted altogether the imperial-cosmopolitan formation in a second, more distinctly revolutionary wave of vernacularization.[9] In short, the vernacular had to come to terms with the oral poetic, according to Nagaraj, and it did so in multiple and complex ways, not by instituting one sweeping, categorical binary between orality and writing.

This is perhaps even truer in Marathi vernacularization, where there was never an "imperial redefinition of poetics" in the Kannada style. There was no Marathi *Kavirājamārga* to reconfigure Marathi poetics in the mirror of the superposed tradition. This is in part because, as Christian Novetzke has amply demonstrated, Marathi vernacularization did not follow the imperial culture-power trajectory that Pollock identifies as the dominant paradigm of vernacularization.[10] For most of its history, Marathi literature was written outside of royal courts and without royal patronage. There is some evidence in Mahanubhava sources that a nascent literary court had begun to take shape in the final decade of the thirteenth century, under the rule of the last Yadava king, Ramdev (r. 1271–1311), but this was very short-lived.[11] The Delhi sultanate, whose incursions began as early as 1296, successfully annexed the whole of the Yadava region and made Devgiri their provincial capital by 1318. Thus Marathi did not hold imperial status as a language of dynastic rule over a Marathi-speaking polity for long under the Yadavas, though Ramdev appears to have aspired to something of the sort toward the very end of his reign.

Though the first Marathi literary texts seem to have appeared first in the late thirteenth century, during the reign of Ramdev, they continued to be written unabated over the turn of the century into the fourteenth, the fifteenth, and the sixteenth centuries, contradicting the all-too-common characterization of the period after the fall of the Yadavas and the rise of the Marathas as the "Dark Ages" of Marathi cultural decline under "Muslim rule."[12] The continuity of vernacular writing over the period of transition from Yadava to sultanate rule is what, in fact, evinces the relative independence of Marathi vernacularization from the royal centers of power and patronage. There is no evidence of direct literary patronage of Marathi by any of the sultanates that ruled over Marathi-speaking regions for the next three centuries in the manner, for example, of the patronage of Telugu literature by Sultan Ibrahim Qutb Shah (r. 1550–1580) of the Golconda dynasty. But there is no denying that Marathi literature continued to be written during the age of the sultanates as powerful religious-literary sects came to dominate the decentralized vernacular spaces fostered, as Richard Eaton has shown, by the administrative practices of the sultanates.[13] Marathi language and poetics also influenced and were influenced by the syncretic literatures and theologies of the sixteenth and seventeenth centuries, as seen, for example, in the *cakkī-nāmā* poems of the Bijapur Sufis. Given this, we might do better, Pushkar Sohoni contends, to think of the vernacular not as a singular language but as a "space," a "regional episteme," a multilingual and religiously diverse "lifeworld."[14]

Marathi literature emerged and developed in the shared everyday vernacular spaces, "at the crossroads of towns and cities, among networks of villages linked by trade and roving preachers, under trees, outside temples and monasteries, amid farms and homes."[15] And these spaces were—and in some ways still are—resonant with public recitations, discourses, theaters, performances, songs, and poetries of all kinds. Though he misapprehended the threat to Marathi during sultanate rule, S. G. Tulpule was right that, in the absence of courtly patronage, the "the religious institutions of Mahārāṣṭra like the *kīrtana*, *bhajana*, *purāṇa* and *gondhaḷa*, and the folksongs of women" came to the "aid" of Marathi writing.[16] By calling these oral traditions "institutions," Tulpule conveys their historical weight and substantiality. This is not orality conceived as the mess and tangle of "demotic" impermanence, but orality structured by well-known, self-aware, long-established, and continuous traditions of composition and performance. There are, as folk studies scholars have pointed out, many more such oral "institutions" in the landscape of the everyday than even mentioned by Tulpule or can be fully accounted here. Working their way through villages, towns, and cities on any given day are the *potarāj*, a traveling devotee of the goddess; the *vāsudev*, a traveling devotee of Krishna; the *bharāḍī*, a devotee-performer of Bhairav; as well as *dhangars*, Nath *yogīs*, Sufi *pīrs* and fakirs, Jain monks and nuns, and so on.[17] Many such oral performers are vividly depicted in the thirteenth-century works of the Mahanubhavas, and many songs, among them women's *ovīs*, are included in these texts. The everyday world is a space populated, in short, by diverse and influential interlocutors, not a passive audience. Vernacularization is thus better understood, I explain in this chapter, as the process of making literature with a "new sense of the listener as a partner-interlocutor."[18]

The vernacularization of Marathi is, in other words, the work of interweaving the novel practices of writing in Marathi with the long-abiding, everyday oral poetics of the region. Just as royal courts promoted a certain high-poetic aesthetic based on superposed models and theories of *kāvya*, so did the space of the everyday shape a new vernacular written aesthetics through the models, motifs, meters, lexicon, and concepts circulating in the oral landscape. Women's songs of the grind mill, in particular, are so woven into the fabric of the everyday that their reach and influence would have been impossible to avoid. Important aspects of the quotidian in Marathi literature are drawn from the labors, speech genres, poetic motifs, and tropes of this influential oral poetic tradition. In Marathi poetry, as arguably in other *bhakti* poetic traditions of the North and South, women's oral poetic genres played a constitutive literary role.

Literarization and Colloquialization

When a language is first put into writing for documentary purposes, Pollock calls this "literization," but vernacularization involves a second and more crucial process he calls "literarization," the development of the literary and expressive capacities of a language in and through the modality of writing. "Writing literarily," he argues, "can only emerge out of a matrix of preexisting and dominant literatures." The vernacular writer "achieves expressivity" in the new language "by appropriating and domesticating models of literary language use from superposed cultural formations."[19] According to Ollett, literarization "involves the building up" of the "rules, procedures, norms, or models" of literarity and "the production of texts in accordance with them."[20] Though Ollett and Pollock have slightly different theories of literarization, both see it as a process of "building up" distance between the literary and the everyday. "Literarization," Ollett writes, "is always accompanied by a rarification of discourse."[21] The argument that the "spoken" language is *made* literary ignores the complex and layered language of the everyday, suffused as it is by song and prayer and oral poetries and performances.

Colloquialization maps a countervailing trajectory to literarization, a movement from the literary toward the spoken and oral. H. C. Bhayani uses this concept to explain the development of Prakrit and Apabhramsha in relation to Sanskrit. Although, Bhayani writes, the origins of Prakrit and Apabhramsha remain unknown:

> The same factors were responsible in the case of both Prakrit and Ap[abhramsha] for their successive formation and subsequent standardization for literary purposes, the 'high' language becoming fixed by standardization etc. moved farther and farther away from the ordinary language of the people, creating thereby an ever-widening communication gap. To bridge this gap, there starts a process of colloquializing the archaic literary language at various levels. In course of time this mixed language becomes again standardized and the colloquializing process is repeated.[22]

Bhayani describes a kind of ebb and flow in the history of Prakrit and Apabhramsha, both of which reached from time to time into the colloquial, while still maintaining—through a countervailing process of "standardization for literary purposes"—their transregional, courtly, cosmopolitan character as languages of literature. Bhayani calls Prakrit a colloquialized form of Sanskrit and Apabhramsha a "colloquialized form of literary Prakrit."[23] This does not mean they were spoken languages but rather that, as literary languages, they turned to the colloquial, the regional, the *deśī*, at various points in order to break out of the stultification of a rarified literary discourse. "Literary Apabraṁśa, like the literary Prakrits," though rarified, attempted "to a limited degree to adopt its morphology and expressions and, to a slight extent, its lexicon to the constantly changing spoken idioms of the period," Bhayani writes.[24] The openness to "reinforcement through an undercurrent of living speech forms" undermines the "rigidity" that can develop in "a highly standardized literary language, fostered in the linguistic surroundings of centuries of aristocratic and stylized traditions."[25] Bhayani's argument suggests something of a "linguistic drift" over time in the direction of the colloquial, not in one language, but as fitting for the polyglot landscape of premodern South Asia, in the dynamics of at least three languages of literature, and perhaps more if we think about how this process continued into vernacularization. "Drift" refers to the cumulative, sometimes subtle changes in language over long spans of time. "Linguistic drift," Sapir writes, "has direction."[26] Sapir was focused on the "unconscious" changes in spoken language, but colloquialization in literary texts is the result of specific literary choices in response to specific historical circumstances. We will have to leave it to Indologists to debate Bhayani's perspectives on Prakrit and Apabhramsha specifically, but the concept of colloquialization is a useful analytic, as attested in literary history, to avoid pitting the sung and the written, the oral and the literary, and even the superposed and the vernacular languages as binary opposites.

T. S. Eliot acknowledged something of the process of colloquialization in English literary history:

> Every revolution in poetry is apt to be, and sometimes to announce itself to be, a return to common speech. That is the revolution which Wordsworth announced in his prefaces, and he was right: the same revolution had been carried out a century before by Oldham, Waller, Denham and Dryden; and the same revolution was due again something over a century later. The followers of a revolution develop the new poetic idiom in one direction or another; they polish or perfect it; meanwhile the spoken language goes on changing, and the poetic idiom goes out of date.[27]

Eliot here suggests a similar back and forth between rarification and colloquialization, a dialectic of weaving and unraveling, two countervailing processes of literary making always in tension. A quantitative study of informal and oral style in English fiction, essays, and letters written between the seventeenth and the nineteenth centuries seems to support Eliot's observation. The authors of the study, Douglas Biber and Edward Finegan, found a discernible "drift" toward the colloquial from the seventeenth through the nineteenth centuries.[28] The use of "private verbs" (think, feel), the second person, *wh*-questions, emphasis, present tense verbs, active voice, and less abstract referents are some of the features that create an oral style in English. There were many such oral markers in seventeenth-century writing, but also a move toward more formal and elaborated style in the eighteenth century against which Romanticism inspired a gradual move back to oral styles in the nineteenth century (499). Looking at the long-term trends, Biber and Finegan found that by the modern, post-1865 period, all three genres of writing in English were considerably more oral in style than the style that dominated seventeenth-century writing (507). They connect this historical trajectory to transformations in mass literacy and democratization.

A similar colloquialization over the course of the twentieth century, perhaps also connected to democratizing trends, created literary space for Anand Yadav's rural language in his memoir *Ploughing*, and for Yadav's inclusion of his mother's grind mill verses in that memoir. It is what led to Sopan Dev's recognition of the poetry in his mother Bahinabai Chaudhari's oral verses in the 1950s, and Indira Sant's argument in *Songs of a Beautiful Woman* that the grind mill *ovī* is a poem. Yet colloquialization is not only a modern phenomenon on the subcontinent; it goes back to the very founding of Marathi literature in the thirteenth and fourteenth centuries. Eight centuries before Yadav included his mother's *ovīs* in his autobiography, the *Līḷācaritra*, the biography of an incarnated god, gave women's *ovīs* written form for the first time.

Colloquialization is not, I want to make clear, an argument about the linguistic genealogy of Marathi.[29] Rather, it is important to the ways Marathi came to be and know itself as a literary language, whatever the specifics of its linguistic history. Like many vernaculars, especially those of the North, Marathi was heir to the conceptual literary schema of "co-figuration" that Ollett argues structured Prakrit and Apabhramsha as alternatives to Sanskrit.[30] Ollett writes that in the North, "the vernaculars were largely thought of as a further iteration of Apabhramsha, which was itself conceived of as a kind of iteration of Prakrit."[31] Perhaps the text that best shows Marathi literarity to be on an iterative spectrum of intensified colloquialization is Mahadaise's *Dhavaḷe* (ca. 1285), a narrative poem on the marriage of Rukmini and Krishna. This work is likely the very first extant narrative poem in Marathi, and it was written, not in the *ovī* like most other early vernacular poetic works, but in the Apabhramsha poetic form of the *dhavala*. This work, notable if only for its early attribution of authorship to a woman, is almost always left out of studies of vernacularization. I return to it and its remarkable author in the final chapter.

I would like to broaden the concept of colloquialization beyond grammatical and linguistic markers to include the literary movement toward oral compositional styles and forms, as well as motifs, themes, and even subjects derived from oral verbal art, especially song. Colloquialization encompasses an aspiration within written literature for the ease of expression, purpose, vigor, reach, audience, emotional effects, and aesthetic attributes of orality. Mikhail Bakhtin comes close to the concept of colloquialization in the broader literary and not simply linguistic sense in his discussion of "familiarization" in literature. Students of literature have likely heard of the Russian formalist concept of "defamiliarization," a modernist literary technique meant to make the ordinary and the mundane seem strange in order to disrupt habitual and routinized thinking. Here Bakhtin calls attention to an opposite technique, one that he argues to be equally disruptive to the literary status quo: "When the task was to destroy traditional official styles and worldviews that had faded and become conventional, familiar styles became very significant in literature. Moreover, familiarization of styles opened literature up to layers of language that had previously been under speech constraint. The significance of familiar genres and styles in literary history has not been adequately addressed."[32] Bakhtin's notion that "familiarization" in literature brings language that had once been "under speech constraint" into the literary is one way of characterizing the turn to the colloquial as important to the processes of vernacularization.

The prolific and high-literary sixteenth-century poet-philosopher Dasopant (1551–1615) illustrates "familiarization" in a humorous story in his massive tome, the *Gītārṇava* (The ocean of Gītā), a commentary on the Bhagavad Gītā inspired by the *Jñāneśvarī* but nearly double in length. The story, published as "A Story of One Sanskrit Devotee," features a debate between two brothers, the elder a zealous champion of Sanskrit and the younger a pragmatic proponent of Prakrit, in other words, everyday spoken Marathi.[33] The proponent of Sanskrit refuses to speak in Prakrit, and this leads to all kinds of humorous escapades and misunderstandings for which he is soundly beaten and driven out by villagers. The wiser younger brother counsels him to recognize the limits of Sanskrit in the world of everyday life, which he calls *saṃsāranagarapeṭhe*, where different "coins" of language circulate.[34] In Marathi, *saṃsāra* means not only "worldly" life as it does in Sanskrit, but household "domestic" life, while *nagara* is the town, and *pethe* the marketplace.

The multiplicity of these everyday spaces is important to the story, since it illustrates how many more spaces there are in which the vernacular, Prakrit, has more currency than Sanskrit, which has a limited sphere of circulation. Sanskrit only has one word for pot, *ghaṭu*, the younger brother says before listing over fifteen extremely colloquial Marathi words for pot, including, for example, the word for a wide-mouthed and narrow-necked pitcher used at the time of milking a cow (*moravā*).[35] He goes on to compare other limited Sanskrit words to the rich lexicon of everyday life. The vernacular words in this section are listed with a certain delight in their sound, precision, and colloquiality, full of the retroflex and hard cerebral consonants of Marathi:

sanavaṭ copaṇ gavhāḷī
cikaṇī panhvaṭ maḷī
cunavaṭ māḷavaṭ khaḷī
khaḷagā khāṭ[36]

Fallow land, loamy earth, soil prepared for growing wheat,
Clay, shaded ground, a river-side garden bed
A limestone quarry, stony and elevated barren ground, a grave
A hollow, muck

These are multiple words for ground, and it becomes evident even when translating them into English how many more words have to be used to get across the meaning of a single colloquial Marathi word. The verse has a rustic musicality to it, almost like a nursery rhyme. The verse form used by Dasopant is, of course, the *ovī*, three-and-a-half lines, with syllables ranging from eight to ten in number in the first three lines followed by a shorter final line. The younger brother says to his prideful, learned brother: "The status you give yourself is in your head, it is not conferred by the people."[37] Only when the Sanskrit proponent gives in and starts speaking in Marathi does he gains a devoted following. That even a high-textual work of this sort makes the case for the importance of the proximate audience illustrates how the space of the everyday shaped Marathi writing in all registers.

Dasopant's concept of the *saṃsāranagarapeṭhe* recalls, perhaps intentionally, a famous marketplace scene from the eighth-century Prakrit work the *Kuvalayamālā* (778 CE) written by the Jain poet Uddyotanasuri. Uddyotanasuri describes a polyglot market scene in which eighteen regional languages (*deśabhāśā*) can be overheard, and he gives examples of words of each language, attributing colorful characteristics to its speakers. This is the earliest textual reference to Marathi, which Uddyotanasuri describes as a language spoken by the "Marahaṭṭhe," a short, dark-skinned, forbearing, and hardworking person who uses words like *diṇṇale* (possibly "given") and *gahille* (meaning "possessed").[38] Since the eighth century of Uddyotanusuri's floruit through the sixteenth of Dasopant's, we see the distinct association of Marathi with the commerce of everyday life. Although Jnaneshvar praises and elevates Marathi as a refined (*nāgara*) language, he also draws on this distinct sense of it as an "ordinary" language when, in the third chapter of the *Jñāneśvarī*, Arjuna demands that Krishna start speaking clearly and provide knowledge in "plain language," in *marhāṭa*.[39] Here Jnaneshvar does not mean Marathi as a language; rather Arjuna uses the word to ask Krishna to explain the obscure, difficult, and philosophical truths in plain, everyday speech. In a clever moment of literary self-reflexivity, Arjuna asks for a vernacularized explanation from Krishna, an unraveling of esoteric truths in everyday language. The image of unraveling or opening up the hidden and the esoteric is a common motif throughout the *Jñāneśvarī*. In this text, the word *marhāṭa* replicates the dual function of the word *prākṛta*. Prakrit is a high-literary language but also serves within the language order as a figure of the spoken, the natural, the unadorned in contrast to the refined, the artificial, and the ornamental Sanskrit.[40] In the same way, *marhāṭa* invokes the everyday, the mundane, the colloquial, even as Marathi is being used as a refined and elevated language of literature by Jnaneshvar.

Jnaneshvar renders the dialogue of Arjuna and Krishna, the heart of the Bhagavad Gītā, as one between intimates, with Arjuna invoking Krishna in the familiar form, often in the structures of maternal address, unmistakably reminiscent of women's song traditions, as I discuss further in the next chapter. Almost all readers are struck by the way the self-consciously literary *Jñāneśvarī* moves between the high artifice of poetic language to the colloquial and familiar style, unraveling the "separation of styles" encoded in the high-literary tradition.[41] Familiar and intimate genres and styles, Bakhtin writes, "are based on a maximum internal proximity of the speaker and addressee."[42] Texts like the *Līḷācaritra* and the *Jñāneśvarī* recreate—dramatize—the proximity of speaker and audience as a structural feature of the written, as does the *abhaṅga* form of *bhakti* poetry. The ongoing banter and conversation between Jnaneshvar and his closest, immediate interlocutor, his brother and guru, Nivrittinath, frames the text of the *Jñāneśvarī*.[43] And in the *abhaṅga* tradition, the poet becomes a speaking figure. It is, however, the Mahanubhavas who develop, not just a work, but a whole new literary form, the *līḷā*, structured by the close, intimate, everyday dialogue between the god Chakradhar and his disciples as the core of the *Līḷācaritra*. The Mahanubhavas bring colloquial Marathi into writing not as a move from the spoken to the written, but as a conscious, deliberate unraveling of the modes of literary writing.

While it is true that South Asian history is not easily grafted onto the binary model of revolutionary reversals and disruptions favored by Bakhtin, there are distinct efforts by the Mahanubhavas to supplant "traditional official styles and worldviews." Anne Feldhaus refers to the immense theological textual corpus of the Mahanubhavas as a "counter-structure."[44] Not only did the Mahanubhavas reject the authorized texts of the Brahminical order, but they wrote their own scriptural texts, and practiced their own methods of writing and reading them with their "own principle[s] of authority . . . hierarchy, and . . . interpretation."[45] This "counter-structure" was a theological-cultural-literary sphere centered not in the Brahminical ecumene or royal court, nor even, in the early period, in the monastery, but insistently and always in the space of everyday life. In addition to the distinctive early scriptural texts, the Mahanubhavas wrote and compiled an enormous archive of literary, philosophical, and commentarial works that rival those of the elite spheres. Ian Raeside lists over three hundred texts written between the thirteenth and eighteenth centuries, most written before the sixteenth century, and this is, no doubt, only a partial account of the literary archive.[46] With these, the Mahanubhavas sought to create an alternative vernacular-theological-literary space, a counter-structure, not just to Vedic but also to the cosmopolitan Sanskrit literary order.

The early Mahanubhavas were anti-cosmopolitan in radically intentional ways, and they drew on the intimate, the familiar, even the scatological in the everyday precisely in order to disrupt "official styles and worldviews."[47]

They were deliberately irreverent when it came to caste, gender, and social rules and open to the initiation of untouchable castes as well as women though Brahmins remained the primary recruits of the early sect. Of Chakradhar's disciples the greatest number were women, many of them widows. The *Līḷācaritra* is a record of his intimate, sometimes problematic by modern standards, dealings with women disciples of various social rank, but it is undeniable that women were central to the vernacular project he set into motion. I return to this point in the final chapter. Some might object to looking at the *Līḷācaritra* and other Mahanubhava scriptural texts as "literature," but it was exactly the "separability principle" that the Mahanubhavas unraveled in the Marathi vernacular turn. There are numerous more recognizably literary works in the earliest Mahanubhava archive, like Mahadaise's *Dhavaḷe* (Wedding songs, ca. 1285), Narendra's *Rukmiṇī-Svayaṃvar* (The marriage of Rukmini, ca. 1292), and Bhaskar's *Śiśupālavadha* (The killing of Sisupala, ca. 1313), all poetic renderings of the story of Rukmini's marriage to Krishna. But these texts, too, had as much theological as literary significance. The Mahanubhavas did not reject all distinctions between written genres, but they did reject any sort of binary that would separate the literary from the theological. They did so without subsuming one into the other.

The First Texts of the Mahanubhavas

Not until the twentieth century, through the meticulous philological work of scholars, did the Mahanubhavas' seminal contributions to the vernacular turn to Marathi come to light. The Mahanubhavas had limited the public circulation of their immense corpus by writing in secret coded scripts, beginning sometime in the late fourteenth century, primarily to protect themselves from persecution by orthodox Brahmins. Until the mid to late twentieth century, the wider Marathi public knew little about the Mahanubhavas' momentous achievements in Marathi writing, beginning with the *Līḷācaritra* (ca. 1278), now widely regarded as the first extant text in Marathi, and its companion volume *Ṛddhipurcaritra* (ca. 1287), an account of the life and times of Chakradhar's eccentric guru, Gundam Raul.[48] Gundam Raul, also known as Govind Prabhu, was believed by the sect to be one of the five incarnations of the Supreme God (*parameśvara*). He is known for his irreverence and play, and he often travesties "official styles and worldviews."[49] It is to Gundam Raul that Chakradhar entrusts his followers at his departure in 1273, and the *Ṛddhipurcaritra* covers the period between 1273 and Gundam Raul's death in 1287. The *Smṛtisthaḷ* focuses on the formation of the sect after the death of Gundam Raul and under the anointed leadership of Nagdev, also called Bhatobas. More than any of the prior texts, the *Smṛtisthaḷ* concerns itself with the literary history of the sect, and an early literary canon begins to come together in it. Several other spiritual texts were written or in the process of being written in the late thirteenth and early fourteenth centuries, including the *Sūtrapāṭh* (ca. 1278–1302), a compilation of Chakradhar's rather distinctive aphorisms as they were recounted by early disciples; the *Dṛṣṭāntapāṭh* (ca. 1280), a recounting of Chakradhar's parables; and the *Mūrtīprakāśa* (ca. 1288), a poetic work on the life of Chakradhar. All three are attributed to the scholar and poet Kesobas. There are numerous other philosophical and theological texts, poetic works, and commentaries. Among these texts, it is the *Līḷācaritra*, the *Ṛddhipurcaritra*, and the *Smṛtisthaḷ* that give us the first extant written records in Marathi of the songs of the grind mill.

Given the immense stature and influence of Chakradhar on these literary efforts, it is understandable why Novetzke would transfer the "author-function" of this early vernacular period to him and interpret the *Līḷācaritra* as a "metonymic biography" that represents "the larger story of Marathi vernacularization itself."[50] Chakradhar is the source and inspiration for the new literary undertakings of this highly textual and literary sect. Yet authorship of the *Līḷācaritra* and the *Ṛddhipurcaritra* is itself much more complicated—and more interesting—than any "great man theory" can accommodate. Though the text depicts Chakradhar's life from approximately 1193 to 1273, it was not written until the last decades of the century, after Chakradhar's purported departure—the Mahanubhavas do not believe he died—in 1273. The decision to write it in a radically new and innovative form marks the beginning of the Marathi vernacular era. The authorship of both the *Līḷācaritra* and the *Ṛddhipurcaritra* is attributed to Mhaimbhat by the Mahanubhavas, though the history of their composition suggests a more complex origin story. Feldhaus, drawing on the *Itīhas*, an undated account of Mahanubhava history, writes that Mhaimbhat and Nagdev began the project of writing the *Līḷācaritra* at Mhaimbhat's suggestion. Yet, Mhaimbhat's method of composition as described in the *Ṛddhipurcaritra* and the *Smṛtisthaḷ*—to ask disciples their stories, to write them down, and with the help of Nagdev and others, to edit and arrange them—suggests a more collaborative, collective authorship.[51] Mhaimbhat could only become a writer of the biography of this God through a process of unlearning his Sanskrit training, and to do that he had to listen to Chakradhar's disciples, foremost among them women. His "authorship," to the extent it can be ascribed to him, is enmeshed in disciples' memories, stories, and songs about their divine founder told in their words and as they remember them. It stands to reason, then, that these very disciples, the primary audience of the *Līḷācaritra* and the *Ṛddhipurcaritra*, played a constitutive role in the composition and writing of the texts. This is true both for the project of writing as envisioned by Mhaimbhat and Nagdev, and for the subsequent reconstructions of the *Līḷācaritra*.

These early texts share history as "reconstructed texts." It is widely accepted by the Mahanubhavas that many texts were lost, including the manuscripts of the *Līḷācaritra*, in the upheavals of the early fourteenth century, spurred by the incursions of the Delhi sultanate into the Godavari River Valley. After "peace and prosperity were restored" a short while later, the Mahanubhavas returned to the Godavari River Valley and began the process of reconstructing the texts.[52] Feldhaus notes that at least thirteen recensions of the *Līḷācaritra*, as well as countless other oral versions, were in circulation at the beginning of the fourteenth century. One of the earliest is believed to have been reconstructed from memory by a woman named Hiraise.[53] All of the main recensions meticulously acknowledge multiple versions and addendums, often citing Hiraise's recension, within the text itself, a protocitational style that encodes the main text with the acts of reconstruction. The trope of the "reconstructed text" is common across cultures and captures a transitional uneasiness about textuality at a time when orality was the more trusted modality. The trope of reconstruction suggests that the text is not a text-artifact, rising above its audience as a permanent object. It is embedded in the world of the proximate audience who knows, remembers, and recomposes the work. The textual is unraveled so that it can again be woven and rewoven; a "reconstructed" text is one that has been returned to the process of making. And this process is preserved in the "final" texts of the *Līḷācaritra* through the addendums and citational references to alternate memories and versions. In this text, the work of making, poiesis, is also clearly the work of making together, a sympoiesis. Sympoiesis, making with rather than against, is a description of a method of composition for a very new, highly original literary genre of *bhakti* poetics introduced by the Mahanubhavas, the *līḷā*.

A New Literary Counter-Form

It is hard to overstate the newness and originality of the Marathi texts of the earliest period in the Mahanubhavas' long literary history. Not only were they in a new literary language, but they also were unlike anything written in cosmopolitan literary spheres, in both form and content. The title of the biography of Chakradhar, *Līḷācaritra*, centers not only the god but his interaction—his play (*līḷā*)—with his disciples in the arena of everyday life. Similarly, the title of the companion volume *Ṛddhipurcaritra* suggests it to be the biography of the village that is the locus of the antics, the play or *līḷā*, of the irreverent Gundam Raul. The word *līḷā* is most widely associated with Krishna's lively, often erotic dalliances and is used to convey the earthly interactions of a divine being incarnated among mortals, predominantly women. For the Mahanubhavas, the term sheds the erotic resonance it holds in the literature of Krishna *bhakti*, but it takes on a new, more colloquial-literary cast and significance: *līḷās* are not only the playful acts of God, but they are also stories about the incarnated Chakradhar and Gundam Raul as remembered, told, and written by the mortals with whom they engaged. Just as the word *līḷā* is meant to capture a playful encounter between divine and human, so the Mahanubhavas' *līḷā* more specifically encodes the encounter—the play—between the written and oral. The authorial stamp of the disciples on the written texts is unmistakable in language, register, form, and content of the *līḷās*.

It is possible that the Mahanubhavas, especially as they undertook the project of writing the *Līḷācaritra*, were influenced by the revolutionary vernacularity of the proximate Kannada literary example of the Virashaivas. Notwithstanding the theological distinctions between them, there are many parallels to be made between the ways that the Virashaivas and the Mahanubhavas related to their respective social and political contexts, but here I focus on the literary parallels. Nagaraj describes the new poetic form of the Virashaivas, the *vacana*, a prose-like, unrhymed, and concise poetic utterance, as a "revolt" against *kāvya*.[54] The *vacana* rejected the courtly high-literary style, which is why Pollock characterizes it as a "decultured form of composition." It was, Pollock writes, "a new literary form, or better an antiform—unversified simple prose."[55] According to Nagaraj, however, the *vacana* was not "decultured" exactly but a turn to oral poetic affordances, what we might call a revolutionary colloquial turn. "The significance of the *vacanakāras* lies," Nagaraj writes, "in their stubborn insistence on bringing the forms of the common folk into literary culture and using them for sophisticated intellectual purposes."[56] The new literary form introduced by the Mahanubhavas, the *līḷā*, is also a simple, concise form in prose, written in a highly colloquial register. It too appears as a "decultured form," a sort of antiform, in its explicit unraveling of the models and expectations of writing. But the *līḷā* also brings into the written an alternative aesthetic drawn from the songs of the grind mill, the most influential of the forms of the common folk. A better term, following Feldhaus's description of the Mahanubhava literary archive as a counter-structure, might be to think of the *līḷā* as a counter-form rather than an antiform, with one clear distinction: its undeniable association with women.

The very word *līḷā* brings the interactions of God with women to the center, not as erotic encounters but as everyday banter and ministrations of care performed throughout the text by women. Mhaimbhat is said to have collected the stories from disciples closest to Chakradhar, and who was closer than the women attending to his everyday needs? The women in the sect were equal initiates with men (in theory). It was often on women's theological questions and aspirations that the Mahanubhava vernacular project was focused. Women's labors in particular are noted and recorded in astonishing detail throughout these texts. While the first generations of Buddhist women wrote poems celebrating their freedom from mortar and pestle in the *Therīgāthā*, the women of the Mahanubhavas, also wandering ascetics, are engaged in daily household labor. The theological focus of the Mahanubhavas was on the worldly, not on escape from the worldly. There are countless *līḷās* depicting the work of women caring for the needs of Chakradhar and of Gundam Raul: details about the kinds of food they made and when; how they cleaned, cooked, and served the food; who was better at making what recipes; how they attended to the culinary preferences of the gods; and how they managed, and sometimes quarreled about, their everyday care. Throughout the *Līḷācaritra* and the *Ṛddhipurcaritra*, women's household labors are prominently rendered in writing, ensuring the vernacular be understood to be as much the language of the household as of the region. The texts even capture the regional variations of words for recipes. For example, in one episode narrated in both the *Ṛddhipurcaritra* and the *Līḷācaritra*, Mahadaise makes sorghum crepes she calls *dhīḍareṃ* for Gundam Raul. When she serves one to him, he gets upset because he says that what she has served is an *āhītā*. Mahadaise explains to him that "in the Gangā Valley [the Godavari River Valley] where I come from, they call it a *dhīḍareṃ*. Here in your Varhāḍ [Vidharba] they call it an *āhītā*." He is not appeased, however, and she has to make a new one for him shaped differently; this satisfies him, and he eats it.[57]

The labors of grinding, pounding, husking, winnowing, cleaning vegetables, cooking, washing, and sewing are prominently depicted throughout the *Līḷācaritra* and the *Ṛddhipurcaritra*, likely because the women (and sometimes men) doing these labors are the ones telling the stories; they are directly involved in the composition of the *līḷās*. And the divine figures do not remain aloof and above these everyday concerns but are at the center of them. In fact, it is this very coexistence of the divine in the mundane, the extraordinary in the ordinary, the colloquial in the textual that the *Līḷācaritra* both records and consecrates as vernacularization. Unsurprisingly then, these thirteenth-century Marathi texts give us our very first written attestations of women's songs of grinding and pounding, several of which were composed and sung by Mahadaise. In addition to being the first woman to whom a written poetic work in Marathi is attributed, she had a reputation in the sect for being an artful composer of *ovīs*. The songs have been an element of everyday life for two millennia, and in texts so faithful to the ordinary and the everyday that they could not have been ignored. Women's *ovīs* stand out as highly crafted and aesthetic oral poems, but they also bleed into and shape the prosaic writing style of the text. These songs are not a mere aside, a tangent, an exception. Rather, they unravel the very heart of the text.

The Oral *Ovī* in Writing

Although women's *ovīs* appear in the *Ṛddhipurcaritra* and the *Smṛtisthaḷ*, the oldest record of women's work songs in Marathi writing is in the *Līḷācaritra*. There are several instances when women are singing *ovīs* in this text, but one important *līḷā* depicts Mahadaise singing while she grinds wheat. The context in which Mahadaise sings these *ovīs* is a common scene of everyday life, with its extremely routine domestic concerns. Baise, one of Chakradhar's first disciples and his primary companion throughout the *Līḷācaritra*, asks Mahadaise to make *lāḍūs*, ball-shaped confections of sweetened semolina, for Chakradhar because Mahadaise was known to make them well. Mahadaise sits down to grind the wheat while Chakradhar eats his meal and takes a nap. When he wakes up, he begins to leave for the temple but stops when he hears Mahadaise's *ovīs*:

On the banks of the Gomati River,
Draped in a blue cloth cover
Is the Emperor of the Gujars,
King Krishna

Draped in a blue cloth cover
The King of the Gujars
Under a ruby canopy
Is Sri Chakradhar

He has a beautiful rosy forehead
He wears earrings
And a royal turban
Sri Chakradhar

His fair skin and arms
Anoint them with sandalwood
May Chakradhar never come
Under the evil eye

Whether I call him father or brother
O my girlfriend
He's my kin, my girlfriend
I want him to come.[58]

In these verses, Mahadaise takes some of the central themes of the grind mill songs—family relationships and friendships—as the figurative vehicle of her *bhakti* centered on Chakradhar. The similarities between the structures, motifs, and form of these verses in this thirteenth-century text and the songs in the contemporary archive of grind mill songs are surprising. Mahadaise's *ovīs* read like a long poem, but each of the verses could be taken as an independent poem, a common feature of *ovīs* even today. She ends with well-known structures of feminine address to *sājaṇī*, a term of endearment for girlfriend, very common in the extant song archive. All verses are three-and-a-half lines; the fourth lines in all but the second verse are shorter, with only four syllables. The first three lines are between five and six syllables, and in the last verse there is a seven-syllable line. The rhyme scheme varies in all of the *ovīs*, rather than following the same rhyming pattern throughout. Grind mill *ovīs* even today are consistently end-rhymed, but do not maintain a single rhyme scheme for *ovīs* in a given sequence. These sorts of irregularities maintain the sung character of the verses even in the written version of Mahadaise's song. The first two lines of the second verse repeat in reverse the opening lines, another common performative aspect of sung *ovīs*. The text maintains the sung character of Mahadaise's *ovīs* by retaining these oral features.

Mahadaise's *ovīs* are expressions of *bhakti*, extolling the beauty of Chakradhar, and in this they are very similar to both contemporary grind mill songs and the *abhaṅgas* of Vitthal-*bhakti* poets who often extol the divinity's beauty. In fact the formal features of her *ovīs* are nearly identical to one variation of the *abhaṅga* used by *bhakti* poets, though they predate any extant *abhaṅgas* as such. Chakradhar is invoked in her song as father, brother, and girlfriend, a trope of kinship more commonly associated with the poetry of Vitthal-*bhakti*, though we do also find such tropes in the contemporary Mahanubhava grind mill songs.[59] Here, for example, are a couple of contemporary Mahanubhava grind mill *ovīs*:

They say the grinding is done
But I take more to grind
I will sing more *ovīs*
For my brother, Sri Chakradhar

Tell me oh my sisters
Who does Chakradhar look like?
He has dark skin
Like a rose among flowers.[60]

Even though the language of the modern *ovīs* is contemporary, we can see that there is continuity in the mode of poetics in Mahadaise's songs from the thirteenth century to today.

While *ovīs* like these elevate and idealize Chakradhar in a familiar *bhakti* poetic mode, Mahadaise's *ovīs* are situated in the context of a prose *līḷā* that records her everyday mundane interactions with the incarnated divine figure himself, and this everyday interaction is juxtaposed to the artful expressions of the song: "As she was singing this *ovī* [*vovī*], the Gosavi climbed down the stairs and grabbed her pestle from behind. When she looked behind her, her head hit the Gosavi's knee. Then the Gosavi said, 'Woman, aren't *ovīs* usually sung to one's father and brothers?' 'Yes, Lord. The Gosavi himself is my father. The Gosavi himself is my brother. The Gosavi himself is my girlfriend and kin.' The Omniscient One said, 'So be it.' "[61] These peculiar narrative details of their interaction—the Gosavi playfully grabbing Mahadaise's pestle from behind, Mahadaise banging her head on his knee as she turns—stand in sharp contrast to the lyrical paeans to Chakradhar in the *ovīs*. There is almost a kind of friction between the idealized image of Chakradhar in Mahadiase's *ovīs* and the everyday, awkward but affectionate interaction between Chakradhar and Mahadaise. The Mahanubhavas are a *bhakti* sect that prioritizes being in the company of an embodied incarnation over more abstract nondualist transcendence or divine unity.[62] This theological worldliness is evident in the inseparability of poetics and prose in the text, just as the song sung while grinding speaks to the embeddedness of *bhakti* in the everyday. We might say that the playful and clumsy interaction illustrates the very kin relations that Mahadaise sings about by unraveling the static poetic image into *līḷā*. This kind of unraveling is central to the very writing style of the *Līḷācaritra*. The prose unravels the poetry of the *ovī*, and in the interaction between the two, we can see the layers within the language and experience of the everyday.

Many *līḷās* feature Mahadaise asking Chakradhar questions that serve as prompts for his theological teachings, but in this *līḷā* the singing of *ovīs* becomes the site of teachings on *bhakti*. In this scene, Chakradhar asks the question and Mahadaise answers it. Mahadaise demonstrates the way that women's *ovīs* can be a vehicle of *bhakti*, and this is theologically sanctioned by Chakradhar. There is one more scene of Mahadaise singing *ovīs* in the *Līḷācaritra*, and another theological conversation about *bhakti* ensues. In this *līḷā*, Mahadaise sings five *ovīs* about the preparations of the mythological figure Akrura, a devotee of Krishna, to meet Krishna in Dvaraka. But Chakradhar asks her why she is singing about Akrura. When she says it is because Akrura is a great devotee, a *bhakta*, Chakradhar reminds her of a central tenet of Mahanubhava *bhakti*: the need to be in the embodied presence of the divine. This episode is grouped among the "Ajñāt Līḷās" or "Līḷās of Unknown Place," which are omitted from the main text, not because they are considered interpolations, but because the place in which they occur is not clear.[63]

This same theologically sanctioned mode of *bhakti* poetics is presented in a comic way in the *Ṛddhipurcaritra* when Gundam Raul reacts negatively to *ovīs* sung by the widow Sadhe:

> 179. Sādheṃ is criticized for singing a folk song [*vovīyā*]
>
> One day Sādheṃ was pounding grain. She began to sing in praise of the Gosāvī. She sang a folk song [*ekī ovī*]: "Govinda is my mother. Govinda is my lady. Govinda wears my baby's garb." [*govindu āi/ govindu bāi/ govindu mājhi bāḷavesī*]
>
> At this, the Gosāvī said, "Die, you! Die, you!"[64]

Notably this thirteenth-century *ovī* is similar to contemporary *ovīs*, showing the long continuity of the song tradition, but it is narrated in a much less serious way. The scene nevertheless provides early textual evidence that the figuring of a male divinity as mother and woman has long been a distinctive feature of women's *ovīs*. The feminizing of Krishna is of course one of the main figurations of divinity by Vitthal devotees, who address Vitthal as a mother (*viṭṭhāī*) and as woman (*viṭṭhābāī*). Still, this episode appears to mock this figuration. Gundam Raul, called Gosavi in the passage, dislikes the *ovī*, perhaps because it is not a particularly well-crafted one. Although the song repeats in content and form Mahadaise's response to Chakradhar, the words, figuration, syllabic structure, and rhyme scheme are much simpler. Sadhe's verse does not have the same sophistication as Mahadaise's *ovīs*, and Gundam Raul is a fastidious musical critic, as the following humorous anecdote suggests:

> 141. He criticizes singing.
>
> A Mahātmā and his wife came along, bringing a stringed instrument with them. They plucked at the string and began to sing a song.
>
> As they begin to sing, the Mahātmā sang in one mode [*rāga*], his wife in another mode [*rāga*] and they played the instrument in a third mode [*rāga*].
>
> And the Gosāvī said, "Die, you miserable wretches!"
>
> And they kept silent.
>
> Then the Gosāvī left.[65]

Gundam Raul is displeased, not because this holy man and his wife are singing, but because they are singing badly! Perhaps he dislikes Sadhem's verses for the same reason. The scorn for Sadhe's verses in *Ṛddhipurcaritra* and the elevation of Mahadaise's in the *Līḷācaritra* suggest that perhaps there was some attention accorded to the aesthetics of the *ovī*, although it also shows the iconoclasm of the sect, its irreverence and humor.

Just as the *Līḷācaritra* embeds the divine teachings of Chakradhar in conversations with disciples, songs are situated within a conversational matrix in this text. That is to say, the songs are an aspect of everyday discourse, though also marked as distinct by certain poetic features. Many of Chakradhar's teachings emerge in response to questions raised by disciples, most often women. Similarly, songs are responsive. For example, one woman in *Līḷācaritra* is a figure named Demati, a widow from Paithan with whom Baise quarrels. Baise demands that Demati be thrown out because she quarrels too much. Chakradhar orders Demati to leave the next morning, but before she leaves, Demati sings this song:

Hari, my feet won't do
What I ask them to do
Who are we supposed
To go to?

At your feet my heart
Is alive with color
Why, O Kanha,
Do you send me away?

Even the hard mind
Of the passionless yogi
Is charmed and pulled
by you.[66]

Demati's verses are called *ovīs* in the *Līḷācaritra*, but they are very different in form and substance from the *ovīs* sung by Mahadaise. They are more akin to the song-form known as *gauḷaṇa*, or songs in the voice of dairy maids, often featuring the love play between Krishna and Radha. Demati's song impresses Chakradhar enough that he gives her permission to stay.

Although there is formal distinction between Mahadaise's grind mill *ovīs* and Demati's more elevated song, the fact that both are called *ovīs* in the text shows how connected the very idea of the *ovī* was to women's song.

When the songs of women, like Mahadaise's or Demati's *ovīs*, are inscribed into the text of the *Līḷācaritra*, there is no definite line separating them from the rest of the writing, except in print where they are sometimes highlighted or indented. The distinction, in other words, between *ovī* (*padya*) and *līḷā* (*gadya*) is not always absolute or immediately discernible. There are times when the songs bleed into the prose. For example, when Chakradhar asks Mahadaise about the *ovīs* she has sung, her response, though presented as prose, is an embedded *ovī*: "The Gosavi himself is my father. The Gosavi himself is my brother. The Gosavi himself is my girlfriend and kin." The syntactical parallelism and parataxis create rhythm like an embedded *ovī*. The arrangement of the three sentences as asyndeton gives her response a crisp, sung character: *gosāvīcī bapu: gosāvīcī bhau: gosāvicī sājaṇī gota*. This kind of permeability between verse and prose is not an exception in this text. Indeed, the very unusual prose style of the *līḷā* may, in fact, follow the contours of the grind mill *ovī*.

Singing Prose

The *līḷās* in *Līḷācaritra* and the *Ṛddhipurcaritra* are written in brusque, short, simple, unadorned sentences. Parataxis is a prominent feature in the style of these texts. Often there are one-word sentences, and these follow one another in an abrupt and sudden fashion with almost no transitional or coordinating or subordinating words or clauses. It would be mistaken, however, to assume that the *Līḷācaritra* is simply unmediated realism or ethnography. The brevity of the sentences, their punctuated juxtaposition, are not representative of actual speech. It is a chosen style of writing modeled not on speech but on the oral poetics of the *ovī*. S. R. Kulkarni, a noted musicologist, suggests that sometimes there is a certain cadence and rhythm inherent to the prose writing of the *Līḷācaritra* that recalls the *ovī*.[67] *Kāvya*, Kulkarni reminds us, is divided into *padya* (verse), *gadya* (prose), and *miśra* (mixed) by the Sanskrit theorists, and further that prose can and often does have many poetic features. It is true that the *ovī's* syllabic flexibility makes it easy to fit almost anything into its structure, but in the *Līḷācaritra* the syntax creates the cadence of the short, paratactical lines of women's oral *ovīs*. In fact, the *Līḷācaritra* unravels the literary as it creates a very new style of writing in the *līḷā*.

A *līḷā* in which the Sanskrit scholar Sarangpandit first realizes Chakradhar's divinity is particularly interesting for the way it unravels a representative of the Brahmin ecumene. Sarangpandit is a complex Brahminical figure in the *Līḷācaritra*, one who is, at first, an eager devotee of Chakradhar, but who later breaks with him and even betrays him.[68] In this early, *līḷā*, he is shown to interrupt his own textual discourse on a *purāṇa* to go to Chakradhar with manuscript in hand. He asks him, "Lord, people used to get a natural kind of joy from Shri Krishna Chakravarti. Can that be found anywhere else?" Chakradhar's response comes in an embedded verse: "Look at it, ask about it, discuss it. Then it is where it is" [*pāhīje: pusīje: carcije: mā āti: teth āti*].[69] Feldhaus's translation maintains the poetic cadence and captures the parataxis of the Marathi text. Like the *ovī*, Chakradhar's response is a quatrain, though the longer line is the last one. The first three sentences, all one word, are in the imperative case and end-rhymed, while the last is a very condensed sentence that releases the rhythm. The rhyming and parataxis continue a bit more in the description of Sarangpandit's trance when he hears Chakradhar's words, evident even to non-Marathi readers: *āṇi stīti jā**lī**: bhogī**lī**: bhaṅga**lī***.[70] There is a distinct song-like quality to these one-word sentences. The last two words have three syllables each with a further consonance conjoining them, while the assonance if the "ī" is emphasized. Feldhaus translates this as: "With that, Sarangpandit went into a trance. He experienced the trance, and then after some time, it broke."[71] By adding phrases like "with that" and "and then after some time," Feldhaus adds hypotactical connections that mitigate the extreme parataxis of the original, but it is hard to see how any translation could maintain the parataxis and strong sound patterns of the Marathi text without a serious stylistic issue. In the Marathi it reads very crisply and stands out as poetic utterance. Sarangpandit comes from the world of Sanskrit texts to Chakradhar, but his momentary state (*stīti*) of unraveling, his trance, is narrated in the counter-form of the *līḷā*, which follows the cadence and style of the *ovī*.

The bleeding of song into prose is not restricted to the *līḷās* that feature songs or the speech of the divine. The style permeates the text in unexpected ways. Here is another example in one extremely short *līḷā* at the beginning of the *Līḷācaritra,* in the section titled "The Solitary Period." This section narrates Chakradhar's origin story and tells us about his early life as a solitary wandering ascetic before he has followers. The text begins, not with Chakradhar, but with the figure Cangdev Raul, the third of the five main incarnations, the pentad, of the Supreme God. Mahanubhavas believe that Cangdev left his body in order to avoid the sexual provocations of a *yoginī*. He then entered the recently deceased body of the son of a Gujarati minister. The term used for the divine figure in the early part of the text is Gosavi, which could refer to any of the three contemporaneous incarnations, Cangdev Raul, Gundam Raul, and Chakradhar. The term shows the continuity between the figures as part of the godly pentad of the one Supreme God. The second *līḷā* narrates what "the Gosavi," in other words Cangdev Raul, was doing after he had attained divine status. I have highlighted the end-rhymes here to show the verse pattern:

> *gosāvī dvārāvatiesi kharāṭevari bīdī jhā**ḍīti:** mag supīṃ puñje bha**riti:** srīmūguṭāvari ṭhe**viti:** gomatīe madheṃ ghā**līti:** supeṃ margu pragaṭe: kharāṭeni vidyā*[72]

There is exact rhyme in the last syllable of the first four sentences, *ti*, but also an imperfect rhyme in the second to last syllables that reinforces and strengthens the end-rhyme, thus emphasizing the rhyme overall. The first sentence is long, and all the words end with an *i*-sound, while the next three sentences are short and paratactical. The four together form a quatrain. In the oral *ovī* we sometimes find this arrangement of a longer opening refrain, followed by two or three shorter lines. The syntactic parallelism and the end-rhymes give the sentences a rhythmical pattern. The last two sentences are unrhymed, the way the last line of an *ovī* might be, recreating the cadence of the *ovī*, its release of the rhythm at the close.

The writing style of the untranslated lines above is reminiscent of the *ovī*, but so are the motifs in the content. Here is Feldhaus's translation: "In Dvaravati, the Gosavi would sweep the streets with a broom. Then he would put the piles of dirt into the winnowing fan and place it on his holy head. He would toss the dirt into the Gomati River. He showed the way with a winnowing fan and knowledge with a broom."[73] In this episode, the Gosavi, who had been given divine powers by the god Dattatreya, holds in his hands the domestic tools of everyday labor: a broom and a "winnowing fan," used as it still is in many parts of India as a dustpan. The incarnated God sweeps the streets with a broom and puts the piles of waste into a dustpan that he carries to the river on his divinely anointed head. Sweeping is not a generic labor in India. It is highly coded as a marker of the lower castes. This is a labor performed usually by the most marginalized members of the household, women of the lowest rank in the patriarchal hierarchy and by people of lower castes in public spaces like the street. The last line, "He showed the way with a winnowing fan and knowledge with a broom" is an aphorism later included, Feldhaus notes, in the *Sūtrapāṭh*.[74] The broom and the dustpan are metonyms of an everyday structured by caste and gender, the broom clearing the "way" and the winnowing fan discarding the waste, perhaps the apparatus of Brahminical learning. The vignette is a perfect illustration of counter-structure. The past is not only swept away, but a new knowledge is conveyed in the metonyms of everyday vernacularity. These illustrate the process of colloquialization, taking us into the deeper deposits of the vernacular. The scene brings to mind Janabai's discovery of the *pothī* in the dung, discussed in the previous chapter. Both the *līḷā* and the *ovī* use emblems taken from the everyday life of marginalized household laborers and women—dung, broom, winnowing fan—as vehicles of theological insight, and of textuality more generally, erasing the "separability principle" that would divide the theological, the written, the aesthetic, and the scholarly from everyday labor and speech.

Looking at the organization of the text as a whole, the paratactical patterning and sequencing in the style of the *ovī* becomes even more evident. Each *līḷā* of the *Līḷācaritra* is compact, compressed, rarely more than a printed page long. A *līḷā* sometimes returns to the same people, town, or house as the *līḷās* that come before it, but with a different focus; or a *līḷā* moves on to the next town or another house, another group of interlocutors. Each *līḷā* is a like a world unto itself, and there is the sense of dwelling, of recurrent return that connects *līḷās*. The brief and charming episodes that depict Chakradhar's interactions with a young girl named Dhanaise are a good example. Each is a vignette of the child's life, and Chakradhar is by turns an observer and participant in her world. In one, he plays cowries with her, but she stops because he keeps winning, while in another he tells her a folktale about a crow and a sparrow. In another, her family dresses her up, and Chakradhar watches as they tease her.[75] The sequencing of these *līḷās* is juxtapositive, without any causal connection or narrative forward movement. Taken together, they are a "mosaic of parceled pictures."[76]

The devotee, or reader make the connections between the sequences. The recurring returns to particular scenes of interaction, like those of Chakradhar and Dhanaise, or Chakradhar and Mahadaise, create continuity but not a temporal or logical or narrative order. Indeed, the only discernible pattern is a geographic one of Chakradhar's constant wandering. Much like the oral sequences of *ovīs*, each *līḷā* remains independent but they are all woven together though implicit, allusive, thematic, affective connections. Like the *ovī*, there are also repeated formulaic threads that connect *līḷās*, just as we see in *ovī* sequences. For example, the phrase "Mahadaise asked" is a similar oral-formulaic thread that runs through the text. Another is the repeated use of structures of direct address, often feminine address. In a great majority of *līḷās*, Chakradhar calls the audience to attention with his direct feminine address of *bāī*, or "my woman," recalling the well-known oral-formulaic refrain of the songs, "I tell you, woman" (*sāṅgate bāī tulā*). I return to this dialogical structure of the *līḷā* when I discuss Mahadaise's role as interlocutor in the final chapter.

Literary Beginnings

The *Līḷācaritra* is an enormous and complex text, and here I have been able to draw out only a bare glimpse of the stamp of women's *ovīs* on the writing of the text. But it is enough to give a sense of the stark difference in the writing style of the two most influential of the early texts of the vernacular era, the *Līḷācaritra* and the *Jñāneśvarī*. It might be tempting to assume that the colloquial, unadorned, paratactic language and style of the *Līḷācaritra* is but a "rustic" origin to Marathi writing before it became a fully realized "literary" language through the processes of literarization. Yet there was little time, if any at all, between the composition of the *Līḷācaritra* and the *Jñāneśvarī*, one intentionally and rigorously colloquial and the other self-consciously high literary in register. The *Jñāneśvarī* is a finely wrought and sophisticated poetic work, but this does not mean that the *Līḷācaritra* was not also a literary text, a product of aesthetic labor. Both are the outcome of a "poetics of work" central to Marathi vernacularity.

The aesthetic sophistication of the *Jñāneśvarī* and the works that soon followed has led some to speculate that "Marathi has long had a literature,

Figure 2.2 Janabai Thorat's grind mill after a grinding and singing session, 2006. Photo by author

well before these . . . texts were composed."[77] The facts seem to suggest a period of what Paul Zumthor calls "formation" that precedes the "manifestation" of new vernacular works, a past "hidden behind the surviving texts" during which the "traditions on which those texts are based were formed."[78] Jnaneshvar and the Mahanubhava writers were embedded in multilingual textual traditions, not only of Sanskrit, Prakrit, and Apabhramsha, but also the proximate vernacular examples of Kannada and Gujarati. It becomes possible to see how a highly innovative and original text like the *Līḷācaritra*, an intentional unraveling of the literary, might be produced alongside the *Jñāneśvarī* without long periods of "building up" of expressive genres and models of literarity. A "manifestation" is an innovation or invention, Zumthor writes, but all inventions "involve a shift of something marginal to a central, functional position; that is, the redeployment of material . . . to serve a novel purpose."[79] There is such a shift in the novel interlinguistic redeployment of the categories of *kāvya* in Marathi composition, in short, literarization, but also the redeployment of colloquial lexicon, oral styles, poetic forms, and expressive genres into writing—in other words, colloquialization. The *Jñāneśvarī* mobilizes the poetics of weaving, sewing, and threading, metaphors of literary composition throughout the subcontinent, while the *Līḷācaritra* mobilizes a poetics of unraveling, a labor associated with grinding and pounding, of removal, reduction, and refining to the most essential articulations. If there is a weaving of the literary in the *Jñāneśvarī*, there is an unraveling of the literary in the *Līḷācaritra*. Yet in both, the reverse is also true. There are moments of astonishing colloquiality in the *Jñāneśvarī*, just as there are high-textual allusions, engagements, and interactions in the *Līḷācaritra*.

Though the Mahanubhavas give us the first written evidence of the songs of the grind mill, this sect did not develop a poetic tradition that engaged with women's songs in the manner of the devotees of Vitthal, who created the *abhaṅga*. Instead, it is in their *prose* writings that we see the most visible imprint of the oral *ovī*. The style of the Mahanubhavas' new genre of *līḷās*: the condensed terseness, the brevity, the parataxis, the abundant structures of feminine address, the highly colloquial register, and the recurrent thematics of women's daily labor are all signposts of the oral *ovī*, evidence of the hand of women's songs in the crafting of this written work. The two primary sects under whose purview Marathi became a literary language enact thus an ongoing dialectic between literarization and colloquialization. At the center of this dialectic is the *ovī*. In turning to the *ovī*, whether in poetry or prose, the new Marathi writers achieved literary expressivity by appropriating, sometimes in subtle and concealed ways, and sometimes through explicit literary envoicement, the expressive structures and motifs of women's songs. The *ovī* might be the best evidence yet of the contributions of "women, *śūdras*, and others" to the vernacular turn to Marathi.

CHAPTER III

The *Ovī*

A Poetics of Work in the Work of Poetics

This is my second *ovī*
What are the rules of *ovī*?
Under the holy basil sits my Rama

—GAVALAN NAWGIRE, VILLAGE WATWADA

The chapter on Janabai in the sprawling hagiographical compendium *Bhaktavijaya*, written in 1762 by the influential poet-scribe Mahipati, features one of the most iconic scenes of Marathi *bhakti*: Vitthal sitting opposite Janabai at the stone mill, helping her grind as she sings. As he does for other laboring poets, Vitthal comes to lend Janabai a hand in her work. He gently wakes her at the crack of dawn, plaits her hair, and seats her at the mill. He tells her that he will pull the mill, that she should only put her hand on it as an occasion (*nimitta*) to sing her songs, recalling the famous proverb among grind mill singers: "No *ovī* comes to mind without holding the handle of the grind mill." The next ten *ovīs* of Mahipati's text are Janabai's songs about the *bhakti* poets (*ovyāṃ santāṃsī gātase*). In the songs she describes Jnaneshvar, Savata Mali, and Namdev as fathers and brothers, a defining trope, as the *Līḷācaritra* makes clear, of women's songs of grinding since at least the thirteenth century.[1] Like Mahadaise's *ovīs* about Chakradhar, Janabai's songs are oral hagiographies of exalted *bhakti* figures.

Janabai sings the songs, as did Mahadaise, in the very presence of the God she worships. Interspersed throughout is the vocative *sājaṇī*, an affectionate address for a loving female friend that Mahadaise had also used. Whereas Mahadaise's *ovīs* are distinguished for their aesthetic qualities and figures of speech embedded in the prose text in which they appear, the language and rhymes in Janabai's song are simpler than Mahipati's own, distinguishing—if ever so slightly—her voice from Mahipati's. Yet just as Mahadaise's *ovīs* bleed into the prose of the *līḷā*, Janabai's *ovīs* are presented in the same *ovī* meter used by Mahipati in the rest of the book, blurring the line between her song and his text. Mahipati thereby captures in a concise way one of the strangest and most unique conundrums in Marathi literature: that a song of the grind mill is called an *ovī*, as is the dominant poetic form of written Marathi literature from the thirteenth through the eighteenth century. What, if any, are the implications arising from this nominal concurrence?

The *ovī* is most commonly defined and described as a syllabic verse form of three-and-a-half lines in which the first three rhyme, and the last is shorter and unrhymed. While this would describe the most ubiquitous structure of the *ovī* in literary texts since the *Jñāneśvarī*, it is also the form of Mahadaise's oral *ovīs* in the *Līḷācaritra*. But oral *ovīs* can also be rhyming couplets, tercets, or quatrains, while the written *ovī*, which came to be known as the literary *ovī* (*grānthik ovī*), can have more than five lines. The syllabic count of a line of the oral *ovī* rarely exceeds eight syllables, while the line of a written *ovī* can sometimes be as long as eighteen syllables. In fact, each line of an *ovī* can have a significantly different syllabic count. The most consistent feature of the literary *ovī* is the shorter, unrhymed final line, but even in this there are some important variations. Although many oral *ovīs* do end in a shorter final line, the grind mill *ovī* can also begin with a shorter opening line. The sixteenth-century poet Eknath is credited with revising the literary *ovī* to have a longer final line that makes the verse a fulsome quatrain, but he inserts an internal rhyme at the caesura of the last line that maintains the rhythmic release—the cadence—of the shorter final line. It is in this unmistakably literary Eknathi *ovī* that Mahipati renders Janabai's grind mill *ovīs* in the *Bhaktavijay*.

By doing so Mahipati admits the possibility of kinship between the oral and the literary *ovī*, but by subsuming Janabai's *ovīs* in his preferred meter, he also enacts an all-too-common ambivalence about women's songs. Where Mahadaise's *ovīs* spill into the prose, shaping the writing with its oral poetic structures, here it is Mahipati's literary *ovī* that shapes Janabai's song. Janabai's song is on the written page, but submerged, like a voice speaking from under water. Mahipati's literary "envoicement" of the grind mill song thus raises some central questions about *ovī* that I pursue in this chapter: "What," as the grind mill song in the epigraph asks, "are the rules of *ovī*?" Was the oral *ovī* the "root" form of the literary *ovī*? Or did women's *ovīs* and the literary *ovī* follow separate metrical paths? And where does the *abhaṅga*, the grind mill *ovī's* closest poetic relative and the dominant vehicle of *bhakti* poetry, come into the picture? Since the oral *ovī* is, without doubt, older than the written, can we call its written form a literarization of the oral *ovī*? Or is the *ovī* itself a sign of colloquialization, as it was in the *Līḷācaritra*? I focus in this chapter on the *Jñāneśvarī*, a text that in many ways is a contrast to the *Līḷācaritra*, especially in its explicitly metapoetic self-reflexivity. In it, Jnaneshvar offers the first literary theorization of the *ovī* as an aesthetic form.

Given the metrical looseness and wide variety of oral and written forms of *ovī*, some scholars have ventured that the word *ovī* does not refer to a specific poetic form at all but rather should be understood as "any form of free composition."[2] In this view, *ovī* is a more general term, like "verse" or "composition," without clear parameters to distinguish it as a specific form. To accept this redefinition, however, would require ignoring centuries of prosodic commentary on the *ovī*, including the descriptions of *ovī* by the first Marathi writers to use it in writing, such as Jnaneshvar, who credits the verse form with an ability to make poetry accessible to a wide audience. It would also mean ignoring the seriousness with which women grind mill singers think about the *ovī*. These women, I have found time and time again, are quite fastidious about what they call an *ovī*, especially when compared to another verse form with which they are almost as equally familiar, the *abhaṅga*. To women, an *abhaṅga* is a specific kind of song written in a book by an elevated exemplar, while an *ovī* is something women made (*jodalela*), or rather "made up" (*manānīc jodalela*) at the grind mill or during other kinds of work. Women, not surprisingly, are rather humble about their *ovīs*. They have a great love and reverence for them, but it is the compositions of elevated poets recorded in writing that they hold in higher esteem.

That a verse form crafted and sung by women, many unlettered and from the most marginalized of castes and communities, shares a name and characteristics with the dominant verse form of high-literary Marathi poetry should give pause and invite inquiry. Yet the fact has not received much sustained discussion. There are generally two approaches: on one side are those who hold the oral and the written traditions of *ovī* to have separate and distinct metrical paths of development, thus requiring little inquiry into the shared name; on the other side are those, probably the greater number, who see women's *ovīs* as the "root form" of the literary *ovī*. R. C. Dhere makes the argument explicitly in his introduction to a newer edition of Sane Guruji's *Strījīvan*. He declares the *ovī* of the grind mill the "original oral *ovī*" (*ādya maukhik ovī*), that "gave birth to the *abhaṅga* and the literary *ovī*" and "ruled over the world of Old Marathi literature."[3] Dhere posits the oral *ovī* as a maternal ancestor of the written *ovī*. There is some truth to this if only in the historical fact that the oral *ovī* preceded the written and is the first textually attested Marathi verse form. But the grind mill *ovī* remained a living and continuous oral tradition that developed alongside the formation of the literary corpus of the written *ovī* and the *abhaṅga* forms. In other words, the grind mill *ovī* was not a distant maternal "ancestor," but always a contemporaneous relative, always being made and remade in conversation with the literary *ovī* and the *abhaṅga*. The relationship of oral and written, the sung and the literary, has a complex—and more interesting—history than a linear genealogy can accommodate.

Unraveling the History of the *Ovī*

A century and half before the first literary use of the *ovī* in written works, women's *ovīs* are described in the twelfth-century Sanskrit encyclopedia, *Mānasollāsa* (ca. 1131) as songs "sung in Maharashtra by women while pounding" (*mahārāṣṭreṣu yoṣidbhirovī geyā tu kaṇdane*).[4] In other words, the first attestation of the *ovī* is as a women's work song. The *ovī* is one of several song forms listed in this section of the *Mānasollāsa* that are associated with specific occasions and contexts, including daily labor, festivals, weddings, and feasts. These are verse forms meant for worldly occasions, what Someshvara calls *prabandha laukika*, or "worldly compositions." Eight-and-a-half centuries later, this is how Urmila Pawar, a Dalit feminist writer, describes women's *ovīs*: "Women sang songs all the time, while sweeping the front courtyard and polishing it with dung, at the time of husking, sifting, and cleaning rice grains and putting them into containers."[5] The songs were also sung, she writes, at weddings and festivals (worldly occasions), and many of the examples she gives are grind mill songs.[6] After conversion to Buddhism, Dalit women "learned to sing songs without using the names of gods and goddesses," and they composed many new grind mill songs about Ambedkar.[7] Pawar shows how the "original oral *ovī*" is not some distant ancestor from the past, but a continuous tradition, responsive to change. When *ovīs* are sung in the fields they are called field *ovīs* (*śetātil ovyā*), though these might be grind mill songs sung to a different rhythm and melody. Lullabies are women's work songs (*aṅgāī* or *pāḷaṇā* or *hallara*), also often in the *ovī* form.[8] As Tara Bhavalkar points out, lullabies can be *ovīs* of the grind mill but sung to a different melody and beat. The songs of grinding are the most prolific genre of women's songs, the one that influenced all other song forms. Since grinding was a daily labor, rather than seasonal or intermittent or occasional, the context alone set the stage for the generation of an immense volume of songs that blend with and travel into many other genres and traditions.

A century or so after *Mānasollāsa*—and still decades before any extant written Marathi literature—the *ovī* is again attested as a song form in the influential Sanskrit musical compendium, the *Saṅgīta-Ratnākara*, written by Sharangadeva in Devgiri during the reign of the Yadava king, Singhana (r. 1200–1245). Sharangadeva categorizes songs into two groups: *gāndharva*, songs that are rule-bound and of divine origin; and *gāna*, songs that are regional in origin (*deśī*), less bound by rules, and pleasing to the people (*tadgānam janarañjanam*).[9] This division roughly maps onto a classical / popular divide, and it is in the latter category, as *gāna*, that the *ovī* is described as being pleasing and popular to the people (*janamanohara*):

> 304. It's sung in a regional language [*deśabhāṣayā*], with three line-breaks and alliteration—
> And if it has the word *ovī* at the end, then the experts call it *ovī*.
>
> 305. Each and every one of the three lines can be different in terms of meter,
> And with alliteration from word to word that is variously located at the start, middle or end.
>
> 306. The *ovīs*, which delight the people [*janamanohara*], are to be sung with various meters,
> And they are arranged in three lines, with alliteration, and with Prakrit words.[10]

In this description, the *ovī* is not a meter but rather a form that can be sung in various meters or melodies, evidence that metrical variability has been

Figure 3.1 Lakshmibai Gavale picking cotton in a field in Shirad Shahapur in the Hingoli district as she sings *ovīs*, 2007.
Photo by author

Figure 3.2 Yamunabai Jadhav (now deceased) sitting at a grind mill for a recording session in Shirad Shahapur, 2007
Photo by author

a long-recognized feature of the *ovī*. Notably, alliteration at the beginnings and in the middle of words, and not just end-rhymes, is outlined here as a marker of the *ovī*. This is exactly what we saw in the prose sections of the *Līḷācaritra* analyzed in the previous chapter. Sharangadeva delineates three lines, not the more common three-and-a-half lines, as the form of the *ovī*. The three-lined *ovī* recalls the Kannada *tripadi*, also a verse form that straddles the sung and the written and associated with women's labors of grinding. There are numerous examples of three-lined grind mill *ovīs* in the Marathi song archives as well. The *ovīs* sung by the widow Sadhe in a humorous episode of the *Ṛddhipurcaritra* is an example of a three-lined *ovī*: "Govinda is my mother. Govinda is my lady. Govinda wears my baby's garb [*govindu āi / govindu bāi / govindu mājhi bālavesī*]."[11] A written work attributed to Mahadaise, the *Mātṛkī-Rukmiṇī-Svayaṃvar*, is also written in the three-lined *ovī*. The *ovīs* sung by Mahadaise in the *Līḷācaritra* and in the *Smṛtisthaḷ*, which also includes a song sung in *ovī* by another woman named Nakaise, are three-and-a-half lines, with the last line shorter and unrhymed. The fact that both varieties appear in thirteenth- and fourteenth-century texts suggests the fluidity of the *ovī*. The three-and-half line *ovī*, which became standardized in literary texts after the *Jñāneśvarī* and Narendra's *Rukmiṇī-Svayaṃvar*, is also attested in the Mahanubhava texts as an oral form.

According to Sharangadeva, "experts" recognize an *ovī* by the actual use of the word *ovī* at the end of a verse. The description of the *ovī* as having a repeated word *ovī* or *ūvī* at the end is also mentioned in a verse in the *Mānasollāsa*: "If it ends with the sound '*ūvī*,' then the experts should deem it to be an *ovikā*."[12] His description aligns with a common way of singing grind mill songs evidenced in a 1997 recording from western Maharashtra available in The Grindmill Song Project database.[13] In this recording, each line of an *ovī* ends with the repetition of the word or sound *ūvī*. For example:

Sita is leaving for her forest exile—*ūvī*
A cow has blocked her path—*ūvī*
Don't go far—*ūvī*
In exile, O Sitabai—*ūvī*[14]

This uncanny resemblance between a thirteenth-century description of *ovī* and a contemporary singing practice brings to light the relative stability and continuity of this song tradition. In the recording, one woman sings a line, and other women join in at the end to sing the word *ūvī* in unison. This singing practice appears to be very similar to the repetition of words and phrases like *elelo elelo* and *aiyyasa* that Vijaya Ramaswamy describes as a common feature of Tamil field labor songs.[15] According to Ramaswamy, such words do not have a semantic function but rather serve to mark time in rhythmical, punctuated singing that coincides with the requirements of heavy field labor. In the case of the *ovī*, it is possible that the end of a line of *ovī*—where the word *ūvī* is interjected—corresponds to the timing of rotating a grind mill. But as I explained earlier, there is no necessary rhythm to the rotation of the mill. The word *ūvī* seems to indicate line endings of the verse as much as it does any inherent timing of the labor itself. In other words, it is possible that the metrical form drives the cadence of the grinding and not the other way around.

Dhere suggests that women's song practice of repeating *ūvī* at the close of a line is evidence of the etymological origins of the word *ovī* in the songs of the grind mill rather than in the word *ovaṇeṃ* or weaving.[16] But what if these were not mutually exclusive etymologies? That is to say, even if the name of *ovī* came from a singing practice such as described in the *Saṅgīta-Ratnākara*, the word *ūvī* itself may still have a connection to the metaphor of weaving. Spinning, threading, and weaving are common and ancient metaphors for storytelling, singing, composing, and writing around the world. They are especially well-known in the Greek tradition, which has supplied English with terms like text and ode and rhapsody, with their origins in words for weaving and sewing. The rhapsodes (from *rhaptein,* to stitch, and *oide*, ode or song) of ancient Greece were oral epic performers who "stitched together" songs into longer stories.[17] There are similar weaving analogies in Sanskrit as well. The first to come to mind is the term *sūtra*, meaning "thread," which came to denote a genre of aphoristic prose writing of the post-Vedic period that aimed "to present the essence of some doctrine systematically in a compact form."[18] The Mahanubhavas unraveled the conventions and expectations of this genre in the *Sūtrapāṭh*, a collection of the highly colloquial aphorisms of Chakradhar. "There can be no doubt," Jan Gonda writes, that the word *sūtra* "is taken from the image of weaving and of woven material made out of threads."[19]

The labors of weaving and carpentry are used as analogies for verse making in the Vedas themselves.[20] The Sanskrit verbs *ūya* and *vāyaḥ*, which mean "to weave, sew," perhaps have an etymological relationship to the *ūvi* or *vovī* of women's songs.[21] A common colloquial pronunciation of *ovī* is *vovī* or *vaī* or *ūvī*, as discussed above. In Old Marathi texts, *ovī* is commonly spelled as *vovī*. A *vahī* is also the Marathi word for notebook, a book "stitched together," and it is also the name of a verse form, as noted earlier, for performance traditions associated with goddess worship. The word *ovī* may be cognate, through the Indo-European etyma of *au̯-*, *au̯ē*, to many other words meaning "to weave" across the span of Indo-European languages, including the English "weaving"; "weaving" and "wove" appear to be cognates of *ovī* especially noticeable in its older spelling and pronunciation as *vovī*.[22]

In the Ṛgveda, weaving is used as a metaphor for women's song making:

> Just for this one, for Indra, even the ladies, the Wives of the Gods,
> **wove a chant** at the Vr̥tra-smashing.[23]

Here the women's act of singing in praise of Indra is described as weaving (*ūvuḥ*), whereas the male poet of this hymn, Nodhas, describes his own poetic composition as carpentry, suggesting a gendered contrast between the song making of women and men.[24] The possible connection of *ovī*, especially women's pronunciation of it as *ūvī* (in the singing style discussed above) to *ūvuḥ* is palpable. Many scholars have attempted to elaborate the history of *ovī* by its etymology, but often only in a narrow sense. What seems more compelling is to see the use of this term as reflective of the weaving and sewing metaphors ubiquitous in the song archive itself. Given that grind mill singers themselves use textile imagery in their songs, there is some support for the possibility that the *ovī* carries the long memory of an ancient connection to textile metaphors in poetry and song. In Greek literature, as in many oral traditions like those of Native Americans, weaving was strongly associated with women's creative work, as it also seems to be in this Vedic hymn. But in South Asia, weaving is the work of whole castes, though women are prominent in this labor in some parts of the country. The labor with which women in South Asia are consistently, continuously, primarily associated, however, is grinding and pounding.

In describing the labors of composition as weaving and unraveling in the context of a labor of grinding, the women who composed at the grind mill themselves seem to acknowledge song-making as a distinct labor. The very fact that women call these verses *ovīs* suggests a poetic, not merely a functional, understanding of the act of composition and singing, a recognition of the labor of poetic making. Work songs are often reduced to their function, and tied to the immediacy of the laboring context, but the imagery in the songs themselves suggests aesthetic intent. "In a fictional way," Paul Zumthor writes of work songs, "the apparent relationships are reversed. The work can seem to be nothing more than the auxiliary of the song."[25] As one grind mill song from the collection of unraveling-heart songs describes it:

While grinding and pounding
I unraveled my heart
My throat is worn out
Pulling this stone mill

daḷatā kāṇḍatā
hurada mājha ukalala

jāta yā vaḍhatānā
kanṭha mājha sukala[26]

To the singer of this verse the physical effects of grinding and pounding are felt in the throat, not the arms or hips or body. The image captures exactly Zumthor's point: the work of grinding is depicted as an auxiliary of song making, of the unraveling of *ovīs*.

The *Saṅgīta-Ratnākara* also includes a *mārga*, in other words, a traditional, more elevated and rule-bound song form called *oveṇaka*, which seems to have a connection to the weaving metaphor.[27] Rhythm is dominant in this song form, and thus Sharangadeva includes it in the chapter on *tāla* or rhythm, rather than in the section on popular, regional (*deśī*) song forms where we find description of the *ovī*. Nothing in the characteristics of the *oveṇaka* suggests it to be related in any way to the *ovī* except in the matter of the name, evident especially when *ovī* is Sanskritized, as it sometimes is in Mahanubhava texts, as *ovikā* or *ovanikā*. The *oveṇaka* may, however, be connected to a song form called *ōvanige* attested in a 1077 inscription at Humcha, a small town in the Shimog district in southern Karnataka and dated to the reign of the Chalukya king Vikramaditya VI (r. 1076–1126 CE). One small verse in this inscription extols a ninth-century Ganga king named Shivamara, the purported author of a now lost work called the *Gajāṣṭaka*, a poem in eight parts about an elephant, which the inscription claims was sung in *ōvanige* and *onakevāḍu*.[28] As I understand it from scholars of Kannada, there is much debate about how to interpret this inscription.[29] There is no definitive source text for the meaning of *ōvanige*, but *onakevāḍu* seems to be a clear reference to pestle songs. *Onake* is defined in *Kittel's Kannada-English Dictionary* as a "large wooden pestle for pounding rice and other things," while *vāḍu* (or *pāḍu*) means to sing.[30] Was *ōvanige* a type of work song similar to *onakevāḍu*? Or were the two paired here because one was an elevated but popular form, perhaps the *oveṇaka* described in the *Saṅgīta-Ratnākara*, and the other an everyday, domestic form?[31]

While there may be no direct connection to *ovī* in this inscription, it does shed light on the importance of women's orality for the dissemination of a high courtly work written by a king. The editor of the *Epigraphica Carnatica*, Benjamin Lewis Rice, interprets the inscription to mean that the *Gajāṣṭaka* is "a poem of such power that it would make a dumb man speak."[32] This seems a sort of backhanded acknowledgment that the literary work was influential outside the elite literary sphere, the "dumb man" perhaps meaning women to Mr. Rice. This Humcha inscription appears to be what Nagaraj was referring to when he said that though there is inscriptional evidence that Sanskrit literary culture was held in high esteem in Karnataka, "there is also evidence that *dēsi*, or vernacular, forms, too, were used to measure the popularity of a work."[33] Even when a work was written for a court, in other words, a poet might aspire to a wider audience beyond the courtly one. All in all, neither the inscriptional evidence nor the descriptions of *deśī* song forms in Sanskrit texts enforce anything like a necessary "separability principle" between the oral and the written, between "high" courtly works and "folk" forms. They instead show complex and ongoing entanglements, a process of literary making encoded in the very form of the *ovī*.

"What Are the Rules of *Ovī*?"

Dictionary definitions of *ovī* often include both women's oral *ovī* and the literary *ovī*, but the relationship between them is never specified. Here, for example, is Molesworth's entry for *ovī*: "ओवी **ovī** *f* (ओंवणें [*ovaṃṇeṃ*]) A stanza of a particular measure of Prákrit verse. (2) A light air sung by women whilst grinding, lulling infants &c. Ex. हातीं खुंटा आल्यावांचून ओवी सुचत नाहीं. (3) The member of a loom, consisting of cords called गोमटा, through which proceed, alternately raised and depressed, the threads of the warp. Often used *pl* ओव्या."[34] Molesworth's first definition of the literary *ovī*, which he describes as "a stanza of a particular measure of Prákrit verse," follows a verse categorization laid out in the 1860 book *Vṛttadarpaṇa* (Mirror of meters), by Parashuram B. Godbole.[35] Godbole was a towering figure in colonial literary circles, more widely known for his anthology of Marathi literature *Navanīta*, commissioned by the British for use in classrooms. In *Vṛttadarpaṇa*, Godbole set out to write a handbook of Marathi poetic meters for students and aspiring poets. There were other Marathi poetic treatises in circulation in the eighteenth and nineteenth centuries, but they focused primarily on the elevated quantitative meters inherited from Sanskrit and Prakrit that came to prominence in Marathi poetry of the seventeenth and eighteenth centuries, and often excluded the *ovī* and *abhaṅga*.[36] By including *ovī* and *abhaṅga*, Godbole departs from these earlier treatises, but he does not mention women's oral *ovīs* in his book at all, deriving his examples entirely from the written literary corpus.

Godbole was on the committee of learned Brahmins who served as Molesworth's native consultants for the dictionary project, but Molesworth often clashed with this group, complaining that they preferred "high Sanskrit" to everyday Marathi.[37] Molesworth intended to include the "common," the "local," and the "coarse," not only the "learned" and "recondite" words found in writing or used by Brahmins in the dictionary, but he often encountered resistance from his committee.[38] This might provide some clue as to why Godbole's *Vṛttadarpaṇa* does not discuss the oral *ovī*, and why Molesworth includes women's *ovīs* as his second definition, (though even Molesworth overlooks the *dhangar ovī*).[39] Molesworth goes on to cite the well-known proverb alluded to by Vitthal in Mahipati's chapter on Janabai: "No *ovī* comes to mind without holding the handle of the grind mill." Yet Molesworth's two definitions of *ovī* sit side by side, like the definitions of any other polysemic word. It is common practice to put the historically older usage first, but Molesworth puts the literary *ovī* first, though it was the oral that was historically prior, as attested by the *Mānasollāsa* (ca. 1131). Likely, Molesworth understood them as coequal verse forms, one literary and the other oral, since both were contemporaneous.

Godbole categorizes *ovī* and *abhaṅga* as Prakrit forms, by which term he means not the ancient language of Prakrit but a certain popular register of Marathi, and he groups them with other popular Marathi forms, like the *sākī*, *diṇḍī*, *dohā*, and *ghanākṣarī*, most of which are composed in the quantitative meters. The two main metrical categories that Godbole outlines as central to Marathi poetry are the *akṣaragaṇavṛtta* or *vṛtta* meters inherited from Sanskrit poetry; and the *jāti* or morae counting meters inherited from Prakrit and Apabhramsa. The *vṛtta* class is made up of syllabic-quantitative meters in which both the weight (long or short) and the number of syllables are counted and arranged into feet (or *gaṇa*) in accordance with specific proscribed patterns. In *jāti* or moric meters, on the other hand, only the weight, not the number of syllables, is important. Short syllables are counted as one and long syllables as two, and it is the total morae, sometimes arranged into *gaṇas* or feet, that matters. Both *vṛtta* and *jāti* meters were used in Marathi poetry as early as the fourteenth century by Mahanubhava poets, but they became more prominent in the eighteenth century. The pressing of Marathi syllables into the highly ordered quantitative requirements of the *vṛtta* meters often resulted in an artificial style that came to characterize an elevated genre of poetry called *paṇḍit kāvya.* This highly ornate style was epitomized by the verbal and metrical ingenuity of Moropant (1729–1794), the elite poet of the Peshwa period, but it came to be viewed with much suspicion after the colloquial turns of the nineteenth and twentieth centuries, inspired in part by the influence of British Romanticism. The *jāti* meters, however, more suitable for song, came into vogue in the highly popular performance genres of *povāḍa*, *lāvaṇī*, and *nāṭya saṅgīt*, as well as in the neo-Romantic Marathi poetry of the late nineteenth and early twentieth centuries.[40]

The *ovī* and *abhaṅga*, being primarily syllabic forms, diverge significantly from both classes of quantitative meters. According to Philip Engblom, the *ovī* and the *abhaṅga* "testify to the extreme attenuation of the quantitative principle that had been basic to the preceding stages of the Indo-Aryan languages." Engblom connects the prosodic basis of the *ovī* and the *abhaṅga* to the linguistic particularity of Marathi, rather than to any metrical ancestor. "All syllables in spoken Marathi," he points out, "tend towards equality of quantity, and . . . [the *ovī* and *abhaṅga*] simply reflected that development."[41] Of course there is no one spoken register of Marathi; there are many registers contingent on region and caste, but the purely syllabic basis of the *ovī* and the *abhaṅga* allows for colloquial diversity.[42] The flexibility and structural openness to the spoken and colloquial—to the language and poetics of the *audience* of literary works—is perhaps one reason for the overwhelming preference of Marathi poets for the *ovī* and *abhaṅga* during at least the first four centuries of Marathi literature, which developed in the space of the everyday rather than for and in elite spheres.

The earliest Marathi poetic treatise on the *ovī* thus far known is the *Mahārāṣtra Kāvyadīpikā* (Light on the poetry of Maharashtra) written in 1618 by the Mahanubhava poet Lakshadhira, and it likewise declares the *ovī* to be a "creation of Maharashtra's ingenuity" (*mahārāṣtra yuktī yojunī*).[43] Lakshadhira treats the *ovī* as a syllabic form. Unlike nineteenth- and twentieth-century scholars, he neither makes any effort to trace the metrical origins of *ovī* to the superposed meters, nor to "Prakritize" or reformulate the *ovī* by imposing a system of *gaṇas* or moric categories on it. Instead, one of the chief goals of *Kāvyadīpikā* seems to be to rein in the ever-lengthening line of the literary *ovī* by identifying as corrupt (*bhraṣṭa*) and nonstandard (*te apramāṇa mudrā bolije*) any *ovīs* with less than five or more than sixteen syllables. When he specifies that the *ovī* must have at least five syllables, he means the sung form, since *ovīs* with less than eight syllables were most certainly oral *ovīs*. Lakshadhira suggests thereby a long continuity between oral and written *ovīs*. He does assign specific names for sixteen different varieties based on syllabic count and lines numbers, but this effort to systematize the dizzying metrical variety, also attempted by later scholars, has never gained much traction. The singular and more general term *ovī* has persisted throughout the last eight centuries of Marathi poetry, suggesting that flexibility has always been understood—since the early thirteenth-century *Saṅgīta-Ratnākara*—to be inherent to the *ovī* as a form. Except for the *abhaṅga*, no other names supplanted or supplemented the idea of the *ovī* as a variable, flexible, and loosely syllabic poetic form used in written as well as oral compositions.

M. T. Patwardhan's foundational metrical treatise *Chandoracanā* (Composition of poetic forms), published in 1937, was the first to propose a third and separate metrical class for the *ovī* and *abhaṅga* as supplement to the *vṛtta* and *jātī* categories. Patwardhan called this class *chanda,* and this three-fold classification of *jātī*, *vṛtta*, and *chanda* has since held sway in Marathi poetics. "In the Chandas metres," Patwardhan explains in his English preface, "all syllables whether short or long are treated uniformly as long. This kind of verse does not appear in classical Sanskrit and though Vedic metres are called Chandas the difference of short and long appears to be observed in them."[44] Patwardhan is partly refuting V. K. Rajwade's argument in his foundational 1904 essay "Marāṭhī Chanda" (Marathi meters) that *ovī* and *abhaṅga* were direct descendants of syllabic Vedic meters (*vaidik chandacīṃ rupāntareṃ*).[45] Patwardhan instead looks at *ovī* and *abhaṅga* as musical forms. While Rajwade had drawn on Vedic meters—from the six-syllabled *gāyatrī* to the eighteen-syllabled *dhṛti* meter, to name the syllabic varieties of *ovī* and *abhaṅga*, Patwardhan counters by drawing on the names of Prakrit *jātī* meters for the different metrical varieties of *ovī* and *abhaṅga*. He argues that though they are syllabic, the *ovī* and *abhaṅga* are regulated by the rhythm inherent to their sung performance, which requires that each syllable be treated as long, as two morae. Better known by his pen name, Madhav Julian, Patwardhan was a well-known poet affiliated with an influential poetic coterie called the Ravi Kiran Mandal, or Sunbeam Club, which promoted poetry meant to be sung rather than recited or read so as to make it more accessible to a wider swath of the population. The kind of poetry that developed out of this tradition was overwhelmingly in the *jātī* or moric meters, and it was sung by select musicians in a classical, *rāga*-based style on popular radio programs that appealed—and still does—to the urban middle classes. Patwardhan valued musicality as a marker of good poetry, indeed as its defining feature. But as mentioned in chapter 1, he also lays out a graph on the spectrum of poetic possibilities between pure song and purely written poetry, and on that graph, he places the literary *ovī* (*grānthik ovī*) at the furthest end from song.

Patwardhan, Rajwade, N. G. Joshi, and H. D. Velankar, the most influential modern theorists of the *ovī*, all refuse to draw a hard line between the written and the sung *ovī*, assuming a continuity that gives historical priority to the sung. Rajwade draws on several examples of women's *ovīs* and children's songs, weighing orality and syllabic flexibility as the determinant factors in both Vedic antecedents and the *ovī* and *abhaṅga*. He quotes several opening lines of grind mill songs, writing that "the girls (*porī*) sing everything from six-syllabled *ovīs* to ten-syllabled *ovīs*," a variety mirrored, he says, in the written *ovī* tradition since the time of Jnaneshvar.[46] Similarly, Patwardhan draws on grind mill and festival songs for his examples of the metrical variety of the *ovī* form.[47] Velankar introduces an alternative, somewhat tortuous metrical genealogy and etymology in his speculation that the *ovī* form, and the word *ovī*, descended from the Apabhramsha *ardhacatuṣpadī*, which "gained popularity among the early Marathi-speaking masses influenced by the Apabraṁśa poets." He writes that:

> Women appear to have composed and sung their songs in this metre while doing their work, or while enjoying their leisure on the household swings. The songs with which they lulled their babies to sleep in their cradles, or with which they tried to forget the hard labour involved in their daily grinding of corn, were also without doubt, composed in this same metre. Later on, the metre came to be called *Ovī* and is preserved in practice even till to-day, though, in course of time its origin from the Apabraṁśa parent was altogether forgotten.[48]

Velankar includes the expansive range of women's *ovīs*, from the grind mill to the crib to the swing, but he argues that the *ovī* entered women's oral poetry through the popularity of an Apabhramsha song form. Given that the labor of the grind mill has been a fact of life in South Asia for two millennia, however, there is no reason to believe the songs to be a derivation of a later literary song form. Indeed, the "extreme attenuation of the quantitative principle" in the prosodic basis of the *ovī* suggests a distinct, independent metrical lineage. The name *ovī*, as well as the textile imagery in the song archive, support the possibility that the *ovī* has, perhaps, a more ancient past, even if we cannot specify any known ancestor.

Nevertheless, Apabhramsha songs, as also *gāthās* and other meters and song forms, likely influenced how the *ovī* developed over time. Just as in the twentieth century women began to sing the songs of the grind mill using tunes from film songs, it is possible that Apabhramsha and other songs shaped women's songs at various points in the formative period of the Marathi language. There is also no doubt that both Sanskrit and Prakrit poetry influenced how Marathi poets understood the *ovī*, and how it came to be figured and conceptualized in the literary sphere. That is to say, when Marathi poets took to the *ovī*, they brought the apparatus of the superposed poetics to bear on a process we might describe as the literarization of the *ovī*. But the *ovī*, too, had its own plans and brought with it its own apparatus of orality, tugging the literary toward the colloquial. It is the dialectical tension between literarization and colloquialization that best describes the long history—and many forms—of the *ovī* in written literature.

The third definition of *ovī* in Molesworth's dictionary is worth returning to here. It also comes from the world of labor, specifically the labor of weaving: an *ovī* is "a member of a loom." This is a highly evocative definition that seems to support the etymological connection of the *ovī* to *ovaṇeṃ*: to thread, sew, weave, knit. Molesworth's attention to the lexicon of the everyday brings into view an important, implicit connective thread between the three definitions of *ovī* he provides: whether in its oral, everyday form at the grind mill or its literary form defined by Molesworth as "a stanza of a particular measure of Prákrit verse," the *ovī* is associated, either directly or analogically, with a labor of the hands. It is in the tension generated by two kinds of labor, grinding and weaving, that we can trace the development of the *ovī* into its two main branches, the sung and the written, the lyric and the narrative. What is the significance of the centrality of labor, even if analogical, to poetic form and to the work of developing the literary qualities of the *ovī*? What, in other words, is the relationship of the poetics of work to the works of poetics? There is, as I show below, a "poetics of work" undergirding both oral and written *ovī* traditions, labors that are not wholly separate and independent but always engaged in relations of tension and dialogue.

Jnaneshvar's *Ovī* Between Song and Poetry

For the very first writers of Marathi the oral and the sung were never outside the purview of writing, not in the earliest Mahanubhava prose texts—which included a plethora of songs embedded in a new literary style influenced by them—and not for several centuries in the development of *bhakti* poetry in the *abhaṅga* form. The poetic texts of the thirteenth century, Mahadaise's *Dhavaḷe*, the *Jñāneśvarī*, and Narendra's *Rukmiṇī-Svayaṃvar*, are all rendered in poetic song forms, with Mahadaise's in the Apabhramsha song form of the *dhavala* (I return to this text in the final chapter). Jnaneshvar's and Narendra's works are rendered in what came to be known as the literary *ovī* (*grānthik ovī*). A little known Mahanubhava poet named Murarimalla appears to have been the first to theorize the literary *ovī* (*aisīhīṃ grantha ovanikā*) in his 1638 work, *Darśanaprakāśa*. He describes it as a *sākhaḷī*, a necklace or chain.[49] Although Jnaneshvar's and Narendra's works came to exemplify the literary *ovī*, both poets clearly considered the *ovī* to be a song form. Like the word lyric, the *ovī* carries its history as song into writing. Yet these first works are better understood, not as literary trees growing from oral roots, but rather as trees growing in the same forest ecosystem as the oral forms. The turn to the *ovī* by poets like Jnaneshvar and Narendra is an interlinguistic turn from within the literary sphere to a new literary language and a new colloquial form, the *ovī*. This colloquial turn is not a complete break with the inherited textual-literary models of Sanskrit, Prakrit, and Apabhramsha, but rather a new iteration of the literary in a vernacular language, Marathi, whose poetic qualities were already being developed in the oral and the sung.

Jnaneshvar presents the *ovī* as a *deśī* form. *Deśī*, a category of the superposed literary tradition, refers, Nagaraj reminds us, not only to the regional language but to "a cluster of metrical forms and poetic structures."[50] The *Saṅgīta-Ratnākara* classified the *ovī* as a *deśī prabandha,* and it is possible that the early poets knew of this classification. Narendra's work, in particular, engages the technical musical lexicon in minute detail in his descriptions of the performance of an oral bard, thus showing his erudition and likely familiarity with the *Saṅgīta-Ratnākara.* The very categorization of the *ovī* as *deśī* stakes a claim for its inclusion in the cosmopolitan literary order. Here's how Jnaneshvar puts it:

Through the refined beauty of the *deśī* [*deśīyecini*],
Peace vanquishes the erotic
Then the *ovī* becomes
An ornament of poetics

deśīyecini nāgarpaṇeṃ
śāntu śruṅgārāteṃ jiṇeṃ
tari oṃviyā hotī leṇeṃ
sāhityāsi[51]

Jnaneshvar is describing *how* the *ovī* enters the literary and becomes (*hotī*) an ornament. *Leṇeṃ*, which means ornament, is the Marathi word for *alaṅkāra*, which also means ornament or figure of speech in Sanskrit poetics. He seems here to acknowledge the novelty of the *ovī* in the space of the literary as an originally *deśī*—oral—poetic form. Jnaneshvar associates both the *deśī* and the *ovī* with the *rasa* of peace (*śāntarasa*).[52]

Narendra, whose *Rukmiṇī-Svayaṃvar* was written in roughly the same period as the *Jñāneśvarī*, justifies his use of the *ovī* meter in a similar way:

This Marathi speech (*bol*) is full of *rasa* (*rasik*)
On top of that I will show the power (*bika*) of the *deśī* (*deśīyeciṃ*)
That's why the verses (*śloka*) of this exposition
Are in the form of *ovīs* (*voviyeceni*)[53]

To Narendra the *deśī* includes not only the Marathi language but also the verse form of the *ovī*. Through the *ovī* Narendra will "show the power of the *deśī*." Narendra, too, specifies the *rasa* of peace to be the goal of his work. There is a long discussion of this *rasa* in the Sanskrit tradition. The eminent Marathi scholar Sadanand More has pointed out the influence on Jnaneshvar of Anandavardhana's ninth-century *Dhvanyāloka* (Light on implicature), and of Abhinavagupta's tenth-century commentary *Locana*

(The eye). To Anandavardhana "peace," the experience of freedom from the sensual, is the predominant *rasa*—the aesthetic essence—of the *Mahābhārata* as a work of poetry.[54] Jnaneshvar, in turn, makes an argument for the worthiness of the *ovī* as a poetic form because through it the *rasa* of peace can conquer the erotic *rasa (sṃgārarasa)*, the dominant *rasa* of *kāvya*. There is a clear rejection here of the "separability principle," the idea that poetry must rise above all purpose or religious intent to be pure art. Both Jnaneshvar and Narendra write poetry with full attention to aesthetics but without separation from theological purpose.

Jnaneshvar clearly understood the *ovī* to be a song form given the number of times he uses the words "sing" and "song" when discussing his composition. Thanking his brother and guru, Nivrittinath, for inspiring him to write this work, he says, for example:

> In that way, you made it possible for me
> To sing in *ovīs* [*voṃviyā gāvo*] the Gītā,
> The Sovereign of Divine Knowledge
> And the Seat of all Science[55]

Certainly, Jnaneshvar is having some fun punning with the title of the Gītā, but his wordplay often condenses multiple possible meanings into a single verse. Toward the end of the text, for example, Jnaneshvar reflects on his own poetic practice and goals in writing in Marathi and in the *ovī*. The section is a veritable metapoetics. I quote only a few of the verses here and more below:

> For this reason, I told the meaning
> of the Gītā in Marathi
> I made it easy and pleasing
> For all these people [*lokāṃ*][56]
>
> When the colors of Marathi speech
> Embrace the body of the Gītā
> Even if the singer is deficient
> The meaning will not be limited[57]
>
> So I say sing the Gītā
> In the art of singing [*gāṇiveṃ*], it becomes an ornament.

Even if on its own it will not have faults
It will still bring the Gītā.[58]

In that way, I made this work
In the charming *ovī* meter,
Which shows off in the art of singing [*gāṇivetem̱*],
and is colorful even without the Gītā[59]

Jnaneshvar is playing throughout these verses with various words for song and singing (*gīta*, *gāṇiva*) because they are important both to the title of the original Sanskrit text *and* to the verse form of the *ovī*. Jnaneshvar is surely distinguishing here the Sanskrit and Marathi versions based on the fact that the latter is in the sung *ovī*.[60] His description of the "colors of Marathi speech" seems to acknowledge the colloquial diversity of Marathi. These verses suggest that the *Jñāneśvarī*, a Marathi work in the *ovī* form, can stand on its own independently of the Sanskrit Gītā. The word *gāṇiva* in the third and fourth verses means "skill, artistry in singing."[61] It is the musical counterpart to the word that Jnaneshvar uses for poetry, *kavitva*. Both terms signify the aesthetic craft, process of making and doing, rather the end product, the song (*gāṇa/gīta*) or the poem (*kavitā/kāvya*) respectively. Where the title of the Sanskrit work, Gītā, indicates it is a finished work, Jnaneshvar's insistence on words like "sing" or "singing" or "the skill of singing" returns the text artifact to an active and living vernacular making. Recall that women's *ovīs*, too, present texts like the *Jñāneśvarī* as always in the process of being made (*kāḍhalī/lavalī*).

The word *ovī* in Marathi carries the memory of song into its literary form in a way not unlike the word *gāthā*. Andrew Ollett describes *gāthā* this way:

According to the derivation from the verbal root *gā*, "to sing," the word *gāthā* refers to sung verse. This highlights one of the tensions inherent in Prakrit poetry. Sheldon Pollock has argued that "the realm of the oral, specifically the sung" lies outside of "the sphere of literary culture." Where are we to place Prakrit *gāthās*? Are they closer to the songs that one might sing to pass the time at the grinding stone, or to the literate productions of professional poets? I have argued . . . that Prakrit texts helped to establish "the sphere of literary culture" where works of art, *kāvya*, were produced. . . . The *gāthā*, like Prakrit itself, thus seems to stand between two categories that have been essential for conceptualizing and historicizing cultural practices in India: on the one hand, the oral, musical, and sung; on the other, the literate, textual, and recited.[62]

This positioning of *gāthā* "between" the binary of professional poets and grind mill singers sounds like the *ovī*, which also straddles the space between the oral and written modes of verse making in Marathi. Yet I want to make it clear that there is little to suggest a direct metrical line of descent from *gāthā* to *ovī*.[63] The prosodic basis of *gāthā* is quantitative, while the *ovī* is syllabic. Though both share the characteristic of the shorter final line, the *gāthā* is always a couplet, whereas the *ovī* can be anywhere from two lines in the sung form to the predominant three and a half, or more, in written works. But there are some important similarities in how the *gāthā* and the *ovī* functioned and are figured in their respective literary arenas. Just as the *gāthā* did for *kāvya* in the Sanskrit Cosmopolis, so the *ovī* helped to establish the "sphere of literary culture" in Marathi writing, with the "oral and sung" inscribed in its very name. Just as the *gāthā* became the predominant form of Prakrit poetry, so the *ovī* in Marathi. If the *gāthā* is the "only meter to have entire works written about it,"[64] the *ovī* is the singular subject of the earliest premodern treatise on Marathi poetics, Lakshadhira's *Mahārāṣtra Kāvyadipikā*. Wherever the *ovī* is used in the early literature, it is highlighted and extolled. These functional and figurative similarities between the *gāthā* and the *ovī* evidence the influence of colloquialization on the formation of Marathi literarity, but not a direct metrical link between the two verse forms. It would not be a stretch to suggest that the *gāthā's* place "between" the oral and the sung functioned as literary precedent, a conceptual space created and inherited from Prakrit, for the colloquial turn to the *ovī* in Marathi literature.

Jnaneshvar himself, however, likens the *ovī* not to the *gāthā* but to the *anuṣṭubh*, and he justifies his turn to the *ovī*, not as a vernacular contrast to the Sanskrit meters, but rather as a continuity. Following the Bhāgavata Purāṇa (1.4.25), Jnaneshvar believed that Vyasa had written the *Mahābhārata* in a way that made the teachings of the Vedas accessible to "women, *śūdras*, and others." But accessibility is not purely a linguistic issue for Jnaneshvar. Rather, he gives the poetic meter, the *anuṣṭubh*, a communicative power beyond that of mere words, beyond language:

As when a mother sits
to breastfeed her baby,

she gives him only
the amount he needs.

Or as a clever man
Invents a fan
To bring under control
the boundless wind

So [Vyasa] crafted into the *anuṣṭubh*
What cannot be reached by words alone
To bring women, *śūdras*, and others
Into understanding[65]

It is clear here that Jnaneshvar believed that the *anuṣṭubh*, notwithstanding the Sanskrit language, was widely accessible to all those excluded by the high classical and Vedic traditions.[66] The *anuṣṭubh*, also called the *ślōkaḥ*, is a flexible, octosyllabic quatrain that resembles the *ovī* in several ways. It is an ancient Vedic meter that not only perdured into the classical period, but became the most popular meter, used ubiquitously in the epic and puranic traditions. Like the *ovī*, it is primarily syllabic and highly flexible, though it does admit of some patterns of regulated long and short syllables.[67] The fact that Jnaneshvar's *ovī* overwhelmingly stays within eight to eleven syllables might be attributed to the influence of the eight-syllable *anuṣṭubh* and eleven-syllable *triṣṭubh* or *upajāti* meters dominant in the Sanskrit Gītā of which his text is a vernacular rendering. In short, in the forging—the weaving—of the written *ovī*, other literary meters likely had their hand.

According to Jnaneshvar, the experience of the Gītā, which he believes is simultaneously theological and aesthetic, is not accessible by words alone; it cannot be reached through words alone (*śabdeṃ jeṃ na labhe*). Rather, it becomes accessible through the crafting of words—their sounds as well as their sense—into a concise metrical arrangement, in other words, into poetry. The *anuṣṭubh*, according to Jnaneshvar, makes the ineffable comprehensible and accessible, like the fan does the boundless wind, like a mother who feeds her baby only in small amounts. The poetic meter brings the experience of the divine within reach of those with the least access to it, the traditionally excluded and marginalized, "women, *śūdras*, and others." The similes of the breastfeeding and the fan enact what they are describing: they put into concise, accessible imagery his literary choices in order to speak to the new audience of Marathi-speaking "women, *śūdras*, and others." These similes colloquialize the high literary at the same time that they insist on an aesthetic vehicle for divine teachings. What the *anuṣṭubh* meter does for the Sanskrit text, Jnaneshvar believes, the *ovī* will do for Marathi.

The *ovī* is lauded by Jnaneshvar as the most accessible in a verse that is perhaps the most well-known of his statements on the *ovī*:

> In this *ovī* meter,
> Easily understood by even a child (*ābālasubodheṃ*)
> I wove the syllables
> Of the pleasurable *rasa* of Brahma (*brahmarasasusvādeṃ*)[68]

Here Jnaneshvar explicitly invokes the household in his declaration of the *ovī* as something so accessible that even a child could understand it. Yet this trope of poetic accessibility, even the explicit reference to children, was not unknown in the superposed tradition. Ollett cites a poet of the tenth century, Siddharshi, who notes at the beginning of one of his works that "Sanskrit and Prakrit are the two languages worthy of preeminence, and among them Sanskrit resides in the hearts of self-styled scholars, while Prakrit, beautiful to the ear, awakens true wisdom even in children."[69] Clearly this kind of figuration of Prakrit, an example of its own colloquial aspirations, shaped Jnaneshvar's understanding of Marathi, except that this time it was no mere figuration. The *ovī* is, indeed, accessible to "women, *śūdras*, and others." Even if the trope of accessibility has a conceptual basis in the superposed literary tradition, it is through colloquialization that the *ovī* brings its long memory of song into writing, and Jnaneshvar opens up—unravels—the literary sphere to the excluded.

Jnaneshvar describes his own labor of making poetry as a weaving or threading of syllables, *akṣareṃ gunthalīṃ*, as one might string pearls in a necklace or flowers in a garland. Garlands, necklaces, and jewelry are common metaphors for literary works in the superposed literary traditions, yet Jnaneshvar is not calling his text a garland or a necklace. He is rather describing the activity of making, of weaving or threading the syllables (*akṣareṃ gunthalīṃ*). The Tulpule and Feldhaus dictionary defines *gunthaṇeṃ* as *ovaṇeṃ*, or "to wreathe; to interweave."[70] Indeed, Jnaneshvar explicitly describes himself interweaving two traditions: the easily accessible, well-known *ovī*, invoked metonymically by reference to the child (*ābālasubodheṃ*), and the highest experience and joy of divine experience (*brahmarasasusvādeṃ*). This image of interweaving is reinforced by the dyadic parallel structure of his *ovī*, the first two lines on the *ovī* and the last two on his act of weaving the syllables of divine experience. The two compound terms *ābālasubodheṃ* and *brahmarasasusvādeṃ* are thus juxtaposed, seeming opposites, that he weaves together. In other words, Jnaneshvar is himself describing the work of poetics as an interweaving of the oral and the written, the *deśī* vernacular and the superposed tradition. And he does this by maintaining the *ovī's* "poetics of work" as an act of making, rather than as a text artifact.

In the *ovīs* that precede his description of making poetry in the *ovī* above, Jnaneshvar includes several conventional analogies for works of literature, including ornaments, necklaces, garlands:

When a beautiful body is not draped in ornaments
It would still be a bare beauty
As it is also when wearing them
Which is more appropriate?

Or though it is the nature of a pearl
To complement gold,
The pearl is still in itself worthy
Unattached from it.

Or as in the coming of spring,
the fragrance in jasmine flowers
is not diminished whether they are
loose or woven variously.[71]

These *ovīs* have been interpreted to mean that Jnaneshvar is claiming a place for his Marathi rendering as a distinct work, not one that needs to accompany the original Sanskrit text. In most print editions, the Sanskrit verses of the Gītā are inserted (not always in the exact same places in all editions) so that Jnaneshvar's Marathi verses can be read alongside them. This is also common in oral recitations of the *Jñāneśvarī*. But here he seems to be making a claim for the beauty of the pearl, the flower, and the beautiful body on their own, separate from the gold chain, the thread, the jewelry. The imagery suggests the independence of his work from the Sanskrit original, not only as theological text but as a work of poetry.

The Marathi rendering—imaged as the pearl without the necklace, the jasmine flower without the garland, the beautiful body without ornaments—is described as an unraveling, an undoing. These are images of deconstructed necklaces and garlands. The imagery invokes the two kinds of *ovīs*, but it associates Marathi with the unraveled work of art. The juxtaposition of the unadorned body, unattached pearl, and the single jasmine flower with the ornamented body, the string of pearls, and the garland of flowers conveys beautifully the distinction between the *muktaka* or independent verse form of the oral *ovī*—especially the single pearls and flowers—and the concatenation of *ovīs* through the activity of weaving, threading, sewing that constitutes the literary *ovī*. The fact that Jnaneshvar describes himself as threading together syllables or letters is an image of poetry making, a reference not to literature as aesthetic artifact but as a poetics of work. Far from accepting *kāvya* as an "autonomous 'aesthetic sphere' with its own theoretical self-understanding (*sāhityaśāstra*)" distinct from all "religious" and "worldly" forms of verbal making,[72] Jnaneshvar conceives of his work as a weaving together of the worldly and otherworldly, the everyday with the superordinate.

Jnaneshvar takes a profoundly new direction in his founding poetics by seeking to bring *kāvya*, not only theology, out of its rarified, sequestered arena into the world of everyday *bhakti*. His opening invocation and salutation to Ganesh is an amalgamation of the separated fields of knowledge and poetics inherited from the high literary traditions. He describes the Vedas, Purāṇas, the six philosophical/logical systems of thought, the epics, and the art of poetry as parts of one body of Ganesh in clear rejection of any sort of "separability principle." And in bringing literary texts and traditions together and unifying them, Jnaneshvar emphasizes their poetic and aesthetic contributions, while poetics and aesthetics are, he suggests, the best form for theology. The divine words (*śabdabrahma*) of the Vedas are the beautifully adorned image of Ganesh (*mūrti suveśa*).[73] The *Smṛti* texts are his beautiful and graceful limbs, while the eighteen *purāṇas*, through their ways of poetry (*padapaddhatī*), adorn his body with jewels of theories.[74] Here we find another compelling imagery of weaving as poetry making:

> The beauty of poetic compositions [*padabandha*]
> is his colorful clothing
> Where the poetic devices [*sāhitya*] are woven
> with fine shimmering threads.[75]

The opening invocation of the *Jñāneśvarī* establishes that Marathi writing, especially poetry, emerged in deep engagement with the literary concepts established by a long and robust history of *kāvya*. One need not deny the formative role of writing and of the literatures of the Sanskrit tradition in Marathi literarity, in other words, literarization, to see also the skillful hand of oral poetries in the development of its expressive and aesthetic capacities, in short, colloquialization. Jnaneshvar's conception of literature as a making, as poiesis, comes not from the superposed conceptual framework extolled in this image of Ganesh but from his colloquial turn to the *ovī*. The *ovī* is an unraveling and a weaving. While each grind mill *ovī* stands on its own as an independent poem, the literary *ovī* and the *abhaṅga* are "strings" or necklaces or garlands of verses. Two kinds of labor, grinding and weaving, come to distinguish two compositional modes of *ovī*.

Two Literary Styles, Two Modes of *Ovī*

As discussed in chapter 1, parataxis is one of the grind mill *ovī's* central structural features: an intentional removal of connective and transitional words, lines, and verses, an unraveling of the threads so that the *ovī* becomes a concise and concentrated articulation of experience, image, story, or emotion. The labors of reduction, removal, and concentration inherent to grinding and pounding are an analogue to the art of editing and removing and concentrating in the composition of the *ovī*. This is the style that is so influential in the writing of the *Līḷācaritra*. In direct contrast to this paratactic style is the development of hypotaxis as a structural feature of the literary *ovī*, imaged as a labor of weaving, sewing, or threading. The "poetics of work" in the *ovī*, both grinding and weaving, finds structural expression in this distinction between the paratactic and the hypotactic styles. Jnaneshvar uses the metaphors of threading and stringing to describe his act of literary composition— *akṣareṃ gunthalīṃ*—while the poetics of women's *ovīs* and the style of the *Līḷācaritra* rely on an unraveling, an undoing.

There are no "strings" or garlands of grind mill *ovīs*, only a shower of loose flowers, like the loose *līḷās* of the *Līḷācaritra*. Sequencing and connectivity emerge through patterns of syntax, repetition, structures of feeling. Each *ovī*, like each *līḷā*, still remains independent. With this kind of paratactical sequencing there is often no temporal, causal, or narrative forward movement, but rather a kind of return or dwelling within a particular experience, story, emotion, or thought through different imagery and scenes. In the literary *ovī*, by contrast, we find the increased use of hypotaxis: more linking, subordinating, comparative, and coordinating words, within and between *ovīs,* as a marker of its elevated style. In the *Jñāneśvarī* there is an abundance—an overabundance—of subordinating and conditional conjunctions that thread verses together, such as "just as / so" clauses (*jaiseṃ/taiseṃ*); "if/then" clauses (*jar/tar*); the ubiquitous "or" (*kāṃ / na tari*); "then" (*taiṃ*); "but, however, or still" (*pari*); "because of" (*tava, mhaṇoni*); "by that" (*teṇe*); and so on. Below I translate a bit more literally the same *ovīs* quoted earlier, to give a sense of Jnaneshvar's emphatic hypotaxis:

> A beautiful body is not draped with ornaments
> **Yet still** that would be a free beauty
> **But even** wearing [them] it [the beauty] is there
> **In that way,** which is more appropriate?
>
> *sundar āṅgīṃ leṇeṃ na sūye*
> ***taiṃ*** *to mokaḷā śṛṅgāru hoye*
> ***nā*** *leileṃ* ***tarī*** *āhe*
> ***taiseṃ*** *keṃ ucita*[76]
>
> **Or just as** it is in the nature of a pearl
> To give honor **also** to gold
> **But even otherwise** it brings honor
> To its own detached form.
>
> ***kāṃ*** *motiyāñcī* ***jaisī*** *jātī*
> *sonayā****hī*** *mān detī*
> ***nātarī*** *mānavatī*
> *aṅgeṃci saḍīṃ*[77]

It's apparent here how very conscientiously Jnaneshvar weaves the words, lines, and even the two separate *ovīs* together with overabundant hypotaxis. Sometimes, the linking words seem unnecessary, but the fact that he inserts them, often in every line or two, shows how intentional Jnaneshvar is about weaving and tying the verses together. It suggests, in one way,

Jnaneshvar's acute awareness of the parataxis in the oral forms of the *ovī* thereby driving his efforts to counter by adding all manner of hypotactic netting. Hypotaxis is also evident in verb endings and other grammatical features of Marathi like post-positions that create causal, temporal, or logical connections between words and lines and verses.

Perhaps a good comparative example is to look at the verses that draw on the imagery of weaving and sewing as a metaphor for poiesis in both the song archive and the *Jñāneśvarī*. Recall the *ovīs* from the first chapter, when women sing about the written works of the *bhakti* poets as an act of sewing or embroidery. Here is one example:

In the city of Pandharpur
My father buys a blouse
O Eknath, make a stitch with
a needle and thread of gold

gāva paṇḍharīta
coḷī gheto mājhā bāpa
sonyācā suī dorā
ṭipa ṭāka ekanātha[78]

A more literal translation of the verse would be, "In Pandharpur town / my father buys a blouse / gold needle thread / Make a stitch, Eknath." For the purpose of translation, I added a "with," but this does not do much to mitigate the ideogrammatic layering of images here. The dyadic scaffold of two images, buying a blouse in Pandharpur and Eknath's stitching, are also paratactically arranged, without any temporal or narrative transitions. The thread and needle are metonyms for the labor of making—and they are placed next to the apostrophe to Eknath. More precisely, the gold needle and thread serve as metonyms *within* the metaphor of sewing as writing.

Here are two verses from the *Jñāneśvarī* in which Jnaneshvar uses *ovaṇeṃ* or weaving to describe how Krishna made the world. Krishna uses the word *vovileṃ* (*ovaṇeṃ*):

Whether it is seen or unseen
It is all Me in Myself
I hold the world
As [*jaiseṃ*] a string does pearls

I created beads of gold
These I wove [*vovileṃ*] with gold thread
Just so [*taiseṃ*] I hold the world
From the outer to the innermost.[79]

In the second *ovī*, there is gold thread and gold beads and an act of threading that reveal the intertextual netting between women's and Jnaneshvar's *ovīs*. There is also dyadic parallelism in Jnaneshvar's *ovīs* that recall the structure of the grind mill *ovī*. The first two lines of each *ovī* form one unit, while the last two complete the thought with another unit. Yet, Jnaneshvar adds "just as / just so" (*jaiseṃ/taiseṃ*) connecting the first to the second in a clear and explicit relationship. Jnaneshvar thereby transforms metonomy, a figure of speech dominant in the grind mill *ovī*, into simile. Where gold thread and gold needle function as metonyms in the songs, the gold thread and gold beads are woven into a simile in Jnaneshvar's *ovī*. Krishna makes and holds the world "like" or "as" he weaves gold beads on a gold chain.

The hypotactic style becomes more evident in Marathi poetry in the growing prominence of the simile over metaphor and metonymy. Indeed, Jnaneshvar does not only have a simile here or there within a verse; rather his *ovīs* are often long strings of similes, as briefly seen above in the similes of jasmine flowers, pearls, and jewelry. Sometimes his similes are epic similes, extended over several verses, woven together through explicit hypotaxis. Readers of Marathi literature will recognize the abundance of similes as a feature of elevated poetry, but this is not to say there is no metaphor or metonymy in the literary *ovī*. In fact, even in Jnaneshvar's *ovī* above, there is an embedded metaphor in Krishna's description of world making, poiesis, in the making of gold beads. But there are very few similes in the grind mill songs, which favor the more immersive and intense and concise indwelling of metaphor and metonymy. Similes are more explicit, the comparison explained by the poet, whereas metaphor and metonymy maintain an empty space at the center of the analogy, which listener or reader must enter.

This distinction between the paratactic and hypotactic style helps us to distinguish two modes of *ovī*, and two literary styles. The hypotactic style is developed in the literary *ovī*, whose lines grow longer to accommodate it. Longer lines move the *ovī* toward recitation rather than song, to something more resembling stichic poetry, though with a release of the stichic rhythm in every final, unrhymed shorter line, thus maintaining a quasi-stanzaic form. The dyadic parallelism that makes each *ovī* a tight unit is also further loosened as the literary *ovī* is elongated. These differences map onto a distinction between *ovī* in the *lyric* mode and *ovī* in the narrative mode. These are not, however, necessarily mutually exclusive, nor are they divided into silos of orality and writing. There is a constant tug and pull between these styles, between the two modes of *ovī*. The poetics of one involves an unraveling, while the poetics of the other a stitching together. Just as singers at the grind mill draw from the narratives and texts they hear, so the poets of the page draw on the lyric intensity, the conciseness, the intimacy, and the dialogical structure of the unraveling heart of women's songs.

The *Ovī* Intertext

Jnaneshvar's intended audience is "women, *śūdras*, and others." The singers of the grind mill are, in other words, included as explicitly intended interlocutors, hence his choice of the *ovī*, easily accessible even to a child (*ābālasubodheṃ*), and the sometimes startlingly colloquial analogies woven throughout the text. In turn, there are grind mill *ovīs* in which women describe being in the audience listening to the *Jñāneśvarī*:

> To Jnaneshvar I sang my second *ovī*
> I will gain experience listening to the *Jñāneśvarī*
>
> *dusarī mājhī vavī jñāneśvarālā gāīlī*
> *jñāneśvarī aikun mī anubhava gheīna*[80]

This *ovī* is about the very act of listening to the *Jñāneśvarī*, most likely during an extended, often week-long, oral recitation of the text known as a *pārāyaṇ*. The singer anticipates gaining experiential knowledge (*anubhava*) simply by hearing the text. Indeed, this is the promise of the fruits of hearing (*phalaśruti*), that Jnaneshvar himself makes at the end of the *Jñāneśvarī*:

Just as one does not have to wait
Until a sandalwood tree
Is in bloom
To enjoy its fragrance

So, when this work is heard,
A deep absorption in the divine [*samādhī*] will set in
As soon as a person listens to this exposition
Won't it create [for listening to it] an addiction?[81]

When women sing about gaining *anubhava* by listening to the *Jñāneśvarī*, they seem to be indirectly invoking this verse. Poet, performer, and audience are meant to experience *samādhi* through the recitation or performance of the text, through what Norman Cutler describes as the "triangulated communication" between poet, audience, and God.[82] But this *ovī* itself is evidence that the listener is not merely the passive audience of this triangulated communication; she is also the composer or singer of a responding verse, putting two modes of *ovī* in dialogue. Listening prompts the listener's response in the form of the *ovī*. It is true that the addressee of the grind mill songs is always other women, or the grind mill itself, but the *ovī* above is explicit about another addressee: "To *Jnaneshvar*, I'll sing my second *ovī*."

Jnaneshvar's audience and devotees address him, not as a distant founding poet or elite, learned figure, but as *maulī*, a highly colloquial and affectionate address for "mother." Maternal address and metaphors of maternal kinship abound in both the grind mill songs and the *bhakti* tradition in Maharashtra. Here, for example, is an *abhaṅga* about Jnaneshvar attributed to Janabai:

O My girlfriend, my companion, [*sakhiye sājani*]
Jñānābāī, a doe, mother [*māy*] of my faun,
Cow of mother loving devotion [*bhakti vatsācī*]
Why are you so late? I am weary without you
I've sat down to grind, come quickly, says Jani[83]

Janabai calls on Jnaneshvar as a woman, *Jñānābāī*, and as a girlfriend and mother figure to come and grind with her. She speaks with the presuming urgency of a child calling out for her mother. An invitation to the grind mill is, metaphorically, a call to intimate dialogue at the site of sympoiesis.

There are abundant examples of maternal figuration in the *Jñāneśvarī* as well. We see it most poignantly in Jnaneshvar's depiction of the mother-child relationship between Krishna and Arjuna. The colloquial register of Arjuna's conversation with Krishna, the easy familiarity shared between the two, is striking and recalls the figure of the mother in the grind mill *ovīs* as well as the figure of Vitthal as a mother:

O God, you yourself are my teacher
So why shouldn't I satisfy my wish?
Why should I defer to anyone?
You are my mother [*māy*][84]

In this *ovī* Jnaneshvar uses an extremely colloquial Marathi word for mother (*māy*), the same word used by Janabai when she calls for Jnaneshvar. The word both invokes and generates an experience of maternal care. R. C. Dhere has pointed out that Krishna is also addressed as "mother" by Arjuna when Krishna reveals his cosmic form in chapter 11 of the Gītā. In the corresponding Sanskrit verses of the Gītā, Krishna is called father of the universe (*pitā'si lokasya*) and their relationship is cast as that between father and son (*pite'va putrasya*), friends (*sakhe'va sakhyuḥ*), and lover and beloved (*priyaḥ priyāyā'rhasi*).[85] Distinctively, in Jnaneshvar's Marathi rendering, Krishna is also addressed as mother using very intimate, colloquial structures of maternal address, such as *maulī* or as above, *māy*. Though there is no explicit mention of Vitthal in the *Jñāneśvarī*, this maternal figuration seems to prefigure the Varkari *bhakti* expressive mode. Arjuna describes Krishna's revelation of the cosmic vision as a mother opening up her blouse to feed her child:

Now what is there to show?
What even the Upanishads never reached
For That, you untied for me the knot
Of the heart of existence[86]

The words I have translated as "knot of the heart of existence" (*jivhārīṃcī gāṃṭhīṃ*) are deeply evocative in Marathi and hard to translate. *Jivhārā* is a very embodied, physical word for the affective center of emotion, the heart, the living essence of a thing. Dhere writes, "Arjun calls the Lord 'mother,' and expresses supreme joy that that mother has untied 'the knot of the essence of existence' for him. Each and every mother loosens 'the knot of the essence of existence' and gives her child the nectar of her heart to drink."[87] Dhere's English translator, Anne Feldhaus, adds an endnote to clarify for non-Marathi readers: "The reference here is to a mother nursing her baby. She first unties the knot beneath her breasts that holds her blouse closed."[88] In the verse, as well as in Dhere's interpretation of the verse, we hear a strong echo of the grind mill songs, not only in the maternal figuration of Krishna, but also in the "suggested" image of the *coḷī*, worn by women over the breasts, knotted at the center but unraveled to feed the devotee by a generous and motherly god.

There is more to the image here than even suggested by Dhere. The very notion of untying knots or releasing secrets of the heart is an echo of the unraveling heart. Here is another grind mill *ovī* about the unraveling heart:

As the mill turns, my dear
I sing *ovīs* of deepest feeling [*jivābhāvācyā vovyā*]
I unravel my heart
To my mother mill [*jātyā māulīcyā*][89]

The description of the *ovīs* as *jivābhāvācyā vovyā*, as lyrical utterances emanating from the deep interiority of the heart, echoes Jnaneshvar's word for the secret meaning of life, *jivhārīṃcī gāṃṭhīṃ*. *Gāṃṭhīṃ* means knots, ties, which in telling the secret of the universe to Arjuna, Krishna unravels, invoking both modes of *ovī*, a weaving and an unraveling. In both verses—the oral and the written—the act of speaking, of revealing, of opening up are described as an untying, as unraveling of the heart. Here, in the center of the narrative *ovī* is the unraveling heart of the lyric *ovī*. Two modes of *ovī* are, in other words, enmeshed, not separate or opposed. We can't know for certain that *ovīs* of the unraveling heart were sung during Jnaneshvar's time, of course, but given the antiquity of weaving as a metaphor for the composition of songs and poetry, it would not be unlikely that this sort of imagery was prevalent in the songs even then. The dialogue between Krishna and Arjuna is structured very much like the intimate proximity of the singers at the grind mill, as a conversation between mother and child. The *Jñāneśvarī*, writes Sadanand More, is like "the advice given by a mother to a child."[90]

Sadanand More links the ubiquitous maternal imagery in the *Jñāneśvarī* to Jnaneshvar's elevation of the *rasa* of peace (*śantarasa*) over the erotic *rasa* (*śṛṅgārarasa*), as we saw in the *ovī* discussed above. This imagery of motherhood, he argues, conveys the *rasa* of peace in the most poetic way.[91] Dhere suggests a more anthropological explanation. He connects the maternal imagery of *bhakti* to the way the deity Vitthal absorbed, transformed and sublimated the not-entirely peaceful motherhood of the numerous goddess figures and cults across the village landscapes.[92] These are valid interpretations, but they miss the most obvious source of the maternal figuration and feminine addressivity in the *Jñāneśvarī*: the *ovī* itself, a form that moves and travels, but carries in its many varieties certain basic parameters, motifs, and structures drawn from women's lives and labor. Because the *Jñāneśvarī* was written for "women, *śūdras*, and others," for the singers of the grind mill, his *ovī*, though figured and shaped by the conceptual structures of the superposed poetic tradition, still nevertheless remained in deep conversation with women's songs. There are moments when it is clear that the *Jñāneśvarī*, a high literary text, absorbs the "speech genres," in other words, the poetics, of its intended audience of "women, *śūdras*, and others." In turn, listening to the *Jñāneśvarī* impels, not merely a silent and passive embodied experience, but poiesis— women's songs that respond back to the texts women hear. Jnaneshvar is often given the status of the First Poet of Marathi, but his own poetic utterance engages the words and speech genres of his audience. Bakhtin reminds us that any verbal making, whether the *Jñāneśvarī*, the *Bhaktavijay*, a *kīrtan,* or a song sung while grinding is but "a link in a very complexly organized chain of other utterances."[93] Which came first, song or text? Who copied whom? These are not even the right questions. "The utterance is related," Bakhtin writes, "not only to *preceding* but to *subsequent* links in the chain of communication."[94]

Dhere is right in one sense, perhaps, about the rule of the "original oral *ovī*" over Marathi literature, but not in a linear, genealogical, or etymological sense. It is the lyric power (*bika*, as Narendra put it) of women's songs that remains a vital presence in Marathi expressivity, especially in *bhakti* poetics. There are aspects of the *Jñāneśvarī* that draw specifically on the *ovī's* lyric mode, developed over the centuries in women's songs. And this lyric intensity of the *ovī*, its poetics of unraveling, was important to the *Līḷācaritra*, and as we will see in the final chapter, to Mahadaise's *Dhavaḷe*, even though it is not written in the *ovī*. Unlike the *Līḷācaritra*, the *Jñāneśvarī* does not explicitly mention women's *ovīs*, but the poets who follow Jnaneshvar's literary lead—Namdev, Tukaram, Janabai, just to name a few—did draw explicitly on the grind mill songs in creating their prodigious poetic corpus of *bhakti* poetry. Janabai's grind mill songs in the *Bhaktavijay*, transcribed by Mahipati into his own literary *Eknāthi ovī*, are about these poets who generated their enormous corpus of poems in devotion to Vitthal. In depicting Janabai singing about these poets at the grind mill, Mahipati admits, albeit with hesitation and only partially, the centrality of the songs of the grind mill to the very structures of *bhakti*. While the Mahanubhavas continued to create an enormous archive of high literary works in the literary *ovī*, it was these *bhakti* poets devoted to Vitthal, the ones who claimed Jnaneshvar as their mother (*maulī*), who returned the *ovī* to the provenance of song in the form of the *abhaṅga*.

CHAPTER IV

Bhakti as Poiesis

A Dialogue in Verse

That softhearted God said
My Jani, get up to grind
The devotees will be waiting
For the dawn temple prayers

While he grinds and pounds,
His five-gem necklace sways
O Lord Vitthala
Janabai sings ovīs

—GRIND MILL SONGS, INDIRA SANT, COMP., *MĀLANAGĀTHĀ*

In many a grind mill song, Vitthal sits grinding with Janabai in her hut while she sings her own *ovīs* of *bhakti*. The temple priests wait for him, but Vitthal sits—indeed prefers to sit—with Janabai immersed in her songs. In many versions of this story, including in Mahipati's chapter on Janabai, Vitthal leaves his necklace and silk shawl in Janabai's hut as he rushes back to the temple after the grinding is done draped in Janabai's coarse blanket. The priests are appalled and immediately accuse Janabai of theft. When they find Vitthal's necklace in her hut, they sentence her to death by impaling, but at the moment of impalement, the spear turns to water and all hail Janabai's *bhakti*. Until this public incident, her *bhakti* was unrecognized, sequestered at home, at the grind mill. Far from public gatherings and temple rituals, the silent dawn hours when women sit to grind and sing *ovīs* are, Vitthal's presence with Janabai makes clear, no less a scene of *bhakti* than a *kīrtan* or a *bhajan*. At the grind mill, *bhakti* is not an event set apart from everyday life. It is everyday life. The songs give words to the longing for presence, participation, and fullness we have come to associate with *bhakti*, but always within and inseparable from the worldly, everyday experiences of the

Figure 4.1 Painting on the wall of the Sant Janabai Temple in Gopalpur, a hamlet just outside of Pandharpur. The painting shows Vitthal's necklace and shawl on the clothesline behind them, along with Janabai's patchwork blanket.

laboring body, of kinship and friendship, of exile and alienation. This "poetry is not a luxury," to draw on Audre Lorde's words, but "carved from the rock experiences of daily life."[1]

The enormous volume of grind mill songs, like the ones that tell the story of Janabai, should be enough to make the case for their inclusion in any study of *bhakti* poetics, yet the songs remain conspicuously absent in studies of *bhakti*, even in those that attend to its oral and performative modalities. There is something about the liminality of the songs, perhaps, that has led to their exclusion. Because they are sung at home, often in that fleeting, solitary time between night and day, they are not seen as properly "performative," but being oral, they are rarely seen as literary. They straddle the public and private spheres, and they defy the temporal boundaries of history. For the most part it is difficult to date the songs. Were the verses above composed before or after Mahipati's chapter on Janabai, which recreates the exact same scene? It is hard to say for certain, but there is, even in the question, an admission of the deep and abiding relationship between *bhakti* poetics and the grind mill song tradition.

It is true that the songs are inclusive, not bound by sectarian lines, perhaps another reason they have been neglected in *bhakti* studies. Yet the tropes of *bhakti* are ubiquitous in the numerous "semantic classes" of the song archive. The very first written attestations of the songs in the earliest Mahanubhava texts are, as we have seen, songs of *bhakti* centered on Chakradhar. There are songs on dozens of deities, and, just as we find in the written corpus of *bhakti* literature, there are numerous songs on the figures and stories of the *Rāmāyaṇa*, the *Mahābhārata*, and the *purāṇas*. One finds grind mill songs on Jesus Christ and on the Buddha composed in the modes of *bhakti*; in Muslim women's songs centering Allah, the overlaps between *sufi* and *bhakti* modes are evident, invoked also in the *cakkī-nāmā* poems of the Sufi poets.[2] There are songs on elevated modern historical figures like B. R. Ambedkar and Mohandas Gandhi, secular subjects but ensconced in the figurative tropes of *bhakti*.[3] In her autobiography, Urmila Pawar writes about how Dalit women, after their conversion to Buddhism, learned to sing their songs without the names of gods and goddesses, yet the tropes and poetics of *bhakti* remained especially strong in songs about Ambedkar and Buddha.

There is no denying, however, that the songs on Vitthal are the most copious genre within the song archive, and in this chapter, I focus primarily on them. Even today, the relationship between the grind mill songs and Vitthal *bhakti* is renowned in Maharashtra. The most famous opening, oral-formulaic refrain, "This is my first *ovī*," is almost always followed up by the closing refrain, "Come to me, Vitthala" (*ye re bā Viṭṭhalā*). To say that more than a third of the hundreds of thousands of songs of the grind mill collected over the last century specifically invoke Vitthal *bhakti* in some way is not an exaggeration. There are countless songs about Vitthal's temple, the city of Pandharpur, the annual pilgrimage, the texts, the *kīrtans*, the *bhajans*, the poets. There are, in fact, over a thousand songs on Janabai alone in the digital archive at The Grindmill Songs Project, and I have recordings of even more. There are songs about every *bhakti* poet, and an extensive family drama featuring the deeds of the wayward Vitthal and his often-exasperated wife Rukmini. "Who is Jana to you?" Rukmini demands to know from her husband after he spends the night at Jani's hut. He is quick to reassure Rukmini in another set of *ovīs* that she is his sister (*dharmācī bahīṇ*) or his helpless child (*lekaru*).

In these songs we have an immense archive of oral *bhakti* poetry, composed over the centuries by women, many from the most excluded castes and communities; it is as copious and as influential, as immersive and as captivating, as any written corpus of *bhakti* poetry. That such an enormous oral archive of *bhakti* exists is remarkable enough, but when listening it becomes quite apparent that the songs of women form one of the two major verse traditions of *bhakti* in Maharashtra. *Bhakti* poetry composed by elevated exemplars and the songs of women composed daily at the grind mill make up two distinct and copious genres of Marathi verse, but these two verse traditions are not in fact separate and self-contained. Rather they are engaged in ongoing conversation; they speak within each other's speech genres and poetic structures. This continuous dialogue, the commerce between *ovī* and *abhaṅga* gives form to the very architectonics of *bhakti*.

The overwhelming evidence of shared poetic structures, motifs, symbols, and speech patterns between women's *ovīs* and the *abhaṅgas* should be enough to dislodge the longstanding categorical divide between them. The *abhaṅga* is a poetic form meant to be sung and is metrically related to, and sometimes even metrically indistinct from, the oral *ovī* of the grind mill, yet the two are held worlds apart: one admitted to the literary canons of poetry; the other banished from the literary by the presuppositions that accompany its categorization as folksong (*lokagīta*).[4] In fact, the *abhaṅga* developed alongside and in direct engagement with the songs of the grind mill, just as the songs of the grind mill continued as an oral *bhakti* tradition alongside and in engagement with the corpus of poetry composed by the *sants* and recorded in writing between the thirteenth through the seventeenth centuries. The songs of women have shaped the poetry of elevated *bhakti* authors and texts as much as written texts have shaped the song tradition. It is the dialogics of the grind mill, its context of shared labor, its structures of address, its intimate unraveling of the heart that provide us with an apt analogy for the circulation of *bhakti* as a continuous dialogue in verse between poets, oral and written, each the audience of the other.

Bhakti at the Grind Mill

Bhakti is not merely one semantic class of grind mill songs among many others. In fact, *bhakti* is less a semantic class, or even a genre of songs, than the principal poetic *mode* of the songs of the grind mill. There are, in fact, many songs that depict the very act of singing at the grind mill as an obligation bestowed by Vitthal himself:

Don't put grist in the mill silently
My friend Vitthal has given me family
To my heart's content.

jātyālā vairaṇa nakā ghālū mukyānī
dhanabhara gota dila Viṭṭhal sakhyānī[5]

My friend Vitthal has sent us a message:
Don't sit silently at the chariot of Rama

sāṅgunī dhāḍīla Viṭṭhala sakhyānī
rāmācyā rathāvarī naye basū mukyānī[6]

In the first verse, singing is seen as an act of gratitude for all that Vitthal, figured here as a close friend (*sakhā*), has provided. Having enough food to grind and a big family to feed are, after all, fruits of abundance even if the labor itself is arduous. In the second verse, Vitthal himself directs women to sing at the grind mill. This verse features yet another figuration of the grind mill as the wheel of the chariot of Rama. The grind mill is, as we have seen, also figured as God himself in the ubiquitous apostrophes to Lord Mill (*jātyā iśvarā*). As a directive from Vitthal, the imperative to sing rises above the hierarchies and oppressive demands that structure the household lives of women. It is not an imposed, inescapable, daily labor like grinding, but poiesis, an act of making one's life mean more than the immediate, the functional, the necessary, the imposed. In and through these songs, women make a lyrical space that Tara Bhavalkar calls *svagata*, a "belonging to oneself" or "passing to one's own mind, spoken to oneself, apart."[7] There are many other verses that warn that if a woman doesn't sing while grinding, the holy man or sage (*ṛṣī*, *gosāvī*) will refuse to take their flour as alms.[8] Such verses connect the very act of singing at the mill to *bhakti*, no matter the subject or deity invoked.

The centrality of *bhakti* to the grind mill song tradition, not only as a class or genre but a mode of singing, as a defining structure of the songs, calls to mind the intense theological focus of African American spirituals, the work songs of enslaved Africans of the United States. The compositional contexts of each song tradition, the system of Atlantic slavery and the manifold and complex systems of caste patriarchy and enslavement, are distinct, yet there is something in the concentrated theological focus of each work song tradition that suggests a fruitful comparison. Though the spirituals were crafted in the midst of the most brutal conditions of labor, they are not named for their functionality, so focused are they on the religious, the "spiritual" questions. Similarly, though *ovīs* cover a wide range of topics, they are best known for the songs on Vitthal, and beyond Vitthal, as songs of *bhakti* in the broader sense. The spirituals engaged the Bible as the enslaved encountered it through sermons, storytelling, hymns, and sometimes covert literacy. The songs of the grind mill drew from the numerous texts, poems, and songs of *bhakti* encountered by women through diverse performance and recitation traditions in the oral landscape of Maharashtra. Neither song tradition was sequestered and separate from the dominant order; both engaged and responded to the world around them.

"The clue to the meaning of the songs," the renowned Black theologian Howard Thurman writes, "is to be found in religious experience and spiritual discernment."[9] Thurman neither dismisses the theology as merely conventional, nor does he subsume the theological into the sociological and political conditions of the enslaved as later commentators were wont to do. Thurman writes, "Whether the song uses the term, Jesus, or the oft repeated Lord, or Saviour, or God, the same insistence is present—God is in them, in their soul, as they put it, and what is just as important, He is in the facts of their world. In short, God is active in history in a personal and primary manner."[10] This theological focus did not "paralyze action," as later Black poets and activists would allege, "but made for detachment from the environment so that they could live in the midst of the traffic of their situation with the independence of solitude" (43). There is a parallel here between Thurman's description of the songs as creating "independence of solitude" and Bhavalkar's characterization of women's songs as *svagata*. Both see the songs as creating a space—personal, theological, conceptual, aesthetic, political—that is otherwise denied by oppressive regimes of labor, albeit differing in kind and context. The "center of focus was beyond themselves," Thurman writes, "in a God who was a companion to them in their miseries even as He enabled them to transcend their miseries" (42). This seems an apt description of Janabai grinding with Vitthal in her hut while the temple Brahmins are outraged.

Like the spirituals, women's songs are widely known as "sorrow songs" even more than as songs of *bhakti* precisely because they articulate the "miseries" of everyday hardship. Recall the Prakrit verse of the Jain poet Sanghadas, who describes women's singing as a kind of lamentation. Some of the most poignant of such songs develop a critique of everyday life as *saṃsāra*, a theologically loaded term that casts mundane, worldly existence as a cycle of unwanted rebirths from which a true seeker pursues freedom. *Saṃsār* in Marathi (spelled without the final "a" to distinguish the Marathi usage) is also a value-neutral term for married life, domesticity; it is used even more specifically as a collective noun for the accoutrements of domestic life, such as pots and pans and grind mills. In the Janabai temple in Gopalpur, for example, there is a room with Janabai's *saṃsār*, meaning her grind mill and kitchenware (see figures 4.2 and 4.3).

Janabai was never thought of as a married woman, but she was tethered to domestic labor and thus to *saṃsār* in this narrower sense. For the grind mill singer, *saṃsār* is their own everyday life of hardships and oppression:

> This is no *saṃsār*,
> It is an iron shackle
> Those who can't handle it
> Should go to a far country
>
> *Saṃsār navha lokhaṇḍācī beḍī*
> *jyālā hoīnā tyāna jāva deśodhaḍī*[11]
>
> This is no *saṃsār*
> It is a sacred thread of iron
> If she dies everyday
> Then you could say she wins the day
>
> *Saṃsār navha āhe lokhaṇḍī jānava*
> *mēlyā jhāla tīna rōja maga jitala mhaṇāva*[12]

These *ovīs* rather starkly present *saṃsār* as an iron yoke, even a shackle, weighing down the body, an imagery of everyday life as oppressive

Figure 4.2 In the Gopalpur Sant Janabai Temple, male priests of the Gurav caste lead visitors and devotees in turning what is believed to be Janabai's grind mill as they sing grind mill songs about Janabai.

Figure 4.3 What is believed to be the original grind mill belonging to Janabai at the Gopalpur Janabai temple.

hardship. These are not the shackles associated with Atlantic slavery, of course, but they show that these women experience their domestic life as ruthless servitude, even a type of enslavement, even a living death. In these *ovīs*, *saṃsār* is not an abstract theological concept but a description of everyday social conditions and experience. The second verse, for example, is darkly ironic. The sacred thread (*jānava*), worn over the torso by upper-caste men after their boyhood initiation ceremony, is described here as made of iron. The thread is a symbol of their "twice born" status, when their bodily birth is purportedly transcended by a spiritual "rebirth." It is a symbol of the man's freedom from his bodily birth. For the woman singing the *ovī*, however, the iron *jānava* represents women's "initiation" into a life of caste and patriarchal servitude and hardship, an iron tether of subjugation. While the first verse was sung by a woman of the Maratha caste, the second verse was sung by Gita Chawre, a Dalit woman identified in the The Grindmill Song archive as *navbaudha* or "Neo-Buddhist." In her verse, the *jānava* or sacred thread becomes a poignantly ironic metonym of the "sex-gender-caste complex" that Shailaja Paik calls "caste slavery."[13]

The only escape, the first verse asserts, is leaving the country, an impossibility for most women, or, as several verses in this class suggest, death itself, revealing the absolute oppression of caste slavery. Indeed, there is an enormous and somewhat perplexing corpus of songs on death in The Grindmill Songs archive, verses in which women imagine their own deaths, their funerals, the reactions of their family and so on.[14] There is a similar emphasis on death in the spirituals, Thurman points out, which registers, in one sense, a protest against enslavement, death being preferable to a life of enslavement. But it also affirms life as an existence that cannot be "measured by what oppressors could do to the physical body."[15] Women's songs of death, perhaps, do something similar. Though yoked by *saṃsār*, women carve out a space of existence, *svagata*, through poiesis in their songs. Though the songs often contend that only death is an escape, the song itself maintains the possibility of other imaginings. "The song," writes Paul Rekret of work songs, "acts as the residue of that which still might be."[16] The song is a life-wish that carries the singer through and beyond the death wish.

At the grind mill, there is less focus on "freedom"—both in its modern political sense and its theological sense as a liberation from worldly life—than in the songs of the enslaved Africans, which posit the "promised land" as the place of striving, of freedom from enslavement. In the grind mill songs we find instead an abiding focus on connection, intimacy, and belonging. Ordinary, everyday life is figuratively spatialized in the songs as both *sāsar*, the alienating home of in-laws, the locus of *saṃsār*, and as *māher*, the comforting home of the mother. Where there is loveless suffering, hardship, and alienation there is *sāsar*; and where there is intimacy, support, belonging, and love there is the home of the mother, *māher*. *Sāsar* and *māher* are also used by *bhakti* poets to convey the tensions between alienation and belonging, separation and intimacy, and "power and protest" that animate *bhakti*.[17] *Sāsar* and *māher* are the two poles of a dualism inherent to the stone mill itself, an instrument of rock-hard and inescapable daily labor on the one hand, and the site of conversation, sharing, affection, and above all, verse-making on the other. The grind mill is both the seat of hard labor, *sāsarvās*, and of belonging where *māher* is realized. When women and the *bhakti* poets who envoice them in their *abhaṅgas* sing about going to Pandharpur to visit Vitthal, they are daughters traveling to their *māher*, the home of Vitthal figured as their mother. *Māher* is the "promised land" of the grind mill singers, and it is neither otherworldly nor a revolutionary cry for freedom. It is a lived space of *bhakti*, of sympoiesis, immanent in the interstices of the everyday. It is a space *made by the songs*, by *bhakti* as poiesis.

Many scholars have noted that the devotees of Vitthal remain within the confines of *saṃsāra* as a sect of householders rather than of renouncers and ascetics.[18] In several Hindu theologies, *saṃsāra* is denigrated as an earthly, worldly life of illusory traps and bodily deception. In the *bhakti* traditions of Maharashtra, however, the word *saṃsār* becomes more palimpsest than a purely inherited theological concept. It invokes, sometimes even conflates, domestic life with the cycle of rebirths, but often the colloquial sense dominates the strictly theological sense. If what characterizes and distinguishes the theological orientation of the devotees of Vitthal is that they follow the "householder path" (*gṛhasthāśrama*), then it is in no small measure women's household lives that provide the poetic structures and the figurative vehicles of *bhakti*. Even the Mahanubhavas—being an ascetic sect whose initiates renounced marriage and domestic life to wander—remain nevertheless engaged, as the early texts amply show, with the everyday household labors of women. I suggest it was, in large part, the continuous engagement of *bhakti* with the grind mill song tradition that kept both the corpus of *abhaṅgas* and also the prose works of the Mahanubhavas centered on the household.

In this domestic space of *saṃsār*, riven by brutal labor, alienation, and hardship, Vitthal is made present by the songs, like Jesus in the spirituals, "in a personal and primary manner." Karen Pechilis Prentiss writes that "poets who write or sing *bhakti* poems in regional languages are involving themselves; they are making God theirs."[19] Prentiss draws on Charles Hallisey's illuminating discussion of *mamāyana*, an analogue for "devotion" in Buddhism, to draw out the specificity of what it means to translate *bhakti* as devotion. Hallisey describes *mamāyana* as "the complex attitude recognized by the linguistic action of calling an object, 'mine.' "[20] He emphasizes the illocutionary force of certain linguistic patterns—like deixis and the use of possessives and honorifics to address the Buddha—that are the generative markers of *mamāyana.* Such linguistic patterns, which encode the here and now of the speaker or singer, point to the object of devotion using possessive pronouns (*our* Buddha or more intensely *my* Buddha) and also to the speaking subject (the me, the I), generating thus the self-involvement that distinguishes devotion from other kinds of religiosity.[21] This is not unlike the pattern of self-involvement that Thurman describes in the spirituals. There are rich possibilities here for a deeper comparative study of *bhakti*, *mamāyana*, and the spirituals that are beyond the scope of the present study.

Possessive pronouns and structures of address are also ubiquitous in women's song traditions, where friends, daughters, sons, mothers, brothers, gods, goddesses, poets and many others are referred to as "mine" (*mājhā/ī*). Indeed, the very concept of *māher* is a spatial figuration of *mamāyana*, a space of belonging to, rather than separation from. In women's *ovīs*, gods, poets, epic and puranic figures come into the present lives of women and become theirs. This kind of intimate speech draws elevated figures into everyday commerce with the most marginalized members of the household and of society. Thus, the grind mill singers' Vitthal never stays put in his temple. He wanders beyond the temple walls, joins his devotees in the fields, at the river, in their households, and in their labors: grinding with Janabai, pulling cattle with the untouchable poet Chokhamela, reading texts with Tukaram:

At Tuka's house, **my** Hari reads a *pothī*
Reading *pothi*, Hari is weary
O Vitthal of Pandharpur
Come and visit **me**

sant tukāyācyā gharī
pothī vāca ***mājhā*** *harī*
pothī vācunī harī śinalā
paṇḍharīcyā pāṇḍuraṅgā
bheṭa de **malā**[22]

At Sant Chokhoba's house
My Hari pulls cattle
Pulling cattle Hari is weary
O Vitthal of Pandharpur
Come and visit **me**

sant cokhobācyā gharī
ḍhora vaḷī ***mājhā*** *harī*
ḍhora vaḷūnī harī śinalā
paṇḍharīcyā pāṇḍūraṅgā
bheṭa dere ***malā***[23]

Hari is another name for Vitthal, and in these songs, he is "**my** Hari" (***mājhā*** *harī*), which brings Hari into the present—the here and now—an example of *mamāyana*. The use of the possessive is almost insistent here. The poets Tukaram (*tukyā*) and Chokhamela (*cokhobā*) are also addressed using hypocoristic nicknames that generate familiarity and closeness. At the end there is an invitation for the god of Pandharpur to visit "me" (*bheṭa dere malā*). There is not only longing for Vitthal here, but a sense of belonging to Vitthal, to Hari, to Tukaram as *Tukyā* and Chokhamela as *Chokyā*. They are all made "mine." In these songs, as Prentiss herself so aptly puts it, women "are making God theirs." *Bhakti* is, in other words, not only embodiment, nor merely an illocutionary act that has immediate, pragmatic consequence, but an active and ongoing *making*. It is poiesis.[24]

The *Bhakti* Intertext as Poiesis

In his preface to Bahinabai Chaudhari's posthumously published book, her son Sopan Dev writes about how his unlettered mother composed her affecting oral poetry. "My mother was naturally gifted with poetry," he writes, and "because of *kīrtans* and other storytelling performances (*kathākīrtanādī*), my mother had gained wide cultural knowledge (*bahuśrutapaṇā*)."[25] The literal translation of what he describes as her wide knowledge, *bahuśrutapaṇā*, would be something like, "the condition of having heard many things." The term suggests an erudition gained through deep engagement with the oral life of texts. Sopan Dev describes how, as a child, he once read out the story of Savitri from his school textbook. Savitri is a famous epic and puranic figure, renowned for following her deceased husband, Satyavan, into the afterlife to save him from death. She succeeds in freeing Satyavan from the grip of the God of Death, Yama, by impressing Yama with her eloquence, knowledge, and devotion, her *bhakti*. Sopan Dev writes:

> I read that lesson out loud with great pomp. My mother came close and listened very carefully, and I thought, what is my uneducated mother going to understand? The following morning, she got up at dawn to grind. As soon as the grind mill started whirring and the sweet sound of her *ovīs* fell from her lips to my ears, I went to her and settled my head in her lap. Mother was singing *ovīs*:
>
> Savitri, Savitri, the shadow of Satyavan
> As soon as Satyavan left, behind him she ran
>
> *sāyatrī sāyatrī satyevānācī sāvalī*
> *nighe satyavān, tyācyā māghūna dhāvalī*
>
> I only remember these two lines now. All the other *ovīs* are unfortunately lost. After she was finished grinding, I asked Mother, "Who taught you these *ovīs*?" She said, "I was singing a song I made myself on the lesson you read to me yesterday." Hearing her response, I was amazed.[26]

Bahinabai's verse is a response to the story read by Sopan Dev. Sopan Dev is astonished that his mother, not unlike the legendary Savitri herself, is eloquent and knowledgeable, able to compose verse at a story's first hearing. Although it does not come through in the translation above, Bahinabai's response to Sopan Dev's question is written in the spoken inflections of the Khandesh region, just like her poems. Her colloquial idiom contrasts with his language of book learning, but she is engaged with that book learning. The songs are not, Bahinabai shows us, natural, spontaneous, preliterate, or outside of the sphere of the textual and the superordinate, even when they accompany the most everyday labor. We get a glimpse here of the many genres embedded in Bahinabai's poetic composition: a story that is first attested in the *Mahābhārata* and circulates widely in all kinds of tellings—including *purāṇas*, *kīrtans*, dramas, and even modern school books—is woven into concise *ovīs* in Bahinabai's own regional idiom, her poem thus entering a "chain of utterances," a vast intertext of story and song, writing and orality that undergirds *bhakti* poetics.

Like Sopan Dev, I have often asked women how they knew or learned the *ovīs* they sing. The preponderant response was always *aikun māhitī,* meaning that they know by listening. This is a kind of oral literacy, in which the aural is at the center of the oral. In a free-wheeling conversation I had with several women from whom I had recorded grind mill songs in the village of Shirad Shahpur in 2006, I repeatedly heard the phrase *aikun gāṇa mhaṇāyaca,* meaning, "Having listened, you sing the song."[27] There is actually little temporal distinction between listening and singing in the Marathi expression, *aikun gāṇa mhaṇāyaca,* calling to mind Bakhtin's insistence on the simultaneity of speaking and listening. Speaking and listening are not discrete and opposed activities that occur sequentially but are simultaneous: "The speaker listens, and the listener speaks."[28] Bahinabai listened, and she composed, and Sopan Dev was astonished. Women describe the song tradition in almost exactly the opposite way than it is generally understood, as an "oral" tradition, one that is spoken or sung. It is, rather, as an "aural" tradition that songs—and texts—are given authority and legitimacy. Most women I talked to did not value "originality" in songs, which they viewed suspiciously as "making up" verses. A verse *heard*, a verse that is "*made* mine," has more value than one merely "made up." Listening is never passive, in other words; it is itself a form of poiesis.

These women, like Bahinabai Chaudhari in the early twentieth century, were and still are, an important audience of the texts and performances of *bhakti*—*kathakīrtanādī*—but they have mostly been seen as a passive one. They are the listeners toward whom the poetics of *bhakti* are aimed, but whose own *bhakti* expressivity remains, as it were, outside the conceptual field of poetic circulation. Norman Cutler's triangulated schema of *bhakti* poetic circulation includes movement between poet, God, and audience, but the audience remains a sort of faceless and silent entity at the receiving end.[29] In truth, *bhakti* circulates, not in a closed triangular circuit, but much more freely across the great expanse of the underview. Every utterance, Bakhtin writes, is a response, an active listening, and thus already saturated with the words and speech genres of the listener, actual and imagined, intended and unintended. Every verbal event is "a link in a very complexly organized chain of other utterances."[30] In the universe of *bhakti* composition and performance, there is no great divide between poet, performer, audience, and public; every poem sets the stage for a new poem, every performance for a reperformance in the "chain of utterances"—the mycorrhizae—that connect literary texts, grind mill songs, *kīrtans*, *bhajans*, folk theater, and a plethora of oral and written genres. Listening is the compositional engine. Hundreds of songs composed by women about being in the audience of *bhakti* performances and textual recitations show women's active participation, the continuity of poiesis.[31] The very existence of these songs shows that women have never been mere listeners, that their listening was also, at the same time, speaking, composing, responding—of "making mine."

A large corpus of diverse *ovīs* on women's experiences at text recitations and *kīrtans* shows the ways that they make space for themselves within the *bhakti* arena—in particular through the use of deixis, possessive pronouns, hypocoristic address, and metaphors of kinship. There are, for example, numerous verses in which women sing about a *kīrtan* taking place in their own courtyard or in front of their own house, or they sing about being related to a performer. It's important not to assume that these are all merely literal reports. Rather, these songs create self-involvement in *bhakti* spaces though such poetic structures of *mamāyana*. Here is one example:

In Pandharpur
A clamor of cymbals and drum
My baby wears anklets with bells, O woman
He rises to perform *kīrtan*

paṇḍharapurāmandī
ṭāḷamṛdaṅgācī ghāī
bāḷā paijaṇa bāī
kirtanāle ubhī rāhī[32]

The singer is a Dalit woman named Mahananda Ujgare. She is singing about being in the audience and listening to the bustle and excitement of a *kīrtan*, and the performer is the singer's own child, whom she calls "baby," another example of hypocorism. By making the performer her son, her baby, she makes the experience of the *kīrtan* "mine." The figurative use of kinship as a metaphor is central to all *bhakti* poetry, but here the common maternal figuration is reversed: the song is from the perspective of the mother, not the child. Even if this song were once originally about an actual experience of listening to one's own child performing *kīrtan*, it becomes a song sung by many, not for its literal, biographical content, but for the intimacy and belonging—*mamāyana* or *bhakti*—it generates. The singers of the grind mill convey the realities of exclusion and alienation, of *sāsarvās*, in many songs about Janabai and Sita and their daily lives. Yet they also sing verses about the texts and performances and pilgrimages of *bhakti* not as mimesis but as poiesis, not simply a reenactment of what is but of what one wishes, hopes, imagines, and aspires. That is, through these songs, women create belonging—*bhakti*—for themselves in spaces where they are not always included or seen or heard.

In a lot of songs, the performer of a text or a *kīrtan* is depicted as Vitthal himself. He is, to invoke Thurman again, active in "a personal and primary manner." Here is a verse about going to a textual recitation, a reading of a *pothī* by Vitthal:

I'm going to the reading,
Girlfriends, save me a place
Dark-skinned Panduranga is performing
A diamond under the stars

Pothīlā mī jāte,
sayāno tumī jāgā dharā
Sāvaḷā Pāṇḍuraṅga
ubhā cāndaṇī khālī hīrā[33]

The *ovī* suggests that Vitthal (Panduranga) is "standing up" under the stars as the performer or reciter of the *pothī*. Like the woman's child in the previous *ovī*, Vitthal—everyone's God, a mother—creates a sense of belonging at the event. The address to women friends, *sayāno*, frames this verse with a request for space, for inclusion, at the text reading, one that her female companions can ensure. Another verse declares Janabai to be the performer of the text:

In Pandharpur
Women throng every street, every nook
Janabai is reading the sacred book.

paṇḍharapurāta galogalī āyābāyā
pothī vācatī janā bayā[34]

Pandharpur is widely depicted throughout the *bhakti* poetic corpus as a feminine sanctuary, a *māher* or mother's home. Here the throngs of women who have traveled to Pandharpur find their sense of belonging from Janabai, who is addressed as "Jana Bayā," an affectionate hypocorism of *bāī*. We have here presence and participation, a fullness of *bhakti* in the city of Pandharpur. Many of these songs are about the actual pilgrimage to Pandharpur in which women do participate vigorously in song and play.

There are also numerous songs about the act of overhearing a *bhakti* performance from a space outside the arena of public performance:

This is my first *ovī*
I sit grinding
The calling of God's name
Booms through the tenement

pahilī mājhī ovī mī basate daḷīta
parabhu nāmācā gajara ghumato cāḷīta[35]

The *kīrtan* described in the *ovī* is in or around a tenement complex (*cāḷīta*), perhaps in the courtyard, but the woman composing is inside her home, at her grind mill. The singer overhears the *kīrtan* and describes the sounds of collective, joyous recitation of the divine name common in the participatory segments of a *kīrtan*. The words *nāmācā gajara* also invoke a well-known *abhaṅga* by Namdev. Here is one verse from Namdev's famous poem invoked by the grind mill singer:

The calling of God's name
Booms on the banks of the Bhima
Listen how they proclaim your glory!

nāmācā gajara garje bhimātir
mahimā sāje thora tuja aikā[36]

Both the Namdev poem and the grind mill *ovī* are about the poetic performance of *kīrtan*, but each poet approaches the performance from different spaces. The poet Namdev, believed to be the founder of *kīrtan* in Maharashtra, is leading the *kīrtan* he is describing, and his addressee is none other than Vitthal himself, whom he advises to listen (*aikā*) to the resounding performance in his honor—Namdev uses the familiar second person possessive to address Vitthal as "your" (*tujā*). In Namdev's poem, the attendees are learned sages, gods, and even the Vedas personified. The poem dramatizes Cutler's model of *bhakti poetics* as a triangulated verbal event between poet, audience, and God. Namdev directly addresses Vitthal himself and draws in the participation of the audience in a collective experience of exuberant participation in the cosmic *kīrtan*. The grind mill *ovī*, on the other hand, puts before our eyes a solitary woman overhearing a *kīrtan* as she labors at the grind mill in the tenement building where she lives, but as she sings her own verse in response, she opens up the closed triangle into an "endless chain of utterances."

Another *ovī* creates a similar scene of overhearing a *bhakti* performance, this one a story about Rukmini and Vitthal:

Below the town,
Rukmini harvests fenugreek
So sweet is the sound she overhears,
Lord Vitthal reading the book

gāvācyā khālatī
Rukhmīṇ khurapatī methī
aśī mañjuḷa aiku yetī
devā iṭṭhalācī pothī[37]

Rukmini is imagined here as working outside the boundaries of the town, in a field of fenugreek, and far from the public performance arena where Vitthal is reading a *pothī*. The words *aiku yetī* suggests overhearing, not merely hearing. Though they are not intended for her, the sounds are mellifluous (*mañjuḷa*). In this and in the previous *ovī*, the women listen while engaged in labor, at home or in the field, in spaces that might be called more private than public. Susie Tharu and K. Lalita observe that "the women poets of the *bhakti* movements did not have to seek the institutionalized spaces religion provided to express themselves, and women's poetry moved from the court and the temple to the open spaces of the field, the workplace and the common women's hearth."[38] Tharu and Lalita are talking about poets like Janabai, but verses like this one show that the "open spaces of the field, the workplace and the common women's hearth" are saturated by a grind mill poetics of *bhakti*. And though both verses above describe *bhakti* spaces outside the "institutionalized spaces religion provided," they continue to speak to the *bhakti* public, and in doing so, they create a liminal, more inclusive shared geography, a *māher*.

It is the integration of the separated fields of religion, poetry, and everyday life—a refusal of the "separability principle"—that maps the poetic geography of the grind mill songs. The singers of the grind mill use their poetics of the everyday to retell, recreate, and respond to "received" texts and performances they hear in the vernacular mode, connecting their everyday life to *bhakti* texts, poems, and performances. "If we consider vernacularization in relation to the topos of everyday life, and by extension to an immanent critique of social difference," writes Christian Lee Novetzke, "then this allows us to see that the process of vernacularization occurs long before vernacular literatures arise."[39] Novetzke is speaking here of the turn to the vernacular audience within the Sanskrit textual tradition, but his point is perhaps better illustrated in the ongoing exchanges between orality and textuality evident already within the oral traditions. Is not the *Sītāyan* a vernacularization of the *Rāmāyaṇa*, one in which "the topos of everyday life" expands at the center of its retelling? I'm referring here to Novetzke's definition of vernacularization as "the strategic use of the topos of everyday life within a social, political, artistic, linguistic, and cultural process in which the quotidian ("ordinary," "everyday") expands at the center of a given region's public culture."[40] But vernacularization also involves the opposite and simultaneous trajectory through which the textual and the superordinate enter and expand at the center of the everyday through oral poetic engagements and reenactments.

Guy Poitevin sees women's retellings of texts in the grind mill songs, like the *Sītāyan*, as evidence of the creative limits on women's self-expression, whereby the ideological patterns of "received," male-authored texts serve as "the mirror of a restraining tradition." Women's "range of innovation," Poitevin writes, "is therefore extremely narrow. Attempts of autonomy follow paths already marked out."[41] It is a common charge leveled at work song traditions, which are often denigrated as derivative, as secondary. Yet Poitevin assumes that there exists some "range of innovation" that isn't similarly "limited." This is exactly the assumption that Bakhtin is at pains to call out in "The Problem of Speech Genres." All utterances—written as well as spoken—are shaped and formed as responses to an already ongoing conversation, he argues. The *Jñāneśvarī* is considered a founding text of Marathi poetry and *bhakti*, but it, too, is "limited" by the Gītā of which it is a retelling and a response, and by the superposed models of literarity inherited from Sanskrit and Prakrit texts. The *Jñāneśvarī* also works, as we discussed in the previous chapter, within the speech codes and poetic models of its vernacular audience of "women, *śūdras*, and others." *Bhakti* texts work within the "limits" and structures of the oral poetic traditions no less than the songs composed by women at the grind mill work within the "limits" of the texts. To put this differently, Jnaneshvar's engagements with the oral poetic free him from the limits of the superposed written inheritance, just as the texts expand women's compositional horizons beyond the local, the immediate, the proximate. Each is the audience of the other. This intimate exchange, this tug and pull between text and song, between the literary models and the oral ones, structures the very form of the preferred poetic vehicle of the *bhakti* poets, the *abhaṅga*.

The *Abhaṅga*

The enormous corpus of *bhakti* poetry centered on Vitthal comes in a variety of poetic forms and genres, many of which feature female envoicement. Eknath is famous, for example, for his *bhāruḍs*, a dramatic song form written in a highly colloquial and performative register featuring the voices of women and lower castes. There are also a significant number of *gauḷanas*, songs in the voice of Radha or a female cowherder, featuring the love play between Krishna and Radha.[42] This variety of verse forms is noted in the grind mill songs. Here, for example, are a couple of verses from the over two thousand verses sung by Rama Ughade, who belongs to the Dhangar community settled in a western Maharashtrian village:

My baby is very set
On going to hear *bhāruḍ*
I tell you, baby, you still have
Your childhood

bhāruḍī jāyālā bāḷa mājhyālā laī dhyāna
sāṅgate bāḷā tulā tujhā hāye lahānapaṇa[43]

My own, he sang
a *gavaḷanī abhaṅga*
I tell you, woman
He performed the *bhajan*

gavaḷaṇīcā abhaṅga mājhyānī gāīlā
sāṅgate bāī tulā ubhā bhajanī rāhilā[44]

There is a deep sense of belonging and ownership conveyed in these verses. I found variations of both sung by another woman from a different caste and village, which in itself tells us not to look at them too literally. The verses speak through the structures of *mamāyana* to convey a deep appreciation for the *bhāruḍ* and the *gauḷana*.

It is the *abhaṅga*, however, that reigns supreme in the Marathi *bhakti* corpus centered on Vitthal, as we see in the sheer volume of poetry in the *abhaṅga* that emerged between the thirteenth and seventeenth centuries. In the song archive, this abundance is noted in the imagery of the blouse, *coḷī*, covered in *abhaṅgas*:

Rukmini's blouse
Is filled with *abhaṅgas*
The God Vitthal has put on
The *Jñāneśvarī*

rukmīṇīcī coḷī
abhaṅgānī bharalī sārī
devā Viṭṭhalāne
lāvalī jñāneśvarī[45]

The dyadic verse juxtaposes—puts into conversation—the *abhaṅgas* teeming on Rukmini's blouse and the *Jñāneśvarī* being performed by Vitthal.

The *abhaṅga* is so associated with Vitthal that some have argued that its very name derives from the description of Vitthal as "*abhaṅga* Vitthal," in other words as "undivided Vitthal."[46] Bhakti poetry is often colloquially referred to in Marathi as *abhaṅgavāṇī*, the "speech" of *abhaṅgas*. To say that the *abhaṅga* has an oral life is to say that it is sung, and the primary venue for this is the *bhajan*, which is an integral part of *kīrtan*. But there are *bhajans* outside of *kīrtan*, and these tend to be more informal, decentralized, local, and participatory gatherings. *Abhaṅgas* are most often sung to rhythmical cycles called *bhajanī thekās*, which are eight or sixteen beat cycles that pair well with verses of six to eight syllables. One interesting argument about the origin of the name of the *abhaṅga*, a topic of some controversy in Marathi scholarship, is that it came from a specific rhythmic pattern (*tāla*) called *abhaṅga tāla* included by Sharangadeva in a list of over a hundred *deśī* or regional *tālas* in the *Saṅgīta-Ratnākara*.[47] The *deśī tālas*, according to the musician and musicologist Keshavchaitanya Kunte, are "patterns of clapping or accent percussion instruments." The *abhaṅga tāla* has four beats, which are "roughly similar to the pattern of the cymbal playing (*ṭāla*) practiced . . . even in today's *bhajan* singing."[48] At least one scholar has surmised that the name of the *abhaṅga* might have arisen from the *abhaṅga tāla*.[49]

There are two *abhaṅgas* attributed to Namdev, both of uncertain date and authorship, but likely one of the earlier efforts to set out metrical parameters for the *abhaṅga* form.[50] In the first of these, Namdev sets out detailed rules for the *abhaṅga*: there are, he says, three and-a-half lines, with a total of eighteen syllables, six per line in the first three lines, and four syllables in the last line, thus totaling twenty-two syllables.[51] The other *abhaṅga* describes the other variation as a couplet with lines of equal length totaling sixteen syllables, thus eight syllables per line.[52] These two *abhaṅga* varieties correspond exactly to the two varieties, the *devadvāra* or "big" *abhaṅga* and the *devīvara* or "small" *abhaṅga* that Godbole describes in his 1860 *Vṛttadarpaṇa* (Mirror of meters).[53] Neither Namdev nor Godbole makes reference to the overlaps between the *abhaṅga* and the grind mill *ovī*, but later scholars like H. D. Velankar and N. G. Joshi declare that the *abhaṅga* is nothing more than the "original and purer form" of the sung *ovī*.[54] Joshi writes, "There is an indissoluble relationship between the grind mill *ovī*, the *ovī* sung while grinding and pounding, and the *abhaṅga* of the *Vārkarīs*."[55]

But it is important to acknowledge that though undoubtedly intended for song, the *abhaṅga* was never completely oral in the way that the grind mill *ovī* is oral. It has literary features that appear to be shaped by textual traditions, including the efforts at metrical classification as we see in the Namdev *abhaṅgas*. For one thing, *abhaṅgas* are a strophic form of the *ovī* in which one rhyme scheme prevails in all verses. This is in distinct contrast to grind mill *ovī* sequences in which the rhyme scheme, and often the syllabic counts, vary from verse to verse. Thus grind mill verses, even when sung in sequence, remain an independent verse form, whereas the *abhaṅga* is a concatenation of verses, of *ovīs*, each verse connected to the previous by subject matter, syllabic parameters, and rhyming patterns, which are clasped together at the end with a signature verse. Another theory about the origins of the name *abhaṅga* suggests that it refers to the idea of binding and stringing individual *ovīs* together—creating a unity, an "unbrokenness" (*a-bhaṅga*) between verses. Velankar writes:

> In the early days of its currency, the word Abhaṅga must not have signified any simple metre. It only meant an "unbroken or musically uninterrupted" group of stanzas composed in the Ovī meter. It may indeed be pointed out that the word retains this sense even to-day. To sing an Abhaṅga means, to sing not this or that stanza, but a group of stanzas forming a unity owing to the common idea and concluding portion, containing the name of the poet and such other things.[56]

This integration of each verse into a larger whole is most evident when we contrast it to the grind mill *ovī*, which is *bhaṅga*—that is to say, each verse remains separate from another. To describe a poem as *a-bhaṅga*, which literally means undivided, implies an inherent contrast to the independent verse form of the grind mill *ovī*. In this specific structural way, the *abhaṅga* seems closer to the literary *ovī* than to the grind mill *ovī*.

The feature that perhaps most clearly distinguishes the *abhaṅga* from the grind mill *ovī* is the "concluding portion, containing the name of the poet." As John Stratton Hawley notes in his landmark essay on this topic, "it is a virtual requirement of the genre" of *bhakti* poetry that "the poet's name appear in the last one or two lines as a sort of oral signature."[57] Hawley calls the signature "oral" for good reason, yet the practice of authorial self-naming is not usually a common feature of oral traditions. "To refer to the author," Paul Zumthor writes, "is the mark of literacy."[58] Grind mill *ovīs*, for example, are consistently indifferent to claims of authorship. The verses are sung and reperformed without need to distinguish the composer of the verse from the one singing it. This does not mean, however, as Ruth Finnegan points out, that oral compositions are necessarily "collectively authored."[59] When a verse is sung, the singer's experiences and emotions are put into verse. The singers make each verse their own by inhabiting and transforming it to fit the needs and context of her own idiom and purpose. When grind mill singers are singing about the *bhakti* poets, they often use the poets' signatures—Jani says (*janī mhaṇe*)—narratively, but they never name themselves as composers of verse, even when the verses might be their own novel compositions.[60]

S. G. Tulpule points out that the word *abhaṅga* is almost never used in extant Old Marathi texts to refer to the verse form of *bhakti* poetry. Rather it seems to mean "the colophon or the signature of the author appearing at the end of the composition."[61] In the story about King Ramdev attempting to buy the authorship of Narendra's *Rukmiṇī Svayaṃvar* in *Smṛtisthaḷ*, what the king asks for is the *abhaṅgu* of the text: "Then the King said, 'Give me the authorship of this work' [*yā granthācā* ***abhaṅgu*** *maja dyāvā*].[62] Anne Feldhaus and Tulpule translate the word *abhaṅgu* to mean "authorship" here. A. R. Priolkar points to an entry for *abhaṅgu* in a 1626 Portuguese-Konkani dictionary, where it is defined as *fim de escriptura*, in other words, "colophon."[63] This connects the word *abhaṅga* to the signature line or signature verse that is one of the *abhaṅga*'s main features, though perhaps not in the strictly etymological sense implied by Tulpule.

Indeed, the practice of naming oneself as poet within a poem has a rather long and hoary literary history. The practice appears as early as the *Therīgāthā*. As Charles Hallisey notes in the introduction to his translation: "One of the peculiar features of the *Therīgāthā* is . . . often the *therī* addressing herself, but thus also identifying herself as the author of the poem."[64] The authorial signature is also a common feature of Prakrit and Apabhramsha poetry, where poets might use their own names or self-identifying phrases or words called *cinha*s or *lāñchanas*. Jnaneshvar uses an authorial signature line in the *Jñāneśvarī*, often at the beginnings or endings of chapters (for example in the very first verse of the text), as does Narendra in the *Rukmiṇī-Svayaṃvar*, the *abhaṅgu* that the king presumably wished to purchase. The Prakrit *cinha* and *lāñchana* are both also used in Marathi to mean something like stamp or seal, similar to the modern Marathi words *nāmamudrā* or *bhaṇitā* used by Marathi scholars for the signature of the *abhaṅga*. The signature is perhaps most well known in South Asia as a feature Urdu poetry, in particular the ghazal, where it came to be known as *takhalluṣ*, a "pen name" chosen by a poet. While some scholars attribute this convention of the ghazal to the rise of Sufi poetry outside of the courts, the practice seems to be well attested in courtly Persian poetry going back to the tenth century.[65] Drawing on its well-attested practice in archaic and ancient Greek poetry, this trope of self-naming has come to be known in English as "sphragis," which also means stamp or seal. According to the *Oxford Classical Dictionary*, sphragis is a literary motif in which an author "names or otherwise identifies himself or herself, especially at the beginning or end of a poem or collection of poems."[66] There are at least a couple of examples of its use by Shakespeare. For example, the closing couplet at the end of Sonnet 136 is a veritable signature verse: "Make but my name thy love, and love that still / And then thou lovest me, for my name is Will."[67]

Though a mark of the literary, authorial self-naming is also a practice that clearly evokes the experience and aesthetics of orality. It makes the poet a figure in their own poem, and this figure becomes a sort of bridge between the textual and the oral, marking the points of contact and exchange between them. In her study of Occitan, Middle-High German, and Castilian songbooks of the twelfth and thirteenth centuries, Marisa Galvez finds ample evidence of what she calls "nominal self-invocation" in the early European vernacular lyrics. The gesture, Galvez argues, metonymically invokes both "the troubadour in the process of singing" and "the lyric corpus of his or her texts," connecting the oral and the written, the performative and the scribal.[68] The name of the poet is a "deictic principle within the lyric" but also serves as an extrinsic "rubric for the body of songs."[69] That is, the name invokes the oral performance of the poet but is also used to organize songs in the songbooks. The latter, paratextual sense of the author becomes more prominent as writing becomes the dominant modality of the lyric. In the case of the *abhaṅga*, we not only have songbooks—*bāḍas*, *pothīs*, and then *gāthās*—the latter organized by the name of the author, but we also have ongoing and continuous oral traditions, like the grind mill song tradition, *kīrtan*, and *bhajan* that perform and reperform the name of the poet alongside and in engagement with the texts. The *abhaṅga* is not an isolated unit, in other words, but one part of a "chain of utterances" that make up the intertextual web of *bhakti* expressivity. In the practice of "nominal self-invocation" in *bhakti* poetry, the poet invokes or addresses him or herself in the poem, but the poet is figured, made a palpable and intimate presence, not alone by the signature line of the *abhaṅga*, but by all the *ovīs* and *kīrtans*, the manuscripts, texts, and hagiographies occasioned by the "speaking name" of the poet. The poet is not only invoked by name but becomes a figure who enters into the present of every reperformance. The name of the author dramatizes—or rather reperforms—the poet in the act of speaking, capturing an oral event as a structural feature of the poetic form itself.

Perhaps one answer to the conundrum of authorship in *bhakti* poetry—the fact that many poets sing under the name of Janabai or Namdev—might lie in the lyrical mode of the *abhaṅga* itself. Each performance of the *abhaṅga*, whether in a *bhajan* or *kirtan*, recreates the poem as event. Just as the singer of the grind mill verse becomes the "I" of the song whether she has composed the verse or not, so the one who sings or recites the *abhaṅga* takes on the "speaking name"—*nomen loquens*—of the author of the *abhaṅga*. This is quite different than saying that the authorship is composite since it maintains the figure of a singular author, making the authorship figural. The concept of "figural" makes room for the continuity between past and the present, the permanent and the changing, the original and the iteration, the oral and the written.[70] Figural authorship is, I think, a more apt term for the kind of dynamic authorship that we see in *bhakti* poetics. Poets are not understood to be a composite of many performers and poets over time. They are always understood as singular, yet they become capacious enough to take on ever new articulations and utterances in their "speaking names."

Both the grind mill *ovī* and the *abhaṅga* alike are created for reperformance, but in oral poetry, Zumthor points out, the "role of the performer counts more than the role of the composer."[71] I would add to Zumthor's formulation, at least when it comes to the songs of the grind mill, that the oral centers the listener no less than the performer through structures of direct address and apostrophe. The songs use common oral refrains like "I tell you, woman" (*sāṅgate bāī tulā*), or they address girlfriends, mothers, sisters, gods, and even the grind mill. These take the place of what might be the signature in an *abhaṅga*. Both the speaker and listener are centered in the refrain "I tell you, woman." The "I" is inhabited by the singer, but the "you" (*tulā*), the listener, the other woman (*bāī*), comes to the fore through the emphatic and repeated direct address. In each song, the lyrical mode overtakes the narrative, and we enter into a shared space between speaker and addressee, between singer and listener. Where the *abhaṅga* centralizes the teller, the poet, through authorial self-invocation, the songs of the grind mill centralize the listener, the addressee. The two verse forms thus form two components of a whole bound to each other in dialogue. This is *bhakti*, not only as poiesis, but as sympoiesis. The "I" of the named author, like the "I" of any lyric utterance, is open to anyone who sings the poem, but the poet becomes a figure in the poem only through the verse dialogue between poet and audience, singer and listener, *ovī* and *abhaṅga*. The oral *ovī* of the grind mill song tradition has been at least as influential and generative an interlocutor of *bhakti* poetics as any written text or any *kīrtan* that is its oral venue.

No wonder, then, that a*bhaṅgas* are steeped in the structures, motifs, and tropes of the grind mill songs. We can see in an *abhaṅga* attributed to Namdev how it bridges and binds together the speech structures and poetic models of the textual and the oral traditions, invoking the Gītā and the *Mahābhārata* on the one hand, and women's songs on the other:

The world is thick and dense
When will this grinding end?

Life is the stone mill and Karma its handle
Four women pull the stone roller

When you pour hatred as grist into the mill, the self will benefit
Know that the one who must go will be no more

One hundred and one Kauravas were ground as grist
Know that the same thing happened to the Pandavas

In the grind mill Nala, Nila, and Mandhata
Were ground to flour in a twinkling

Even pulling, I cannot pull against the pull of *saṃsāra*
Sit down there opposite me and give me a hand

Nama says, Vithoba is the *maher* of the wretched,
Let us sing songs of Pandharpur always[72]

The poem invokes the crucial chapter 11 of the Gītā in which Krishna reveals his frightening cosmic form to Arjuna. Namdev symbolically represents the cosmic cycle of worldly life revealed by Krishna as a grind mill. The grind mill becomes an emblem of *saṃsāra*, the ruthless grinding down of living beings caught in the cycle of birth and death. The poem says that the Pandavas and Kauravas, opposing sides representing good and evil in the great war that is the center of the *Mahābhārata*, are equal in the fate of *saṃsāra*. Worldly attainments and power, such as those of kings, are nothing but grains ground by the cosmic mill of *saṃsāra*. Though textual references to the Gītā are clear, *saṃsāra* in this *abhaṅga* refers not just to the theological concept, but to a woman's household life of hard labor, *saṃsār* in the more colloquial sense. The *abhaṅga* is clearly drawing on the ways in which women themselves sing about their *sāsarvās* or suffering, of *saṃsār* as an iron yoke, a daily hardship. Importantly, Namdev's poem ends, not with other worldly liberation, but with the image of singing together at the grind mill. The grind mill is the seat of *saṃsār* but also of *maher*. The deictic markers of "you," the invitation to sit "over there" bring the poem into the present, into the lyrical space of *bhakti*, of *svagata*.

If the songs move from the grind mill to the world of texts and elevated figures, *abhaṅgas* often take us from the texts to the intimacy at the grind mill, to the immanence of *bhakti* in the everyday. There is a constant tug and pull, a back and forth, a weaving and unraveling between *ovī* and *abhaṅga*. The poetics of the grind mill saturate the *abhaṅga*, just as the songs of the grind mill carry the poets, the figures, the performances, the stories, and the poetry of *bhakti* into the everyday. It is, however, not only the abundant shared poetic resources that show the commerce between the *ovī* and the *abhaṅga*, between song and text, but rather something even more fundamental, more structural. The dialogical verse-making of the grind mill, its context of shared labor, its direct structures of address, of the responsive understanding of a proximate listener also give structure to the *abhaṅga* as a form. Intimate speech, Bakhtin writes, is "imbued with deep confidence in the addressee, in [her] sympathy, in the sensitivity and goodwill of [her] responsive understanding. In this atmosphere of profound trust, the speaker reveals [her] internal depths."[73] This is as good a description of verse-making at the grind mill as of *bhakti* expressivity more generally.

Besides the symbolism of the grind mill, there are many other features that show the engagement between the *abhaṅga* and the grind mill *ovī*, such as the figuration of Pandharpur as *māher*, the invocation of the male Vitthal as a mother and a woman, the poet's adoption of the voice of the daughter-in-law, the dialogical and intimate forms of address, the parataxis, and so on. Here, for example, is one *abhaṅga* by Tukaram in which he uses the verb *ovaṇeṃ* to describe the activity of singing at the grind mill:

This is my first *ovī*,
I will weave [*ovīna*] the three worlds
I will sing pure Panduranga [Vitthal]

This is my second [*dusarī*] *ovī*,
There are no others [*dujeṃ*] anywhere
I meet Panduranga in the people and in nature

This is my third *ovī*
She has no place for
Other gods among the people and in nature

This is my fourth *ovī*,
I poured the grist in the mill
I will sing of Panduranga till the end

My fifth *ovī* is for my *māher*
I will sing without pause O Panduranga

This is my sixth [*sāhāvī*] *ovī*
All six systems [*sāhā*] have evaporated
I met my ideal teacher Pandurang

This is my seventh [*sātavī*] *ovī*
I remember [*āṭhaveṃ*] him all the time
Panduranga is sitting in my eyes

This is my eighth *ovī*
For twenty-eight yugas,
Panduranga has been standing at the Chandrabhaga River

This is my ninth *ovī*
The grinding is completed
I have escaped the death of *saṃsāra*[74]

This *abhaṅga* is overt literary envoicement of a woman singing at the grind mill using the well-known formulaic structure of an *ovī* sequence, "This is my first *ovī* . . . This is my second *ovī*," and so on. Each of Tukaram's verses has the conceptual dyadic structure and paratactic style of the grind mill *ovī*. There is no connecting word between the introductory line *pahilī majhī ovī* and the next lines, just as in grind mill verses, and no hypotactic weaving of the verses to create transition and continuity as we found in the *Jñāneśvarī*. Each of Tukaram's verses could stand on their own. In the *abhaṅga* above, the phrases and lines within each verse are arranged paratactically just as they would be in the grind mill songs, with connections between them implicit rather than explicit. In other words, it is an *abhaṅga* that, both in underlying structure and overt presentation, takes the form of a grind mill verse. A broader review of the corpus of *abhaṅgas* will show that parataxis is quite common in the *abhaṅga*, especially in the poetry of Tukaram, who uses it masterfully to create compressed, dense, and ideogrammatic poetry.

So, what makes this poem an *abhaṅga* rather than a written grind mill *ovī* sequence? Each verse follows the pattern of 6-6-6-4 with an *abbc* rhyming pattern, a perfect example of a *devadvāra abhaṅga* or "big" *abhaṅga* as described by Namdev and Godbole. Unlike when grind mill *ovīs* are sung in sequence, Tukaram carries the *abbc* rhyming pattern consistently through the whole series of ten verses. In the grind mill song sequences, the rhyme scheme would likely alternate between *abab, abcb, abba*, or *abbb,* or there might even be a variation between couplets, tercets, and quatrains. Where the grind mill songs describe singing as an unraveling of the heart, Tukaram's *abhaṅga* describes singing through the metaphor of weaving, invoking the etymology and literary history of *ovī* as *ovaṇeṃ*: "I will weave [*ovīna*] the three worlds."

Finally, the poem ends with one of the most important markers of the *abhaṅga*, Tukaram's signature line in the tenth verse, his "nominal self-invocation":

This is my tenth *ovī*
Saṃsāra should not have
Ten incarnations, says Tuka.

With his characteristic wit and brevity, Tukaram's ending quip suggests that while Vishnu has ten incarnations, *saṃsāra* or worldly existence should not. In other words, there should not be ten rebirths into *saṃsāra* but rather liberation from it. In each of the verses, in fact, Tukaram puns on the number of the verse. I included the Marathi words in the translation above to highlight this. His signature in the final verse acts as a clasp that brings the concatenation of verses to a neat conclusion. In doing so, it also brings Tukaram as a speaking figure right into the time of the poem's utterance, creating a bridge to a conversation with his interlocutors.

The trope of the signature line is duly accepted as an invitation to dialogue in the song tradition. There are *ovīs* in the song archive in apparent response to this particular *abhaṅga*, showing women's deep familiarity with Tukaram's corpus:

> This is my ninth verse
> There are ten incarnations
> *Saṃsāra* should be taken away
> Says Tuka
>
> *navavī mājhī ovī*
> *dahā avatāra*
> *nyāve saṃsāra*
> *tukā mhaṇe*[75]
>
> This is my eighth verse
> I sang eight incarnations
> Tukaram says *saṃsār* has been completed
>
> *āṭhavī mājhī ovī*
> *āṭha gāile avatāra*
> *tukārāma bole*
> *purā jhālā saṃsāra.*[76]

These *ovīs* also engage the word play on the number of the verse just as in Tukaram's poem. An actual *ovī* sequence may not be structured in as cohesive a manner as Tukaram's poem, however. Tukaram can appear or be invoked anywhere in the sequence, and the numerical sequence might not even be sung sequentially at the grind mill. Yet, the *ovīs* clearly engage

Tukaram's poem. The signature line is being used narratively to report what Tukaram has said about *saṃsār* in his poem, but at the same time, it also calls forth Tukaram as a figural presence, the singer inhabiting his "speaking name" and making it hers. It is the dialogical engagement between Tukaram's *abhaṅga* and women's *ovīs*, each envoicing the other, each shaped by the speech of the other, that brings into view, through a dialectic of weaving and unraveling, the *bhakti* intertext. The grind mill songs are perfectly open about their engagements with the textual and performance traditions of *bhakti*, as are *abhaṅgas* about their engagements with the songs of the grind mill, yet the processes of textualization that developed over the course of the seventeenth and eighteenth centuries often obscured this dialogue, concealing the contributions of women and their songs.

The Closed Heart of Texts

Bahinabai Chaudhari quite openly showed her admiring poet son Sopan Dev how she listened to the text he was reading and then composed her *ovīs* based on it. Women's deep admiration for *abhaṅgas* and texts like the *Jñāneśvarī* is etched all over their *coḷīs*, their blouses. You might say they wear their unraveling heart on their sleeves. The textual tradition, however, has never been forthright about its engagements with women's songs, at least not since the early texts of the Mahanubhavas. In the *Bhaktavijay*, Vitthal is so enchanted by Janabai's songs that he puts them on paper. "I like Jani's songs," he says to himself, "that's why I picked up a pen and sat down to write them myself."[77] This is not an entirely novel act in Marathi literature, as we have amply documented, yet when Jnaneshvar comes into the room where he is writing, Vitthal quickly hides his "inkstand, pen, and paper." "The vernacular," Nagaraj reminds us, is often "an act of concealment," and here Vitthal enacts this impulse to conceal.[78] Jnaneshvar is not so easily fooled, however, and exclaims: "Vyasa, Valmiki, and the other great poets (*mahākavī*) attained prestige by describing you, and now if you should write Jani's songs, the poets (*kavi*) will laugh at you!"[79] Vitthal admits to feeling "doubt" (*āśaṅkā*) about his recreant writing activity, but he decides to involve the society of *bhakti* poets in a "fathomless divine play" that brings the deep anxiety triggered by his act of writing Janabai's compositions into the open. Her verses are good enough in their place in the oral, but can they be accepted, the chapter asks, as *bhakti* poetry?

Vitthal defends his writing by extolling the poetic qualities of Jani's songs, describing them as loving (*premaḷ*) and full of *rasa* (*rasāḷ*).[80] Given that Vitthal is God, Jnaneshvar is left with little room to argue, and he accompanies Vitthal to introduce Janabai as poet to the society of poets assembled at the house of Namdev. Jani is already known as a servant or slave in Namdev's house, but Vitthal intends to introduce her as poet. She is outside gathering dung when she is called in by Namdev's mother, Gonai, who had earlier beaten her while she slaved away in household chores. Janabai has to wash the dung from her hands before she enters. When she falls to Vitthal's feet, he delivers the authenticating declaration to the gathered poets. "I wrote down Jani's songs," he assures them, "and this brought me no loss of status whatsoever. I declare an oath and lay my testimony at your feet that you should know Jani's spoken language (*prākṛt bhāṣaṇ*] as itself the *rasa* of Self-Bliss. . . . You will find Me in the courtyard of all who read (*vācīla*] Jani's spoken words (*bolaṇīṃ*)."[81] Jani's *prākṛt bhāṣaṇ* means Marathi, but it specifically signifies the everyday speech and songs of a lowly household servant, a *dāsī*. By putting her spoken idiom, her *oral* poetry, into writing, Vitthal consecrates Jani's compositions as literature worth reading. Since Jani has God himself as her scribe, Jnaneshvar declares, "Who will call her a slave?"[82] This comment suggests *dāsī* and poet to be mutually exclusive identities, though Janabai is both.

Indeed, in Mahipati's rendering, the verses that Vitthal writes are not the *ovīs* Janabai sings at the grind mill. They are verses she composes in her mind at the temple, not at the grind mill or in her hut, but those which Vitthal overhears telepathically while he is at Namdev's house.[83] In this small detail we have a decontextualization of Jani's compositions from the world of everyday labor, almost as if to say that only when separated from the grind mill could they be written. Only when Janabai's compositions move from the laboring body to the mind, from the household to the temple, do they make it on to paper through Vitthal's pen. When she is singing her songs at the grind mill, Mahipati calls her songs *ovīs*, but when Vitthal is talking about writing her verses, he uses the words *padeṃ*, *abhaṅga*, and *kavitva* to describe her compositions. A *pada* is an elevated song form often composed in the quantitative *jāti* meters for *kīrtan,* performed in the classical style of *rāga*. *Abhaṅgas* by Mahipati's time had already gained literary status as *kavitva*, Jnaneshvar's term for the skill and art of composing poetry. Although Vitthal loves Jani's songs, his act of writing is an effort to extricate the *ovī* from the *abhaṅga*, separate the oral from the literary, elevating the latter to the status of *kavitva*.

Mahipati's chapter on Janabai ends with a famous scene, repeated in many a *kīrtan*, in which Vitthal assigns scribes to the poets: "'Now, divide up the scribes,'" (*lekhakācī karā vāṃṭaṇī*), he tells the gathering of poets. "Words that come from the mouths should be written down."[84] This scene overlaps with a famous poem attributed to Janabai that catalogues the scribes of ten poets, beginning with Jnaneshvar's family:

Chidanand Baba wrote the words
Of Jnanadev's *abhaṅgas*

Sopan wrote Nivritti's speech, [*bol*]
Jnanadev Mother Mukta's sayings [*vacanem̧*]

Shama the blacksmith would write for Canga
Khecar was writing for Parmananda

What Purnananda would tell [*sāṅge*], Parmananda would write
Bhagavanta found happiness in Ramananda

Vasudev was Kurma's scribe [*kāīta*]
Kashiba Gurav was Savata Mali's

Anantabhatta was Chokhamela's ablution [*abhyaṅga*]
That's why Nama's Jani has Panduranga[85]

As is evident in this poem, there were a lot more words to denote the oral than the written, and it is as if the very multiplicity of orality were being funneled through a singular scribal sieve. While the oral is signified through words like *bol* (speaking), *abhaṅga*, *vacanem̧* (also the name of the short verse form of the Virashaiva poets), *sāṅge* (telling); the written has one main word, *lihiṇe*. Notably missing in the list of oral forms is the *ovī*, which has been banished from the scene of *bhakti* altogether, and that, too, in a poem purportedly by Janabai.

The poem ends, significantly, with Jani and Chokhamela, two poets whose caste and slave/servant status put them farthest from the resources of writing. The last line of the poem introduces a new metaphor for writing that is significant: "Anantabhatta is Chokhamela's ablution [*abhyaṅga*], / That's why [*mhaṇonī*] Nama's Jani has Panduranga [another name for Vitthal]." The word *abhyaṅga* means ritual bath or the ritual rubbing of oils and herbs on the body before the bath. Describing writing as a ritual bath, a ritual cleansing, has obvious caste implications. Chokhamela is a self-described poet of the Mahar caste. Defining the scribal act as a ritual bath implies that it will purify the oral compositions of the untouchable poet; the Brahmin scribe Anantabhatta will cleanse the composition originating from the mouth of Chokhamela, washing away the corporeal touch of the untouchable poet.[86] Once the verses have been written, they will no longer be tainted by the corporeality of the oral. The last line connects Jani to Chokhamela, suggesting that Jani needs Vitthal to purify her compositions, not only because of her own outcaste status as a *dāsī* but also, perhaps, because of her insistent connection to the labors of the body, to the grind mill. This is certainly a far cry from the scribal objectives that guided Mhaimbhat in the writing of the *Līḷācaritra*.

Clearly the elevation of writing we see evidenced in this poem and in the *Bhaktavijaya* comes, not from an imperial redefinition of poetics in the Kannada style, but from a much lower echelon of imperial regimes: the scribal elite. Marathi scribal communities gained new prominence in the sixteenth century when the Bijapur sultanate declared Marathi the official language of law and administration, establishing "a political and judicial framework that in turn allowed for the emergence of a public, vernacular space."[87] We might locate the profusion of narrative poetic works from the mid-sixteenth century onward, as well as the birth of new written genres like the *bakhar* and the *mestak*, in this new "vernacular space" marked by the assumption of literary gatekeeping privileges by a scribal elite dominated by Brahmins.[88] Prachi Deshpande has written about the continuing spread and intensification of scribal practices and communities in the seventeenth century under the Marathas as the administrative apparatus spread further into rural areas.[89] The rise of the scribe turned philosopher-poet Ramdas (1608–1681) revitalized an orthodox sectarianism in this period, led by Brahmin scribes disaffected in their administrative roles. Ramdas promoted writing and copying as a devotional and ethical practice thus redirecting scribal practices from administrative to religious affairs to "assert Brahmin social authority."[90] In monasteries (*maṭhas*) throughout the Marathi-speaking regions, Ramdas followers' practices of writing generated an enormous archive of manuscripts, notebooks, and other kinds of texts and correspondence that nudged literary endeavors toward the high-textual.[91]

The influence of the Ramdas sect on Mahipati and on the textualization of the poetry of the Varkari *sants* is considerable. It's worth keeping in mind G. N. Devy's insight that "sects and not periods chapterize the Indian literary past," and that "sects thrive not on the rejection of the past but on a selective renewal of the past."[92] Indeed, Mahipati's very depiction of God as scribe must be attributed in large part to the influence of the Ramdas sect, which had taken on the "selective renewal" of Varkari poetry through scribal practices guided by their own sectarian caste orthodoxy. I suspect that the poem about scribes attributed to Janabai was, if not written by Ramdas devotees, then at least performed by them in *kīrtans* and recorded in writing or even revised by them. It would not surprise me if it were a scribe of the Ramdas sect who introduced the metaphor of the ritual bath into the final verse given the caste orthodoxy of this sect.

With this proliferation and elevation of practices of writing, *abhaṅgas* came increasingly to be recorded and collected in performance notebooks and manuscripts, and eventually in massive print collections or *gāthās*, codifying thereby a new distance between them and the songs of the grind mill.[93] Indeed *abhaṅgas* came to be composed in writing by the seventeenth century, as the biography of Tukaram attests. It is widely believed that, as a *śūdra*, Tukaram's act of writing his own poems and his growing stature as poet and *sant* threatened Brahmins. He was compelled, according to Mahipati's account in another hagiographical compendium, the *Bhaktalīlāmṛta*, to throw his notebook of poems into a river after a Brahmin named Rameshwar Bhatt attacked him for overstepping his caste boundaries. Tukaram's great offense lay, not in composing verses in the oral modality acceptable for women and those of lower castes, but in *writing* his own verses. The notebook miraculously resurfaces undamaged after thirteen days, restoring Tukaram's faith in his own poetic calling and his *bhakti*.

During the thirteen days, however, with his precious notebook of poems under water, Tukaram is depicted by Mahipati as overcome with deep self-doubt and despair: "Now, this is the end of the path of *bhakti*. I lie wholly at your feet. Words no longer give clear delight in this world full of bombast. It is as if the made up *ovīs* sung at the grind mill are to be taken as true. Such is the condition of my life, I feel, O Lord of Pandhari. Now this is the end of my efforts. Why should I uselessly winnow chaff? I have resolved in my mind that I will not easily lift a pen again."[94] Here, Mahipati's Tukaram describes *ovīs* sung at the grind mill as *laṭakyā*, which I have translated as "made up," but which also means false, deceitful, untruthful. Mahipati is associating the *ovīs* with the everyday townspeople who taunt Tukaram. Yet the term *laṭakyā* also recalls the way women singers themselves often denigrate songs that women compose or "make up" on their own. Being at the lowest rungs of the caste patriarchy, women's "made up" songs are viewed with deep suspicion. Mahipati's description of *ovīs* as *laṭakyā* comes in the midst of Tukaram's monologue of writerly angst and self-doubt about his skills as a poet. The description is meant to draw a contrast between women's *ovīs*, dismissed as "made up," and Tukaram's written *abhaṅgas*, which are seen as *kavitva*. For Mahipati, what distinguishes and elevates Tukaram's compositions is that they are written. Mahipati's version of this story thus enacts a separation between the *abhaṅga* and the *ovī* that has persisted in the subsequent literary elevation of the *abhaṅga* and the marginalization of women's *ovīs* in the arena of *bhakti* poetics.

The grind mill singers themselves have never abided by this effort to separate Tukaram from them, however. One *ovī* puts it succinctly:

The *abhaṅgas* of Panduranga
Are in the mouths of great and small
Tuka left after printing his book of songs

Pāṇḍūraṅgācyā abhaṅga
Lahānathorāñcyā mukhā
Gāthā chāpunī gelā Tukā[95]

In this *ovī*, the word for printing, *chāpaṇeṃ*, also means "to stamp" something, recalling the terms for the signature verse as a stamp—*sphragis, cinha, bhanitā*. The term seems to work on several levels, implying that Tukaram put his stamp—his signature—on the songs that are in the mouths (*mukhā*) of people. Yet it is also a reference to Tukaram's written text, his *gāthā*, the printed edition. The name of the poet, too, works at the dual level, invoking both the oral poet and his written text. There is no necessary separation between these two facts of Tukaram's contributions. His *abhaṅgas* float at the confluence of the oral and the written, the river here marking the fluidity between the two. The "drowned manuscript" is a common motif throughout the subcontinent, and it is usually interpreted in one of two ways: as a symbol of the oral tradition or as a symbol of the permanence of writing, signaled by its indestructibility.[96] These need not be mutually exclusive interpretations. The whole point of symbolism is that it contains, within the concrete tangibility of the symbol, multiple and even opposing significations at once. Perhaps the drowned manuscript is a symbol of the confluence of oral and written, its inseparability, as succinctly articulated in the *ovī* above.

It was paradoxically Bahinabai, the seventeenth-century woman disciple of Tukaram, considered to be one of the last poets of this tradition, who gave us the enduring image of a temple—a literary pantheon—to describe the literary canon of *bhakti*, an emblem of its completion, its end:

> With the blessings of the *sants*, a building is erected
> Jnaneshvar laid the ground and raised a temple
> His servant Namdev, he built the interior
> Eknath's *Bhāgvata* provided the pillars
> Tuka has become the steeple, sing in praise steadily,
> Bahini, flag fluttering, described the temple.[97]

Jnaneshvar and Namdev, followed by Eknath and Tukaram, laid the foundation and built the pillars of the literary tradition; Bahinabai sings, while Tukaram forms the spire, the pinnacle, its completion, and fulfillment. "The temple becomes a static standing thing," Ramanujan writes in his introduction to the *vacanas* of the Virashaivas, "that has forgotten its moving credentials."[98] The Virashaivas maintained the tension between the moving, itinerant bodies of the saints and the static temples, but Bahinabai's poem presents the *abhaṅga* tradition as a completed artifact, a frozen and fixed work of art, rather than an ongoing process of making.

It is rather ironic to describe the *bhakti* tradition as a temple when so many poets in Bahinabai's own literary lineage write about their painful experiences of exclusion and banishment from Vitthal's temple in Pandharpur, including Namdev himself. In a famous legend, the massive stone-carved Shiva temple in Aundha Nagnath turned itself so it could face Namdev as he resumed his *kīrtan* outside after being kicked out of the temple by Brahmins. The poets who did not always have access to Vitthal's temple are the very ones also excluded from Bahinabai's poem; she herself, along with all the dozens of women poets that came before and after her, as well as Dalit poets like Chokhamela and Soyarabai, sits outside the structure. To his credit, Vitthal was never at ease in the temple, according to numerous legends and grind mill songs, just as Chakradhar refused to stay in any one place. Vitthal was always looking for a reason to escape, often to meet Janabai at the riverbank or in the grasses outside the temple, to sit with her and grind or wash clothes while she sang her *ovīs*. In this space of the underview, the songs and poems and texts kept on being made and remade, performed and reperformed.

Did the separation of the *abhaṅga* from the *ovī* by the new regimes of writing that developed during the seventeenth century lead to the decline of the *abhaṅga* tradition? The poet Dilip Chitre calls Tukaram "not only the last great Bhakti poet in Marathi but . . . also the first truly modern poet."[99] And the reason for that might well be that writing began to elevate itself over orality in the arena of poetics. The relationship between scribe (*lekhak*) and poet (*kavi*) depicted in Janabai's poem and in Mahipati's *Bhaktavijaya* captures a specific historical crisis in the long-established relationship between poetry and orality that had perdured in Marathi poetry from the thirteenth through the seventeenth centuries. Mahipati's depiction of God as a scribe shows the elevation of the scribe and of writing, but it also suggests the need to justify the scribal act, especially when it comes to writing the oral poems of a figure like Janabai. The scribal act was still considered secondary to the "art of composing poetry" (*kavitva*), but it gained prominence just as the *abhaṅga* tradition began to wane, after Tukaram, in the seventeenth century.

Still, it is clear that the elevation of writing and the proliferation of manuscript cultures "did not displace orality's authority" completely.[100] The eighteenth and nineteenth centuries saw the growth of the popular oral-performative traditions of *povāḍa*, *lāvaṇī*, and *nāṭya saṅgīt*, not to mention the continuity of *kīrtan, bhajan*, and of course, the grind mill song tradition. Texts continued to make their way back to women through *kīrtans*, recitations, songbooks, and anthologies, and the *bhakti* intertext continued to be woven and unraveled within the song tradition of the grind mill as well as other performance traditions that perdured long after the seventeenth century. You could say, in fact, given the power and prominence of the Ramdas sect over the textualization of the poetry of the Varkari poets, that women's songs of the grind mill became even more important to the continuity of *bhakti* as an ongoing and inclusive dialogue in verse.

And Janabai is one poet in particular who remained steady at the confluence of *ovī* and *abhaṅga*, who even Mahipati could not separate from the *laṭakyā ovīs* of the grind mill. So much so, indeed, that she compelled Mahipati himself to write about Vitthal's deep appreciation for the songs of the grind mill.

Janabai sustained the centrality of *bhakti* as poiesis in her very figuration as both a *dāsī* at the grind mill and a poet admitted into the society of poets by Vitthal's authenticating declaration. The women who sing about her refused to accept the separation of poet from *dāsī*, the written from the oral. As the written tradition attempted to elevate Janabai from laboring *dāsī* to poet, the songs of women continuously unraveled this figuration. In their songs, Janabai is always the lonely and exiled *dāsī*, laboring away in everyday tasks, the one who makes Vitthal hers through her *bhakti*, just as the women make Janabai theirs in their songs through a figuration that connects Janabai to their own present lives. Here is a beautiful song sequence I recorded from Janabai Thorat in Bhendegaon:

This is what Vitthal says,
Jana, let's go to the grasses

asā iṭṭhala manīta
calā janā gavatālā

Jana, let's go to the grasses
Around the Chandrabhaga River

calā janā gavatālā re
candrabhāgecyā bhavatālā

Near the Chandrabhaga River
There the breeze is blowing

candrabhāgecyā bhavatālā
tīta pavana mātalā

This is what Vitthal says,
Come, Jana, let's go wash the clothes

asā iṭṭhala manīta
calā janā dhuyā jāū

Let's go wash the clothes, Jana
Let's wash the silk garments

calā janā dhuyā jāū
pāṭāvāca dhuna dhuū

Let's wash the silk garments
And look for sandalwood stones

pāṭāvāca dhuna dhuvū
āni candanācyā śīḷā pāhu

Janabai washes the clothes
Over here, Vitthal gathers them up

janābāī dhuna dhutī
yaha iṭṭhala karī goḷā

Let's go, Jana, let's hurry
Or they will curse you at home

Cala janā lavakarī
Śivyā detīla tulā gharī[101]

These *ovīs* depict the intimate space shared by Janabai and Vitthal near the river Chandrabhaga, which flows in front of Vitthal's temple in Pandharpur. Through the use of the present tense and deictic markers like "here" and "there," these verses create the "effects of presence" so essential to the lyric and to *bhakti* as *mamāyanā*. Characteristically, Vitthal is not in the temple, but out wandering with Janabai, in the grasses where the wind blows by the water. It is Vitthal who invites Janabai to go there, and it is Vitthal who suggests they wash the clothes that she must wash. It is he who helps her wash, and it is he who reminds her that she better get back before she is scolded for being late. The *ovīs* are sequenced together through repetition and by carrying over the final line of one *ovī* into the opening line of the next *ovī*, creating a movement and flow that isn't quite captured in a transcription and certainly lost in translation. There is some narrative forward movement by the last verse, but the verses mostly proceed through a movement of recurrent return, a dwelling on the banks of the river. The last verse works as volta, a return to Janabai's condition of servitude, which the previous verses momentarily put into suspension. Though it says little, the stories of all the torture and violence that Janabai experiences as a *dāsī* in the house of Namdev are conjured up as background in Vitthal's worry that they should hurry back, that she may be scolded or punished.

In singing these *ovīs*, even though she did it for my recording, Janabai Thorat created—through poiesis—a momentary, intensely felt space of *bhakti*, not just theological but aesthetic and lyrical, a space of solitude at the banks of the holy river in Pandharpur where the lonely Janabai dwells with Vitthal. The breeze, the grasses, the sandalwood stone, the silk

Figure 4.4 Janabai Thorat grinding in her thatched dwelling located on her farmland in Bhendegaon, Hingoli district, in 2006.
Photo by author

garments, and the company of Vitthal alleviate Jana's everyday servitude, just as the songs that women compose create their own space to make something, the song, beyond the labor imposed, impressed, coerced, and necessary. Vitthal helps create a space of *svagata* for Janabai in the song, just as, in the act of composing and singing at the grind mill women create a space to "live in the midst of the traffic of their situation with the independence of solitude."[102] By making Janabai theirs, these women composers of the grind mill help to generate the figure of Janabai that follows her into the written text, into Mahipati's chapter, and into the *abhaṅgas* and poetic works attributed to her. They refuse to abide by her apotheosis as poet and not *dāsī*. These songs live in the signature line of Nama's *dāsī* Jani, which invites the participation of "women, *śūdras*, and others," not only as audience but as makers and poets and singers of *bhakti*. The figural authorship of Janabai makes room for the "made up" verses of the "absent and invisible" as poetry within the written-performative arena of *bhakti*. Like Mahadaise before her, Janabai brings a poetics of the grind mill, a "poetics of work" into "works of poetics."

CHAPTER V

Women and Vernacularization

The Founding Poetics of Mahadaise and Janabai

The grinding is done,
I am gathering the flour, O God
I had gone to listen
To the Book of Knowledge

—INGULE MANDA, VILLAGE MANJRAT

I will take knowledge
I will scrape it up

—SAVITRIBAI PHULE

"In Maharashtra," the formidable Eleanor Zelliot observed, "an extraordinary number of women sang their devotional songs in Marathi."[1] This could be an apt description of women's songs of the grind mill, but Zelliot was referring to the women poets of the Varkari sect, composers not of *ovīs* but of *abhaṅgas*. Indeed, dozens of women poets composed poetry, mostly *abhaṅgas,* centered on Vitthal *bhakti* between the thirteenth and seventeenth centuries, some with only an extant *abhaṅga* or two to their name, but enough to make their presence and participation known. There were, no doubt, even more women who composed, sang, and wrote under the names—the *nomen loquens*—of these women poets, the practice of figural authorship bringing many more into the world of poetry than is discernible to us in the surviving texts. Women also figured prominently in the early Mahanubhava community as Chakradhar's earliest and most numerous disciples. Hundreds of women, many of them Brahmin widows, took active part in the sect in its earliest years, their lives, labors, questions, quarrels, and songs taking center stage in the foundational written texts of the vernacular era, ostensibly written to meet women's thirst for a "knowledge" long denied them. Yet women's participation has hardly gotten the attention it deserves in the annals of Marathi literarity.[2] What impelled women's active participation in these vernacular poetic communities? In what ways did women's avid and abundant participation shape the vernacular poetic communities? Is there something in the highly developed and influential oral poetic tradition of the grind mill that made women's early and prominent literary participation possible?

Mahadaise and Janabai are uniquely positioned to offer us some insights into these questions. Where Mahadaise composed the very first written attestations of the grind mill songs in Marathi, Janabai's *abhaṅgas* dwell at the confluence of *bhakti* poetry and the grind mill *ovī*. At the same time, both Mahadaise and Janabai are the professed authors of important written works that came to form defining canons of narrative poetry in Marathi. Mahadaise's *Dhavaḷe* is arguably the first of many poetic renderings of the story of Rukmini's marriage to Krishna, known widely as the *Rukmiṇī-Svayaṃvar* (The marriage of Rukmini). It is a story about how Rukmini actively subverts her brother's attempts to arrange her marriage to King Shishupal by planning her own abduction by and marriage to Krishna. Raeside lists eight independent versions of the *Rukmiṇī-Svayaṃvar* written by Mahanubhava poets between the thirteenth and seventeenth centuries, and there are dozens more versions by well-known poets of different sects, including Eknath and Dasopant.[3] Similarly, Janabai is the author of the *Hariścandra Ākhyāna*, a Marathi rendering of the pan-Indic legend of Harischandra, a king of Ayodhya who gives up his kingdom and sells his family into slavery to meet the tests of goodness concocted by the wily sage Vishvamitra. The thirteenth-century Kannada poet Raghavanka is credited with the first vernacular rendering of this story (ca. 1225), and over the next four centuries it comes to be written in several regional languages of the subcontinent.[4] Janabai's work is one in a long line of versions by well-known and elite narrative poets, including Vishnudas Nama (ca. 1550–1610), Krishnayagnavalki (1548–1613) Mukteshvar (1606–1680), Shridhar (1658–1729), and Moropant (1729–1794), just to name a few of the most well-known. Many of these same poets also wrote their own versions of the *Rukmiṇī-Svayaṃvar.* To my knowledge, the only versions of these stories attributed to women poets are Mahadaise's and Janabai's . Both feature strong female characters, and both are well represented in the grind mill song archive. Interestingly, while most other Marathi versions of these poems are written in the literary *ovī* or sung by women at the grind mill in the oral *ovī*, neither Janabai nor Mahadaise writes in the literary *ovī*. Mahadaise's story is in the *dhavala* form, while Janabai's is in the *abhaṅga* form. Even so, both "works of poetics" are clearly shaped by the *ovī's* "poetics of work."

Mahadaise was a contemporary of Jnaneshvar, and *Dhavaḷe* was composed in the same period as the *Jñāneśvarī*. In fact, given that Mahadaise's composition is attested in the *Ṛddhipurcaritra*, which was ostensibly written circa 1287, it is quite probable that *Dhavaḷe* is the first extant work of narrative poetry in Marathi, though it is almost universally overlooked by scholars of vernacularization. Christian Lee Novetzke does suggest in a footnote the possibility of *Dhavaḷe* being the first work, but he focuses on the *Jñāneśvarī* as the "first explicitly *literary* text," a "vernacular manifesto" that becomes "the foundation of Marathi literature up to the present."[5] The importance of the *Jñāneśvarī* in Marathi literature cannot to be disputed, of course, but as I demonstrate in this chapter, Mahadaise's *Dhavaḷe* was not just the first work, but also the first *literary* work. It is generally assumed that *Dhavaḷe* was not influential enough to hold a foundational position because the Mahanubhavas sequestered their literary archive with secret scripts beginning in the fourteenth century. But if the *Līlācaritra* can be celebrated as a first text, though its circulation was also limited until the twentieth century, then why deny that status to Mahadaise's composition? Indeed, the influence of *Dhavaḷe* is apparent in later renderings of the story within the Mahanubhava archive and possibly also outside the sect. More importantly, however, Mahadaise's foundational role cannot be limited to specific citable influence; to this day, women's work remains at a disadvantage on that measure. Mahadaise's foundational contributions are evident rather in the way that she makes visible the shaping influence of women's oral traditions on Marathi literature. *Dhavaḷe*, as well as Mahadaise's authorial contributions to texts like the *Līḷācaritra*, brings into view the subterranean exchanges of the underview in the development of vernacular poetics in Marathi.

Though there is less historical certainty about Janabai's floruit than Mahadaise's, Janabai is also believed to have been a contemporary of Jnaneshvar and a *dāsī* in the house of Namdev. Jnaneshvar and Namdev respectively embody the principles of book learning (*jñāna*) and recitation of the name (*nāma*) that structure the very way *bhakti* came to be conceptualized and understood in the Varkari sect. As a figure at the margins of this dynamic, Janabai becomes an important third foundational figure of the vernacular *jana*, carrying in her "speaking name" the *bhakti* of countless women who compose and sing at the grind mill. It is therefore significant that she is positioned by the devotional tradition itself as a contemporary of the founding poets, whether this has a historical basis or not. Where Jnaneshvar as the learned scholar poet and Namdev as the founder of *kīrtan* come to represent "the tension between intellection and emotion" that constitute *bhakti* as a "theology of embodiment,"[6] it is Janabai who illuminates the themes, motifs, and expressive structures of *bhakti* as everyday poiesis, as sympoiesis.

It is true that the *Hariścandra Ākhyāna* was almost certainly composed no earlier than the sixteenth century and was possibly the work of a later poet writing under the *nomen loquens* of an earlier Janabai. It is also possible that the historical floruit of the first Janabai was itself later. There can be no definitive solution to this historical uncertainty, but there is no doubt that Janabai's figural authorship opened the door for many to compose under her speaking name. By "figural" I do not mean that Janabai's authorship is not real, or that there is no historical Janabai. And I do not mean figurative authorship as a contrast to literal. Rather, I mean that her authorship is the outcome of a constant negotiation between Janabai as a historical figure and the figure of Janabai that emerges in the enactments and reenactments of the poems attributed to her in the songs of the grind mill, in texts and hagiographies, and in performances of all kinds. She is a figure who is always brought into the present as a maker and "speaker" of poems, "a speaking name" for the marginalized and excluded women she calls forth. We do not know much in the historical sense about the Janabai who authored the *Hariścandra Ākhyāna*, but it is undeniable that a poet who called herself Nama's Jani is the self-named author of this work. Whether she is the "original" Janabai or a later Janabai, her authorial name as a figure of the excluded and marginalized *jana* shapes the telling of this story so that it centers the suffering, enslavement, and ultimately heroic redemption of a woman, Queen Taramati.

Just as Janabai leads us inexorably to the songs of the grind mill, so she helps to excavate Mahadaise's figural authorship, her formative authorial contributions beyond *Dhavaḷe* to founding texts like the *Līḷācaritra*. Though Mahadaise is more textually and historically attested as an author than Janabai, Mahadaise too takes on the mantle of figural authorship. She becomes a figure of the broader vernacular audience of women whose ways of speaking and singing come to shape the literary contours

Figure 5.1 Painting of women grinding by M. V. Dhurandhar (1867–1944). From the Collection of Prem Kandwal, printed with permission by Prem Kandwal

of the first texts written in the Marathi language, especially the *Līḷācaritra*. Thus, though Mahadaise and Janabai are professed, historical authors of specific written works, they both do something more; the poetry attributed to each brings into view the oral-textual intertext inherent to vernacular literarity. Their authorial names become "speaking names" through which many women participate as poets and authors in the making of the vernacular literary. It is in this sense that they can be seen as founding poets. They bring into view an alternative story of the founding aesthetics of Marathi literature, one that highlights the contributions of "the extraordinary number of women who sang their devotional songs in Marathi."

Women and Vernacularization: An Untold Story

In some ways, the pervasive and striking presence of women in the early vernacular communities in Maharashtra is comparable to the prominence of women in the rise of the vernaculars in Europe. Yet Sheldon Pollock, who argues at length for a comparative analysis of vernacularization in Europe and South Asia, wholly ignores gender in *The Language of the Gods in the World of Men*. Gender hardly gets a mention in the numerous vernacular traditions of the subcontinent covered in the massive anthology *Literary Cultures in History: Reconstructions from South Asia*, which Pollock edited. Even D. R. Nagaraj's essay on Kannada vernacularization in that volume, the most attentive to the compositions of "the absent and the invisible," does not mention women's contributions specifically. Novetzke's *Quotidian Revolution* offers an important response to Pollock's study by showing that gender and caste were indeed central to Marathi vernacularization, and that the literary did develop first in the *bhakti* mode in Maharashtra.[7] Yet his study situates women as part of a *bhakti* public "constituted primarily by passive attention," not as active "partner-interlocutors" in the making of vernacular literature.[8]

By contrast, substantial scholarship does exist—more than can be adequately summarized here—on the role of women in the rise of vernacular literatures in Europe.[9] "The first one who started to write poetry in the vernacular," Dante famously wrote in *Vita Nuova* (ca. 1292–1295), "started to do so because he wanted to make his words comprehensible to women, who found it difficult to follow Latin verses."[10] Herbert Grundmann, an early scholar of European vernacularity whose work seems to have had a significant influence on Pollock, argued (back in 1935) that it was not only because women did not know Latin, as Dante contended, but because of "the extraordinary (one might almost say excessive) zeal of women of this time for reading and writing—for books" that "a vernacular literature hence arose for them."[11] Unlike knights and even sometimes court poets of the medieval era, women of the courtly classes could read and write well.[12] Grundmann argues that women's practices of reading and writing impelled the turn to the vernacular.[13] "The fact that women began regularly to cross and blur the border dividing the people's language from literature," he writes, "was obviously the strongest, most decisive spur to dissolving the strict division between Latin literature and nonliterary speech—that language previously deemed unworthy of script."[14] While women have long been recognized as the intended addressees of poets and writers in the European vernacular turn, feminist scholars pointed out that they played an active role in shaping which texts were translated and how. Joan Ferrante maintains that because women participated in choosing, soliciting, patronizing, and shaping texts through active interactions with male scribes, scholars, theologians, and poets, they should be recognized as collaborators in the authorship of early vernacular texts.[15] The turn to the vernacular also unleashed a wave of women-authored works, both in lyric poetry and religious writings of nuns and mystics of the medieval era.[16]

Even though women were also a decisive catalyst of the vernacular turn to Marathi, there are some important differences in the South Asian context to keep in mind. The women involved in European vernacular projects were from the literate and aristocratic classes, while in the Marathi vernacular turn, it was women outside of royal courts and religious institutions, women of much lesser means and literary backgrounds, who took on important roles. Even though many Mahanubhava women of the early sect were Brahmins, most were also widows with little societal standing. Marathi literature not only developed outside of royal courts but among sects that challenged the caste and gender hierarchies within the everyday "public." Furthermore, "book learning" in Marathi vernacularity was never restricted to literacy, as this grind-mill *ovī* succinctly shows:

I can't read
The book of Jnaneshvar
That doesn't stop by father Vitthal
from giving it to me

ginyānācī pothī
malā vācāyā yēinā
iṭṭala mājhā pitā
malā detā nā rāhīnā[17]

Here the "book of Jnaneshvar" could also be translated as the "book of knowledge." In Maharashtra, as in Europe, women blurred the border dividing the people's language from literature, but their zeal for books and knowledge was often manifested in avid engagements with the oral-textual interweb of *bhakti* literarity, rather than through the courtly arena of circulating texts and letters. Indeed, many Sanskrit works, especially epic and puranic texts, had a robust oral and public life.

The early Mahanubhava texts paint a vivid picture of this oral-textual landscape in the thirteenth century. The *Smṛtisthaḷ* describes how, for example, the poet Bhaskar, called the "Lord of Poets" or Kavishvar by the Mahanubhavas, "expounds" (*vyākhyā karīt hote*) on a Sanskrit text and attracts the whole town to listen: "One day Kaviśvar was sitting right at the side of the river. (*Addendum:* He was reciting something—to whom is not known. But he was expounding a Sanskrit text.) And one after another, people [*loku*] were drawn to him. He evoked intense emotion. The whole town [*nagara*] was attracted."[18] The passage goes on to describe the poetic beauty (*rasu*) of Kavishvar's discourses, suggesting them to be in verse, though it is not clear if these were in the vernacular. Also unspecified is who "the whole town" or the "people" refers to, but the audience is clearly the wider "*bhakti* public." Women were active participants in this *bhakti* public. Even though female literacy was not as widespread in the everyday world of thirteenth-century Maharashtra as among the female aristocracy of early vernacular Europe, there was widespread interest among women in the texts—both Sanskrit and later Marathi—that came to form the *bhakti* literary corpus.

Women were never merely a passive audience. Even at the earliest stage, texts were not only written for women, but by women. It is likely that Mahadaise, a Brahmin widow from a highly learned family, and the Janabai who authored the *Hariścandra Ākhyāna* were both literate. Besides *Dhavaḷe*, there are two other works attributed to Mahadaise, including another retelling of the story of Rukmini's marriage in simpler *ovīs* sequenced in the order of the Marathi syllabary called the *Mātṛkī-Rukmiṇī-Svayaṃvar* (Abecedarian marriage of Rukmini), and a collection of seventy-five or so *ovīs* known as the *Garbhakāṇḍa Ovyā* (*Ovīs* of the inner sanctum).[19] There are also other women writers among the Mahanubhavas. Hiraise is known for her purportedly oral reconstruction of the *Līḷācaritra* after it was lost or destroyed at the turn of the fourteenth century, but she is also credited with another work called *Nāmamahimāvarṇana* (An account of the importance of the name) that suggests she too may have been literate.[20] The most prolific of the women writers of the early period appears to be a woman named Nagaise, a child-widow who took initiation in the sect through the influence of her famous literary uncle, the poet Bhaskar. There are at least six commentarial and philosophical works attributed to her, though several are no longer extant.[21] More research on these and other women Mahanubhava writers is needed.

Janabai, perhaps surprisingly, has also long been associated with textuality, whether through the assignment of Vitthal as her scribe or in her own self-proclamations of literacy as evidenced in a famous *abhaṅga*: "Woman, I learned to write from the king of noble gurus (*sadgururāyā*)."[22] More than 350 extant poems have been attributed to Janabai, and while many clearly overlap with oral-performative traditions of the grind mill and with *kīrtan*, there are some that constitute literary work in the common understanding of that term as a written work. These include the *Hariścandra Ākhyāna* and other stories from the *Mahābhārata*, some available only in fragments but enough to take her seriously as a narrative poet. One extant narrative poem is titled *Thālīpāk* and focuses on the plight of Draupadi in an episode in the *Mahābhārata* when she has to feed the foul-tempered sage Durvasa who unexpectedly visits the Pandavas' forest-abode during their exile. Janabai also seems to have written a work called the *Draupadīvastraharaṇ*, on the famous gambling scene in which the Pandavas lose Draupadi in a dice game, and Krishna comes to rescue her from the Kauravas. Unfortunately, this work is only extant in quoted form in an essay by A. R. Ajgaonkar.[23] All three stories focus on consequential female characters, and all are narrated in the small *abhaṅga* in the concise style of the grind mill *ovī*, so that they appear to have been written by a single author and to belong together as a set. Indeed, the poet Mukteshvar, the grandson of Eknath, also wrote these same three stories; there are astonishing verbatim overlaps between Mukteshvar's and Janabai's texts, as N. G. Nandapurkar has established, and between the works of Vishnudas Nama and Janabai, placing her firmly within a textual—and not only an oral-performative—tradition.[24]

There were numerous other women poets of the Varkari sect—an extraordinary number—who composed *abhaṅgas* in the everyday spaces of the *bhakti* public. Many, like Janabai, were from marginalized and impoverished castes and classes, or they were exiled Brahmins. Besides Janabai, the most well-known are Soyarabai and Nirmalabai from the Mahar caste, wife and daughter respectively of the more famous fourteenth-century poet Chokhamela; Muktabai, an accomplished *yoginī* and sister to Jnaneshvar; and Kanhopatra, a courtesan ostracized by "respectable" society but given refuge in the sixteenth century by Eknath. A surviving *abhaṅga* or two have been attributed to a dozen or so women poets associated with Namdev, and several to female disciples of Tukaram. The most famous and prolific of these was Bahinabai, who wrote about the abusive wrath unleashed by her orthodox Brahmin family against her determined pursuit of her "gift of poetry" (*varadāna kavitvāce*).[25]

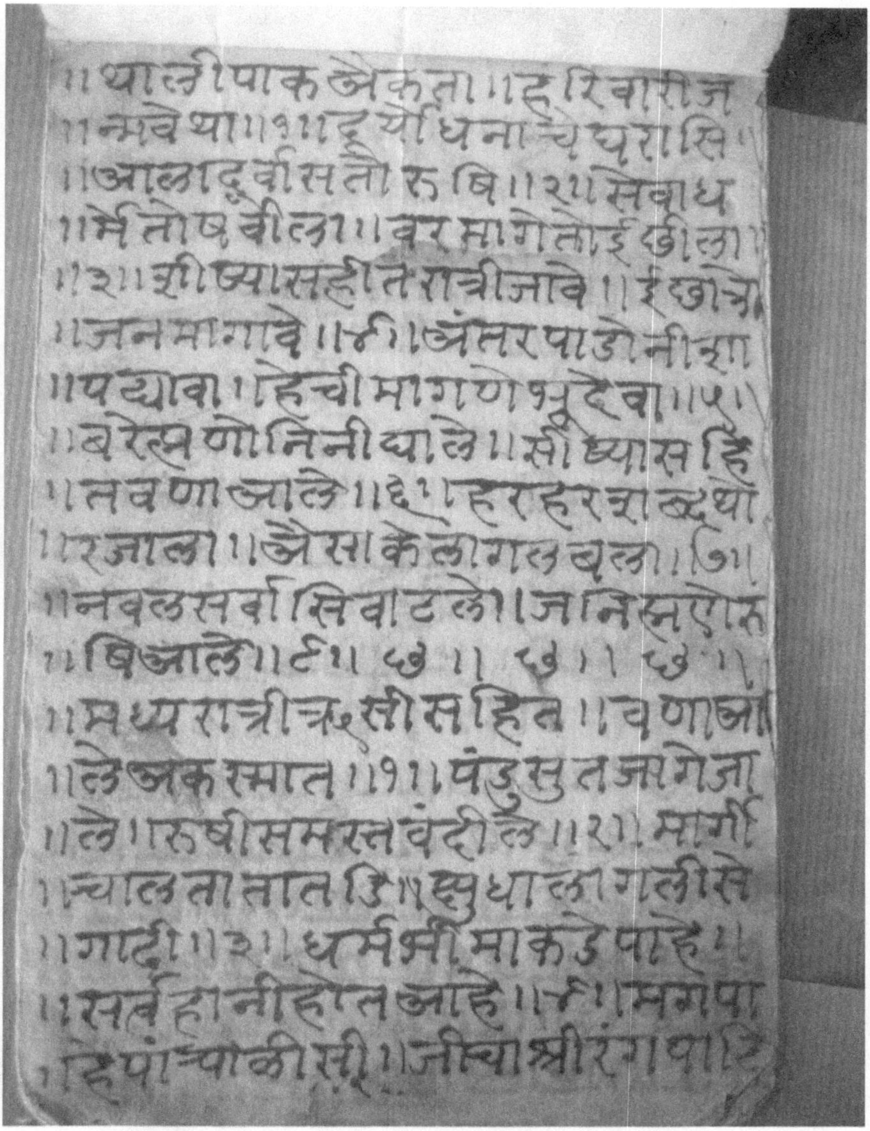

Figure 5.2 Photo of the first page of Janabai's "*Thālipāk*" from manuscript no. 516/235, in the manuscript collection of the Rajwade Samshodhan Mandal in Dhule, Maharashtra, 2009. No date is evident in the manuscript. No manuscripts of Janabai's *Hariścandra Ākhyāna* were found in the course of my research.
Photo by author

In the multilingual South Asian context the distinction between literary languages and "nonliterary speech" was, perhaps, not as strictly binary as Grundmann argues the Latin and the European vernaculars were.[26] Apabhramsha and Prakrit mediated between Sanskrit and the vernaculars, destabilizing the dichotomy between the "literary language" and so-called nonliterary speech, according to H. C. Bhayani, through ongoing processes of colloquialization, as I explain in chapter 2. It is well-known that both Prakrit and Apabhramsha were associated with women's speech and songs, even within the Sanskrit literary corpus. According to Andrew Ollett, though Prakrit literature was courtly in style and register, it was also considered to be and figured as more accessible to women and "more open to women's participation than Sanskrit."[27] Indeed, the foundational work of Prakrit literature, the *Sattasaī*, features numerous poems in the voices of women, with a cast of characters central to women's songs—husbands, brothers-in-law, traveling visitors to the village, mothers, aunts, girlfriends, and mothers-in-law. Yet because these *gāthās* are written in a courtly style and register, their apparent connections to women's songs have not received the attention they deserve. An insightful dissertation on the *Sattasāī* concludes that though "it would be reductive to claim that the *Gahākośa* [*Sattasāī*] is unmodulated Sātavāhana-era women's folk music," the work nevertheless "carries and has retained, perhaps purposefully, something of this character."[28]

There may be room for comparison between the female-voiced lyrics of the *Sattasaī* and extant manuscripts of female-voiced love lyrics in the earliest strata of vernacular poetry in Europe—*chanson de femme* in Old French, *cantigas de amigo* in Galician-Portuguese, *frauenlieder* in Old German to name a few. Known subsequently as "woman's song," these manuscripts constitute some the earliest uses of European vernaculars in lyric poetry. Yet like the *Sattasaī*, most are authored by men or by anonymous poets and written in a courtly style for a courtly audience. There have been scholarly efforts to trace these songs to "preliterate songs actually composed by women" in the European vernaculars, just as some scholars see the trace of folksongs in the *Sattasaī*. But this effort has largely remained speculative, "since no genuinely oral and popular examples survive" in the European archive.[29] Grundmann cites Charlemagne's 789 CE injunction forbidding nuns from writing down *winileodos*—"by which he must have meant love songs, communal songs or all worldly, popular poems"—composed and sung by women, as proof of the widespread existence of women's oral traditions.[30] Anne Klinck lists many Church injunctions against women's song traditions in Europe, arguing that the "regularity of these prohibitions" shows how "ineradicable" women's song traditions were.[31] Yet such injunctions also attest to the intentional separation of women's songs from written texts in the European lyric archive. The gendered divide between song and poetry, between women's expressive forms and writing was, these injunctions suggest, more a forced outcome than the inevitable consequence of an aesthetic "separability principle."

By contrast, one of the most distinctive aspects of Marathi vernacularization is the manifest inclusion of women's songs in texts like the *Līḷācaritra*, the *Ṛddhipurcaritra*, and the *Smṛtisthaḷ*. Though Mahanubhavas later issued injunctions against singing as well, these early texts give written form, and thus literary status, to numerous songs by women, in particular those of Mahadaise but also of several other women. Placing these early textual attestations of women's songs alongside the enormous oral archive that was amassed over the course of the twentieth century shows that women's songs have neither been "preliterate" nor entirely separate from the world of texts for at least the span of the vernacular era and likely before that. The fact that within so-called nonliterary speech one finds copious repertoires of oral poetry that engage the texts of the dominant literary order further complicates the constructed binary between cosmopolitan and vernacular, literary language and everyday speech, poetry and song.

Women became "the strongest, most decisive spur" in Marathi vernacularization by bringing this oral-textual interweb into the vernacular project. Whether singing about Sita from the *Rāmāyaṇa*, or Rukmini from the *Bhāgavata Purāṇa*, or Taramati from the various puranic and vernacular renderings of the Harischandra story, women clearly and obviously engaged the oral-textual traditions around them. Mahadaise and Janabai wrote about Rukmini and Taramati in founding works of Marathi literature by drawing on the modes of expressivity in women's song traditions. Both Mahadaise and Janabai show in their respective poetic works and figural authorship that a deeply entwined oral-textual intertext was foundational to Marathi writing, that the vernacular turn was, in a real and substantial way, responsive to and shaped by, not only women, but women's oral poetic traditions.

In the Company of Women

Though there are important theological distinctions between them, both Mahanubhavas and Varkaris are Krishnaite sects, and just as Krishna famously reveled in the company of cowherding women, Chakradhar and Vitthal are also surrounded by women.[32] Chakradhar was, of course, a historical being, incarnated and embodied at a particular historical time, but this distinction would not necessarily be meaningful to the devotees of Vitthal for whom Vitthal became present in their songs and poems about him. Chakradhar's choice of the company of women, his insistence on wandering, and on stepping outside the structures of power and comfort are not entirely unlike the legendary wanderlust of Vitthal, though the geographies of their wanderings were distinct. Chakradhar wandered through the villages and towns of Maharashtra, refusing to consecrate any one place, whereas Vitthal's wandering in and around Pandharpur make it the center of the universe for his devotees. The *Līḷācaritra* is mapped along the routes of Chakradhar's wanderings, just as the stories and legends of Vitthal's wanderings around Pandharpur make up a significant portion of the songs and poems of devotees. In thousands of grind mill songs, Jani's Vitthal, like Mahadaise's Chakradhar, strays outside the comforts of home and temple to the fields and the humble abodes of his devotees. Both are gods who surround themselves, not with the powerful, but with the least powerful, in everyday spaces that sometimes transgress the bounds of convention and hierarchy. Both gods are comparatively less amorous, the poetry and writings inspired by each focused, not on the tropes of erotic desire usually associated with Krishna's dalliances with women, but on the mundane, everyday world of women's labors.

There is sometimes a suggestive shadow of eroticism in Vitthal's preference for Janabai's company. In the *Bhaktavijay*, Vitthal is described as spending the night in intimate conversation with Janabai on her bed in her hut. Rukmini's anguish over Vitthal's constant pull to Janabai is the subject of numerous songs of the grind mill:

There Rukmini has blocked
Her husband against the wall

Tell me the truth, Vitthala
Who was Jana to you?

This is what Rukmini says,

Where are you going?
And the oil lamp burns eternally
And you go on making me wait for you.

yāta rukamīṇīna patī
āḍavīlāya āḍabhītī

khara saṅgāvo iṭṭalā
janā tumcīna kona vhotī
aśī rukmīṇa mhaṇatī

tumhīn kuṭha jātāya
ān jaḷatāta nandādīpa
ān vāṭa pāhāyalā lāvītāya[33]

In response to Rukmini's anguished questions, Vitthal tells her not to worry, that Janabai is merely his sister in dharma (*dharmācī bahīṇ*) or his child (*lekaru*), thus undercutting the erotic possibilities of their bond. It is hard to know whether these are merely "cleaned-up" versions of now forgotten songs that might have had more erotic content, but it is nevertheless true that Vitthal's engagement with Janabai mostly involves work—grinding, sweeping, collecting dung, doing laundry together—both in the extant poems attributed to her, in copious grind mill songs, and in the written hagiographical tradition. Whatever eros there might be between Vitthal and Janabai, it is mostly that between mother and daughter, not lovers.[34] The deflection of the erotic puts the focus on women's theological aspirations for knowledge, for books.

There is a poignant scene in the *Līḷācaritra* that illustrates this very point. The scene features the Brahmanical figure Sarangpandit, an elite Sanskrit scholar drawn to Chakradhar's teachings, though he ultimately betrays him in the end by colluding with the Brahmanical powers. One day he visits Chakradhar only to find him surrounded by a throng of women. Sarangpandit wanted to have Chakradhar to himself for a learned dialogue and is full of contempt for the women. He thinks to himself, "How these plump women have encircled him like slender betel vines! All of them should be rounded up and sent to the Telugu land to husk and grind rice grains. Then I would be able to be alone in the Gosavi's presence!" Chakradhar, reading Sarangpandit's thoughts, is displeased and says to him, "Why couldn't plump women surround me like slender betel vines out of a desire for dharma? . . . You have a soul. Do they have a soulette? Does one God protect you and another God protect them?"[35] Chakradhar centers women's "zeal" for theological knowledge, for dharma, repudiating Sarangpandit's innuendo. And Sarangpandit seems to think that husking rice in the Telugu land is an activity far from theological relevance, but the *Līḷācaritra* repeatedly undercuts this presumption by showing Chakradhar engaging with the minute details of women's labors, preferring their company over that of elite scholars and royalty.

Indeed, Chakradhar avoided association with the Yadava kings, even the ones who admired him, like Mahadev (r. 1261–1270). One *līḷā* is quite explicit about his reason for this:

> The omniscient one said to Baïse, "My woman, Mahadev is an estimable person. He will come for *darśan*, he will hand over the kingdom to me, and he himself will become my servant." "Is that so, Baba?" asked Baïse. "Then, my children, there will be no place left for you." "Oh, no, Baba!" said Baïse. "I will prevent that day from coming," said the omniscient one. "Make preparations for us to leave."
>
> Baïse made all the preparations, and the Gosavi left.[36]

Chakradhar knew that accepting royal gifts or patronage would shift the space of his teachings to a royal sphere that would exclude women like Baise. Chakradhar had first met Baise, then called Nagubai, during his solitary period of wandering. Baise is the most prominent woman in the text, the manager of Chakradhar's everyday life, and his constant interlocutor, the "*bāī*" invoked by Chakradhar in numerous *līḷās*. She was a Brahmin widow who had been living by herself in a hermitage as a respected ascetic with disciples of her own when she met Chakradhar. In their first encounter, she had made Chakradhar sit on the floor to eat, while she sat on an elevated platform propitiated by her disciple. Then, one day, Baise went into a trance, had a realization about her ego, and became one of Chakradhar's first disciples.[37] The *Līḷācaritra* introduces numerous such women spiritual seekers of thirteenth-century Maharashtra, many of them Brahmin but with low social standing as widows. These women are the nonelite analogue to the courtly women of the European vernacular projects. A series of disputed *līḷās* in the *Līḷācaritra* suggests that it was, in fact, Chakradhar's association with such women that brought down the ire of the powerful Brahmins of his time.[38] While the *līḷās* depicting Chakradhar's punishment at the hands of the Brahmin elite of the Yadava court are disputed by Mahanubhavas, Chakradhar's purposeful distance from the courtly sphere in favor of the company of ordinary women is evident throughout the text.[39]

Not only is Chakradhar's decision to prioritize the company of women important, but so is the way Chakradhar's choices are written in the text of the *Līḷācaritra*. In the *līḷā* above, Chakradhar's dealings with the Yadava king are narrated through a conversation between Chakradhar and Baise. When Chakradhar and Baise go into hiding to escape the king, it is Baise who finds out the news about the king's attempted visit from a group of dairy maids she meets while fetching water. Baise asks these women how they had returned so early from the town where they sell their milk and yogurt, and they tell her that they sold out their wares quickly because the king and all his men had been in the town. She reports this conversation to Chakradhar, and this is the interaction recorded in a *līḷā*.[40] The narrative structure of the *līḷā* centers women's voices, not only Baise's but also the dairy maids', ordinary working women, engaged in their daily labor of fetching water.

Meeting Baise marks a major transformation in Chakradhar's life that is textually encoded as a transition from the "Solitary Period" to the "First Half." The "Second Half" begins when Nagdev, also called Bhat or Bhatobas, a common address for a Brahmin, takes initiation in the sect. Affectionately addressed by Chakradhar with the more diminutive nickname Monkey (*vānar*), Nagdev becomes the anointed continuator after Chakradhar's departure. But Baise is Chakradhar's closest and constant companion and interlocutor, the caretaker of his everyday needs. Her everyday labors include cooking, cleaning, sewing, bathing, and massaging Chakradhar; she also manages other disciples and visitors. Baise's labors are abundantly described throughout the text, never separated from daily theological conversations. With women as his most ubiquitous interlocutors, Chakradhar and the text that records his *līḷās* thus embed theology in the minutiae of women's everyday lives.

The women surrounding both Chakradhar and Vitthal thus help to reconfigure what it means for these gods to be in the company of women by clearly rejecting the erotic aesthetics of *kāvya*. The everyday village world described in the *Līḷācaritra* and in *ovīs* and *abhaṅgas* is quite distinct from the pastoral eroticism of the everyday village world of the *Sattasaī*, for example. Women are not the sexualized object of the erotic *rasa*. Instead, the focus in early vernacular texts and poems is on women's mundane lives and their ways of speaking and singing *to each other*. Furthermore, the gods become the primary audience for songs and poems composed by women poets. Chakradhar is the one who listens to Mahadaise's *ovīs* in the *Līḷācaritra*, and Gundam Raul is the attentive audience of *Dhavaḷe* in the *Ṛddhipurcaritra*. While Vitthal visits and labors with numerous devotees, he is depicted as the audience—and later the scribe—of Janabai's songs in the *Bhaktavijay*.

Indeed, with God as her audience, Mahadaise takes on a distinctive role in the composition of the *Līḷācaritra*. The textualization of Chakradhar's life story is retrospective, after all, and marks the beginning of the vernacular moment as a literary phenomenon. And because Baise commits suicide when she gets a false report of Chakradhar's death, she is not present when the project of writing the *Līḷācaritra* is undertaken.[41] Mahadaise thus becomes one of the central narrators and composers of the text, not only as an individual author but as figural author, a "speaking name" for the vernacular public of zealous and engaged women. Ian Raeside acknowledges her central authorial role when he attributes authorship of the *Līḷācaritra* to "Mhāimbhaṭa with some help from Mahādāisā,"[42] Yet even this attribution does not adequately account for Mahadaise's essential contributions, nor those of many other women, to the writing of this text.

Mahadaise's Figural Authorship

Jnaneshvar's foundational position in Marathi literature is conveyed in the fact that he is remembered and addressed as *maulī*, a colloquial, affectionate form of maternal address that brings the scholarly male poet into relations of maternal intimacy with his devotees. In contrast, Mahadaise (sometimes Mahadamba, Mahadāī), which means Great Mother, is an elevating, honorific title. The maternal address is not uncommon in the languages of the subcontinent as a way of showing respect to women; the *āī*, or *aïsā/se* or *aüsā/se* suffix attached to the end of women's names appears throughout the Mahanubhava corpus as an example of this widespread practice. Mahadaise is sometimes addressed by what is presumably her birth name, Rupai, which also has the suffix *āī* at the end. For Mahadaise, then, the fact that she is called "mother" is not what distinguishes her status; rather the prefix *mahā/mahat*, meaning "great," elevates a common maternal address to a title. There is a story about how Mahadaise got her new name in the "Ajñāt Līḷās" (Līḷās of unknown place). Although not considered part of the main text, these are often appended to the end of the *Līḷācaritra*. In one such episode, titled "The Renaming of Rupāī as Mahādāī," we get the story behind Mahadaise's title:

> One day Mahadaise told this story to the Gosavi: "Lord, the grandmother of Vayanayaka was named Mahadaise. She was very learned. Lord, she had studied a great deal. The Goddess *Mhāḷasā* was pleased with her. The Goddess herself spoke to her. She was the family priest [*purohit*] for King Mahadev. The king used to ask her all manner of things. She used to see the future. One time she even defeated great scholarly men in debate. That's how learned she was. I know nothing, Lord. The Omniscient One said, "Woman, she was Mahadaise to the king, and you are Mahadaise here. As she used to talk to him, you should talk to me. Then Mahadaise said, "What's this, Lord?" The Omniscient One said, "I myself will speak with you!"[43]

Vayanayaka was Mahadaise's father, and the elder Mahadaise mentioned here was her own great grandmother, renowned for being a learned woman who knew the Vedas and served as a family priest for the Yadava king Mahadev.[44] Mahadaise feels lacking in comparison, and Chakradhar assuages her self-doubts by granting her new status as Mahadaise. By giving her this title, Chakradhar creates a position for her among his followers that functions as a sort of parallel to the position and status of her grandmother in the court of Mahadev. The new name elevates Mahadaise in the sect in recognition of her aspirations and "zeal" for learning and erudition. She is recognized, thus, as his primary vernacular-intellectual interlocutor. "I myself will speak with you!" he declares.

Indeed, Mahadaise is frequently depicted in ardent theological pursuits. She is shown to regularly attend text recitations called *purāṇas*, not unlike the twentieth-century poet Bahinabai Chaudhari, whose deep knowledge (*bahuśrutapaṇā*) of texts and traditions comes, according to her son Sopan

Dev, through her participation in *kīrtans* and oral recitations. While Chaudhari was unlettered, however, it seems likely that Mahadaise knew how to read and write. Given her purported family background, it would not be unreasonable to assume that Mahadaise knew at least some Sanskrit, and that she likely wrote her own *Dhavaḷe*. Many *līḷās* are structured by Mahadaise's deep and penetrating theological questions. Several are dialogues between Chakradhar and Mahadaise on texts like the Bhagavad Gītā and the Bhāgavata Purāṇa after Mahadaise has attended a *purāṇa*, likely an oral recitation in which Sanskrit texts were recited, perhaps accompanied by oral commentaries in Marathi. Jnaneshvar is believed to have engaged in such recitations, and the *Jñāneśvarī* is itself structured as just this kind of an oral discourse. In the *Līḷācaritra*, the audience and the interlocutor of these texts is Mahadaise.

Mahadaise becomes a figure in the text of the book-hungry vernacular audience of women, the ones who surround Chakradhar like slender betel vines. The conventionalized refrain, "Mahadaise asked" (*Mahadāïse pusalīṃ*), points us toward all these women, just as the text is rife with Chakradhar's interactions with numerous women. This phrase becomes an important rhetorical device that structures many a *līḷā*.[45] Whereas Janabai's figural authorship emerges in the signature line "Says Jani," or "Says Nama's Jani," Mahadaise's figural authorship is signaled by the ubiquitous phrase "Mahadaise asked":

> Mahadaise had come back after listening to a *purāṇa*. **Mahadaise asked**, "Lord, the teller of the *purāṇa* [*purāṇik*] said that Sri Krishna Chakravarti is the incarnation of God and Arjuna is the incarnation of man. Both have equal learning. Is this true, Lord?"
>
> The omniscient one said, "My Woman [*bāī*], what this and that poet knows, I will tell you here. Sri Krishna is Parmeshvar's incarnation. Arjuna is a *jīva*, a living being. Because he studied the fourteen systems of knowledge, he gained equal footing with Krishna. Arjuna was learned in all ways of knowing except one."
>
> "I see, Lord. Which one was that?"
>
> "My woman, that one was knowledge of Brahma."
>
> "Is that so, Lord?" Then continuing on this, **Mahadaise asked**, "The *purāṇik* said that among devotees there is no *bhakti* like that of Arjuna for Krishna. Is this true, Lord?"

> The omniscient one said, "That's true, My Woman. Arjuna asked the kind of questions that could be resolved only by Krishna Chakravarti himself. Arjuna's questions were as if Krishna's own knowledge of Brahma were being put into words."
>
> "Is that so, Lord?" On this **Mahadaise asked**, "In the Bhagavad Gītā, Sri Krishna says, 'Among the Suns, I am Vishnu; among the stars, I am the moon; among the gods, I am Indra; among the Gandharvas, I am Chitraratha.' There were a lot more like this. But how can this be, Lord?"[46]

In a very concise manner and simple Marathi words this *līḷā* presents a vernacular discussion of the Bhagavad Gītā in the form of a dialogue. Notice the number of times the phrase "Mahadaise asked" appears in this exchange. Her questions prompt the details of Chakradhar's reading of the Bhagavad Gītā. The structure of the *līḷā* sets up an implicit analogy between the Arjuna and Krishna dialogue that is the topic of discussion and the Mahadaise and Chakradhar dialogue that is its vehicle. When Chakradhar says that Arjuna's *bhakti* lies in his learned questions, the kind that only an incarnated god could answer, Mahadaise's persistent and abundant questions come to mind. Mahadaise thus plays a role in the *Līḷācaritra* not unlike that played by Arjuna in the Gītā; each is the interlocutor who calls forth divine knowledge. Whereas a warrior is God's interlocutor in the age of Krishna, a woman is God's interlocutor in the vernacular age of Chakradhar. The warrior of the Sanskrit text is replaced by a woman in the vernacular text, enacting a major shift in the field of divine revelation and of writing. Instead of the courts and battlefields of kings and warriors, Chakradhar's teachings emerge in the space of everyday life, in conversations with women.

Mahadaise's role, however, goes far beyond that of audience because she delivers a Marathi rendering—a vernacularization—of lines from the Bhagavad Gītā in this episode. She does so in an embedded verse, with end-rhymed lines of equal syllabic length.[47] Here Mahadaise contributes to the written text as a figure of the vernacular audience, who reenacts and recomposes the text in verse, just as Bahinabai Chaudhuri had recomposed the story of Savitri into a verse after Sopan Dev had read the story out loud. Song blends into prose in the figural authorship of Mahadaise. Indeed, the whole *līḷā* becomes an intimate dialogue, not unlike that at the grind mill. Mahadaise's questions and Chakradhar's responses are succinct and move back and forth in a swift and brusque fashion, eased by direct and intimate structures of address. She addresses him as *jī*, a supplicating honorific more common today in Gujarati and Hindi, which following Feldhaus I have translated as "Lord." The feminine addressivity of Chakradhar's response to Mahadaise is marked here and throughout the *Līḷācaritra* by the ubiquitous use of the vocative *bāī*, translated following Feldhaus as "my woman." Chakradhar's feminine address echoes the common oral refrain of the grind mill songs, *sāṅgate bāī tulā* ("I tell you, woman"). Grind mill singers address their grind mill as a god (*jātyā iśvarā*), just as Mahadaise addresses Chakradhar. The intimate dialogue at the grind mill is evoked in the rhetorical structure of this *līḷā*, through which Chakradhar's teachings are unraveled, opened, divulged, not unlike the depiction of the Arjuna and Krishna dialogue in the *Jñāneśvarī* discussed in chapter 3. In other words, women's ways of speaking, singing, and conversing with each other provide the rhetorical structure for many such *līḷās*.

Though the "Mahadaise asked" device is especially noticeable in the "Second Half" of the *Līḷācaritra*, it makes its first appearance at the very beginning of the text, in the fourth *līḷā* of the "Solitary Period." This is the crucial *līḷā* in which Chakradhar discloses his complex origin story. The *līḷā* opens with the phrase, "In Hivarali, Mahadaïse asked" (*Hivaraḷiyeṃ Mahadāïsīṃ pusaleṃ*). This *līḷā* reveals that Chakradhar and the revered holy man Cangdev Raul, the third of the five incarnations of the Supreme God, were one and the same. Cangdev Raul "gave up his body" to escape the sexual advances of a female ascetic, Chakradhar tells Mahadaise, and he entered the body of the son of a Gujarati minister who had died at the same moment:

> And **Mahadaïse asked** the Gosavi [Chakradhar], "So, Lord Gosavi, are you this minister's son from Gujarat?" "Yes." "How did they let you leave?" Thereupon he told her the story of the Ram pilgrimage.
>
> At their lodgings, Mahadaïse said, "Abai! Abai! Our Gosavi is really Cangdev Raül of Dvaravati." "Is that so, Rupai?"[48]

Surely there were other ways to narrate this very complex origin story. Why maintain the conversational structure centering Mahadaise, especially in the section on Chakradhar's "Solitary Period"? Rather than merely telling the story, the text records Mahadaise's realization of this truth about Chakradhar's origins. The *līḷā* also says that Chakradhar told her "the story of his Ram pilgrimage," which is narrated a few *līḷās* later in a much more straightforward third-person perspective: "Once the omniscient one said. . . ."[49] There is no explicit mention of Mahadaise in this later *līḷā*, but the earlier one has already set up the framework of Mahadaise as the listener of Chakradhar's revelation and thus also the implicit teller of it in the text, a record of the simultaneity of listening and speaking implicit in Mahadaise's figural authorship.

Toward the end of the *Līḷācaritra*, which focuses on Chakradhar's preparations for his departure, the phrase "Mahadaise asked" appears in almost every *līḷā* of the last sixty or so *līḷās*.[50] She and Nagdev are the primary figures in these final *līḷās* because, while Chakradhar names Bhatobas as the preceptor after his departure, he also "entrusts" Mahadaise specifically to him. To this Bhatobas replies, "Lord, who am I? She is well-versed in the *purāṇas*, adept at debate and dialogue, and very learned. Who am I, Lord?"[51] And, indeed, the *Smṛtisthaḷ*, the text that focuses on sect formation and continuity under Nagdev's leadership after the death of Gundam Raul, shows not her dependency on Nagdev so much as her contributions, which are acknowledged later when Nagdev says, "The old woman is the protector of my *dharma*."[52] Indeed, the importance of the old woman as a figure of the vernacular audience is evident in a another episode. The *Smṛtisthaḷ* records the ways that Nagdev, like Chakradhar before him, continually had to redirect Brahmin followers away from their Sanskritic and high-literary proclivities, to unlearn their training, to listen and write in response to the vernacular audience, especially women. The poet and Sanskrit scholar, Kesobas, for example, wrote a narrative poem in Sanskrit on the life of Chakradhar, an abridged Sanskrit *Līḷācaritra* of sorts, titled *Ratnamāḷa Stotra* (Hymn of the garland of jewels), the title itself a sign of the ornamental threading and weaving of the literary. According to the *Smṛtisthaḷ*, this text is praised by Nagdev, but when Kesobas wants to translate a chapter of the *Sūtrapāṭh* into Sanskrit, Nagdev forbids him: "And Bhaṭobās said, 'Don't do that, Keśavdev. That will deprive my old ladies [*mhātāriyā*]."[53] The word Feldhaus translates as "deprive," *nāgavtila*, has a dual meaning. It means both "not to catch or be caught," and "to make someone naked; to remove someone's clothes."[54] Bhatobas is telling Kesobas to avoid Sanskrit because the old women will not be able to catch or understand it. There is also the added connotation, perhaps, that the Sanskrit will expose their lack of literacy; it will humiliate them. The reference to old women recalls the *Therīgāthā*. *Therī* or *therikā* means "old woman." Many of these poems deal with aging, not as a thing to avoid or escape, but as a kind of freedom from the sensualities of youth. This is, perhaps, another sign of the rejection of the erotic *rasa*.

The *Smṛtisthaḷ*, like the *Līḷācaritra*, also includes Mahadaise's *ovīs*. Where her *ovīs* in the *Līḷācaritra* had been about Chakradhar, the *ovīs* in this text are about Nagdev and Mhaimbhat. When she sings them, Nagdev calls her a *siddha*—a term for a spiritual adept who has reached the pinnacle of practice. Mahadaise's first *ovī* is about the anointing of Nagdev by Chakradhar, while the second features Mhaimbhat:

Laying his hand
On the shoulder of Nagdev
King Chakradhar
Took his leave

Wearing gold-woven silk,
A scarf tied at the hip
Mhaiya came
To meet the Lord.[55]

Each verse is independent, though loosely connected by the overall purpose of extolling Chakradhar's continuators, Nagdev as preceptor and Mhaimbhat as the named author of the *Līḷācaritra* and the *Ṛddhipurcaritra*. Mahadaise calls Mhaimbhat "Mhaiya," a hypocoristic nickname, and portrays him as a sort of Brahmin dandy. This may have an ironic edge, a chiding to put Mhaimbhat in his place. Such indirect or ironic speech would not be outside the conventions of the *ovī*, and there are episodes in which Mahadaise scolds Mhaimbhat to keep him in line. The indirection and irony in Mahadaise's *ovī* speaks volumes about Mhaimbhat's role as purported author of the *Līḷācaritra*.

The idea of Mhaimbhat's authorship of the *Līḷācaritra* has been maintained by the Mahanubhavas for the last eight centuries, and he is depicted in all the texts as the one who collects, transcribes, and writes the stories. The question is not whether Mhaimbhat should be credited with authorship—that he has been so credited is a fact—but rather what this authorial attribution reveals to us about authorship itself. Whether it was intentional or not, in the figure of Mhaimbhat as author there is an embodied enactment of literary colloquialization. Like Mahadaise, Mhaimbhat is himself a figure in the text, whose journey from elite and egotistical Brahmin to humble disciple to writer of the sacred texts is a story told in the texts themselves. Mhaimbhat's acts of writing are acts of envoicement, often of female envoicement, centering Chakradhar's primary vernacular interlocutors, most prominently women—and especially Mahadaise. The "Mahadaise asked" trope, as well as the ubiquitous female addressivity of Chakradhar's speech in the text, anchor it to women's vernacular, oral modes.

In a substantial sense, the *Līḷācaritra* is a collectively authored text, a record of the stories of disciples written in their colloquial codes. But it would not be accurate to see it as merely a transcription of the spoken and oral. The consistency of style and focus, the development of the new literary form of the *līḷā*, attest to its careful composition. The method of writing is guided by an aesthetics of reduction, compression, and unraveling associated with the grind mill, and these are aesthetic labors no less than the elaborate weaving and threading of the high literary style. In other words, colloquialization is not a simple record of the demotic, a mere transcription of the spoken, it is an intentional literary labor that is immanent to the literary sphere. The text unravels the codes of literarity embedded in the very apparatus of writing, a resource that had been kept scarce by cosmopolitan regimes of caste and gender exclusion, by making visible the authorial contributions of women, revealing thus the underview that undergirds the very idea of authorship, even as or perhaps because it is attributed to a figure of the Brahmin ecumene, Mhaimbhat. If the superposed literary models mask engagements with women's oral forms through rarification of language and form, like the *gāthās* of the *Sattasaī*, then the "author" of the *Līḷācaritra* works to expose, unravel, bring into the open the shaping influence of women's orality to the project of writing.

In this, Mahadaise's coauthorial role is undeniable. The phrase "Mahadaise asked," which becomes a conventionalized refrain that structures much of the *Līḷācaritra*, also travels to other texts attributed to Mhaimbhat. It appears frequently in the "Ajñāt Līḷās" and also in a work called the *Śrīkṛṣṇacaritra* (The life of Krishna), a collection of *līḷās*, some from the *Līḷācaritra* and others of unknown sources, in which Chakradhar narrates stories about Krishna. The *Śrīkṛṣṇacaritra* is generally attributed to Mhaimbhat and is meant to be a companion volume to the *Līḷācaritra*, but with a focus on puranic stories about Krishna retold from the perspective of Mahanubhava theology.[56] Some versions of the *Līḷācaritra*, like that edited by Hari Narayan Nene, remove many of the *līḷās* structured by the "Mahadaise asked" trope likely presuming them to be part of the *Śrīkṛṣṇacaritra*. It is, in any case, an independent literary work and deserves much more literary attention than it has received or that can be given here. It is one more text that highlights Mahadaise's figural authorship, in particular her important collaborative role in Mhaimbhat's writing projects. In fact, Mhaimbhat's meddling role in the composition of Mahadaise's *Dhavaḷe* is even more illuminating.

Mahadaise's *Dhavaḷe*

There is an important and much neglected example of Mhaimbhat writing under Mahadaise's figural authorship when he takes it upon himself to write a "Second Half" (*Uttarārdha*) for her *Dhavaḷe*. This act, though it was undertaken ostensibly to elevate Mahadaise's literary status, has served instead to depreciate Mahadaise's signal literary contribution in *Dhavaḷe*. An episode narrated in the *Smṛtisthaḷ* is the source of the widely accepted belief that Mahadaise is the author only of the "First Half" (*Purvārdha*) of *Dhavaḷe*. In this episode, Mhaimbhat, accompanied by another scholarly poet named Lakshmidharbhat, asks her to "complete" the *Dhavaḷe*:

> One day Mhāībhaṭ and Lakṣmīdharbhaṭ said to Mahādāïsē, "why don't you go on with the *Rukmiṇī Svayaṃvar*?"
>
> Mahādāïsē said, "How can I do it? At that time the Gosāvi [i.e. Gundam Raul] gave me a boon, and that is why I was inspired." Mhāībhaṭ and Lakṣmīdharbhaṭ said, "Then we will make up the words, and you sing them."
>
> Mahādāïsē agreed. So they made up the words and composed the verses, and Mahādāïsē sang them.
>
> In this way the second part was completed.[57]

Mhaimbhat and Lakshmidharbhat transform Mahadaise's authorship of *Dhavaḷe* into a figural authorship under whose sign *they* continue the story in *her* voice and style. They seem to think it perfectly acceptable to write *as Mahadaise*—in her speaking name—and continue a work she had composed, perhaps because Mhaimbhat has been doing something of this sort in the *Līḷācaritra* and in other writings already. Their work of composing this "Second Half" is described as quite laborious in the original Marathi. A more literal translation would be something like, "they wrought and wrought the verses into purity, and Mahadaise sang them."[58] It required great labor, the episode suggests, to achieve the ease and purity of Mahadaise's orally inflected writing style, which corroborates the point that recreating an oral style in writing requires literary labor. This particular episode makes overt the practice of men composing "female-envoiced" poetry, common throughout South Asia, in the *bhakti* and Sufi modes. Though their intention was not to steal her authorship, they easily and readily appropriated a woman's poetic text; they wrote a second part by calling her work incomplete . Their actions are then openly revealed in the *Smṛtisthaḷ*.

The Marathi scholar Suhasini Irlekar has raised a profound question about this whole incident: Did Mahadaise herself consider *Dhavaḷe* incomplete when Mhaimbhat and Lakshmidharbhat came up with the idea to write a "Second Half?" Irlekar reads Mahadaise's refusal to write a "Second Half" as indicating that she considered the work already finished.[59] Mhaimbhat and Lakshmidharbhat impose their own literary sensibilities on Mahadaise and take it upon themselves to "improve" her work—an experience not uncommon in the history of women's writing. While Irlekar attempts to trace different textual sources for each half, the larger distinction lies in the fact that Mhaimbhat and Lakshmidharbhat want to follow the story to the ending told in the Bhāgavata Purāṇa, drawing on it as a Sanskrit source text, while Mahadaise sought to tell a story addressed to a specific vernacular audience and time, responsive to their vernacular sensibilities and expressive forms.[60] Grind mill *ovīs* draw on texts and stories in ways that serve the time in which they are composed and sung, bringing epic and puranic figures into their present, and this is the style that undergirds the "first half" of *Dhavaḷe*.

It turns out that this divergence in the compositional objectives of Mhaimbhat/Lakshmidharbhat and Mahadaise was immensely consequential. Mhaimbhat substantiates Mahadaise's authorship of *Dhavaḷe*, but he also manages to diminish its importance as the inaugural (extant) narrative poem in Marathi by suggesting that it was incomplete, and that only a "First Half" was authored by Mahadaise. This whole incident is all the more mystifying because Narendra's *Rukmiṇī-Svayaṃvar* was elevated as one of the great Seven Books (*sātī grantha*) of the sect even though it is available only in incomplete form in the Mahanubhava archive.[61] The propagation of the belief that Mahadaise only wrote one half has no doubt contributed to the neglect of *Dhavaḷe* in studies of the vernacular period. Consequently, Mahadaise is rarely acknowledged as one of the first poets to write in Marathi, though she is given the title of *adyakavayitrī,* the first *woman* poet.

Importantly, the episode in *Smṛtisthaḷ* also suggests that Mahadaise's *Dhavaḷe* was known at the time as *Rukmiṇī-Svayaṃvar.* The title *Dhavaḷe* seems to have come later, perhaps as a way to distinguish her work from all other versions of the *Rukmiṇī-Svayaṃvar,* in particular the one written by Narendra. The title is in the plural form, *Dhavaḷe* (Wedding songs) which implies that it is a random collection of songs rather than the unified narrative poetic work that it is. To Mahadaise, the story was no doubt as important as the poetic form; in fact, the content of the story cannot be separated from the choice of this form. The story is centered on Rukmini's quest to marry Krishna. Rukmini's brother Rukmi has a rivalry with Krishna and arranges his sister's wedding with his ally Shishupal to thwart her choice. Rukmini, however, takes matters into her own hands and dispatches a messenger to Krishna to urge him to come and save her from this forced marriage. Krishna famously abducts Rukmini, and a war ensues. The story was important to the Mahanubhavas in both theological and literary ways. It puts in story form the love and longing for an incarnated and embodied God, illustrating the unique *bhakti* of their sect. Rukmini enjoyed the company of God incarnated.

The compressed, intense, paratactic style of Mahadaise's composition contrasts markedly with the elevated, ornate, hypotactic style of Narendra's work, but an interesting poetic paradox emerges here. While Narendra's *Rukmiṇī-Svayaṃvar* is in the literary *ovī* meter, it makes clear nods to the Sanskrit poetic heritage, while Mahadaise's poem, written in a much simpler, colloquial register, is in an inherited poetic form, the *dhavala.* Indeed, the very fact that it is in the *dhavala* differentiates Mahadaise's telling from oral versions that might have been circulating at the time, possibly in the oral *ovī.* The *dhavala* is not an attested Marathi oral form, as far as I have been able to discern, but an Apabhramsha form used in songs of praise for a king, a hero, or a groom depicted as a *dhavala* or "a white bull." Several varieties of *dhavala* are described in prosodic texts like *Svayambhūchandas*, an eighth-century handbook on Prakrit and Apabhramsha meters attributed to the Apabhramsha poet Svayambhu; and the *Chandonuśāsana*, an eleventh-century treatise on Apabhramsha poetry penned by the Jain scholar Hemachandra.[62] The *dhavala* is also described as a *prabandha laukika*—a worldly composition—in the *Mānasollāsa* in the same section that includes a description of the *ovī*. It is described as an Apabhramsha wedding-song form specifically. Bhayani suggests that the *dhavala* may even date back to the time of the Satavahanas in the first and second centuries.[63]

While more common in early Gujarati literature, the *dhavala* has a rather restricted purview in Marathi literature, where it is almost singularly associated with the *Rukmiṇī-Svayaṃvar*.[64] To my knowledge, Mahadaise's is the only Marathi literary work exclusively written in the *dhavala* form; other works include or mention *dhavala* as a song sung at Krishna's wedding. Mahadaise's *dhavala* is a quatrain of two end-rhymed shorter lines followed by two end-rhymed longer lines in varying moric or *jāti* meters. She was the first to bring the *dhavala* to Marathi poetry to write the story of Rukmini's wedding as a narrative poem, and all later versions also connect the form to the story of Krishna and Rukmini's wedding. In this startling, discrete fact, her contribution to Marathi narrative poetry is evident and undeniable.

A *līḷā* in the *Ṛddhipurcaritra* depicts an oral occasion for Mahadaise's composition of *Dhavaḷe*. The episode begins when Mahadaise encounters a woman selling beautiful nuptial crowns—called *bāśiṅga*—and she buys one for Gundam Raul, who is called Gosavi in the *Ṛddhipurcaritra*. Remember that Gundam Raul is a god who is known for his mischievous play and disregard for social rules and boundaries. Wearing this *bāśiṅga* excites Gundam Raul so much that that he orders the preparations for his own wedding. It is not clear whether this was meant to be an actual wedding or only play, but as the elaborate cooking and decorating begins, a man offers his daughter to Gundam Raul, and he does not refuse her. Gundam Raul experiences the wedding as a reenactment of Krishna's wedding to Rukmini, the very subject of the *Dhavaḷe*. For example, at one point, Gundam Raul tells a woman who offers him food that he has already eaten in the palace of Rukmini.[65] Both Krishna and Gundam Raul are, after all, incarnations of the one Supreme God. At a certain point, Mahadaise begins to sing wedding songs or *dhavalas*:

> Then Mahādāïse sang wedding songs [*dhavala*].
>
> The Gosāvī said, "Oh, drop dead! Sing! Sing, I tell you!
>
> Mahādāïse said, "What should I sing, Lord?"
>
> The Gosāvī said, "What should I sing, Lord?" The Gosāvī said, "Oh, sing about Kṛṣṇa and Rukmiṇī, I tell you. Sing about how grandly the horns were played, I tell you."
>
> And Mahādāïsē was inspired. She immediately began to sing about Rukmiṇī's engagement ceremony. She sang the verse, "Surely he touched her in her soul."[66]
>
> And the Gosāvī said, "Oh, yes! Yes! Surely he touched her in her soul."
>
> Then Ābāïsē said, "Oh Lord, please get up. Eat your evening meal."[67]

This episode situates Mahadaise's *Dhavaḷe* in a performance context appropriate to the form of the *dhavala*, not only a wedding, but one that is a reenactment of Krishna's wedding to Rukmini. The episode includes an actual line from *Dhavaḷe*, creating a sonorous intertext between her work and the *Ṛddhipurcaritra*.

Though presented as a song sung by Mahadaise, there is no doubt that *Dhavaḷe* is a written narrative poem. In fact, Mahadaise's performance of *Dhavaḷe* for Gundam Raul functions as a sort of a counter-performance to Narendra's presentation of his *Rukmiṇī-Svayaṃvar* in the court of the Yadavas. Just as King Ramdev suggested, or rather challenged, Narendra to write his poem, Gundam Raul is the one who suggests Mahadaise sing *dhavalas* about "Kṛṣṇa and Rukmiṇī." While Mahadaise's audience is God incarnate, far and above any king, the irreverence and mad play of Gundam Raul dismantles and unravels any sort of literary pretentions of the sort held by Ramdev. When Narendra joins the sect after rejecting the king's offer to buy the authorship of his *Rukmiṇī-Svayaṃvar*, the *Smṛtisthaḷ* declares, "Then, from that time on, the work *Rukmiṇī-Svayaṃvar* came to belong to the order."[68] In another episode of the *Smṛtisthaḷ*, Mahadaise rebukes a woman for singing the *Rukmiṇī-Svayaṃvar* during her wandering.[69] Though the incident came to be used by the Mahanubhavas to support injunctions against singing in the sect, it also seems to have literary significance. Mahadaise's admonishing of the woman seems to be an effort to reign in its proliferation in order to canonize it in the literary archive of the sect.

Nowhere in the *Ṛddhipurcaritra* is there any indication that the *Dhavaḷe* is incomplete. In actuality, Mahadaise ends her story with a dramatic culminating scene when Krishna steals Rukmini away on his chariot. When Rukmini climbs on to Krishna's chariot, she puts a garland on him as the gods celebrate and sing their praises:

Putting the garland on him
The young one looked at Krishna
How the unmanifest Brahma took form!
The Supreme Lord has manifested!
Her eyes welled up, words bursting with emotion
[She said] to the Compassionate Lord
What you did today was pure and true.[70]

This is the penultimate stanza of the *Dhavaḷe.* The final one is her signature verse. This certainly does not sound incomplete. Rather, it reads like a conclusion, one that presents the meeting of Rukmini and Krishna on the chariot as the climax of divine union. This union is consecrated by the garland that Rukmini puts on him. In other words, the wedding is implicit here, and when she performs it for Gundam Raul, this appears to be the point that Gundam Raul loses interest and walks away. In the "Second Half," Mhaimbhat and Lakshmidharbhat narrate the war that ensues between Rukmi's and Krishna's armies after this abduction, and after Krisha's forces win, they narrate in great detail an official, conventional wedding, one more acceptable to orthodox sensibilities.[71] In contrast, Mahadaise's ending recalls the brevity and dramatic intensity of women's *ovīs.* It puts the lyric mode at the center of the narrative.

In the contemporary women's song archive, Rukmini is a favorite figure.[72] There are over two thousand verses on Rukmini in the grind mill archive, many on the marriage of Rukmini and Krishna/Vitthal. There are numerous verses describing Vitthal wearing a nuptial crown—the *bāśiṅga*—recalling the scene in the *Ṛddhipurcaritra* when Mahadaise buys one for Gundam Raul in the chapter on *Dhavaḷe*:

What is that music
playing in Pandharpur?

Wearing a gold nuptial crown (*bāśiṅga*),
God is getting married.

paṇḍharapurāta
kāya vājata gājata
sonerī bāśiṅga
lagna devāca lāgata[73]

The uncanny overlaps here between the depictions of Gundam Raul and Vitthal give us a glimpse of the underview that seems to undergird the episode in the *Ṛddhipurcaritra*, which recreates exactly the scene being described in this *ovī*. The episode about the woman whom Mahadaise admonishes for singing the *Rukmiṇī-Svayaṃvar* provides some evidence that the story had wide appeal and oral circulation in the thirteenth century as well. If this episode and the song archive can be taken as evidence of the continuous interest of women poets and singers in the figure of Rukmini, Mahadaise's choice to render this story over the numerous other puranic stories available to her has deep significance. We might see it as a response to women composers, shaped by addressivity to this vernacular audience. There are numerous *ovīs* in the contemporary song archive that specifically engage the texts of *Rukmiṇī-Svayaṃvar* as well, narrating scenes from the texts in the concise, paratactic style for which the oral *ovī* is known:[74]

Rukmini's mind can't accept
Shishupal as the groom
Send a letter to bring
The God of Dvaraka

śiśupāla navaradeva
yeinā rukhamīṇīcyā manā
patrīkā dāvūnī deva
dvārakecā ānā[75]

This *ovī* compresses the story into a highly condensed articulation. This is the style we see re-created in Mahadaise's *Dhavaḷe*, which also moves through the scenes with artful brevity, though using a more literary language and style. In Mahadaise's telling, when Rukmini decides to take matters into her own hands to avoid marriage to Shishupal, she summons

Sudev to go to Dvaraka to convey her message to Krishna. This scene occurs in the tenth verse in Mahadaise's *Dhavaḷe*, but this same episode does not take place until the 647th verse of Narendra's version. In fact, it takes two hundred more verses before Sudev finally enters Dvarka in Narendra's telling![76] When the messenger in Mahadaise's story conveys Rukmini's "request" (*vinatī*) to Krishna, he does so in a single verse:

Bhimaka's beautiful daughter, Rukmini,
Abounding in beauty, allure of the three worlds,
She has sent a plea (*vinatī*) to you:
O Lord, King of the world, the Refuge of Devotees
If you are the Protector of the Displaced, then come, O Murari![77]

This episode is narrated in one *dhavala* verse in Mahadaise's telling. The last two lines are Rukmini's own words. By contrast, in Narendra's text, the messenger, Sudev, suggests to Rukmini that she write down her plea (*vinatī*) in a letter, so Rukmini takes a palm leaf (*bhūrjapatra*) and a pen made from the stem of a lotus flower (*kamaḷanaḷācī lekhanī*) and writes a brief account of her situation beseeching Krishna to come and save her. The letter is nine *ovīs* long, but after that, it takes Narendra two hundred or so *ovīs* describe Sudev's journey through the enchanting gardens and forests of Krishna's kingdom.[78] The grind mill *ovīs*, of course, wrap up several episodes in a single verse. A couple of lovely, concise *ovīs* about Rukmini's letter in the grind mill archive suggest it to be a common motif in the songs as well, though the letter doesn't appear in Mahadaise's version:

She wrote a letter,
She sent it to the far country
Rahi-Rukmini, a bride
In King Bhimaka's house

lihila patara
dhāḍīla deśāvarī
rāhī rukhamīṇa navarī
rājā bhimakācyā gharī[79]

She wrote a letter
The letter is stamped with a yellow seal

How Rukmini writes!
God smiled to himself.

lihila patara
patrikāvara pivaḷa ṭhasa
rukhamiṇīnī lihila kasa
deva manāta hasa[80]

The second verse packs a great deal of narrative into its condensed form, not only Rukmini's writing of the letter and her yellow seal, but Krishna's affectionate reaction after reading it. The songs assume knowledge of the texts and stories and instead focus on the intense emotional moments in the story, expressed in the lyrical mode. It is exactly this concentrated intensity that Mahadaise brings to the final scene of her story, which dwells in that moment of ecstatic union, when Rukmini is in the proximate presence of Krishna. Indeed, the ending throws a new light on Mahadaise's own experience of proximity to the incarnated, embodied god Chakradhar, the very experience captured in the *Līḷācaritra* through the trope of "Mahadaise asked." In her story about the union of Rukmini with Krishna, she entwines the theological and the literary, capturing in poetry that euphoric moment when the *bhakta* finds herself in the presence of her incarnated, embodied god.

The figure of Rukmini connects Mahadaise to her literary descendant Janabai through the underview. In the grind mill songs, Rukmini is always a wife-figure, associated with the ornaments of marital life, like bangles, vermilion, fancy blouses, and saris, in contrast to the poverty of the lonely Janabai. Janabai has none of the emblems of marriage or opulent luxury, but she often has Vitthal's attention and company. The grind mill songs plumb the depths of Rukmini's wifely angst as a counterpoint to the songs about Janabai and Vitthal. Vitthal is caught between these two women, but it is *their* emotional lives that the songs narrate. This concentrated focus on Rukmini recalls the ways that women retell the *Sītāyan*. Mahadaise's *Dhavaḷe* follows the way that grind mill singers make women figures from texts and epics the center of their songs, even in terms of the very choice to write this story in the pithy style of the oral *ovī*. This is also the style of Janabai's *Hariścandra Ākhyāna*. Janabai's version of the story of Harischandra focuses on his wife, the Queen Taramati, and just as grind mill singers' songs on the *Rāmāyaṇa* are called the *Sītāyan*, Janabai's story might very well be called the *Tārāmatī Ākhyāna*.

Janabai's *Hariścandra Ākhyāna*

Like the *Rukmiṇī-Svayaṃvar*, the story of King Harischandra forms its own literary canon of Marathi narrative poetry, with a textual lineage that includes some of the most revered and elevated poets of the sixteenth through the eighteenth centuries. Besides the numerous written renderings in Marathi, the story of Harischandra—like the story of Rukmini's wedding—has maintained a wide oral circulation in women's songs, *kīrtans*, folk theater, and other performance genres. There are more vernacular renderings of this story than Sanskrit ones, and Adheesh Sathaye has postulated that it likely had a rich and fluid oral life even before it was textualized in the *Mārkaṇḍeya* and *Devībhāgvata Purāṇas* sometime between the third and the tenth centuries.[81] The choice of rendering this story in Marathi, like the choice to write the *Rukmiṇī-Svayaṃvar*, was also thus conditioned by the tastes and interests of a vernacular audience. The story centers the brutal trials of truth concocted by the sage Vishvamitra to test Harischandra, the king of Ayodhya, on his renowned virtues. Harischandra gives away his entire kingdom as alms to Vishvamitra, and in order to pay additional alms, he sells himself, his wife, and his son into slavery. The story dwells on their intense suffering in the face of their commitment to Harischandra's promises to Vishvamitra. Janabai's version, like the numerous grind mill songs about this story, focuses especially on Taramati's suffering. Although the story of Harischandra is nearly the opposite of the story of Rukmini's marriage in its primary focus on suffering and loss, rather than love and ecstatic divine union, Janabai's telling brings focus to Taramati's choices in a way not unlike the focus on Rukmini's choices in the *Rukmiṇī-Svayaṃvar*.

Was Janabai's the first written version of the story of Harischandra in Marathi literature in the same way that Mahadaise's *Dhavaḷe* was, in all likelihood, the first version of the *Rukmiṇī-Svayaṃvar* in Marathi poetry? It is certainly possible but hard to say with any certainty. Though Janabai is believed to have been a contemporary of Namdev in the late thirteenth and early fourteenth centuries, the story appears to be of a later period, a fact especially evident when the story is read alongside Mahadaise's *Dhavaḷe*. The language and grammar are, without doubt, more modern than what we find in her story. There is always the possibility that the language of Janabai's story was modernized in the course of its manuscript transmission over the years, especially if oral performance was its primary intent. The Mahanubhavas used secret coded scripts to maintain their manuscript archives, so perhaps the writing was more carefully transmitted than would be the case for popular and widely circulating works like the poems attributed to Janabai. On the other hand, it is also possible that the story was written by a poet of a later historical floruit under the figural authorship—the signature—of Janabai. Or even that Janabai was always a figure of a later historical floruit than the one suggested by the hagiographical tradition. We may never find a satisfactory answer to this authorial conundrum, but we do have the texts to attest to a poet Janabai who wrote this story.

Janabai's *Thālīpāk* is cited as being in the oldest known manuscript source of *abhaṅgas*, the Dhule Manuscripts, with a colophon of 1631–1632.[82] This allows us to tentatively conclude that not only *Thālīpāk* but the *Hariścandra Ākhyāna* were composed before 1631. Whatever the exact date of composition, these texts put its purported author Janabai sometime in the sixteenth or seventeenth century, in a period we might call a Second Vernacular moment, distinct from the thirteenth and fourteenth century, but equally important. In some ways, Marathi vernacularization had an opposite trajectory to that of Kannada vernacularization. In Kannada literature, the second vernacular revolution saw the Virashaiva repudiation of royal influence, which brought oral aesthetics of the *vacana* into literary prominence; while in Marathi, this better describes vernacularization in its earliest phase with the Mahanubhavas's "counter-structure" of literarity. The second vernacular revolution in Marathi was more tied to spaces created by the imperial elevation of scribal communities, first by the sultanate rulers and then the Marathas. The growth of practices and genres of writing in Marathi in this period created the conditions for the textual blossoming of narrative poetry in the age of Eknath. Novetzke pinpoints this same period as the one that "produced the phenomenon of anamnetic authorship associated with Namdev."[83] This was not only because of the oral influence of *kīrtan* but also because of the increased focus on writing, which brought questions of authorship into crisis. If this period saw the proliferation of Namas, then it likely opened up the space for many Janis to write under the figural authorship of "Nama's Jani," though this does not mean that the Janabai who wrote the story of Harischandra was biographically attached to any one specific Nama.

With the possible exception of Janabai's story, the earliest, written version of the Harischandra story in Marathi is in fact Vishnudas Nama's *Hariścandrapurāṇakathā* (ca. 1580) which was translated into Portuguese sometime between 1610 and 1633 by Dom Francisco Garcia, a Jesuit who came to India in 1602.[84] This puts Vishnudas Nama's story within the same time frame as the colophon of the earliest possible record of Janabai's story, though this does little to give us a definitive answer as to which version came first. At least one scholar has suggested that Janabai was the disciple of this Vishnudas Nama, but the vast difference in the treatment of caste and gender in their respective stories suggests otherwise.[85] The name Vishnudas Nama was used by many poets, including purportedly the first Namdev, but there is fair certainty that the Vishnudas Nama who wrote the *Hariścandrapurāṇakathā* lived and wrote in the sixteenth century, and that he was primarily a narrative poet who also wrote a complete eighteen-chapter *Mahābhārata*.[86] Based on the writing style and content of these texts, it does not appear to be the case that he intended to write in the name of the original Namdev, at least not in the longer narrative poems, though there is every likelihood that some of his compositions are mixed into the corpus of Namdev poems.[87] Vishnudas Nama's version must have been fairly well-known in the sixteenth and seventeenth centuries for it to have made its way into the Jesuit archive, and it is certainly the case that Mukteshvar drew on this version, along with Janabai's version, for his own rendering of the poem a few decades later. There are startling, verbatim overlaps between the texts of Janabai, Vishnudas Nama, and Mukteshvar to an extent that, in modern times, would be seen as a serious case of plagiarism, but these textual overlaps show that the story took on its own vernacular identity. Writers turned to other Marathi texts, rather than to the Sanskrit versions, to write their stories.

Mukteshvar's *Hariścandrākhyāna* became the most well-known in Marathi literary history; it was included in the *Navanīt*, the first anthology of Marathi literature compiled for the classroom by Parshuram Godbole in the nineteenth century.[88] Mukteshvar has a highly ornate style that differentiates his telling from others, but it is clear that he relied heavily on Vishnudas Nama's and Janabai's texts, not only for episode order and plot but also for characterization, descriptive details, and metaphors.[89] These overlaps are quite significant, but we can also see the distinctions that highlight Janabai's compositional style on one end and Mukteshvar's on the other. Take, for example, an early scene of the story in which the sage Narada is shown in the court of the gods extolling the virtues of Harischandra. His speech pleases the sage Vasishta, who was Harischandra's guru, but it displeases Vasishta's rival, the sage Vishvamitra. Janabai's two verses on this are quite succinct:

> Listening to Narada's story (*goṣṭa*)
> Vasishta was happy (*sukhāvalā*)
>
> Vishvamitra got angry (*kopalā*)
> How they inflate that student![90]

Here Janabai's paratactic style is evident in the way Vishvamitra's words are tacked on without any transitions or introduction. The brevity in her narration and the compact verses recall the style of the grind mill *ovī*. In Vishnudas Nama's version, he opens with a much longer description of Narada's speech in the court of the gods, after which he adds:

> Then Vasishta was happy (*santośalā*)
> At that time Vishvamitra got angry (*kopalā*)
> Just like ghee poured into a fire.[91]

There is similarity in Janabai's verses and the first two lines of Vishnudas Nama's three-and-a-half line literary *ovī*, but in the hypotactic style of more elevated Marathi poetry, Vishnudas Nama adds a simile at the end, comparing Vishvamitra's anger to a fire into which ghee, like Narada's speech, has been poured. Mukteshvar takes this simile and further embellishes it, but his opening is a near duplication of Janabai's verse:

> Listening to Narada's story (*goṣṭī*)
> Vasishta was happy (*sukhāvalā*)
> Thundering in the court, he said in all of creation
> Harischandra has no comparison
>
> The wick of Narada's words
> Lit a fire of anger in the earthen pot of Vishvamitra's mind

On top of that, the ghee of Vasishta's words
Made the flames grasp the sky.[92]

Such embellishments are the mark of the elevated style. The first two lines are a verbatim copy of Janabai's, but the divergence between the compositional aesthetics are starkly evident, Janabai's paratactic brevity and Mukteshvar's hypotactic weaving and lengthening. Between the texts there is a sort of tug and pull between colloquialization and literarization. Nandapurkar, following a careful excavation of over thirty verbatim overlaps between Janabai's and Mukteshvar's *Hariścandrākhyāna*, concludes that "Mukteshvar's *Hariścandra Ākhyāna* is an improved and longer version of Janabai's *Ākhyāna*."[93] A. N. Deshpande's historical overview of Marathi literature concludes that "Mukteshvar was indebted to Janabai in his rendering of the *Hariścandra Ākhyāna*. For this story, the accomplished and elite poet Mukteshvar, a master of Sanskrit poetics, had to take the help of the simple but pure-hearted Janabai."[94] Deshpande further surmises that Janabai got the story from folk sources.

It is likely that oral versions of the story of Harischandra circulated widely throughout the region and influenced Janabai, but Janabai's story is also firmly situated in a textual nexus. Like Mahadaise's *Rukmiṇī-Svayaṃvar*, Janabai's storytelling style and aesthetics move between the written and the oral, but the text is very much a written work. One might say that Janabai puts the story through the grind mill of a women's oral tradition, only to bring the work to the written page in a more concentrated form. Her version is written in the *abhaṅga* and thus is quite distinct from the other two versions that are in the literary *ovī*. Though the *abhaṅga* is intended for song and performance, it has literary contours as I explained in chapter 4. She writes in the "small" *abhaṅga*, what Godbole calls the *devīvara abhaṅga*, a rhyming couplet of eight or nine syllables, which gives the narration a brisk pace, accentuated by her paratactical style of narration. This form favors concentrated lyrical intensity over extended narration. Unlike Mukteshvar and Vishnudas Nama, Janabai does not divide the story into long chapters (*prasaṅgas*). Rather, each episode is a concatenation of a dozen or more verses clasped at the end by Janabai's signature line, variously "Says Nama's *dāsī* Jani," or "Says Jani" or "Says Nama's *dāsī*." Whereas the author's name only appears at the end of long chapters in Mukteshvar's and Vishnudas Nama's versions, Janabai's authorial presence is pervasive throughout the text because of the brevity of her style and the *abhaṅga* form. The repeated authorial signature line pulls Janabai's story into the orbit of the literary and written, but it also pulls the figure of Janabai into the telling of the story.

Janabai the poet and storyteller thus becomes a figure within the poem, and in doing so, she makes her own story a part of the larger story told. If Mahadaise's story of Rukmini's wedding is an allegory of her own experience of being in the company of God incarnate, as the ending of her work suggests, then this story of Harischandra speaks to the exile, labor, suffering, oppression, enslavement, and *bhakti* that are central to the figuration of Janabai. This story depicts enslavement, understood clearly as the selling of humans into bondage and labor, when Harischandra, Taramati, and their child Rohidas stand in the market square in Varanasi to sell themselves in order to pay the debt of alms Harischandra has promised to Vishvamitra. The figuration of Janabai as *dāsī* brings special poignancy to her version that heightens the emotive experience of their ordeal. There is a notable affinity between the story of Janabai the *dāsī* and the experiences of Harischandra, Taramati, and even Rohidas the child as utterly destitute and dependent slaves at the mercy of their masters. In this work, we get a picture of the way that devotion and actual enslavement—*dasatva* in both senses of this term, as I discussed in the introduction—are conjoined and collapsed in the figure of Harischandra and his family, just as they are in the figure of Nama's *dāsī* Jani, a devotee and a slave/servant.

The enslavement and suffering of Harischandra and family are common themes taken up in the grind mill songs.[95] A popular *ovī* with dozens of variations in the song archive focuses on this exact scene:

People are put up for sale
Just beyond Kashi,
One buys Rohidas,
Another buys Taramati

kāśīcyā palīkaḍaṁ
manuṣyācī vikrī hotī
koṇī ghyā rohīdāsa
koṇī ghyā tārāmatī[96]

Notice that the second *ovī* focuses on Taramati and the child Rohidas, not Harischandra. There are also songs that take Harischandra to task for selling his wife and child. Harischandra and Taramati have to do domestic labor in the same way that Janabai is described doing domestic labor:

> King Harischandra
> And his Queen Taramati
> Carry water in the house of
> A cremation keeper in Kashi.
>
> *harīcandra rājā yācī*
> *tārāmatī rāṇī*
> *kāśī khaṇḍāmadhī*
> *vāhī ḍomyā gharī pāṇī*[97]

The juxtapositive parallelism between the first two lines, which emphasize the royal status of the characters, with the next two lines that emphasize their work as slaves to the cremation grounds keeper, himself at the lowest rungs of the caste hierarchy, captures concisely their loss of status. Yet this loss of wealth and social status is what elevates their moral status in the story.

Although there are significant verbatim overlaps in all the Marathi texts of this story, Janabai's story diverges in important ways in the depictions of enslavement, caste, and gender by aligning more with the grind mill songs' treatment of these themes. Vishnudas Nama's and Mukteshvar's versions of the story valorize the orthodox caste order, whereas Janabai's minimizes these aspects of the story.[98] There are numerous examples, but I mention two here. In one scene Harischandra is in the forest when two dancing girls are sent by Vishvamitra to seduce Harischandra. Both Vishnudas Nama and Mukteshvar include extended insults against these women for their lowly status as untouchables and prostitutes, whereas Janabai's text does not include offensive language against them.[99] In another episode of Vishnudas Nama's story, Taramati learns that her son Rohidas has been bitten and killed by a snake (really Vishvamitra in disguise) while she is serving dinner to Brahmins, but she continues serving the Brahmins and waits until they have burped their contentment before running to search for her son. She even asks her "master" for permission.[100] Janabai condenses this scene, the grind mill poetics evident in the editing. Taramati does not serve food to Brahmins in her story, and she drops everything the minute she gets the news and runs weeping to her son, putting the thematic emphasis on motherhood over caste duties.[101]

For Janabai, Taramati ultimately emerges as the central character, just as in Mahadaise's story the focus is on Rukmini. Although Harischandra and the child suffer, most of the scenes in Janabai's story dwell on Taramati's suffering. Taramati attempts *sati*, experiences the apparent death of her son twice, and is almost killed by the hand of her own husband because she is accused of being a child-eating witch. Much of the emotional weight of the story is created by Taramati's suffering at separation from her son. At end of the story, after they pass the brutal tests that Vishvamitra puts them through, it is Taramati who wins over the gods when she asks to be given a son like Rohidas, a husband like Harischandra, and a supplicant (*yācaka*) like Vishvamitra in every life.[102] Although this scene is in almost all Marathi versions, Janabai's text centralizes Taramati by omitting parts that highlight Harischandra's greatness, creating a dramatic poignancy to her words and experience. Taramati is thus brought forward as the embodiment of virtue in Janabai's telling. Whether Janabai's version was written before Vishnudas Nama's and Mukteshvar's or after, she exercises creative license in shaping the story through an aesthetics of reduction, removal, and editing—a grind mill poetics.

Far from being merely the audience of the vernacular turn, both Mahadaise and Janabai hew out their own responses to texts and stories as they retell them in the manner and style of the songs of the grind mill, with a concise focus that edits out all that does not contribute to the essential experience of the women characters. This is what countless unnamed women at the grind mill were already doing in their songs. This poetics of work involves sifting, editing, removing—like threshing, pounding, grinding—to recreate the story in its most concentrated, dramatic form. The vernacular innovation, the colloquial literary turn in the works of Mahadaise and Janabai lies in bringing a poetics of the grind mill into writing. Both Vishnudas Nama's and Mukteshvar's Harischandra stories include long descriptions of Harischandra's wealth and power, as well as discourses on what it means to be a good king, but these parts of the story are pared away by Janabai to highlight Taramati's emotional and physical experiences of loss, exile, enslavement, separation, and finally triumph. In the *Dhavaḷe* Mahadaise similarly pays little attention to the conflict between Krishna and Rukmini's brother, though Mhaimbhat does return to these characters and their ensuing war in his "Second Half." But Mahaidaise's own rendering of the *Rukmiṇī-Svayaṃvar* cuts out the war, as well as the long descriptions of palaces, armies, and gardens that we find, for example, in Narendra's version.

That a story centered on a woman, rather than on warring epic heroes, becomes the inaugural extant work of Marathi literature is a sign of the hand of women in the making of vernacular literature. Just as the grind mill songs narrate specific scenes and stories in discrete, concise, and independent verses, Mahadaise chooses to write a specific and discrete story, trimmed, like the songs of the grind mill, of all narrative details and poetic embellishments that detract from the intense and dramatic focus on Rukmini's desires and actions. Similarly, Janabai's editorial choices provide a counter-poetics of unraveling to the works of Vishnudas Nama and Mukteshvar, though it remains impossible to be certain about whether her text historically preceded theirs. Whether she was engaging the Marathi versions, Sanskrit versions, the Kannada version, the oral poetic and performative versions, or any versions before her own, it is clear that her telling concentrates the story so that a more intense version focused on the themes of *bhakti*, with Taramati as the central figure. An aesthetics of the unraveling heart shapes the way that Janabai reworks the story of Harischandra into the story of Taramati's trials and triumphs and in the way that Mahadaise narrates, in terse and succinct poetry, the story of Rukmini's longings and machinations to ensure that she marries the man of *her* choice, not her brother's or father's.

Although rarified literarity prefers the abundant hypotactic style of verse "garlands" and "necklaces," Mahadaise and Janabai bring a different aesthetics of brevity and lyrical intensity to literature. It is a poetics that values the unsaid, the empty spaces left in parataxis, the intimacy of dialogue in the lyrical utterance, felt as the unraveling heart. This is a founding poetics that travels through the underview of Marathi literarity for centuries, so that even poets of the highest rarified style, like Moropant, were occasionally pulled by it. Moropant wrote intricate, verbally complex poetry in quantitative meters, but he also composed shorter works influenced by the poetics of the grind mill for the daughters of his patron, such as *Songs on Rukmini's Abduction* (*Rukmiṇī Haraṇ Gīt*) and *Songs of Sita* (*Sitāgit*).[103] Admittedly, such works were the exception in Moropant's enormous corpus, but by the later nineteenth century, partly influenced by European Romanticism, there was a colloquial turn against the high style to more expressive and lyrical poetry. Kedar Kulkarni points out, for example, that the nineteenth-century intellectual Vishnu Krishna Chiplunkar (1850–1883) set forth a poetics of simplicity and "heart-melting" (*hṛdayadrāvak*) lyrical expression as far superior to the elaborate, technical proficiency of the high style. Kulkarni argues that it was not only European Romanticism that influenced Chiplunkar, but that Chiplunkar "re-gifted" the Sanskrit aesthetic heritage to the field of the literary, thus "refashioning romanticism with a concrete Sanskrit poetic nexus."[104] But perhaps the poetics of the grind mill was also an unacknowledged third interlocutor in these reconceptualizations, especially in the elevation of lyric poetry? What is "heart-melting" if not another way of describing the unraveling heart? This colloquial turn in the redefining of the literary set the stage for the twentieth-century acknowledgement of women's *ovīs*, to quote Sane Guruji again, as "a beautiful and refined literature" (*sundar abhijāt vāṅmay*).[105]

As figural authors, Mahadaise and Janabai represent, embody, and connect even us, who have only textual access to their works centuries later, to the poetic aspirations and oral poetics of the countless, unnamed women composers of the grind mill, the "absent and invisible" far from royal courts and Brahmin ecumenes. Mahadaise's presence as an interlocuter in the *līḷās*, her persistent questions captured by her identifying signature, "Mahadaise asked," and her textualized songs and poems show us that Marathi vernacularization developed—at its founding—in dialogue with the complex and abundant oral landscape of the everyday, especially with women's songs. Her figural presence as the female interlocutor of Chakradhar in the Mahanubhava texts anticipates the figural authorship of Janabai, even though it is Janabai, more known in Maharashtra, who leads us back to Mahadaise's contributions. Janabai, an important figure in the continually unfolding story of *bhakti* opens and widens the space of the literary, revealing the unexpected amalgamations of high and low, literate and oral, local and translocal, vernacular and cosmopolitan that went into the making of literature in Marathi. The two poets together illuminate why women were so prominently represented in the vernacular communities of *bhakti*, and what their contributions brought to the forging of the literary. It turns out that not only women but also the oral poetic tradition they created were "the strongest, most decisive spur" to the vernacular turn.

All this does not mean that we discount the specific affordances of writing or the great works of literature. The *Jñāneśvarī*, in particular, is an extraordinary literary achievement and needs far more attention as a literary, not just theological, work. The study of the massive corpus of poetry written by the Mahanubhavas also awaits further study. Yet Mahadaise and Janabai are the ones who make it clear that such literary works are embedded in, indeed reliant on, a vast poetic network, a conversation and exchange, not only with the rarified models of literarity but also with the poetics of the *jana*. What happens to literature in the hands of the vernacular *jana*, the "women, *śūdras*, and others," expelled from the literary arena by caste and gender exclusive regimes of writing? It is unraveled and remade and rewoven in songs, oral poetries, and also in written texts; this active making—poiesis—is at least as important to the literary as the passive consumption of a thing already made, the artifactual text, reified for the pleasure of a few. For those of us interested in the literary contributions of the "absent and the invisible," the underview reveals that "women, *śūdras*, and others" sang, wrote, rewrote, debated, retold, transformed, and contributed to the forging of the literary throughout its history. The underview shows us that the literary is most compelling when it is not an artifact, fixed and frozen in time, but is returned to the process of making, unmaking, and remaking, of weaving and unraveling—of literarization, rarification, standardization, yes, but followed inevitably by colloquialization. Without this turn to the colloquial, literature ceases to have relevance. The reason to take Janabai and Mahadaise seriously as literary "founders" is that they put us in contact with the vast underview of situated and embodied poetics of the grind mill at the very heart of one of the most elite endeavors in South Asian history: writing literature.

Postscript

Contra Conclusions

Indian literary historiography is like entering the mythical Naimisharanya [sacred forest]. In it any story will work, but no story will be the complete story. It will give rise to a thousand 'Once upon a time' but will not admit a definite conclusion. Every conclusion must stay perpetually tentative . . .

—G. N. DEVY, "*OF MANY HEROES": AN INDIAN ESSAY IN LITERARY HISTORIOGRAPHY*

In this vast forest
Who is speaking? Listen!
Sita has no one
But jujube and acacia tree-women

—SARU MAGAR, THE GRINDMILL SONGS PROJECT

I first heard the songs of the grind mill in the 1980s when my father sat down to record the songs of my grandmother and great aunts on a cassette player that he had brought with him from the United States to India. I remember thinking then that my grandmother did not have a particularly memorable singing voice, but I also remember how moved my father was as he listened. The women encouraged one another, reminding each other of this or that verse, but they also vied for singular attention, for adulation. My great aunt was the stronger singer. She was younger, wore fashionable, low-cut blouses, and had a charming lilt in her voice. She had opted to sing, not the grind mill songs, but film songs, including a famous lullaby from a Marathi film, one that was often on the radio in those years. She impressed my young self greatly, yet her songs were no more or less valued than the others by my father or by anyone else there. I learned later that melodies from film songs often made their way into the grind mill songs, which are ever open to engagement with the texts and songs and performances around them, and that the metrical patterns arising from the labor itself have receded, some melodies now lost forever. At the time of these recordings, I did not really know what grind mill songs were. My grandmother was not, after all, grinding while she sang for the recording. By the 1980s, all the flour for the household was ground weekly at the mill, the *giraṇī*, which happened to be next door to my grandparents' house. Its rhythmic clacking was a constant in the background of long afternoons I spent reading or playing cards with my cousins during summer vacations in India.

The songs were decontextualized then, wrapped in the integument of memory and nostalgia that was impenetrable to me at the time. Many years later, watching my father listen again to the cassette after my grandmother had passed away, I began to sense their enduring power. There was some power of communication in those songs to which I was not quite privy. The songs were not "musical" in ways that matched my expectations of music, and they seemed far away from any poetry I had ever encountered in the classroom. Their plaintive tunes and my grandmother's gravelly voice did not speak to me until I was able to decipher and comprehend the words better, to see for myself how they conjured the presentness of the past, how they put one into the shared time-space of song, how susceptible they made one to nostalgia, even when a connection to the conjured past was, at best, tenuous. Nostalgia is evident in Sane Guruji's adulation of the songs in the 1940s, and in Anand Yadav's memories of his mother's *ovīs* in the 1990s. I saw it in my father and then in myself.

I have had to continually remind myself that these songs come from grueling, backbreaking, and compulsory labor, often turned over by upper-caste and well-to-do women to those whose lives were circumscribed by unforgiving structures of caste oppression and patriarchy. While the hard labor of the grind mill was largely a thing of the past by the time I heard them, the songs lingered and dwelled in the present. "Lost paradises are the only true ones," Herbert Marcuse wrote of nostalgia, "not because, in retrospect, the past joy seems more beautiful than it was, but because remembrance alone provides the joy without the anxiety over its passing and thus gives it an otherwise impossible duration. Time loses its power when remembrance redeems the past." It is not the memory of unforgiving labor, the unbending systems of caste and gender, that linger as nostalgia, but a sense of enduring attachments, everyday intimacy, the freedom of and in song, the anticipation of being heard, the space of *svagata*, the joy and not the anxiety, and no hermeneutics of suspicion, in my view, should diminish these memories or dismiss them. Indeed, even the women whose songs I recorded often recalled their daily grinding with nostalgia, one deepened by genuine experiences of loss. One woman of the potter caste told me it was better than what she currently had to do. With the influx of plastic containers, the labors of the potters had declined. Now, she and her family worked mostly as day laborers in the fields of local, upper-caste farmers. But grinding in her own home for her own family, she said, was never that kind of labor. Loss is a leitmotif of the song tradition, so the songs speak anew to such changes and with contemporary relevance.

It was well after I began my research in 2006 and 2007 that I recalled the memory of my father with his cassette recorder and realized that what he had been doing then was what I set out to do more than thirty years later, after he had passed: record the songs before they too were lost. That sense of holding on to something on the precipice of loss, a sense that has persisted for over half a century among ethnographers, poets, and family members alike who recorded or transcribed verses, only heightens the effect of the songs. The fear of the end, of a conclusion, drives the effort at preservation. The times we are living in now have made ever clearer that there are, perhaps always but certainly now, ways of being on the brink of total extinction. Today soundscape artists are working to capture the very sounds of a natural world on the brink of extinction, and one hopes that we are not relegated to nostalgia about that.

This drive to preserve was something even Mahipati felt as his duty in the late eighteen hundreds when it came to the poetry of the *sants*. In the *Bhaktavijay*, the goddess Sarasvati counsels Vitthal to immediately write down Namdev's words, "as soon as they come out of the mouth," because "when he is asked to repeat them, they'll never come again."[1] Vitthal took the counsel to heart, Mahipati says. So he wrote more than 90 million verses for Namdev, and to these he added even more of his own poems to help Namdev fulfill his legendary vow to write one hundred million verses.[2] By adding his own verses to the mix, Vitthal—and thus Mahipati—seem to concede that they were not written by one individual alone. Many poets helped to fulfill Namdev's vow, including Tukaram, who claimed to have been given the task in a dream by Namdev himself. There is even a legendary belief that Janabai contributed her poems to fulfill Namdev's vow. Though the gods were urging to write and preserve, Mahipati also gives us a glimpse beyond the written archive to that ongoing dialogue-in-verse, that continual process of verse-making that is the underview of *bhakti*. Poetry is not only the poems already written. Poetry is always being made and always being written and rewritten. Today we have the *Nāmdev*

Gāthā, a "finished artifact," with an introduction and conclusion, and the making of *abhangas* in the name of Namdev seems to have receded, but even now it has not concluded.

Recently I shared an iPhone video of some grind mill songs of a woman named Shivakantabai Rawale, which I had recorded in 2020, with an aunt, one of my mother's friends, in the Chicago suburbs. Shivakantabai worked in the house of my maternal uncle, washing clothes and dishes. She had been abandoned many decades earlier by her husband because she could not have children and had been living alone since then, working as a domestic laborer to support herself. She was a rather prickly and dour figure, but in the songs her voice softened, her heart unraveled. She sang of Janabai's *sāsarvās*, her suffering, and I knew she was singing about herself. When I turned to my aunt after the video ended, I found her in tears. She had been taken back to the hardships she had faced with a difficult man for whom she had traveled, as a young bride, across the oceans; now, the songs of one unlettered domestic laborer from a village in Marathwada were unraveling the heart of a woman in Chicago. My aunt told me about her experiences after she gathered herself together, and sometime later she sent me a photo collage she had made. That experience of the song's unraveling had spurred a telling, a making, even in this distant land and time.

What was it about the grind mill that spurred—that still spurs even in the absence of its labor—such poiesis? This long enduring and remarkable song tradition continues to find openings of relevance and engagement even today, yet the practice of singing while working has all but disappeared, especially in the labors of the city, of the industrial and digital age. Song during work is now consumed passively, heard over the radio or through headphones. Songs are largely made by "professionals," not by the laborers, except perhaps in their off hours, during their "leisure time." "Parceled instead as the products of the culture industry," Paul Rekret notes, music has come to be "segregated to the evening and the weekend" as "leisure" came to be defined as a space outside of and opposed to "work."[3] The drive for speed and efficiency overdetermine the time and tempo of modern work, especially in the factory, as the din of machines overpowers human sounds.[4] The modern neighborhood *giraṇī*, where people in cities and villages throughout India take their grains to be freshly ground, is now deafening—no longer the rhythmic clacking I remember from my youth but a clamorous blast, leaving no aural space for listening to music let alone making it while at work. Increasingly, factory-processed flour, sold in supermarkets, is fast replacing even this neighborhood *giraṇī*.

Yet more than a half century after automated mills replaced the hand mill, grind mill songs continue to be sung in various forms and in numerous venues. Though the death knell for this song tradition has been sounding since the mid-twentieth century, we still find, well into third decade of the new millennium, women who know and sing these songs, whether in the fields as they work or at festivals and weddings. The Grindmill Songs Project is ongoing; even today songs continue to be recorded and digitized. I met young women in their thirties and forties during a research trip in 2023 who took pride in knowing the songs, though they learned them as an inheritance from the past. They do not compose songs anymore now that grinding itself is no longer necessary. Though the heavy, grounded stone mill was the generative site of this long-sustained old-growth tradition, the songs themselves circulate widely, as I hope this book has made evident, in the vast and interdependent network of orality and literature and languages—and they continue to circulate now through digital media, albeit in different form and for different purposes.

I am struck by how these songs have endured, how they continue to speak to ever newer generations though the dailiness and vitality of their compositional context is no more. The songs have had immense staying power, and thus have at least a modest claim, maybe a greater one, to that vaunted goal of textuality, permanence. They have achieved this—not through the artifactual, not through preservation in transcriptions and recordings, important as these contributions have been, but rather through the opposite—through their continual remaking, their ongoing unraveling and weaving, their countless and sometimes untraceable transformations. The similarities in expressive tropes, motifs, and poetic structures that we see between the first thirteenth-century transcriptions of *ovīs* in the texts of the Mahanubhavas and the songs collected more recently show us that there was a solid, structural continuity to this song tradition. It is, however, the changes and transformations in the tradition, the protean adaptability of the songs to different times and contexts and even tunes, that has made them perdure. I have drawn guidance from these songs to think about the literary in a different way than I had been trained to do, to unravel its fixed texts, the "Works," and return their literariness to the open space of making—to spaces outside the pantheon, the temple—where Vitthal and

Figure C.1 Janabai Thorat in 2023 listening to a recording of her songs from 2006. She was excited and happy to hear the songs again and began to mouth them, though she no longer had the capacity to sing.
Photo by author

Janabai, Chakradhar and Mahadaise liked to wander, the space where the underview can be felt and experienced.

In focusing on the underview, on the ongoing and continuous exchanges between texts and songs, I intend this book to unravel some knots in order to make visible the ways that orality and writing are interdependent parts of a living and ongoing poetic conversation. It is my hope that future scholars will find new points of entry to continue and expand, to debate and critique, to unravel and remake, everything presented here. There is much about Janabai, as there is about the literature and the song tradition I have discussed, that I did not address in this book with due justice, and I look forward to more scholarship on all of it. In following Janabai to the underview, I lost focus on much of the written poetry attributed to her. Similarly, there are many aspects of the grind mill song tradition—the regional specificity in the language(s) of the songs; the struggles against caste patriarchy in the songs of Dalit women; the changes in songs over time and history—that need further study and elaboration. I have deferred readings of the songs as hidden transcripts of resistance so that their abundant poetic qualities and resonance could be seen and taken seriously. There are, to be sure, clear signs of resistance to (as well as internalizations of) caste and gender ideologies in the songs, just as we find in all literary works, yet restricting our attention to these can lead to the kind of reductionism I have sought to avoid. I have attempted instead to sustain their aesthetic and affective possibilities as forms of lyric. Yet it's also true that the focus of the book on the early *bhakti* sects left little room for what Hema Rairkar identified as the diverse and secular "semantic classes" of the songs; my literary focus left much of the sociological insight, especially on caste and gender, in both the songs and the texts, unattended. One focus will leave out others, and so there is always a need for another unraveling, another weaving.

We have thought, too often and too long, about cultural production as a game of historical winners and losers, a Darwinian struggle for survival. The winners are those extant and preserved in texts, elevated into temples and pantheons, while the vast unknown many, the "absent and invisible," sink into apparent oblivion. The survivors of the "slaughterhouse of literature," are the leaves on Franco Moretti's analogical tree of literature, while the great many, the decaying remains of a great loss, a mass extinction, disappear from view.[5] The prevailing response to this attrition has been to excavate, one by one, the texts of the forgotten and disappeared, to add leaves to the tree through "projects of recovery," to count them and quantify their worth. This work of excavation has been important, bringing back into circulation many written texts of the "absent and the invisible," but it ignores that the leaves are one small element in a vast ecosystem to which the tree belongs, much of it out of view, below land.

There is a difference, G. N. Devy argues, between a literary history cultivated as a garden and one experienced as a forest. "It may be possible to name every tree and count every fruit and flower in a garden," he writes, "but when one is left in the nowhere of a forest without a beginning and without an end in sight, the numerals fail to assist counting and measuring."[6] This "nowhere of a forest" is where the exiled Sita sang her woes to the tree-women, according to the grind mill songs, the place where the songs of women get a hearing.

The truism is that one misses the forest for the tree by focusing on the singular rather than the many, or vice versa, but it turns out that the singular tree is connected to all other trees and species through the vast mycorrhizal network, dependent on the exchanges that run through it. Each tree contains the forest. In her fascinating book titled *The Mushroom at the End of the World: On the Possibility of Life in Capitalist Ruins*, Anna Lowenhaupt Tsing writes: "Below the forest floor, fungal bodies extend themselves in nets and skeins, binding roots and mineral soils, long before producing mushrooms. All books emerge from similarly hidden collaborations."[7] It is such collaboration, convergence, confluence that I have tried to highlight in this book. The leaves, the surviving texts, are only one part of a more complex and vast forest system of literary exchange, what I have called the underview.

Janabai was the one who nudged me to look deeper into the underview that made her poetry, like all poetry, possible. She has been a steadfast companion in this project—sometimes as motif, sometimes as guide, sometimes as poet. Yet I still feel as if she has not quite received the singular attention she deserves. I still find myself hankering for her, for some view—a *darśan*—of her as a living author, a historical poet. I still want to see her leaf on the tree, or better yet to see her as a tree. I still want the words attributed to her to have the weight of her bodily living, knowing full well that though she spoke in the singular, many contributed to her words. Perhaps this is nothing more than what I have been conditioned to want as a student of literature. Or perhaps the very idea of the author, the poet, is nothing more than a figure of this hankering for the person, the human, behind the writing that remembers her. The *bhakti* poets understood this need and placed themselves as figures within the poems, their signature lines adding the weight of their figural presence to the traveling poetic utterance that was enacted and reenacted through time. The lyric form maintains the deep cohabitation and intimacy of speaker and listener, poet and reader, within its structural features. As print technology created ever more distance between the writer and the written, the poet and the reader, the figure of the author grew in stature, in relevance, in the reader's imagination, obscuring the collaborations and convergences at work in the text, the text's interactions with the multiple forms of expressivity around it. The figure of the author became more necessary, as a stand in, for the continuity of dialogue in the Age of Print because we want to have conversations, not only with ideas and abstractions or texts, but also with other humans.

All of this is becoming clearer today, as the very act of writing itself has been automated, erasing even the fiction of the human author, realizing Roland Barthes's prescient declaration of the death of the author, so that there is no "writ*ing*." There is only "the written," a disembodied, artifact generated in an instant, scraped from all our past writing. Not even refined flour but fully baked bread without even the memory of grinding. This might seem like sympoiesis—but it isn't: it ends the dialogue; it presents "the written" as a product, a thing, an artifact; it abrogates our acts of making. Meanwhile we continue to hanker for the face and body, the sound and touch, the messy and imperfect human speaking, singing, and writing. The ability to fully catalogue and encompass all that has been written, said, felt, and thought in the manner of machine intelligence is not what characterizes our human acts, but rather the continuous making, the imperfections, the gaps, and the spaces that we leave for the Other to enter, illuminate, and remake. The tug-and-pull, the incompleteness of each utterance, drives poiesis and sympoiesis. This is the architectonics of the literary.

There has never been a better time to return the concept of the literary from its artifactual apotheosis as written text to the messy grounds of composition and re-composition, from reading and listening to making and remaking, from passive consumption to poiesis and sympoiesis. Poiesis has, of course, been ongoing in the interstices of the industrial and digital age. And forms of poetry—in writing, in song, in spoken word, on social media—continue to circulate widely. I recall a poem, author unknown, that a friend forwarded to me on WhatsApp on the occasion of an important holiday associated with the pilgrimage to Pandharpur. It was a poem about Rukmini and Vitthal, clearly drawing on grind mill songs about Rukmini sulking and upset about Vitthal's wandering attention and his preference for the company of his devotees over her. These were some of the first *ovīs* I remember hearing from Janabai Thorat, but this WhatsApp re-composition, whose origins I could not trace, raised a different point of conflict between Rukmini and Vitthal, the complaint of a modern housewife:

This is how it always is with him
Always his *bhaktas* and his *bhaktas*
What am I here for
Just to do the work?

This digital poem continues the retelling of the stories of Vitthal featuring the voice and perspective of Rukmini; an inheritance of the grind mill songs, but in a different register addressing different concerns. And so, the songs—in some form or another—continue, so ingrained are they in the poetic structures of Marathi, even in a medium so removed from the site of the stone mill.

Who knows whether our times will compel us not only to keep making but also to conceive and theorize more abundant and generous forms of the literary, this time without the petty hoardings, the gatekeeping, the crushing hierarchies? If the advent of capitalism spurred, as Raymond Williams noted, the shift from *poesy*, something that you compose, to *literature*, something that you consume/read, then perhaps our era of late capitalist endings, of ominous threats of extinction, is spurring another historical shift to poiesis and sympoiesis, new forms of worlding with rather than against, to ensure continuity, to defer endings, not only of the poems but of ourselves. The mark of a great work of art or literature or music is that it spurs its audience to make and create, or at least to want to do so. The same is true of works of philosophy, theology, and literary criticism—all the activities that constitute the superordinate sphere. Sometimes the great heights and feats of the expert, the genius, the virtuoso temporarily stun us into silence, compel us to concede the field, to sit back, to consume in admiration. But it is the spirit of my father's impromptu recording session that I return to, that scene where one song has the power to move others to sing, not to sit in admiring silence.

The mark of any great work of literature, philosophy, theology, or literary criticism is that it leads to *more* literature, philosophy, theology, and literary criticism, not that it rises above all efforts and ends the conversation. Any work, including the towering literary work, does not arrive "as the Biblical Adam," as Mikhail Bakhtin puts it; every work, even the purportedly first work, is always a response to an ongoing conversation that precedes and exceeds it. The conversation pushes against the constraints of time and geography, language and social location, and it is not bound to move in any one direction. My aunt, my father, and I entered into the songs, separated by time and geography, imperfectly prepared to receive them, and at a late hour of their history. Yet the songs spurred more making, including this book. I hope *The Unraveling Heart* also feeds the underview and keeps the dialogue of the grind mill turning.

Notes

Introduction and Underview

1. Women poets are the subject of a veritable book industry in Marathi but have not received the same attention in English-language scholarship. There are no English-language monographs on a woman poet of the Marathi *bhakti* tradition. Only one book in English features Janabai substantially: Guy Poitevin and Hema Rairkar, *Stonemill and Bhakti: From the Devotion of Peasant Women to the Philosophy of Swamis* (New Delhi: D. K. Printworld, 1996). A few important Marathi books on Janabai: R. C. Dhere *Nāmayācī Janī* (Pune: Vohra And Company Publishers, 1960); D. B. Bhingarkar, *Sant Kaviyitrī Janābāī: Caritra, Kāvya, Kāmagirī* (Mumbai: Majestic Publishers, 1981); and Suhasini Irlekar, *Sant Janābāī* (Mumbai: Marathi Literature and Culture Association, 2002). The Janabai Educational Foundation, based in her purported birthplace of Gangakhed, also put together an important book, *Sant Janābāī: Caritra va Kāvya* (Gangakhed: Diamond Publication, 2018). The first substantial English-language essay on Janabai was Rajeshwari Pandharipande, "Janabai: A Woman Saint of India," in *Women Saints in World Religions*, ed. Arvind Sharma (Albany: State University of New York Press, 2000), 145–180. See also Irina Glushkova, "Janabai and Gangakhed of Das Ganu: Towards Ethnic Unity and Religious Cohesion in a Time of Transition," in *The Indian Economic & Social History Review* 58, no. 4 (2021): 505–532; Glushkova has also written (in Russian) about the iconography of Janabai at the grind mill and its philosophical implications. I. Glushkova, "The Tool of

Domestic Labor in the Iconography of Janabai's Temples in Maharashtra," *Studia Religiosa Rossica: Russian Journal of Religion* (January 2023): 55-75. See also my own essay, M. Deshmukh, "Mothers and Daughters of *Bhakti*: Janābāī in Marathi Literature," *International Journal of Hindu Studies* 24 (2020): 33–59. For an important, comprehensive dissertation on women poets of the Varkari tradition, see Jacqueline Daukes, "Female Voices in the Vārkarī Sampradāya: Gender Constructions in a *Bhakti* Tradition," (PhD thesis, University of London, School of Oriental and African Studies, 2014).

2. H. D. Sankalia, Shantaram B. Deo, Zainuddin D. Ansari, and Sophie Ehrhardt, *From History to Pre-history at Nevasa (1954–1956)* (Pune: Deccan College Postgraduate Institute, 1960), 489.
3. For numerous references to the mortar and pestle in the Vedas and the Avesta, see Samuel Oliphant, "The Vedic Press Stones," in *Studies in Honor of Maurice Bloomfield*, ed. A Group of His Pupils (New Haven, CT: Yale University Press, 1920), 225–250.
4. Shakuntala Naiknaware, Village Savargaon (Beed District). "I Tell You Woman: Grind Mill Songs of Maharashtra," *The Grindmill Songs Project*, People's Archive of Rural India, https://ccrss.org/database/songs.php?song_id=44660 [Hereafter GSP].
5. See GSP, Semantic Class G:XX-2.19 (G20-02-19), "Daughter-in-law with mother-in-law / Changing times and ways of life," https://ccrss.org/database /songs.php?semantic_class_id=G20-02-19.
6. The foundational essay on this topic is John Stratton Hawley, "Author and Authority in the Bhakti Poetry of North India," *The Journal of Asian Studies* 47, no. 2 (May 1, 1988): 269–290; See also Christian Lee Novetzke, *Religion and Public Memory: A Cultural History of Saint Namdev in India* (New York: Columbia University Press, 2008), 135–139.
7. The 1277 inscription is quoted, partially translated, and analyzed in Christian Lee Novetzke, *The Quotidian Revolution: Vernacularization, Religion, and the Premodern Public Sphere in India* (New York: Columbia University Press, 2016), 96–100.
8. *Saṅgīta-Ratnākara of Śārṅgadeva: Sanskrit Text and English Translation with Comments and Notes, Chapters 2–4*, vol. 2, ed. and trans. R. K. Shringy under the supervision of Prem Lata Sharma (New Delhi: Munshiram Manoharlal, 1989), 4.306.
9. Gregory Nagy, "Genre, Occasion, and Choral Mimesis Revisited, with Special Reference to the 'Newest Sappho,'" in *Genre in Archaic and Classical Greek Poetry: Theories and Models*, Studies in Archaic and Classical Greek Song, vol. 4, ed. Margaret Foster, Leslie Kurke, Naomi Weiss (Boston: Brill, 2019), 32.
10. Novetzke, *Quotidian Revolution*, 291.

11. See entries for *dāsa* and *dāsī*, including all the variations between, in M. Monier-Williams, *A Sanskrit English Dictionary* (Springfield, VA: Natraj Books, 2015), 477. For feminist discussions of the disappeared figure of the *dāsī* in Indian historiography, see Uma Chakravarti, "Whatever Happened to the Vedic Dasi? Orientalism, Nationalism, and a Script for the Past," in *Recasting Women: Essays in Colonial History*, ed. Kumkum Sangari and Suresh Vaid (New Brunswick, NJ: Rutgers University Press, 1990), 27–87. See also Anjali Arondekar, "What More Remains: Slavery, Sexuality, South Asia," in *History of the Present* 6, no. 2 (2016): 146–154. For an effort to excavate evidence of slavery in the texts of ancient India, see Sharad Patil, *Dāsa-Śūdra Slavery: Studies in the Origins of Indian Slavery and Feudalism and Their Philosophies*, 2 vols. (New Delhi: Allied Publishers, 1978).
12. Sumit Guha, "Slavery, Society, and the State in Western India, 1700–1800," in *Slavery and South Asian History*, ed. Indrani Chatterjee and Richard M. Eaton (Bloomington: Indiana University Press, 2006), 164. According to Guha, "the *Rajavyavahārakośa*, a Sanskrit lexicon compiled under the patronage of the first Chatrapati Shivaji in 1676, gave *dasa* (a masculine noun) as the classical equivalent of both *banda* and *ghulam*" (164).
13. Guha, "Slavery, Society, and the State in Western India," 165.
14. Richard Eaton, introduction to *Slavery and South Asian History*, ed. Indrani Chatterjee and Richard M. Eaton (Bloomington: Indiana University Press, 2006), 2–3; Indrani Chatterjee, "Renewed and Connected Histories: Slavery and the Historiography of South Asia," in *Slavery and South Asian History*, 19–20. See also Gwyn Campbell, "Slavery and Other Forms of Unfree Labour in the Indian Ocean World," in *Structure of Slavery in Indian Ocean Africa and Asia*, ed. Gwyn Campbell (London: Frank Cass, 2004), xxii.
15. See, for example, the use of the of the word *gulāmgirī* in poem 34 and poem 37 in Savitribai Phule, *Sāvitrībāī Phule Samagra Vāṅmaya*, ed. M. G. Mali (Mumbai: Government of Maharashtra, 2011), 24–25; 27–28. I thank Christian Novetzke for pointing out these poems to me. See Jotirao Phule, *Slavery*, trans. P. G. Patil, in *Collected Works of Jotirao Phule, Vol. 1* (Bombay: Government of Maharashtra Education Department, 1990).
16. Shailaja Paik, *The Vulgarity of Caste: Dalit, Sexuality, and Humanity in Modern India* (Stanford, CA: Stanford University Press, 2022), 7.
17. Eaton, Introduction to *Slavery and South Asian History*, 2.
18. Chatterjee, "Renewed and Connected Histories," 28–29.
19. Houston A. Baker, *Blues, Ideology, and Afro-American Literature: A Vernacular Theory* (Chicago: University of Chicago Press, 1987), 2.
20. Baker, *Blues, Ideology*, 2.
21. Du Bois was the first to call Black spirituals the "sorrow songs" and give them serious literary attention in *The Souls of Black Folk* (New York: Dover,

1994 [1903]), 155–164. On the songs of the enslaved as an influential lyric tradition, see Lauri Ramey, *Slave Songs and the Birth of African American Poetry* (New York: Palgrave MacMillan, 2008), and Ramey, *History of African-American Poetry* (New York: Cambridge University Press, 2021). On the influence of Black vernacularity on Twain and American literature, see Shelley Fisher Fishkin, *Was Huck Black? Mark Twain and African-American Voices* (New York: Oxford University Press, 1994); There is a great abundance of scholarship on the intersections of the oral tradition and Black literature, but for starters see: Gayl Jones, *Liberating Voices: Oral Tradition in African-American Literature* (Cambridge, MA: Harvard University Press, 1991) and Henry Louis Gates, *Signifying Monkey: A Theory of African-American Literary Criticism* (New York: Oxford University Press, 1988).

22. Sheldon Pollock, "Literary History, Indian History, World History," *Social Scientist* 23, no. 10/12 (October–December 1995), 121.
23. See Anjali Arondekar, *Abundance: Sexuality's History* (Durham, NC: Duke University Press, 2023).
24. See Poitevin and Rairkar, *Stonemill and Bhakti*, 260: "The most essential, permanent . . . dichotomy is to be placed . . . between the oral nature of people's tradition and the elaborate writings of scholars. . . . The dichotomy of oral and written is . . . hidden behind the second dichotomy of the feminine and masculine."
25. For an essential study on women's songs on Sita, see Tara Bhavalkar, *Sītāyan: Vedanā-Vidrohāce Rasāyan* (Pune: Manovikas Publishers, 2023). See also the chapter on the Sita songs in Guy Poitevin, *The Voice and the Will: Subaltern Agency: Forms and Motives* (New Delhi: Manohar, 2002), 46–103.
26. The most comprehensive study to date of the deity Vitthal is R. C. Dhere, *Śrīviṭṭhal: Ek Māhāsamanvaya* (Pune: Padmagandha Publishers, 2004). For the meticulous translation by Anne Feldhaus, see R. C. Dhere, *The Rise of a Folk God: Viṭṭhal of Pandharpur,* trans. Anne Feldhaus (New York: Oxford University Press, 2011).
27. For a collection of contemporary Mahanubhava grind mill songs, see Mangala P. Pathade, *Sarvajña Srīcakradharaviṣayak Saṅkalit Ovīgītāñcā Ābhyās* (MPhil thesis, Babasaheb Ambedkar Marathwada University, 2014), 75–100.
28. Linda Hess, *Bodies of Song: Kabir Oral Traditions and Performative Worlds in North India* (New York: Oxford University Press, 2015), 4.
29. Pollock's foundational paradigm of vernacularization centers the royal court. See Sheldon Pollock, *Language of the Gods in the World of Men: Sanskrit, Culture, and Power in Premodern India* (Berkeley: University of California Press, 2006). Novetzke posits a Brahmin ecumene, patronized by the Yadavas, as central to Marathi vernacularization, but he argues that the first writers, though Brahmins, worked against it to bring literacy into the public space of

the everyday. See Novetzke, *Quotidian Revolution*, 66–73; additional parenthetical page numbers in this paragraph cite Novetzke, *Quotidian Revolution*.

30. Hess, *Bodies of Song*, 17, 94; Shantanu Phukan, "'Through Throats Where Many Rivers Meet:' The Ecology of Hindi in the World of Persian," *Indian Economic and Social History Review* 38, no. 1 (2001): 37. For an extended discussion of ecological literary analogies, see also, Alexander Beecroft, *An Ecology of World Literature: From Antiquity to the Present Day* (London: Verso, 2015), 17–28.
31. I am drawing on this term as used in Kirin Narayan, *Everyday Creativity* (Chicago: University of Chicago Press, 2012), 28–31.
32. Smita Tewari Jassal, *Unearthing Gender: Folksongs of North India* (Durham, NC: Duke University Press, 2012), 38–40.
33. Mary Fuller, "Marathi Grinding Songs," *The New Review* 11 (June 1940): 385. Also quoted in Poitevin, *The Voice and the Will*, 52.
34. Common motifs, scenes, images, expressions, and so on can be found in women's songs on Sita across languages. On North Indian grind mill songs on Sita, see the chapter on "Sita's Trials" in Jassal, *Unearthing Gender*, 155–188. See also, Usha Nilsson, "Grinding Millet but Singing of Sita: Power and Domination in Awadhi and Bhojpuri Women's Songs" in *Questioning Ramayanas: A South Asian Tradition*, ed. Paula Richman (Berkeley: University of California Press, 2001), 137–158. See also Meenakshi Faith Paul, "Sita in Pahari Lok Ramain," in In *Search of Sita: Revisiting Mythology*, ed. Malashri Lal and Namita Gokhale (New Delhi: Penguin, 2009), 147–154. On the South Indian Sita songs, see Velcheru Narayan Rao, "A *Rāmāyaṇa* of Their Own: Women's Oral Tradition in Telugu," in *Many Rāmāyaṇas: The Diversity of a Narrative Tradition in South Asia*, ed. Paul Richman (Berkeley: University of California Press, 1991), 89–113. Also, A. K. Ramanujan, "Two Realms of Kannada Folklore," in *The Collected Essays of A. K. Ramanujan*, ed. Vinay Dharwadkar (New Delhi: Oxford University Press, 2004), 504–505.
35. Poitevin, *The Voice and the Will*, 52
36. Poitevin, *The Voice and the Will*, 61.
37. Richard Bauman and Charles L. Briggs, "Poetics and Performance as Critical Perspectives on Language and Social Life," *Annual Review of Anthropology* 19 (1990): 73.
38. Prabhakar Mande, *Lokagāyakāñcī Paramparā* (Aurangabad: Godavari Publishers, 2011), 228. See also R. C. Dhere, "Sāne Gurujīñce *Strījīvan*," in *Lokasāhitya: Śodh āṇi Samīkṣā* (Padmagandha Publishers, 2014), 136.
39. Mande, *Lokagāyakāñcī Paraṃparā*, 254.
40. See Anne Feldhaus, "Gender and Women in the *Ovīs*," in *Say to the Sun, "Don't Rise," and to the Moon, "Don't Set:" Two Oral Narratives from the Countryside of Maharashtra*, ed. and trans. Anne Feldhaus with Ramdas Atkar and Rajaram Zagade (New York: Oxford University Press, 2014), 108–126.

41. Joyce Burkhalter Flueckiger, *When the World Becomes Female: Guises of a South Indian Goddess* (Bloomington: Indiana University Press, 2013), 21.
42. Richard Eaton, *Sufis of Bijapur, 1300–1700: Social Roles of Sufis in Medieval India* (New Delhi: Munshiram Manoharlal, 2011), 159.
43. Eaton, *Sufis of Bijapur,* 158n56. Eaton spells the term without diacritical marks.
44. I recorded a wedding *cakkī* song sung in Urdu/Dakani by a woman named Hamarbi Sheikh Musa from the village Shirad Shahapur in January 2023. She told me her mother knew many *cakkī* songs, though most women no longer sing them. There are about nine Urdu/Dakani verses by one Muslim woman, Amina Sheikh, in the Grindmill Songs Project archive. See GSP, "Songs by Sheikh Amina," Village Bachoti (Nanded District), https://ccrss.org/database/songs.php?performer_id=763. I thank Pramod Mandade for bringing at least one source on Muslim women's songs to my attention. See Kunta N. Jagdale, *Marāṭhī-Muslim Ovyā (Jātyāvarcyā): Tulanātmak Abhās* (Barshi, Maharashtra: Narayan Jagdale, 2004). Jagdale unfortunately contrasts the terms "Marathi" and "Muslim" in this title, though there are Marathi-speaking Muslim communities in Maharashtra, and very likely some Muslim women composed songs in Marathi as well as Urdu. I have not, however, come across any collection of Marathi songs by Muslim women. This is an area in need of further research.
45. Eaton, *Sufis of Bijapur,* 163–164.
46. Shemeem Burney Abbas, *The Female Voice in Sufi Ritual* (Austin: University of Texas Press, 2002), xx; see also Carla Petievich, *When Men Speak as Women: Vocal Masquerade in Indo-Muslim Poetry* (New Delhi: Oxford University Press, 2007).
47. Eleanor Zelliot, "Women Saints in Medieval Maharashtra," in *Faces of the Feminine*, ed. Mandakranta Bose (New York: Oxford University Press, 2000), 192. See also Daukes, "Female Voices in the Vārkarī Sampradāya," 16.
48. See Justin E. Abbott, trans., *Bahiṇā Bāī: A Translation of Her Autobiography and Verses* (New Delhi: Motilal Banarsidass, 1998 [1929]), 43–44, poem 75; in Marathi, see 216–217, poem 75.
49. Virginia Woolf, *A Room of One's Own* (New York: Harcourt Brace, 1981 [1929]), 93; on Judith Shakespeare, 46–49.
50. Abbott, "Introduction," in *Bahiṇā Bāī: A Translation of Her Autobiography and Verses*, x.
51. Raymond Williams, *Marxism and Literature* (New York: Oxford University Press, 1977), 47. Pages are given in parentheses to cite the remaining quotes in the paragraph.
52. Lydia Goehr, *The Imaginary Museum of Musical Works* (Oxford: Oxford University Press, 1992), 148–149.

53. Goehr, *The Imaginary Museum*, 150. Parenthetical page numbers in the following paragraph cite this work.

54. Pollock, "Literary History, Indian History, World History," 124.

55. Pollock, *Language of the Gods*, 2–5.

56. *Jñāneśvarī* of Jnaneshvar, ed. and with gloss by S. V. Dandekar (Pune: Svānand Publishers, 1976), 18:345.

57. S. G. Tulpule and Anne Feldhaus, *A Dictionary of Old Marathi* (New York: Oxford University Press, 2000), 139.

58. Novetzke, *Quotidian Revolution*, 105. The phrase "women, *śudras*, and others" [*strīśudrādī*] appears in the *Jñāneśvarī* when Jnaneshvar extols the accessibility of the Bhagavad Gītā, which brings the teachings of the Vedas to "women, *śudras*, and others," something that he aspires to in his own vernacular rendering. It is not clear whether Jnaneshvar intended to include Dalit castes in "others" here. See *Jñāneśvarī* of Jnaneshvar, ed. and with gloss by S. V. Dandekar (Pune: Svanand Publishers, 1976), 18.1458; 18.1699. Novetzke writes, "In relation to the Bhagavad Gītā, Jnanadev will declare that the text was explicitly composed for women, low castes and others, yet it could not reach this audience until it was retold in a regional language" (15). I am arguing that women, *śudras*, and others were not only the intended audience of the vernacular text but also contributors to its making.

59. R. C. Dhere, *Sant, Loka aṇī Abhijan (*Pune: Padmagandha Publishers, 2005 [1998]), 18–19.

60. This point was made by Albert Lord. See Albert Lord, *The Singer of Tales*, ed. Stephen Mitchell and Gregory Nagy (Cambridge, MA: Harvard University Press, 2000), 6.

61. Pratima Ingole, *Varhāḍī Lokagītañcā Cikitsak Abhyās* (Pune: Sonal Publishers, 2013), 13–14.

62. *Māṇasollāsa* of Someśvara, vol. 3, ed. G. K. Shrigondekar (Baroda: Oriental Institute, 1961), 4.550.

63. Durga Bhagwat, *Lokasāhityācī Rūparekhā* (Pune: Varada Books, 2017 [1956]), 426–441, 441–454. Mande has three categories, folksongs (*lokagīte*), narrative folksongs or ballads (*lokakathāgīte*), and popular songs (*laukikagīte*). See Prabhakar Mande, *Lokasāhityāce Svarūp* (Aurangabad: Godavari Publishers, 2017), 221, 257, 287.

64. Kedar Kulkarni argues that the *laukiktā* or worldliness of the oral performative genre of *śāhirī poetry* served as paradigm for the reconceptualization of literature by the nineteenth-century intellectual and essayist V. K. Chiplunkar. See Kedar Kulkarni, *World Literature and the Question of Genre in Colonial India: Poetry, Drama and Print Culture, 1790–1890* (New Delhi: Bloomsbury, 2022), 44 45.

65. My approach is greatly influenced by the scholarship R. C. Dhere, who situates his analyses of texts and culture within a larger intertext of *loka* (folk) and *abhijan* (elite) traditions. See, especially, Dhere, *Sant, Lok aṇī Abhijan*. For a similar effort in the field of Sanskrit literature, see also Adheesh Sathaye, "The Scribal Life of Folktales in Medieval India," *South Asian History and Culture* 8, no. 4 (2017): 430–447. For important essays on the relationship of performance and textuality in South Asia, see Francesca Orsini and Katherine Butler Schofield, *Tellings and Texts: Music, Literature and Performance in North India* (Open Book Publishers, 2015); Joyce Flueckiger and Laurie Sears, eds., *Boundaries of the Text: Epic Performances in South and Southeast Asia* (Ann Arbor: University of Michigan Press, 2020), especially Wendy Doniger's essay, "Fluid and Fixed Texts," 31–42; Ludo Rocher, "Orality and Textuality in the Indian Context," *Sino-Platonic Papers* 49, no. 1 (1994): 1–28. On *bhakti* orality and writing in Maharashtra, see Novetzke, *Religion and Public Memory*. An essential study of *kīrtan* is Anna Schultz, *Singing a Hindu Nation: Marathi Devotional Performance and Nationalism* (New York: Oxford University Press, 2013). On keeping oral and written in dialogue see Hess, *Bodies of Song*.
66. The word *vāṅmaya* curiously does not appear in Feldhaus and Tulpule's *A Dictionary of Old Marathi*, nor in the Molesworth dictionary. Jnaneshvar more often uses *sāhitya* and *kavitva* to mean something approximating what we would call literature. For a useful overview of the subtle distinctions between *vāṅmaya* and *sāhitya* in Marathi, see Kulkarni, *World Literature*, 45–48.
67. H. C. Bhayani, "The Rise of Apabhraṁśa as a Literary Language," in *Indological Studies: Literary and Performing Arts, Prakrit and Apabhraṁśa Studies, vol. 2* (Ahmedabad, Parshva Publications, 1993), 26. Kedar Kulkarni makes this same point about literature before the advent of the printing press. See Kulkarni, *World Literature*, 6.
68. Paul Zumthor, *Oral Poetry: An Introduction*, trans. Kathryn Murphy-Judy (Minneapolis: University of Minnesota Press, 1990), 4.
69. See Kirin Narayan, "The Practice of Oral Literary Criticism: Women's Songs in Kangra, India," *The Journal of American Folklore* 108, no. 429 (1995): 243–264. See also Alan Dundes, "Metafolklore and Oral Literary Criticism," *The Monist* 50, no. 4 (1966): 505–516.
70. H. C. Bhayani, *Apabraṁśa Language and Literature: A Short Introduction* (Delhi: B. L. Institute of Indology, 1989), 9–10.
71. See Suzanne Simard et al., "Net Transfer of Carbon between Ectomycorrhizal Tree Species in the Field," *Nature* 388, no. 6642 (1997). See also Suzanne Simard, *Finding the Mother Tree* (New York: Knopf, 2021), 160–161.
72. Simard, *Finding the Mother Tree*, 161.

73. Franco Moretti, "The Slaughterhouse of Literature," *MLQ: Modern Language Quarterly* 61, no. 1 (March 2000): 207–227. Moretti's discussion of the tree as a model for literary history isolates the tree, draws from Darwin, and emphasizes divergence over convergence. See Franco Moretti, *Graphs, Maps, Trees: Abstract Models for Literary History* (London: Verso, 2005), 67–92.
74. Wendy Doniger, "Fluid and Fixed Texts," in *Boundaries of the Text: Epic Performances in South and Southeast Asia*, ed. Joyce Flueckiger and Laurie Sears (Ann Arbor: University of Michigan Press, 2020), 39.
75. A. K. Ramanujan, "Three Hundred *Rāmāyaṇas*: Five Examples and Three Thoughts on Translation," in *Many Rāmāyaṇas: The Diversity of a Narrative Tradition in South Asia*, ed. Paul Richman (Berkeley: University of California Press, 1991), 46–48.
76. M. M. Bakhtin, "The Problem of Speech Genres," in *Speech Genres and Other Late Essays* (Austin: University of Texas Press, 2002), 66.
77. Saru Magar, Village Kumbheri (Pune District), GSP, https://ccrss.org/database/songs.php?song_id=1033. For more than a hundred verse variations of songs on Sita crying in the forest, see GSP, Semantic Class A:I-1.10aii (A01-01-10a02), "Sītā / The forest exile, vanavās, of Sītā / Sītā feels forsaken, lonely, helpless / Help of Jujube tree, Acasia Arabica tree," https://ccrss.org/database/songs.php?group_label=Sita_weeping_in_forest.
78. Phukan, "'Through Throats Where Many Rivers Meet,'" 37. My emphasis.
79. Donna Haraway, *Staying with the Trouble: Making Kin in the Chthulucene* (Durham, NC: Duke University Press, 2016), 58.

1. The Unraveling Heart

1. Anand Yadav, *Nāṅgarṇī* [*Ploughing*] (Pune: Mehta Publishing House, 2017), 262–265, my translation; also quoted in Guy Poitevin, *The Voice and the Will: Subaltern Agency: Forms and Motives* (New Delhi: Manohar, 2002), 50–51.
2. Yadav, *Nāṅgarṇī* [*Ploughing*], 263.
3. Yadav, *Nāṅgarṇī* [*Ploughing*], 265.
4. GSP, Semantic Class D:X-2.7a (D10-02-07a)—"Mother worries for son / Son migrates to Mumbai / Employed in a cotton mill," https://ccrss.org/database/songs.php?semantic_class_title_prefix_id=D10-02-07a.
5. R. C. Dhere, "Sāne Gurujiñce *Strījīvan*," in *Lokasāhitya: Śodh āṇi Samīkṣā* (Padmagandha Publishers, 2014), 137. For references to women's labor songs, including songs of pounding in Tamil poetry going as far back as the first through the sixth centuries, see Vijaya Ramaswamy, "Aspects of Women and

Work in Early South India," *The Indian Economic and Social History Review* 26, no. 1 (1989): 81–99.

6. Thanks to Andrew Ollett for explaining this verse and its context. Andrew Ollett, email to author, July 24, 2022.
7. *Brihat Kalpasutra and Original Niryukti of Sthavir Arya Bhadrabahu Swami and A Bhashya by Shri Sanghadas Gani Kshamashramana thereon with a Commentary Begun by Acharya Malayagiri and Completed by Acharya Shri Kshemakirti*, vol. 3, ed. Guru Shri Chaturvijaya and Punyavijaya (Bhavnagar, Gujarat: Shri Atmanand Jain Sabha, 1992), 747, *gāthā* 2663. I am grateful for Andrew Ollett's help in translating this verse. Any errors are my own.
8. Andrew Ollett, email to author, July 24, 2022.
9. Peter Khoroche and Herman Tieken, trans., *Hāla's Sattasaī (Gāthā Saptaśatī in Prakrit), Life and Love in Ancient India* (Delhi: Motilal Banarsidass, 2014), see poem 39 (Weber 626), 25.
10. A. K. Warder, for example, speculated on the origins of these "pastoral" poems in "folksongs" of the Godavari River Valley. See A. K. Warder, *Kāvya Literature: The Origin and Formation of Classical Kāvya*, vol. 2 (Delhi: Motilal Banarsidass, 1990 [1974]), 182. See also Julie Chiarucci, "Kavva and Kāvya: Hāla's Gāhākosa and Its Sanskrit Successors" (PhD diss., University of California, Berkeley, 2014), 219.
11. *Jñāneśvarī* of Jnaneshvar, ed. and with gloss by S. V. Dandekar (Pune: Svanand Publishers, 1976), 16.334.
12. The first published book of women's *ovīs* appears to be a collection put together, and at least partially composed, by Parvati Gokhale. These are not transcriptions, but poems that women *should* sing, according to the author. See Parvati Gokhale, *Strīgītaratnākar athavā Ābāḷavṛddha Strīyānī Mhaṇaṇyās va Aikṇyās yogya aśī Devādikāñcī Vagaire aśī Gāṇī* (Pune, 1915).
13. Sane Guruji, *Strījīvan* (Pune: Indrayani Sahitya Publishers, 1998 [1940]). There were several important publications on grind mill songs in the 1930s and 1940s. See, for example, Dattatreya Balkrishna Kalelkar and Vamana Krishna Chorghade, *Sāhityācem̥ Mūladhana* (Mumbai: Karnataka Publishing House, 1938); P. S. Gore, *Varhāḍī Lokagite* (Amravati: Seva Publishers, 1940); A. R. Bhagwat, "Maharashtrian Folksongs on the Grind Mill," *Journal of the University of Bombay* 10 (July 1941): 134–186; and "Maharashtrian Folksongs on the Grind Mill, Part II," *Journal of the University of Bombay* 10 (January 1942): 137–174; Kamalabai Deshpande, *Apaurūṣeya Vāṅmaya Arthāt Strīgītem̥* (Pune: Manohar Granthamala Publishers, 1948).
14. Sane Guruji, *Strījīvan*, 3.
15. Deshpande, Apaurūṣeya *Vaṅmaya*, 3.
16. The Maharashtra Government Council on Folk Literature inaugurated a series called the *Mahārāṣṭra Lokasāhitya Mālā* (Maharashtra Folk Literature

Series) in 1956 focused on publishing research on and transcriptions of oral traditions of diverse regional, tribal, and caste communities in Maharashtra. On women's songs, see especially, Sarojini Babar, *Mahārāṣṭra Lokasāhitya Mālā* 2 (Pune: Maharashtra Government Council on Folk Literature, 1957); *Mahārāṣṭra Lokasāhitya Mālā* 3 (Pune: Maharashtra Government Council on Folk Literature, 1959); *Jā Mājhyā Māherā*, *Mahārāṣṭra Rājya Lokasāhitya Mālā* 8, (Pune: Maharashtra Government Council on Folk Literature, 1963); *Striyāmñce Kheḷa āṇi Gāṇī* (Pune: Maharashtra Government Council on Folk Literature, 1977). See also Sarojini Babar, *Folk Literature of Maharashtra* (New Delhi: Maharashtra Information Center, 1968).

17. Studies and collections of grind mill songs, especially ones that focus on regions of Maharashtra that have unique linguistic characteristics, are far too copious to name here, but there are a few foundational ones important to mention. On songs from Marathwada, see, N. G. Nandapurker, *Marāṭhīcā Mohor* (Hyderabad: Jayahind Printing Press, 1953); on songs from Vidarbha, see Vimala Chorghade, "*Mahāvidharbātīl Lokagītāñcem Saṅgīt*" (Pune: Manohar Granthamala Publishers, 1987); on Khandesh, see Krisha Patil, *Ahirāṇī Bolīcyā Itīhāsāsaha: Nātī Gotī*, vol. 2 (Mumbai: Maharashtra Rajya Sahitya ani Sanskriti Mandal, 1990).
18. P. K. Atre, "Preface," in Bahinabai Chaudhari, *Bahiṇāīcī Gāṇī* [Songs of Bahinabai], 1st edition, ed. Sopan Dev (Mumbai: Popular Publishers, 1978 [1952]), 17.
19. See Sheldon Pollock, "Introduction: An Intellectual History of Rasa," in *A Rasa Reader: Classical Indian Aesthetics*, trans. and ed. Sheldon Pollock (New York: Columbia University Press, 2016), 1–14.
20. See Bahinabai Chaudhari, *Bahiṇāīcī Gāṇī* [Songs of Bahinabai], 1st edition, ed. Sopan Dev (Mumbai: Popular Publishers, 1978 [1952]), 19. For the whole poem, see 17–19. For an insightful discussion of this poem see also Rohini Shukla, "Authorship and Generative Embodiment in Bahiṇāī's Songs," in *Transnational Literature* 10, no. 2 (May 2018): 10–11.
21. In my observations, *jāta* is the more common word for grind mill across caste and region. *Gharoṭā* appears to be a derivation of the Sanskrit and Prakrit word for grind mill, *gharaṭṭa*, and is not included in most Marathi dictionaries, nor have I been able to attest to its use in other songs collected in the Khandesh region. It is possible that Sopan Dev changed the more common address to the grind mill, "*jatyā iśvarā*," for a more literary expression, but it is also possible that the word was in use in a local dialect.
22. Indira Sant, comp., *Mālanagāthā*, vols. 1–2 (Pune: Mehta Publishing House, 2013 [1993]).
23. Sant, *Mālanagāthā*, 1:15.
24. Sant, *Mālanagāthā*, 1:4.

25. Sant, *Mālanagāthā*, 1:4–5.
26. For a rethinking of the literary from the vantage point of ordinary language philosophy, see Mary Louise Pratt, *Toward a Speech Act Theory of Literary Discourse* (Bloomington: Indiana University Press, 1977). See also *Toril Moi, Revolution of the Ordinary: Literary Theory After Wittgenstein, Austin, and Cavell.* (Chicago: University of Chicago Press, 2017). These theories rarely take oral poetic forms into account, thus remaining within the binary between ordinary and literary language that they seek to implode.
27. Pratt, *Toward a Speech Act Theory*, 5–6.
28. Barry Sandywell, "The Myth of Everyday Life: Toward a Heterology of the Ordinary," *Cultural Studies* 18, no. 2–3 (January 1, 2004): 160–180.
29. Guy Poitevin and Hema Rairkar, *Stonemill and Bhakti: From the Devotion of Peasant Women to the Philosophy of Swamis* (New Delhi: D.K. Printworld Private Limited, 1996), 260.
30. Sandywell, "The Myth of the Everyday," 175.
31. Yadav, *Nāṅgaraṇī* [*Ploughing*], 263.
32. Yadav, *Nāṅgaraṇī* [*Ploughing*] 263.
33. Yadav, *Nāṅgaraṇī* [*Ploughing*], 264.
34. Janabai Thorat, Bhendegaon, verse recorded by author, June 26, 2006. Personal collection.
35. J. T. Molesworth, *A Dictionary, Marathi and English*, 2nd. ed. (Bombay: Bombay Education Society Press, 1857), 770.
36. M. M. Bakhtin, "The Problem of Speech Genres," in *Speech Genres and Other Late Essays* (Austin: University of Texas Press, 2002), 62.
37. Paul Zumthor, *Oral Poetry: An Introduction*, trans. Kathryn Murphy-Judy (Minneapolis: University of Minnesota Press, 1990), 23. My italics. Zumthor draws from Jacque Dourne, *Le parler de Jörai et le style oral de leur expression* (Paris: Publications Orientalistes, 1976), 272–280.
38. Zumthor, *Oral Poetry*, 33.
39. Ashok D. Ranade, *Keywords and Concepts in Hindustani Classical Music* (New Delhi: Promilla and Company Publishers, 1990), 30.
40. M. T. Patwardhan, *Chandoracanā* (Mumbai: Karnatak Publishing House, 1937), 11.
41. Bob Dylan, *The Lyrics: 1961–2012*, ed. Christopher Ricks, Lisa Nemrow, and Julie Nemrow (New York: Simon and Schuster, 2014).
42. Bob Dylan, "Nobel Lecture," *The Nobel Prize*. Nobel Foundation (June 5, 2017), video and transcript, https://www.nobelprize.org/prizes/literature/2016/dylan/lecture/.
43. Adam Bradley, *The Poetry of Pop* (New Haven, CT: Yale University Press, 2017), 14.

44. Bradley, *The Poetry of Pop*, 14.
45. Bradley, *The Poetry of Pop*, 17.
46. Ted Gioia, *Work Songs* (Durham, NC: Duke University Press, 2006), 37.
47. Ashok D. Ranade, *Lokasaṅgītaśāstra* (Mumbai: Dr. Ashok Da Ranade Memorial Trust, 2021 [1975]), 99. For those interested in the musical study of the songs, see also Sarojini Babar, *Lokasaṅgīta* (Mumbai: Prasiddhi Vibhag, Maharashtra Shasan, 1962).
48. Yadav, *Nāṅgaraṇī* [*Ploughing*], 263. See also. Ranade, *Keywords and Concepts*, 14.
49. Ranade, *Keywords and Concepts,* 14.
50. Ranade, *Keywords and Concepts*, 16.
51. *Māyavātecā Māgovā*, *Dr. Tara Bhavalkar*, video series, Doordarshan Sahyadri, episode 1, 12:16–16:40, YouTube, March 29, 2022, https://www.youtube.com/watch?v=dNa_ZE3sfhk. I am indebted to the work of Tara Bhavalkar, who has written numerous books on women's folk traditions in Maharashtra. Essential reading is Tara Bhavalkar, *Loka Paramparā āṇi Strīpratibhā* [Folk tradition and the representation of women] (Mumbai: The House of Folk Literature, 2002).
52. Marek Korczynski, Micheal Mickering, and Emma Robertson, *Rhythms of Labour: Music at Work in Britain* (Cambridge: Cambridge University Press, 2013), 67.
53. Korczynski et al., *Rhythms of Labour*, 67; the book as a whole draws out these various purposes of "singing at work" in the UK.
54. For the same point about women singers in Kangra see Kirin Narayan, *Everyday Creativity* (Chicago: University of Chicago Press, 2012), 12.
55. Jonathan Culler, *Theory of the Lyric* (Cambridge, MA: Harvard University Press, 2015), 89.
56. Jahan Ramazani, "Lyric Poetry: Intergeneric, Transnational, Translingual?" in *Journal of Literary Terms* 11, no. 1 (2017): 105.
57. Boris Maslov, "Lyric Universality," in *The Cambridge Companion to World Literature*, ed. Ben Etherington and Jarad Zimbler. Cambridge Companions to Literature. (Cambridge: Cambridge University Press, 2018), 136. Maslov draws on Roman Jakobson and the earlier work on parallelism by Alexander Veselovsky to make the case that parallelism is deep structural evidence of both the universality of the lyric and its origin in song. On parallelism as the essential structure of the poetic, see Roman Jakobson, "Grammatical Parallelism and Its Russian Facet," *Language* 42, no. 2. (1966): 399–429.
58. See GSP, https://grindmill.org/. This is the opening page of the website.
59. Alex Preminger and T. V. F. Brogan, eds., *The New Princeton Encyclopedia of Poetry and Poetics* (Princeton, NJ: Princeton University Press, 1993), 880, my emphasis.

60. Janabai Kamble, Village Takali (Latur District), GSP, https://ccrss.org/database/songs.php?song_id=89494.

61. Maslov, "Lyric Universality," 135.

62. Culler, *Theory of the Lyric*, 35.

63. See Albert Lord, *The Singer Resumes the Tale*, ed. Mary Louise Lord (Ithaca, NY: Cornell University Press, 1995), 22–69.

64. M. Monier-Williams, *A Sanskrit-English Dictionary* (Springfield, VA: Natraj Books, 2015 [1899]), 1275.

65. *Māyavāṭecā Māgovā*, episode 1, 24:40, https://www.youtube.com/watch?v=dNa_ZE3sfhk.

66. Howard Thurman, "The Negro Spiritual Speaks of Life and Death," in *African-American Religious Thought: An Anthology*, ed. Cornel West and Eddie Glaude Jr. (Louisville. KY: Westminster Knox Press, 2003), 43.

67. Tulasa Kamble, Village Takali (Latur District). GSP, https://ccrss.org/database/songs.php?song_id=113031.

68. Yadav, *Nāṅgaraṇī* [*Ploughing*], 263.

69. Culler, *Theory of the Lyric*, 14. On poetry's dialogical engagement with multiple genres, see also Jahan Ramazani, *Poetry and Its Others: News, Prayers, Song, and the Dialogue of Genres* (Chicago: University of Chicago Press, 2014).

70. Janabai Thorat, Bhendegaon, verse recorded by author, June 26, 2006. Personal collection.

71. *Śrī Namdev Gāthā: Visobā Khecar, Parasā Bhāgavat, Janābāī Yāñcyā Abhaṅgāsaha [Sakaḷa Santa Gāthā]*, ed. N. Sakhare (Pune: Varada Books, 2002 [1990]), 713, *abhaṅga* 85.

72. Andromache Karanika, *Voices at Work: Women, Performance, and Labor in Ancient Greece* (Baltimore, MD: Johns Hopkins University Press, 2014), 148.

73. Karanika, *Voices at Work*, 145.

74. Karanika, *Voices at Work*, 145–48.

75. Ṛgveda 1.28; English translation from Stephanie W. Jamison and Joel P. Brereton, *The Rigveda: The Earliest Religious Poetry of India, Vol. 1* (New York: Oxford University Press, 2014), 128. They believe this verse depicts an abbreviated domestic soma-pressing ritual using household instruments, rather than the elevated ritual indicated in an older stratum of hymns. See the introductory comments to the translation (126–127).

76. For an overview of the sexual double meanings in the hymn, see Hanns-Peter Schmidt, "Ṛgveda 1.28 and the Alleged Domestic Soma-Pressing," *Electronic Journal of Vedic Studies* 16, no.1 (2009): 3–13.

77. Stephanie W. Jamison, *Sacrificed Wife, Sacrificer's Wife: Women, Ritual, and Hospitality in Ancient India* (New York: Oxford University Press, 1996), 127.

78. Wendy Doniger, "The Zen Diagram of Hinduism," in *The Norton Anthology of World Religions, Vol. 1*, ed. Jack Miles, Wendy Doniger, Donald S. Lopez Jr., James Robson (New York: Norton, 2015), 61. I am referring here to the work of Milman Parry and Albert Lord, who analyzed the performance and poetics of oral bards known as *guslars* in the former Yugoslavia to shed light on the compositional features of Homeric texts. See Albert B. Lord, *The Singer of Tales*, ed. Stephen Mitchell and Gregory Nagy (Cambridge, MA: Harvard University Press, 2000).
79. See poems by "Mutta" and "Sumangala's Mother," for example, in Charles Hallisey, trans., *Therigatha: Poems of the first Buddhist Women*, Murty Classical Library of India (Cambridge, MA: Harvard University Press, 2015), 10–12; 20–21. On possible connections between *Therīgāthā* and women's folksongs, see Barbara Stoler Miller, "The *Therīgāthā*: Women's Songs of Early Buddhism," *Journal of South Asian Literature* 19, no. 2 (Summer/Fall 1984): 129–135. Andrew Ollett calls efforts to link literary meters to folksong "highly sentimental," but there are, besides meter, other poetic tropes, motifs, schemas, that might—even purposefully—invoke women's songs. See Andrew Ollett, *Language of the Snakes. Prakrit, Sanskrit, and the Language Order of Premodern India.* South Asia Across the Disciplines (Berkeley: University of California Press, 2017), 98.
80. Culler, *Theory of the Lyric*, 216.
81. Dundes, "Metafolklore and Oral Literary Criticism," *The Monist* 50, no. 4 (1966): 505–516.
82. For a range of songs on different aspects of singing and composing *ovīs*, including songs about singing together, singing for or with daughters, or about women who can't sing well, see GSP, Semantic Classes A: II-5.3ki to A:II-5.3kxvi, "Labor/Grinding/Singing While Grinding," https://ccrss.org/database/songs.php?semantic_class_title_prefix_id=A02-05-03k01.
83. Sant, *Mālanagāthā*, 1:14
84. Poitevin, *The Voice and the Will*, 60.
85. Paru Bhagat, Village Bahuli (Pune District). GSP, https://ccrss.org/database/songs.php?song_id=6519.
86. Shahu Satpute, Village Akole (Pune District), GSP, https://ccrss.org/database/songs.php?song_id=6517. The word *vāṇī* as transcribed in the GSP with a retroflex *ṇ* might suggest its meaning to be "speech." But, the word is more likely *vanī or vānī* (without a retroflex), a colloquial way to say "like" or "similar to" in rurally inflected Marathi.
87. Poitevin, *The Voice and the Will*, 49.
88. Ruth Finnegan, *Oral Poetry: Its Nature, Significance and Social Context* (London: Cambridge University Press, 1979), 33.

89. Tanha Jadhav, Village Khiri (Ahmednagar District), GSP, https://ccrss.org/database/songs.php?song_id=89163
90. Tanha Jadhav, Village Khairi (Ahmednagar District), GSP, https://ccrss.org/database/songs.php?song_id=40579.
91. Jija Pawar, Village Karegaon (Ahmednagar District), GSP, https://ccrss.org/database/songs.php?song_id=85522.
92. Shanta Giridhar Wahadne, Village Puntamba (District Ahmednagar), GSP, https://ccrss.org/database/songs.php?song_id=58290.
93. Bhama Walung, Village Phakat (Pune District), GSP, https://ccrss.org/database/songs.php?song_id=87863.
94. Sita Marane, Village Siddheshwar (Pune District), GSP, https://ccrss.org/database/songs.php?song_id=13897.
95. Bakhtin, "The Problem of Speech Genres," 65.

2. Colloquial Turns

1. H. D. Sankalia, Shantaram B. Deo, Zainuddin D. Ansari, and Sophie Ehrhardt, *From History to Pre-history at Nevasa (1954–1956)* (Pune: Deccan College Postgraduate Institute, 1960), 489. Varada Khaladkar writes that the saddle querns and mortars (pestles were wooden, so they did not last) excavated in Chalcolithic (ca. 3500–1000 BCE) sites were small in size, enough for one or two handfuls of grain, which suggests that the pounding/grinding was a daily activity. This seems to have largely continued after the rotating mills were introduced. Perhaps something of the continuity of this practice created expectations for freshly processed grain. Even in twenty-first-century India, there is great value placed on recently milled grains over commercially packaged flour sold in supermarkets. See Varada Khaladkar, "The Protohistoric Village: Its Form and Economy in Chalcolithic North Western Deccan" (MPhil thesis, Jawaharalal Nehru University, 1998), 85.
2. Some archeologists believe the rotary querns made their way to India through Indo-Greek contact. For an overview of the different types of querns found, their similarity to those in Greece and England, and their possible origins, see Sankalia et al., *From History to Pre-history*, 482–486.
3. The eighteenth-century *Strīdharmapaddhati* (Guide to the duties of women), written by Tryambakayajvan (1665–1750) for Brahmin women of the court of the Marathas of Tanjavore, includes grinding and preparation of grains as one of the prescribed tasks to be performed by women in the dawn hours. In her translation and commentary on this text, Julia Leslie writes, "Tryambaka now adds the rider that 'this (i.e., all these items of housework)—cleaning

(the house), smearing (the walls and floor with cow-dung), pounding (the grain) and so on—should be done as far as possible by (the wife) herself; alternatively, she may get someone else (such as a servant, daughter-in-law, or even junior co-wife) to do them" (64). See I. Julia Leslie, trans., *The Perfect Wife (Stridharmapaddhati) by Tryambakayajvan* (New Delhi: Penguin, 1995), 58, 64.

4. Sankalia et al., *History to Prehistory*, 489. On issues of commensality, caste and sharing food in the *bhakti* tradition, see John Keune, *Shared Devotion, Shared Food: Equality and the Bhakti-Caste Question in Western India* (New York: Oxford University Press, 2021).
5. Sheldon Pollock, *Language of the Gods in the World of Men: Sanskrit, Culture, and Power in Premodern India* (Berkeley: University of California Press, 2006), 499.
6. D. R. Nagaraj, "Critical Tensions in the History of Kannada Literary Culture," in *Literary Cultures in History: Reconstructions from South Asia*, ed. Sheldon Pollock (Berkeley: University of California Press, 2003), 334.
7. Nagaraj, "Critical Tensions," 334–335. Not all scholars would agree that Sanskrit and "folk structures" are mutually exclusive. Sathaye makes a compelling case against the "false dichotomy" between oral folklore and Sanskrit texts propagated by the "disciplinary gap between Indology and South Asian folklore studies." See Adheesh Sathaye, "The Scribal Life of Folktales," *South Asian History and Culture* 8, no. 4 (2017): 430–432. See also Heidi Pauwels, "The Vernacular Pulse of Sanskrit: Metre and More in the Songs of the *Gītagovinda* and the *Bhāgavata Purāṇa*," *The Journal of Hindu Studies* 13, no. 3 (November 2020): 294–319.
8. See especially the discussion of Nagavarma's tenth-century prosodic text *Chandombudhi* in Nagaraj, "Critical Tensions," 339–341.
9. Nagaraj, "Critical Tensions," 341, 347.
10. Christian Lee Novetzke, *The Quotidian Revolution: Vernacularization, Religion, and the Premodern Public Sphere in India* (New York: Columbia University Press, 2016), 6–11.
11. See Anne Feldhaus and S. G. Tulpule, trans., *In the Absence of God: The Early Years of an Indian Sect: A Translation of Smṛtisthaḷ with an Introduction* (Honolulu: University of Hawai'i Press, 1992), 104–105, chap. 113. This episode mentions two other authors, Salkavi, who wrote a *Ramāyaṇa* and Narsimhakavi, who wrote a *Nalopākhyāna*, presumably both in Marathi, but neither text has survived.
12. Eaton notes the orientalist foregrounding of religion in the very category of "Muslim conquest," especially in contrast to the historically concurrent "Spanish conquest." See Richard Eaton, *India in the Persianate Age, 1000–1765*

(Berkeley: University of California Press, 2019), 3–6. Manan Ahmed Asif locates the demonizing of the "Muslim medieval" in the historiography of the colonial episteme, which divided India's past into "five thousand years" of a "Golden Age" followed by the Dark Ages of Muslim rule and the enlightened modern age of British Colonialism. See Manan Ahmed Asif, *The Loss of Hindustan: The Invention of India* (Cambridge, MA: Harvard University Press, 2020), 28–29. Brajadulal Chattopadhyaya, *The Making of Early Medieval India* (New Delhi: Oxford University Press, 2012), xxvii–xxxi, calls this historiographic trope the "decline syndrome." In Marathi historiography, this "decline syndrome" is evident in how the period between the fall of the Yadavas and the rise of the Marathas is depicted as a dark age of decline. See, for example, S. G. Tulpule, *Classical Marāṭhī Literature: From the Beginning to 1818*, vol. 9 of *A History of Indian Literature*, ed. Jan Gonda (Wiesbaden: Otto Harrassowitz, 1979), 345.

13. Richard Eaton, *India in the Persianate Age, 1000–1765* (Berkeley: University of California Press, 2019), 136–138.
14. See Pushkar Sohoni, "Vernacular As a Space: Writing in the Deccan," *South Asian History and Culture* 7, no. 3 (2016): 3. On the *sufi-bhakti* dialogue, see Dusan Deak, "Maharashtra Saints and the Sufi Tradition: Eknath, Chand Bodhale and the Datta Sampradaya," in *Journal of Deccan Studies* 3, no. 2 (2005): 22–47.
15. Novetzke, *Quotidian Revolution*, 2.
16. Tulpule, *Classical Marāṭhī Literature*, 345. Tulpule claims that Hindu "religious institutions" rescued Marathi from the influence of Persian thereby otherizing Muslim cultural influences, which are considerable in Hindu folk traditions. Oral traditions are quite open to multilingual and multicultural influence, perhaps even more than writing, as we see today in the influence of English on oral culture in India. The idea that oral traditions served as some kind of bulwark against Persian seems, at best, inaccurate.
17. For an overview of the rich diversity of folk traditions, see R. C. Dhere, *Lokasaṃskṛtīce Upāsak* (Pune: Padmagandha Publishers, 2007 [1996]); See also Prabhakar Mande, *Lokagāyakāñcī Paramparā* (Aurangabad: Godavari Publishers, 2011).
18. M. M. Bakhtin, "The Problem of Speech Genres," in *Speech Genres and Other Late Essays* (Austin: University of Texas Press, 2002), 29.
19. Pollock, *Language of the Gods*, 298. Sachin Ketkar critiques the unidirectionality of Pollock's concept of vernacularization and offers "interliterariness" as an alternative term. Where "vernacularization" assumes the "neo-orientalist" primacy of Sanskrit, Ketkar argues, "interliterariness" allows for the engagement of multiple sources and a recognition of the

creative contributions of the receiving language whose "powers of selection" are a sign of an aesthetics inherent to the language. See Sachin Ketkar, "Jnaneshwar's 'Duji Shrushti:' Poetics and Cultural Politics of Precolonial Translation of Dnaneshwari," in *India in Translation: Translation in India*, ed. G. J. V. Prasad (New Delhi: Bloomsbury, 2019), 7–8.

20. Andrew Ollett, *Language of the Snakes: Prakrit, Sanskrit, and the Language Order of Premodern India*. South Asia Across the Disciplines (Berkeley: University of California Press, 2017), 83.
21. Ollett, *Language of the Snakes*, 83.
22. H. C. Bhayani, *Apabraṁśa Language and Literature: A Short Introduction* (Delhi: B. L. Institute of Indology, 1989), 9–10.
23. H. C. Bhayani, "The Rise of Apabhraṁśa as a Literary Language," in *Indological Studies: Literary and Performing Arts, Prakrit and Apabhraṁśa Studies, Vol. 2* (Ahmedabad: Parshva Publication, 1993), 30, 32.
24. Bhayani, *Apabraṁśa Language and Literature,* 10; See also Bhayani, "The Rise of Apabhramsha as a Literary Language," 32–33.
25. Bhayani, *Apabraṁśa Language and Literature*, 11.
26. Edward Sapir, *Language: An Introduction to the Study of Speech* (New York: Harcourt, Brace & World, 1921), 155.
27. T. S. Eliot, "The Music of Poetry," in *On Poetry and Poets* (New York: Farrar, Straus and Giroux, 1957), 23. Although often considered an advocate of rarefication himself, Eliot had what David Chinitz calls an "ambivalent attachment" to the popular culture of his times, in particular jazz, evident in his poetry. See David Chinitz, *T. S. Eliot and the Cultural Divide* (Chicago: University of Chicago Press, 2003).
28. Douglas Biber and Edward Finegan, "Drift and the Evolution of English Style: A History of Three Genres," *Language* 65, no. 3 (September 1989): 487–517. Page numbers in parentheses cite the remaining quotes from this article.
29. There are genealogical connections between Maharashtri Prakrit, Apabhramsha, and Marathi, but there are also formative influences from the languages of the South, as well as from Persian and Hindustani, in the linguistic history of Marathi. See Jules Bloch, *The Formation of the Marathi Language*, trans. Dev Raj Chanana (Delhi: Motilal Banarsidass, 1970 [1941]), 32–33; See also Tulpule, *Classical Marāṭhī Literature*, 311–312. The government of Maharashtra petitioned for and was recently granted recognition of Marathi as a "classical language" by the Ministry of Culture in Delhi based on a proposed continuity between literary Prakrit and Marathi. See Ranganath Pathare et al., *Submission for the Classical Status of Marathi Language to Ministory of Culture, Government of India, by Department of Marathi Language* (Mumbai: Government of Maharashtra, 2013). The authors argue that "Mahārāṣṭrī

Prākṛta, Apabhraṁśa Marāṭhī and Marāṭhī are not three different languages but are three forms of one and the same language" (35).

30. Ollett, *Language of the Snakes*, 122–135.
31. Ollett, *Language of the Snakes*, 161; see also Bhayani, "The Rise of Apabhraṁśa as a Literary Language," 32.
32. Bakhtin, "The Problem of Speech Genres," 97.
33. See "Dāsopantanivedita Ekā Saṃskṛtaniṣṭhācī Kathā [Excerpt of *Gitārṇavā*]," in *Marāṭhī Saṃśodhan Patrikā* 23, no. 2 (January–March 1976): 1–60.
34. "Dāsopantanivedita Ekā Saṃskṛtaniṣṭhācī Kathā," 25, v. 2671.
35. "Dāsopantanivedita Ekā Saṃskṛtaniṣṭhācī Kathā," 25, v. 2673–2676.
36. "Dāsopantanivedita Ekā Saṃskṛtaniṣṭhācī Kathā," 25, v. 2677.
37. "Dāsopantanivedita Ekā Saṃskṛtaniṣṭhācī Kathā," 26, v. 2701.
38. *Kuvalayamālākahā* by Uddyotanasuri, vols. 1–2, ed. and trans. Prem S. Jain (Jaipur: Prakrit Bharati Akademy, 2016), 2:246.15–16. For the possible meanings of the Marathi words, see S. G. Tulpule and Anne Feldhaus, *Dictionary of Old Marathi* (New York: Oxford University Press, 2000), 197, 329. For a translation of this passage, see also Alfred Masters, "Gleanings from the Kuvalayamālā Kahā I: Three Fragments and Specimens of the Eighteen Desabhāsās," *Bulletin of the School of Oriental and African Studies, University of London* 13, no. 2 (1950): 415.
39. *Jñāneśvarī* of Jnaneshvar, ed. with gloss by S. V. Dandekar (Pune: Svanand Publishers, 1976), 68, 3.17 [hereafter *Jñāneśvarī*]. Tulpule and Feldhaus define *marhāṭa* as "in the Marāṭhī language," and in a secondary meaning as "explicit; clear" in Tulpule and Feldhaus, *Dictionary of Old Marathi*, 534.
40. Ollett, *Language of the Snakes*, 115–118.
41. On the "separation of styles," and the blending of the "sublime" with the "everyday" in biblical literature and in early European vernacular literature, see Erich Auerbach, *Mimesis: The Representation of Reality in Western Literature*, trans. Willard Trask (Princeton, NJ: Princeton University Press, 2003), 22–23; 132–133. Auerbach's discussion could be seen as another way of acknowledging "colloquialization."
42. Bakhtin, "The Problem of Speech Genres," 97.
43. Novetzke has an excellent analysis of the "oral presentation style" and "dialogic aesthetic" of the *Jñāneśvarī*, though he traces it back to an "original" compositional context that posits orality as prior to writing. See Novetzke, *The Quotidian Revolution*, 224–229. On Jnaneshvar's appropriation of the oral performance of *dharma kīrtan* as an act of "interliterary" translation, see Ketkar, "Jnaneshwar's 'Duji Shrushti,'" 12–13.
44. Anne Feldhaus, "The Mahanubhavas and Scripture," *Journal of Dharma* 3, no. 3 (1978): 296–297.

45. Feldhaus, "The Mahanubhavas and Scripture," 297.
46. Ian Raeside, "A Bibliographic Index of Mahānubhāva Works in Marathi," *Bulletin of the School of Oriental and African Studies* 23, no. 3 (1960).
47. By scatological, I am referring to the not-infrequent discussion of defecation in the *Līḷācaritra*. For example, in one *līḷā*, Umaise defecates near a man whose bowel movement is full of worms. On seeing this, she says, "What they call hell is right here." Chakradhar overhears Umaise and uses the conversation to impart theological knowledge: "'My Woman,' said the omniscient one, 'for one who knows, hell is right here!'" See Anne Feldhaus, trans., *God at Play*, vol 1. Murty Classical Library (Cambridge, MA: Harvard University Press, 2024), 385-387, FH174.
48. Anne Feldhaus's singular and painstaking work of translation has given the English-speaking world access to several of the most important early texts. The first of the three planned volumes of her translation of *God at Play* (*Līḷācaritra*) has been published at the time of this writing (see note 47 above). For her translation of the *Ṛddhipurcaritra*, see Anne Feldhaus, trans., *The Deeds of God in Ṛddhipur* (New York: Oxford University Press, 1984). See also her edited Marathi text and English translation of the *Sūtrapāṭha* in Anne Feldhaus, *The Religious System of the Mahānubhāva Sect: The Mahānubhāva Sūtrapāṭha* (New Delhi: Manohar, 1983), 173–244. She also translated the *Smṛtisthaḷ* with S. G. Tulpule. See Feldhaus and Tulpule, trans., *In the Absence of God*.
49. For more on Gundam Raul, see Anne Feldhaus, "God and Madman: Guṇḍam Rāuḷ," *Bulletin of the School of Oriental and African Studies* 45, no. 1 (1982): 74–83.
50. Novetzke, *Quotidian Revolution*, 103–104.
51. See Feldhaus, introduction to *God at Play*, xi–xiii.
52. See Feldhaus, introduction to *God at Play*, xv.
53. The Hiraise recension is the basis of the critical edition published by P. C. Nagpure. See *Līḷācaritra*, ed. P. C. Nagpure (Nagpur: Omkar Publishers, 2015) [hereafter *NLC*]. Feldhaus provides an invaluable concordance of six different editions that she consulted in her translation, which is primarily based, however, on the edition by H. N. Nene. I have not looked at all six editions, but I did crosscheck variations between the Feldhaus, Nagpure, and the 1978 Kolte editions. *Līḷācaritra* of Mhaimbat, ed. V. B. Kolte (Mumbai: Maharashtra Rajya Sahitya Sanskriti Mandal, 1978) [hereafter *KLC*]; for the concordance, see the backmatter in Feldhaus, *God at Play*, 687–704.
54. Nagaraj, "Critical Tensions," 361.
55. Pollock, *Language of the Gods*, 433.
56. Nagaraj, "Critical Tensions," 361.

57. Feldhaus, *The Deeds of God,* 88. Mahadaise narrates exactly this episode to Chakradhar in the *Līḷācaritra* as well. See *NLC*, P546.
58. *KLC* U426; *NLC*, U335; Feldhaus, *God at Play* forthcoming: U276; I am grateful to Anne Feldhaus for sharing the drafts of her unpublished translation, which I used as the basis of my own translation, but I did make changes, so any mistakes or problems are my own. I have followed the version in the Kolte edition, which has a slight variation in the final line from the Feldhaus translation. There are also significant variations in the wording and line order of Mahadaise's *ovīs* in the Nagpure edition. The meaning and the overall schema of the *ovīs* is quite similar, however. Given the numerous recensions of *Līḷācaritra*, it is not entirely surprising to find such variation. That there were so many variants shows that orality was a major compositional engine of this text, but this does not mean that any particular *līḷās* should therefore be seen as interpolations.
59. For an example of a few contemporary Mahanubhava women's *ovīs* using the trope of kinship, see Mangala P. Pathade, "Sarvajña Srīcakradharaviṣayak Saṅkalit Ovīgītāñcā Ābhyās" (MPhil thesis, Babasaheb Ambedkar Marathwada University, Aurangabad, 2014), 123–124. There are many tropes in common between the Mahanubhava grind mill songs and the songs of Vitthal. A comparative study of these songs would be a very interesting project.
60. Pathade, "Sarvajña," 123.
61. There are some variations in Mahadaise's *ovīs*, and in the episode as a whole, in the various editions of *Līḷācaritra.* Yet, the basic structure of the *ovī* and the basic interaction is similar. The Kolte edition adds another exchange between Mahadaise and Chakradhar to the end of this *līḷā* in which Chakradhar uses a maternal metaphor to explain to Mahadaise the nature of God's love for living beings. See *KLC*, U426; *NLC*, U334. In the Nagpure edition, these final lines appear in another *līḷā*, *NLC*, U342.
62. For more on Mahanubhava theology, see Antonio Rigopoulos, *Mahānubhāvs* (Firenze: Firenze University Press, 2005), 50 and 54. On the role of other deities in Mahanubhav cosmologies see Anne Feldhaus, "The Devatācakra of the Mahānubhāvas," *Bulletin of the School of Oriental and African Studies* 43, no. 1 (1980): 101–109.
63. The Kolte edition inserts this *līḷā* into the main text of the *Līḷācaritra* right after the one discussed above because of the thematic link and because he believes both take place in the city of Pratishthan (modern day Paithan). See *KLC*, U427; cf. 607.
64. Feldhaus, *The Deeds of God*, 100, *līḷā* 179.
65. Feldhaus, *The Deeds of God*, 95, *līḷā* 141.
66. See *KLC*, U346; the Nagpure edition has several variations in this song. See *NLC*, U380.

67. S. R. Kulkarni, *Ovī te Lāvaṇī: Prācin Marāṭhī Padabandhācī Saṅgīt-Preraṇā āṇi Paramparā* (Dhule: Vani Marathi Pragat Adhyayan Sanstha, 1994), 55–56.
68. For more on Sarangpandit's duplicity, see Novetzke, *Quotidian Revolution*, 194–196.
69. Feldhaus, *God at Play*, 162–165, FH8.
70. Feldhaus, *God at Play*, 164, FH8.
71. Feldhaus, *God at Play*, 165, FH8.
72. Feldhaus, *God at Play*, 2–3, SP2; In the Nagpure edition, the end rhyme of *ti* (a short syllable) is carried through the whole of the *līḷā*. See *NLC*, E2; the Kolte edition frames this chapter as a question and response between Mahadaise and Chakradhar. In his response, the first couple of sentences are not end-rhymed, but the sentences quoted above (with a few interesting variations) are end-rhymed, and here, too, the rhyming carries through to the end as in Nagpure. See *KLC*, E3.
73. Faldhaus, *God at Play*, 3, SP2.
74. Feldhaus, *God at Play*, 651, cf. 6; for an English translation of this *sūtra*, see Feldhaus, *The Religious System of the Mahānubhāva Sect*, 193, *sūtra* 52.
75. For these episodes featuring Dhanaise, see Feldhaus, *God at Play*, 181, FH16; 189, FH22; 191, FH23–24.
76. Auerbach, *Mimesis*, 116. My analysis of the paratactical style of Marathi writing is highly influenced by Auerbach's analysis of a similar style in European vernacular literature.
77. Novetzke, *Quotidian Revolution*, 90. Here is how A. S. Altekar, historian of the Yadava period, puts it: "The mature development of the language as a literary medium, which is to be seen in the works of Mukundarāya and Jñāneśvara, presupposes a literary activity of at least two centuries." See A. S. Altekar, "The The Yādavas of Seunadeśa," in *The Early History of the Deccan*, parts 7–11, ed. G. Yazdani (London: Oxford University Press, 1960), 513–574. See also H. D. Velankar, "Apabhraṁśa and Marāṭhī Metres," *New Indian Antiquary* 1, no. 4 (July 1938): 218; Tulpule, *Classical Marathi Literature*, 314.
78. Paul Zumthor, *Toward a Medieval Poetics*, trans. Philip Bennett (Minneapolis: University of Minnesota, 1992), 35.
79. Zumthor, *Toward a Medieval Poetics*, 36.

3. The *Ovī*

1. *Bhaktavijay* of Mahipati, ed. S. R. Devale (Pune: Sharada Sahitya, n.d.), 21.90–101.

2. See, for example, Guy Poitevin, *The Voice and the Will: Subaltern Agency: Forms and Motives* (New Delhi: Manohar, 2002), 48.
3. R. C. Dhere, "Sāne Gurujiñce *Strījīvan*," in *Lokasāhitya: Śodha āṇi Samikṣā* (Pune: Padmagandha Publishers, 2015), 140.
4. *Mānasollāsa* of Someśvara, vol. 3, ed. G. K. Shrigondekar (Baroda: Oriental Institute, 1961), 4.13. 543.
5. Urmila Pawar, *The Weave of My Life: A Dalit Woman's Memoirs*, trans. Maya Pandit. (New York: Columbia University Press, 2009), 165, EPUB.
6. For example, Pawar, *Weave of My Life*, 115–116.
7. Pawar, *Weave of My Life*, 286, 339.
8. The different words for lullabies can indicate slightly different purposes of each, according to Pratima Ingole, who studied women's songs from the Vidharbha region. A *pāḷaṇā* is sung to protect the baby, while *aṅgāī* and *hallara* are songs to help a child fall asleep. Pratima Ingole, *Varhāḍī Lokagītāñcā Cikitsak Abhyās* (Pune: Sonal Publishers, 2013), 95–102. There is mention of a *hallara* or *hallaru* song in a verse of the *Jñāneśvarī* (12.7) in which Jnaneshvar presents the divine being as a yogic mother lulling her child to sleep.
9. *Saṅgīta-Ratnākara of Śārṅgadeva: Sanskrit Text and English Translation with Comments and Notes, Volume 2, Chapters 2–4*, ed. and trans. R. K. Shringy under supervision of Prem Lata Sharma (New Delhi: Munshiram Manoharlal, 1989), vol. 2, 4.1–3, 210–211. See Shringy's gloss explaining the distinction between *gāndharva* and *gāna* (211).
10. *Saṅgīta-Ratnākara of Śārṅgadeva*, vol. 2, 4.304–306, 306. I am grateful to Adheesh Sathaye for translating these lines for me.
11. *Smṛtisthaḷ*, ed. V. N. Deshpande (Pune: Venus Publishers, [1939] 1960), 179. Anne Feldhaus, trans., *Deeds of God in Ṛddhipur* (New York: Oxford University Press, 1984), 110, 179.
12. *Mānasollāsa*, vol. 3, 4.16.20. This verse from a section of the *Mānasollāsa* appears to have been inserted from one D manuscript dated 1671, produced somewhere in the Deccan by a scribe for a local Yadava chieftain. See G. K. Shrigondekar, preface to *Mānasollāsa* of Someśvara, vol. 3 (Baroda: Oriental Institute, 1961), vii–viii. While only one manuscript attests to this verse and the verse numbers of this section diverge from those in the rest of the chapter, the description nevertheless matches the description of *ovī* in the thirteenth-century *Saṅgīta-Ratnākara*.
13. See GSP, UVS-28-23 recorded in the village Rajmachi in the Mawal district in 1997-03-15, https://ccrss.org/database/recordings.php?tape_id=UVS-28#UVS-28.
14. Lakshmi Umbre, Village Rajmachi (Pune District), GSP, https://ccrss.org/database/songs.php?song_id=31718.

15. See Vijaya Ramaswamy, "Women and Farm Work in Tamil Folk Songs" *Social Scientist* 21, nos. 9–11 (September–October 1993): 113.
16. R. C. Dhere, "Sāne Gurujiñce *Strījīvan*," 139.
17. Gregory Nagy, *Poetry as Performance: Homer and Beyond* (Cambridge: Cambridge University Press, 1996), 60, 69.
18. Jan Gonda, *A History of Indian Literature: Ritual Sūtras*, vol. 1 (Wiesbaden: Otto Harassowitz, 1977), 466.
19. Gonda, *A History of Indian Literature*, 466.
20. For a discussion of carpentry and weaving imagery in the Ṛg Veda, see Tatyana Elizarenkova, *Language and Style of the Vedic Ṛṣis* (New York: State University of New York Press, 1995), 24–26.
21. Arthur Anthony Macdonell, *A Practical Sanskrit Dictionary with Transliteration, Accentuation, and Etymological Analysis Throughout* (London: Oxford University Press, 1929), 275: "वा 4. VÂ IV. P. váya, weave (*also fig. of hymns, speeches, etc.*), compose." See also Vaman Shivaram Apte, *Revised and Enlarged Edition of Prin. V. S. Apte's The Practical Sanskrit-English Dictionary* (Poona: Prasad Prakashan, 1957–1959), vol. 3, 1494: "वे ve 1 U. (वयत\-ते, उत; Caus. वाययत-ते) (1) To weave; सतिांशुवर्णैर्वयत स्म तद्गुणैः N.1.12. (2) To braid, plait. (3) To sew. (4) To cover, overspread. (5) To make, compose, string together."
22. See Proto-Indo-European Etyma, 6. Clothing & Adornment, 6.33 "to weave." Linguistics Research Center, The University of Texas at Austin, https://lrc.la.utexas.edu/lex/semantic/field/CA_WE.
23. Stephanie W. Jamison and Joel P. Brereton, trans., *The Rigveda: The Earliest Religious Poetry of India, Vol. 1* (New York: Oxford University Press, 2014), 180, 1.61.8.
24. Jamison and Brereton, *The Rigveda*, 180, 1.61.4. See Chiara Bozzone, "Weaving Songs for the Dead in Indo-European: Women Poets, Funerary Laments, and the Ecology of **ḱléu̯os**," in *Proceedings of the 27th Annual UCLA Indo-European Conference*, ed. David M. Goldstein, Stephanie W. Jamison, and Brent Vine (Bremen: Hempen, 2016), 3–4. Bozzone writes, "If we admit that women, on some occasions, could weave songs and not just cloth, then we would have an alternative class of IE poets (possibly nonprofessional and possibly not paid) worth considering" (5). For a further suggestion that there might be a technical connection between metrical arrangements of Indo-European poetry and patterns of weaving, see Anthony Tuck, "Singing the Rug: Patterned Textiles and the Origins of Indo-European Metrical Poetry," *American Journal of Archaeology* 110, no. 4 (2006): 539–550. See also Giovanni Fanfani, "Weaving a Song. Convergences in Greek Poetic Imagery between Textile and Musical Terminology. An Overview on Archaic and Classical Literature," in *Textile Terminologies: from the Orient to the Mediterranean and*

Europe, 1000 BC to 1000 AD, ed. Salvatore Gaspa, Cécile Michel, Marie-Louise Nosch (Lincoln, NE: Zea Books, 2017), 421–436.

25. Paul Zumthor, *Oral Poetry: An Introduction*, trans. Kathryn Murphy-Judy (Minneapolis: University of Minnesota Press, 1990), 66.
26. Saru Kadu, Village Wadavali, (Aurangabad District), GSP, https://ccrss.org/database/songs.php?song_id=6525.
27. *Saṅgīta-Ratnākara of Śārṅgadeva*, vol. 2, 5.144–148.
28. See inscription Nr 35 (Nagar Taluq) in B. Lewis Rice, *Epigraphia Carnatica* 8.2 (Bangalore: Mysore Government Press, 1904), 251. I thank Andrew Ollett for helping me to understand this inscription better and Gil Ben-Herut for helping me to translate a few lines of it.
29. T. S. Satyanath, email to author, August 6, 2021.
30. Ferdinand Kittel, *Kittel's Kannada-English Dictionary*, rev. and enl. ed. (Madras [Chennai]: University of Madras, 1968–1971), 323.
31. *Ōvanige* is defined by P. V. Narayana as "a type of verse meant for singing." See P. V. Narayana, Haḷagannaḍa Padasampada (Bangalore: Kannada Sahitya Parishat, 2007), 109. I thank Kamalakar Bhatt for finding and translating this definition. The online *Alar* dictionary defines *ōvanige* as "a kind of poetic composition, either formal or folklore, that is meant to be recited or sung." See https://alar.ink/dictionary/kannada/english/ಓವನಿಗೆ.
32. B. Lewis Rice, Preface to *Epigraphia Carnatica* 8.2, 5.
33. D. R. Nagaraj, "Critical Tensions in the History of Kannada Literary Culture," in *Literary Cultures in History: Reconstructions from South Asia*, ed. Sheldon Pollock (Berkeley: University of California Press, 2003), 339.
34. J. T. Molesworth, *A Dictionary, Marathi and English*, 2d ed. (Bombay: Bombay Education Society Press, 1857), 122. The characters given in the second example are a well-known Marathi proverb: "No *ovī* comes to mind without holding the handle of the grind mill."
35. Parshuram B. Godbole, *Vṛttadarpaṇa*, ed. V. V. Natekar and N. G. Joshi (Baroda: Good Companions Publishers, 1964 [1860]).
36. Patwardhan's historical overview of poetic treatises lists only two Marathi texts as influential in the several that preceded Godbole's *Vṛttadarpaṇa*. One was *Sadvṛttamuktāvalī* (Pearl string of true verse forms) by Niranjan Madhava (1702–1790), a poet-scribe in the employ of the Peshwas. Another influential text was *Chandomanjarī*, by Ramchandra Daivejna, which focused primarily on Sanskrit *vṛtta* poetic meters. See M. T. Patwardhan *Chandoracanā* (Mumbai: Karnatak Publishing House, 1937), 559–560.
37. Sharad Gogate, "James Thomas Molesworth: A Biographical Sketch," in *Molesworth's Marathi-English Dictionary, Sixth Reprint with Corrections* by J. T. Molesworth (Pune: Shubhada-Saraswat Publishers, 1996 [1831]), 16.

38. Right on the first page of the preface, Molesworth cites his inclusion of the word *gāṇḍ*, which he defines as "the posteriors. (2) The anus," as an example of his decision to include the less than "comely" aspects of the language. Molesworth, *Dictionary*, v.
39. See Godbole, *Vṛttadarpaṇa*, 51–52; Molesworth, *Dictionary*, 122.
40. See Philip Engblom, "The Marathi Sonnet: Origins of the Species: A Thesis" (PhD diss., University of Minnesota,1983), 130–137. See also Kedar Kulkarni, *World Literature and the Question of Genre in Colonial India: Poetry, Drama and Print Culture, 1790–1890* (New Delhi: Bloomsbury, 2022).
41. Engblom, "Marathi Sonnet," 77.
42. According to Prachi Deshpande, the rules governing the orthography of long and short syllables became a major focus of debate among grammarians in the nineteenth century, when orthographic conventions were being systematized for textbooks. Debates hinged on whether the rules would follow Sanskrit orthographic conventions or whether the rules would make room for the language of the "ordinary man" (*sāmānya māṇus*). See Prachi Deshpande, *Scripts of Power: Writing, Language Practices, and Cultural History in Western India* (Ranikhet: Permanent Black, 2023), 201–207.
43. See *Mahārāṣtra Kāvyadīpikā* by Lakshadhira, in Annasaheb Adsod, ed, *Kāvyadīpika* (Pune: Snehavardhan Publishing, 2000), 103–110. Raeside notes that this work was not in a secret coded script, so it is possible it had wider circulation beyond the Mahanubhavas. See Ian Raeside, "A Bibliographic Index of Mahānubhāva Works in Marathi," *Bulletin of the School of Oriental and African Studies* 23, no. 3 (1960): 485–486. Lakshadhira also penned a work called *Kavilakṣaṇa-nirṇaya* (Judgment on the characteristics of the poets), in which he identifies and critiques ten different types of poets. The first of these is what he calls *deśavaḷu* or rustic poet: "The rustic poet is like this: / He knows *deśī* not the Sanskrit language. / He can't create (*yojū neṇe*) literature in three genders or three cases." See Adsod, ed., *Kāvyadīpika*, 111–112. Lakshadhira also penned a work called *Jñānamārtanḍa* (The sun of knowledge) in 1622 describing many different literary forms, but I was not able to access this work. See Raeside, "A Bibliographic Index," 482.
44. Patwardhan, *Chandoracanā*, 6.
45. V. K. Rajwade, "Marāṭhī Chanda," in *Itīhāsācārya Vi. Kā. Rājavāḍe Samagra Sāhitya*, vol. 1, ed. M. B. Shah (Dhule: Rajwade Samshodhan Mandal, 1994), 88.
46. Rajwade, "Marāṭhī Chanda," 85.
47. Patwardhan, *Chandoracanā*, 410, 415.
48. H. D. Velankar, "Apabhraṁśa and Marāṭhī Metres," *New Indian Antiquary* 1, no. 4 (July 1938): 217.

49. *Darśanaprakāśa Grantha* of Murarimalla, in *Matiratnākar Grantha 1 va Darśanaprakāśa Grantha 2*, ed. Shankar Narahara Joshi (Pune: Manager Chitrashala Press, n.d.), 14, chap. 9, ll. 15–16.

50. Nagaraj, "Critical Tensions," 334.

51. *Jñāneśvarī*, 10.42.

52. In Novetzke's analysis of this verse, he suggests that the word *nāgarpaṇem*, which I've translated as "refined beauty," might refer to the *nāgarikā* or city slicker in the *Kāmasūtra*, which makes sense given Jnaneshvar's rejection of the erotic *rasa* dominant in *kāvyā* in favor of the *rasa* of peace. See Christian Lee Novetzke, *Quotidian Revolution: Vernacularization, Religion, and the Premodern Public Sphere* (New York: Columbia University Press, 2016), 231.

53. *Rukmiṇī-Svayaṃvar* of Narendra, ed. V. B. Kolte (Nagpur: Arun Publishers, 1966), 9.47.

54. For the influence of Anandavardana and Abhinavagupta on Jnaneshvar's concept of poetics, see Sadanand More, *Trayodaśī: Śrī Jñānadev Sahitya Saṃśodhan* (Pune: Sakal Publishers, 2014), 30–31. From Anandavardhana: "The *Mahābhārata* as a work of doctrine (*śāstranaye*) considers the one supreme goal of man to be *mokṣa* and as a work of poetry (*kavyanaye*) intends the *rasa* of peace, which is a strengthening of the happiness that derives from the cessation of desire, to be the predominant *rasa*" (4.5). See Daniel H. Ingalls, Jeffrey Moussaieff Masson, and M. V. Patwardhan, eds. and trans., *The Dhvanyaloka of Anandavardhana with the Locana of Abhinavagupta* (Cambridge, MA: Harvard University Press, 1990), 692–693.

55. *Jñāneśvarī*, 10.19.

56. *Jñāneśvarī*, 18.1735.

57. *Jñāneśvarī*, 18.173. There are some variations in different editions that can influence the meaning of this verse. The Rajwade edition has slightly different numbering than most other editions, so see verse 18.1714 in *Śrījñāneśvarī*, ed. V. K. Rajwade; 2nd. edition, ed. S. V. Dandekar, B. M. Khuperkar, N. R. Phatak, A. K. Priolkar (Mumbai: Marathi Central Press, 1963). At issue is also the dual meaning of the word *pāṅgeṃ*, which can mean "deep longing" as well as "fault or deficiency." Dandekar's gloss interprets it as meaning that even with a deficiency in the singer's ability to recite Sanskrit, the meaning will not be limited to one region (*ekdeśītva*) (821).

58. *Jñāneśvarī*, 18.1737.

59. *Jñāneśvarī*, 18.1741. In the last line, I have interpreted the term *giteṃviṃṇa* to mean "without the text of the Gītā" following Dandekar's gloss, but others have interpreted to mean "without song," in other words as recitation. See Dandekar's gloss on verses 18.1741 in *Jñāneśvarī*, 821; M. R. Yardi, on the

other hand, translates the verse this way: "So I have composed this work in *ovī* metre which, if set to music, will be found captivating, or if recited, will hold one spell-bound." See M. R. Yardi, *The Jnaneshwari* (Pune: Bharati Vidya Bhavan, 2000), 725.

60. Several scholars use this verse in particular to prove that Jnaneshvar thought of the *ovī* as a song form. See Velankar, "Apabraṁśa and Marāṭhī Metres," 224; N. G. Joshi, *Marāṭhī Chandoracanā: Layadṛṣṭyā Punarvicār* (Mumbai: Mauj Publishers, 2014), 149.
61. S. G. Tulpule and Anne Feldhaus, *Dictionary of Old Marathi* (New York: Oxford University Press, 2000), 200.
62. Bhagwant Deshmukh (no relation) suggests a connection between *gāthā* and women's *ovīs*. See Bhagwant Deshmukh, *Dagaḍī Jātyācā Reśamī Gaḷā* (Pune: Pratima Publishers, 2000), 10. For an overview of perspectives on the *ovī*'s relationship to numerous other meters and forms, see Rohini Tukdev, *Ovī Chanda: Rūp aṇī Āviṣkār* (Pune: Pratibha Publishers, 2004), 36–40.
63. Andrew Ollett, *Language of Snakes. Prakrit, Sanskrit, and the Language Order of Premodern India*. South Asia Across the Disciplines (Berkeley: University of California Press, 2017), 94; Sheldon Pollock, *Language of the Gods in the World of Men*. Berkeley: University of California Press, 2006), 288.
64. Ollett, *Language of Snakes*, 100.
65. *Jñāneśvarī*, 18.1697–1699.
66. See Novetzke, *Quotidian Revolution*, 238–239, for more on Jnaneshvar's understanding of the Gītā as an encapsulation of the Vedas for the excluded castes and women.
67. See the entry for *anuṣṭubh* at *Chandorṇava: A Guide to Sanskrit and Prakrit Meters*, http://prakrit.info/meter/anustubh.html.
68. *Jñāneśvarī*, 18.1742.
69. Ollett, *Language of the Snakes*, 72.
70. Tulpule and Feldhaus, *Dictionary of Old Marathi*, 204.
71. *Jñāneśvarī*, 18.1738–1740.
72. *Jñāneśvarī*, 1.3.
73. *Jñāneśvarī*, 1.4–5.
74. *Jñāneśvarī*, 1.6.
75. *Jñāneśvarī*, 18.1738.
76. *Jñāneśvarī*, 18.1739.
77. Sheldon Pollock, "Literary History, Indian History, World History." *Social Scientist* 23, no. 10/12 (October–December 1995), 124.
78. Tanha Jadhav, Village Khiri (Ahmednagar District), GSP, https://ccrss.org/database/songs.php?song_id=89163.

79. *Jñāneśvarī*, 7.31–32. The second verse is not in the Rajwade edition.
80. Kausalya Gauli, Jalgaon City (Aurangabad District), GSP, https://ccrss.org/database/songs.php?song_id=67013.
81. *Jñāneśvarī*, 18.1743–1744.
82. *Śrī Nāmdev Gāthā*, ed. S. V. Dandekar et al. (Mumbai: Central Government Press, 1970), 933, *abhaṅga* 200.
83. Norman Cutler, *Songs of Experience: The Poetics of Tamil Devotion* (Bloomington: Indiana University Press, 1987), 22.
84. *Jñāneśvarī*, 3.21.
85. S. Radhakrishnan, trans. and ed., *The Bhagavadgita: With an Introductory Essay, Sanskrit Text, English Translation and Notes* (New Delhi: Harper Collins, 2002), 285, 11.43–44. The diacritics follow Radhakrishnan's style.
86. *Jñāneśvarī*, 11.584.
87. R. C. Dhere, *The Rise of a Folk God: Viṭṭhal of Pandharpur,* trans. Anne Feldhaus (New York: Oxford University Press, 2011), 209. To my knowledge R. C. Dhere is the first to analyze the copious maternal imagery associated with Vitthal *bhakti* in detail. See pages 207–220.
88. Dhere, *Rise of a Folk God*, 312n2.
89. Verse in Indra Sant, comp., *Mālanagāthā*, vol 1 (Pune: Mehta Publishing House, 2013 [1993]), 14.
90. More, *Trayodaśī: Śrī Jñānadev Sāhitya Saṃśodhan*, 33.
91. More, *Trayodaśī: Śrī Jñānadev Sāhitya Saṃśodhan*, 34
92. See Dhere, *Rise of a Folk God*, 207–220.
93. M. M. Bakhtin, "The Problem of Speech Genres," in *Speech Genres and Other Late Essays* (Austin: University of Texas Press, 2002), 69.
94. Bakhtin, "The Problem of Speech Genres," 94.

4. *Bhakti* as Poiesis

1. Audre Lorde, "Poetry Is Not a Luxury," in *Sister Outsider: Essays and Speeches by Audre Lorde* (Berkeley: Crossing Press, 2007), 37.
2. The Grindmill Songs Project has only nine verses by one Muslim woman, not devotional songs. See GSP, "The Songs of Shekh Amina," Village Bachoti (Nanded District), https://ccrss.org/database/songs.php?performer_id=763. There are more songs *about* Muslim women. See, for example, Semantic Class A:II-2.13evii (A02-02-13e07), "Women's social identity / Friendly ties / Friendly support / Muslim friends," in GSP, https://ccrss.org/database/songs.php?semantic_class_id=A02-02-13e07. See also 260n44. For songs on Jesus, see GSP, Semantic Class H:XXI-7.1a to H:XXI7.6, https://ccrss.org/database/songs.php?semantic_class_id=H21-07. For songs

on Buddha, see GSP, Semantic Class H: XXI 1.1-1.18, https://ccrss.org/database/songs.php?semantic_class_id=H21-

3. The songs on Ambedkar, almost all composed by women of the Dalit caste, are wide-ranging, some clearly composed closer to when he was alive and others part of the contemporary Dalit movement. Many of these songs draw on *bhakti* tropes and poetic expressions, though the attention to injustice and the explicit call for social movements of the Dalits are quite striking and distinctive in these songs. There is a huge corpus of songs on Ambedkar, far more than on any other historical figure, including many songs on Ambedkar's first and second wives that recall the songs on Rukmini, Vitthal's wife. See all Semantic Classes in GSP, H21–05, "Ambedkar / Struggles for Dalits," https://ccrss.org/database/songs.php?semantic_class_title_prefix_id=H21-05-01a. For songs on Gandhi, see GSP, Semantic Class H:XXI-4 (H21–04), https://ccrss.org/database/songs.php?semantic_class_id=H21-04. There are also a few songs on Jotirao Phule and his wife Savitribai Phule. See GSP, Semantic Class H:XXI-3 (H21–03), "Phule, S. Phule / Social initiative," https://ccrss.org/database/songs.php?semantic_class_id=H21-03.
4. See, for example, Guy Poitevin and Hema Rairkar, *Stonemill and Bhakti: From the Devotion of Peasant Women to the Philosophy of Swamis* (New Delhi: D. K. Printworld Private Limited, 1996), 260.
5. Sulochana Patankar, Village Kule (Pune District), GSP, https://ccrss.org/database/songs.php?song_id=6541.
6. Rama Ughade, Village Gadale (Pune District), GSP, https://ccrss.org/database/songs.php?song_id=6543.
7. *Māyavāṭecā Māgovā: Dr. Tara Bhavalkar,* Video Series. Doordarshan, Sahyadri. Episode 1, 24:40, https://www.youtube.com/watch?v=dNa_ZE3sfhk.
8. There are numerous verses on the injunction to grind. See A:II-5.3kiii (A02-05-03k03, "Labour / Grinding / Singing while grinding / No grinding without singing," GSP, https://ccrss.org/database/songs.php?semantic_class_id=A02-05-03k03.
9. Howard Thurman, "The Negro Spiritual Speaks of Life and Death," in *African-American Religious Thought: An Anthology*, ed. Cornel West and Eddie Glaude Jr. (Louisville, KY: Westminster Knox Press, 2003), 29.
10. Thurman, "The Negro Spiritual Speaks of Life and Death," 41. Parenthetical page numbers in the rest of the paragraph cite this work.
11. Indu Dighe, Village Chachiwali (Pune District), GSP, https://ccrss.org/database/songs.php?song_id=3495.
12. Gita Chawre, Village Taja (District Pune), GSP, https://ccrss.org/database/songs.php?song_id=3502.
13. Shailaja Paik, *The Vulgarity of Caste: Dalit, Sexuality, and Humanity in Modern India* (Stanford, CA: Stanford University Press, 2022), 7.

14. For over seven hundred examples of these songs, see GSP, Semantic Class A02-01-06, A:II-1.6a (A02-01-06a), "Woman's doubtful entity / Imagining one's funeral / One dies alone," https://ccrss.org/database/songs.php?semantic_class_id=A02-01-06.
15. Thurman, "The Negro Spiritual Speaks of Life and Death," 41.
16. Paul Rekret, *Take This Hammer: Work, Song, Crisis* (London: Goldsmiths Press, 2024), 5.
17. For an analysis of *sāsar/māher* as a metaphor of alienation and fulfillment in Tukaram's poetry, see Thomas Dabre, "Sasar-Maher Antithesis in the Abhaṅgas of Tukaram: From Alienation to Fulfillment," in *House and Home in Maharashtra*, ed. Irina Glushkova and Anne Feldhaus (New York: Oxford University Press, 1998), 102–110. See also M. Deshmukh, "Mothers and Daughters of *Bhakti*: Janābāī in Marathi Literature," *International Journal of Hindu Studies* 24, (2020): 33–59, for a discussion of *sāsar/māher* as metaphors in Varkari poetry derived from the grind mill song tradition. For exploration of the question of power and protest in *bhakti*, see John Stratton Hawley, Christian Lee Novetzke, and Swapna Sharma, eds., *Bhakti and Power* (Seattle: University of Washington Press, 2019). Any poetic or song tradition, if it truly speaks to the lived experience of the people who compose and sing, encompass both power and protest, not one or the other.
18. See especially Jacqueline Daukes," Female Voices in the Vārkarī Sampradāya: Gender Constructions in a Bhakti Tradition," (PhD thesis, University of London, School of Oriental and African Studies, 2014), 94–230, for a thorough overview of the literature on Vitthal *bhakti* sect as "a householder path." The two meanings of *saṃsār* are represented in the poetic tradition as a tension between the poets and their wives and/or mothers. The poetry and the hagiographies of Namdev and Tukaram are full of intense arguments between the male poets and their wives and mothers about their prioritizing of *bhakti* over domestic responsibilities as householders. For a discussion of these marital conflicts in the biographies of male *sants*, see Vidyut Aklujkar "Between Pestle and Mortar: Women in the Marathi Sant Tradition," in *Goddesses and Women in Indic Religious Traditions*, ed. Arvind Sharma (Leiden: E. J. Brill), 105–130.
19. Karen Pechilis Prentiss, *The Embodiment of Bhakti* (New York: Oxford University Press, 1999), 23.
20. Quoted in Prentiss, *Embodiment of Bhakti*, 23; see also Charles Hallisey, "Devotion in the Buddhist Literature of Medieval Sri Lanka" (PhD diss., University of Chicago, 1988), 68.
21. Hallisey, "Devotion," 88–91.
22. Lakshmi Satpute, Village Male (Pune District), GSP, https://ccrss.org/database/songs.php?song_id=30221.

23. Savitra Mare, Village Male (Pune District), GSP, https://ccrss.org/database/songs.php?song_id=30222.
24. Rohini Shukla theorizes three different forms of *bhakti* embodiment: embedded, alleviative, and generative. Shukla describes Bahinabai Chaudhari's poems as examples of "generative embodiment" as distinct from the embodiment experienced at *kīrtans*. This is perhaps another way of talking about *bhakti* as poiesis. *Bhakti* at the grind mill should not, I would only caution, be counterpoised to *bhakti* at *kīrtans* so much as seen in continuity and dialogue with it. See Rohini Shukla, "Authorship and Generative Embodiment in Bahiṇāī's Songs," *Transnational Literature* 10, no. 2 (May 2018): 9–12.
25. Sopan Dev, "Mājhī Āī," in *Bahiṇāīcī Gāṇī*, by Bahinabai Chaudhari (Mumbai: Popular Publishers, 1978 [1952]), 31.
26. Dev, "Mājhī Āī," 29–30.
27. Conversation with women, recorded by author, Shirad Shahapur, 2006, https://www.youtube.com/watch?v=cwEQ4sJ8kcU, at 26–28.45.
28. Michael Holquist, "Answering as Authoring: Mikhail Bakhtin's Trans-Linguistics," *Critical Inquiry* 10, no. 2 (December 1983): 311.
29. See Norman Cutler, *Songs of Experience: The Poetics of Tamil Devotion* (Bloomington: Indiana University Press, 1987), 6; See especially Christian Lee Novetzke, *Religion and Public Memory: A Cultural History of Saint Namdev in India* (New York: Columbia, 2008); Francesca Orsini and Katherine Butler Schofield, eds. *Tellings and Texts: Music, Literature and Performance in North India* (Open Book,Publishers, 2015); Linda Hess, *Bodies of Song: Kabir Oral Traditions and Performative Worlds in North India* (New York: Oxford University Press, 2015).
30. M. M. Bakhtin, "The Problem of Speech Genres," in *Speech Genres and Other Late Essays* (Austin: University of Texas Press, 2002), 69.
31. See, as example, GSP, Semantic Class, B:VI-2.9g (B06-02-09g), "Paṇḍharpur pilgrimage / Viṭhṭhhal—the dear one / Katha, Kirtan, Vina," https://ccrss.org/database/songs.php?semantic_class_id=B06-02-09g.
32. Mahananda Ujgare, Majalgaon Town (Beed District), GSP, https://ccrss.org/database/songs.php?song_id=36697.
33. Prabhavati Shinde, Village Gharani (Latur District), GSP, https://ccrss.org/database/songs.php?song_id=36697.
34. Wagh Mahadeo, Village Paritwadi (Ahmednagar District), GSP, https://ccrss.org/database/songs.php?song_id=92400.
35. Yashoda Gaykwad, Village Dhakali Jhari (Latur District), GSP, https://ccrss.org/database/songs.php?song_id=111803.
36. In *Śrī Namdev Gāthā: Visobā Khecar, Parasā Bhāgavat, Janābāī Yāñcyā Abhaṅgāsaha [Sakaḷa Santa Gāthā]*, ed. N. Sakhare (Pune: Varada Books, 2002), 310–311, *abhaṅga* 1103. This poem is not in *NG*.

37. Kalavati Parkhe, Village Vahegaon Majari (Latur District), GSP, https://ccrss.org/database/songs.php?song_id=63313.
38. Susie Tharu and K. Lalita, "Literature of the Ancient and Medieval Periods: Reading Against the Orientalist Grain," in *Women Writing India: 600 BC to the Early Twentieth Century*, vol. 1 (New York: The Feminist Press at CUNY, 1991), 157.
39. Christian Lee Novetzke, *Quotidian Revolution: Vernacularization, Religion, and the Premodern Public Sphere* (New York: Columbia University Press, 2016), 15.
40. Novetzke, *Quotidian Revolution*, 10.
41. Guy Poitevin, *The Voice and the Will: Subaltern Agency: Forms and Motives* (New Delhi: Manohar, 2002), 95.
42. See for example, Eknath's *gauḷanas*, in *Śrī Eknāth Gāthā [Sakaḷa Santa Gāthā]*, ed. N. Sākhare (Pune: Varada Books 2002 [1990]b), 18–49, *abhaṅgas* 51–173; and Tukaram's *gauḷanas* in *Śrī Tukārām Gāthā [Sakaḷa Santa Gāthā]*, ed. N. Sakhre (Pune: Varada Books 2002 [1990]c), 521–542, *abhaṅgas* 3419–3461. Sakhre sets these apart, and he includes them in a section with other female envoiced song forms. For more on Eknath's *bhāruḍs*, see Eleanor Zelliot, "Eknath's *Bhāruḍs*: The Sant as Link Between Cultures," in *The Sants: Studies in the Devotional Tradition of India*, ed. Karine and W. H. McLeod Schomer (New Delhi: Motilal Banarsidass, 1987), 91–110.
43. Rama Ughade, Village Gadale (Pune District), GSP, https://ccrss.org/database/songs.php?song_id=20448.
44. Rama Ughade, Village Gadale (Pune District), GSP, https://ccrss.org/database/songs.php?song_id=20450.
45. Shanta Giridhar Wahadne, Village Puntamba (Ahmednagar District), GSP, https://ccrss.org/database/songs.php?song_id=58290.
46. See an example of this widespread view in N. G. Joshi, *Marathi Chandoracanā Vīkās: Layadṛṣṭyā Punarvicār* (Mumbai: Mauj Publishers, 1964), 135. The Mahanubhavas have no written record of *abhaṅgas*, with the exception of one lone purported *abhaṅga* attributed to Mahadaise. See Raeside, "A Bibliographic Index of Mahānubhāva Works in Marathi," *Bulletin of the School of Oriental and African Studies* 23, no. 3 (1960): 469.
47. *Saṅgīta-Ratnākara of Śārṅgadeva: Sanskrit Text and English Translation with Comments and Notes, Volume 2, Chapters 2–4*, ed. and trans. R. K. Shringy under supervision of Prem Lata Sharma (New Delhi: Munshiram Manoharlal, 1989), vol. 2, 5.247.
48. Keshavchaitanya Kunte, email to author, December 30, 2021.
49. B. B. Chitgupi, "Vithal and Abhang," *Journal of the University of Bombay* 27, no. 2 (July 1958): 20–21.

50. *NG*, 570, *abhaṅga* 1382; 768, *abhaṅga* 2028. The editors cite two different manuscripts as the sources of *abhaṅga* 1382 (570 cf.), and 2028 (768 cf.). They are not dated, and nothing is known about the compilers, making it impossible to determine the date of composition. The poems are not cited as being in the oldest known layer of the manuscripts, the Dhule manuscripts with a colophon of 1631–1632.
51. *NG*, 570, *abhaṅga* 1382.
52. *NG*, 768, *abhaṅga* 2028.
53. Parshuram B. Godbole, *Vṛttadarpaṇa*, ed. V. V. Natekar and N. G. Joshi (Baroda: Good Companions Publishers, 1964 [1860]), 48–50.
54. H. D. Velankar, "Apabhraṁśa and Marāṭhī Metres," *New Indian Antiquary* 1, no. 4 (July 1938): 224.
55. Joshi, *Marāṭhī Chandoracanā*, 126.
56. Velankar, "Apabhraṁśa and Marāṭhī Metres," 220.
57. John Stratton Hawley, "Author and Authority in the Bhakti Poetry of North India." *The Journal of South Asian Studies* 47, no. 2 (1988): 270.
58. See Paul Zumthor, *Oral Poetry: An Introduction*, trans. Kathryn Murphy-Judy (Minneapolis: University of Minnesota Press, 1990), 168.
59. Ruth Finnegan, *Oral Poetry: Its Nature, Significance and Social Context* (London: Cambridge University Press, 1979), 201–206.
60. The *dhangar ovī*, it should be noted, does include one or several signature verses in which the performers give their names and villages, but this is rare in the oral poetic and performance genres and may be a sign of literary influence on this oral tradition. On this practice in the *dhangar ovī*, see Anne Feldhaus, "The Art of the Ovīs," introduction to *Say to the Sun, "Don't Rise" and to the Moon, "Don't Set:" Two Oral Narratives from the Countryside of Maharashtra*, ed. and trans. Anne Feldhaus with Ramdas Atkar and Rajaram Zagade (New York: Oxford University Press, 2014) 26–30.
61. S. G. Tulpule, *Classical Marathi Literature: From the Beginning to A.D. 1818*, vol. 9 of *A History of Indian Literature*, ed. Jan Gonda (Weisbaden: Harassowitz, 1979), 451n749.
62. See Anne Feldhaus and S. G. Tulpule, trans., *The Absence of God: In the Early Years of an Indian Sect: A Translation of Smṛtisthaḷ with an Introduction* (Honolulu: University of Hawai'i Press, 1992), 104–105, and chap. 113. For the Marathi, see *Smṛtisthaḷ*, ed. V. N. Deshpande (Pune: Venus Publishers, 1960 [1939]), 113.
63. See A. K. Priolkar, *Grānthika Marāṭhī Bhāṣā āṇi Koṅkaṇī Bolī* (Pune: University of Pune, 1966), 92.
64. See Charles Hallisey, trans., "Note on the Text and Translation," in *Therigatha: Poems of The First Buddhist Women*, trans. Hallisey. Murty Classical

Library of India (Cambridge, MA: Harvard University Press, 2015), xi; 250n6.

65. See J. T. P. de Bruijn, "The Name of the Poet in Classical Persian Poetry," in *Proceedings of the Third European Conference of Iranian Studies (held in Cambridge, 11th to 15th September 1995).*" Part 2: Mediaeval and Modern Persian Studies, ed. Charles Melville (Wiesbaden: Dr. Ludwig Reichert Verlag, 1999). I thank Sunil Sharma for sharing this essay with me.
66. Deborah Roberts, "Sphragis," *Oxford Classical Dictionary,* March 7, 2016, https://oxfordre.com/classics/view/10.1093/acrefore/9780199381135.001.0001/acrefore-9780199381135-e-6041.
67. William Shakespeare, "Sonnet 136, in *The Complete Works of Shakespeare, Third Edition*, ed. David Bevington (Glenview, IL: Scott, Foresman, and Co., 1980), 1606–1608. See also 135 and 143, where Shakespeare is punning on his name in these sonnets.
68. Marisa Galvez, *Songbook: How Lyrics Became Poetry in Medieval Europe* (Chicago: University of Chicago Press, 2012), 57–98.
69. Galvez, *Songbook*, 61.
70. I am drawing loosely on the discussion of the figural in Erich Auerbach, "Figura," in *Scenes from the Drama of European Literature* (Manchester: Manchester University Press, 1984).
71. Zumthor, *Oral Poetry*, 168.
72. *NG*, *abhaṅga* 288.
73. Bakhtin, "The Problem of Speech Genres," 97.
74. *Śrī Tukārām Gāthā*, 542, *abhaṅga* 3463.
75. Saru Chavan, Village Bangarde (Solapur District), GSP, https://ccrss.org/database/songs.php?song_id=68575.
76. Janabai Khuse, Village Motala (Buldhana District), GSP, https://ccrss.org/database/songs.php?song_id=111671.
77. *Bhaktavijay* of Mahipati, ed. S. R. Devale (Pune: Sharada Sahitya, n.d.), 21.157.
78. D. R. Nagaraj, "Critical Tensions in the History of Kannada Literature," in *Literary Cultures in History: Reconstructions from South Asia*, ed. Sheldon Pollock (Berkeley: University of California Press, 2003), 335.
79. *Bhaktavijay*, 21.166.
80. *Bhaktavijaya*, 21.167.
81. *Bhaktavijaya*, 21.189–190, 192.
82. *Bhaktavijaya*, 21.214.
83. *Bhaktavijaya*, 21.150–51.
84. *Bhaktavijaya*, 21. 206.
85. *NG*, *abhaṅga* by Janabai, 408; also in *Śrī Namdev Gāthā: Sakaḷa Santa Gāthā*, 743, *abhaṅga* 276. Novetzke translates and discusses this same poem for its

strange omission of Namdev, and Pollock uses this poem "attributed to the fourteenth-century Janabai" to show "how prominent writing became in vernacular traditions." Both, however, completely overlook the caste implications of the final line, even in their translations of the poem. See Novetzke, *Religion and Public Memory*, 78; and Sheldon Pollock, *Language of the Gods in the World of Men* (Berkeley: University of California Press, 2006), 307.

86. The editorial footnote to this particular Janabai poem in the *NG* notes a variation of the final line that does not include this metaphor of the ritual bath. This alternative final verse appears in two undated manuscripts that the editors surmise to be 250 years old based on handwriting and paper quality, landing them in the early eighteenth century. There is no indication which or in how many manuscripts the version chosen for the printed anthology appeared, but given that it was chosen, we might surmise it to be more than two manuscripts. Novetzke speculates that this poem may have circulated orally for fifty years or so before being written down and pushes the possible date of its composition back to the mid-seventeenth century. While the date of the poem may be accurate, an oral prehistory to this poem is unlikely given its subject matter, a thing of greater concern to scribes (*lekhaks*) than to any oral (or even written) poets. See *NG*, 983fn1. See also Novetzke, *Religion and Public Memory*, 260fn 9.
87. Richard Eaton, *India in the Persianate Age, 1000–1765* (Berkeley: University of California Press, 2019), 136–137.
88. For more on this, see Sumit Guha, "Serving the Barbarian to Preserve the Dharma: The Ideology and Training of a Clerical Elite in Peninsular India ca. 1300–1800," *The Indian Economic and Social History Review* 47, no. 4 (2010): 497–525. On conflicts between Brahmin and Kayastha scribal elite, see Rosalind O'Hanlon, "Social Worth of Scribes: Brahmins, Kayasthas and the Social Order in Early Modern India," in *Indian Economic and Social History Review* 47, no. 4 (2010), 563–595.
89. Prachi Deshpande, "The Writerly Self: Literacy, Discipline and Codes of Conduct in Early Modern Western India," *The Indian Economic and Social History Review* 53, no. 4 (2016): 451.
90. Prachi Deshpande, *Scripts of Power: Writing, Language Practices, and Cultural History in Western India* (Ranikhet: Permanent Black, 2023), 121.
91. For an analysis of the role of the Ramdasi sect see Deshpande, "Devotional Writing and Literary Archives," in *Scripts of Power*, 126–139.
92. G. N. Devy, *"Of Many Heroes": An Indian Essay in Literary Historiography* (Hyderabad: Orient Longman, 1998), 167.
93. On the *bāḍa* or performance notebook as written-oral archive, see Christian Lee Novetzke, *Religion and Public Memory: A Cultural History of Saint Namdev in*

India (New York: Columbia, 2008), 102–119. For a brief and useful history of the making of *sant gāthās*, see Jon Keune, *Shared Devotion, Shared Food: Equality and the Bhakti-Caste Question in Western India* (New York: Oxford University Press, 2021), 78–82.

94. *Bhaktalīlāmṛta* of Mahipati, ed. Damodar Savalaram et al. (Mumbai: Induprakash Press, 1935), 35.82–84; see also the English translation of the Tukaram chapters of the *Bhaktalīlāmṛta* in Justin E. Abbot, trans. *Tukaram: The Poet Saint of Maharashtra: Translation from Mahipati's Bhaktalīlāmṛta* (Delhi: Sri Satguru Publications: 1996 [1931]), 207, 35.84–85. Abbott's translation of the line about *ovīs* is, "Verses with false sentiment are sung while turning the hand-mill, but one must take them as true" (207, 85).
95. Anusaya Lad, Village Ichalkaranji Shendor (Belgaum District, Karnataka). GSP, https://ccrss.org/database/songs.php?song_id=85793.
96. See, for example, Velcheru Narayana Rao, "Epics and Ideologies: Six Telugu Folk Epics," in *Another Harmony: New Essays on the Folklore of India*, ed. Stuart H. Blackburn and A. K. Ramanujan (Berkeley: University of California press, 1986), 154–155; Pollock, *Language of the Gods*, 310–315.
97. R. R. Gosavi, *Śrīsakalasantagathā*, vol. 2 (Pune: Sarathi Publishers, 2000), 1157, *abhaṅga* 32. This *abhaṅga* is sometimes attributed to Tukaram. For further analysis of this poem and its history, see Deshmukh, "Mothers and Daughters of *Bhakti*," 36–37.
98. A. K. Ramanujan, "Introduction," in *Speaking of Śiva* (London: Penguin, 1973), 20.
99. Dilip Chitre, Introduction to *Says Tuka: Selected Poems of Tukaram*, vol. 1 (Pune: Sontheimer Cultural Association, 2003), xxxi–xxxii.
100. Deshpande, *Scripts of Power*, 119.
101. Janabai Thorat, Shirad Shahapur, recorded June 26, 2006. Personal collection.
102. Thurman, "The Negro Spiritual Speaks of Life and Death," 43.

5. Women and Vernacularization

1. Eleanor Zelliot, "Women Saints in Medieval Maharashtra," in *Faces of the Feminine*, ed. Mandakranta Bose (New York: Oxford University Press, 2000), 192; see also Jacqueline Daukes, "Female Voices: Gender Constructions in a Bhakti Tradition" (PhD thesis, University of London, School of Oriental and African Studies, 2014). Her whole dissertation is focused on examining "why there are so many women associated with the *Vārkarī sampradāya* by considering the function of gender attribution in the discursive construction of the *Vārkarī sampradāya* as a householder path" (17).

2. Women have largely been treated as "add-ons" to the main story of *bhakti* and of literary making in Marathi, the feminist scholar Vidyut Bhagwat observes. See Vidyut Bhagwat, "Heritage of *Bhakti*: *Sant* Women Writings in Marathi" in *Culture and the Making of Identity in Contemporary India*, ed. Kamala Ganesh and Usha Thakkar (New Delhi: Sage Publications, 2005), 171. "The more I read," Jacqueline Daukes writes at the beginning of her comprehensive dissertation on Varkari women poets, "the more I saw that scholarship had been focused primarily on male poet-sants, particularly Jñāneśvar, Nāmdev, Eknāth and Tukārām. It seemed to me that female poet-sants were marginalised as addendums to the male poet-sants and as footnotes to history." See Daukes, "Female Voices," 13. See also M. Deshmukh, "The Mothers and Daughters of *Bhakti*: Janābāī in Marathi Literature," *International Journal of Hindu Studies* 24 (2020): 33–59.
3. For a long list of Mahanubhava versions of *Rukmiṇī-Svayaṃvar* (*RS*), see Ian Raeside, "A Bibliographic Index of Mahānubhāva Works in Marathi," *Bulletin of the School of Oriental and African Studies* 23, no. 3 (1960): 494–495. Eknath's *RS* is still regularly recited by young women who want to get married and is widely available as a printed pamphlet. A small excerpt of Eknath's *RS* on the turmeric ceremony of the wedding is printed in N. Sakhare ed., *Śrī Eknāth Gāthā [Sakaḷa Santa Gāthā]* (Pune: Varada Books, 2002), 654–658. Dasopant's *RS* is quoted in N. G. Joshi, *Marāṭhī Chandoracanā Vīkās: Layadṛṣṭyā Punarvicār* (Mumbai: Mauj Publishers, 1964), 190–191.
4. For an analysis of this story in Sanskrit and a brief overview of its vernacular life, see Adheesh Sathaye, "Why Did Hariścandra Matter in Early Medieval India? Truth, Fact, and Folk Narrative in the Sanskrit Purāṇas," *The Journal of Hindu Studies* 2, no. 2 (November 2009): 131–159. For a translation of Raghavanka's *Hariścandra Kāvyam* (ca. 1225), see Vanamala Viswanatha, trans., *The Life of Harishchandra*, Murty Classical Library of India (Cambridge, MA: Harvard University Press, 2017). *Hariścandra Ākhyāna* of Janabai, in *Śrī Nāmdev Gāthā [Sakaḷa Santa Gāthā]*, ed. N. Sakhare (Pune: Varada Books, 2002), 747–756, *abhaṅgas* 298–320; also see *NG*, 989–1002, *abhaṅgas* 432–454.
5. See Christian Lee Novetzke, *Quotidian Revolution: Vernacularization, Religion, and the Premodern Public Sphere* (New York: Columbia University Press, 2016), 214 and 347n1.
6. Karen Pechilis Prentiss, *Embodiment of Bhakti* (New York: Oxford University Press, 1999), 20–21.
7. For "the absent and the invisible," see D. R. Nagaraj, "Critical Tensions in the History of Kannada Literary Culture," in *Literary Cultures in History: Reconstructions from South Asia*, ed. Sheldon Pollock (Berkeley: University of California Press, 2003), 332. Novetzke, *Quotidian Revolution*, 179.

8. Novetzke, *Quotidian Revolution*, 28. For his discussion of gender and the feminine figuration of Marathi in relation to Sanskrit, see 177–183.
9. On the role of women in European vernacularization, see Herbert Grundmann, "Women and Literature in the Middle Ages: A Contribution on the Origins of Vernacular Writing." In *Herbert Grundmann (1902–1970), Essays on Heresy, Inquisition, and Literacy*, ed. Jennifer Kolpacoff Deane (Rochester, NY: York Medieval Press), 30–55; Joan Ferrante, *To the Glory of Her Sex: Women's Role in the Composition of Medieval Texts* (Bloomington: Indiana University Press, 1997); Alison Cornish, "A Lady Asks: The Gender of Vulgarization in Late Medieval Italy," *PMLA* 115, no. 2 (March 2000): 166–180; June Hall McCash, "The Role of Women in the Rise of the Vernacular," *Comparative Literature* 60, no. 1 (2008): 45–57; Diane Watt, *Women, Writing and Religion in England and Beyond, 650–1100* (London: Bloomsbury, 2020).
10. Dante Alighieri, *Vita Nuova* 16, Frisardi translation, *Digital Dante* (Columbia University), https://digitaldante.columbia.edu/text/library/la-vita-nuova-frisardi/; for more on women as Dante's audience, see also Martin Eisner "Bridge Essay: Vernacularization and World Literature: The Language of Women in the World of God," in *A Companion to World Literature*, ed. Ken Seigneurie (New York: John Wiley & Sons, Ltd, 2020), 685–691.
11. Grundmann, "Women and Literature in the Middle Ages," 47. Grundmann wrote his influential studies of medieval literature in Germany during the Nazi era. For more on his ambivalent status, see Arno Borst, "Obituary Note (1970)," in *Herbert Grundmann (1902–1970)*, 221–249.
12. See, for example, more than two thousand letters in Latin written by women between the fourth and thirteenth centuries, collected, edited, and translated: Joan Ferrante, ed. and trans., *Epistolae: Medieval Women's Letters*, Columbia Center for Teaching and Learning, 2022, https://epistolae.ctl.columbia.edu/.
13. Grundmann tells the story of the court poet and knight Ulrich von Lichtenstein (ca. 1200–January 26, 1275), who was illiterate and would run to his clerk to have letters from the ladies read to him. Once he received a letter from a lady and had to wait for several excruciating days for his clerk. When the clerk read the letter to him, it consisted of a rejection written in ten verses. In other words, the woman was accomplished at writing poetry, while the court poet was not even literate. See Grundmann, "Women and Literature in the Middle Ages," 43–44.
14. Grundmann, "Women and Literature in the Middle Ages," 38.
15. Ferrante, *To the Glory of Her Sex*, 39. See also, June Hall McCash, *The Cultural Patronage of Medieval Women* (Athens: University of Georgia Press, 1996).
16. See McCash, "The Role of Women," 53–54, for a brief overview of what she calls the "unleashing" of women's authorship in several European languages as both the cause and the outcome of the turn to the vernacular.

17. Kurpe Baba, Village Akole (Pune District), GSP, https://ccrss.org/database/songs.php?song_id=13786.
18. Anne Feldhaus and S. G. Tulpule, trans., *In the Absence of God: In the Early Years of an Indian Sect: A Translation of Smṛtisthaḷ with an Introduction* (Honolulu: University of Hawai'i Press, 1992), 108, chap. 120. *Smṛtisthaḷ*, ed. V. N. Deshpande (Pune: Venus Publishers, 1960 [1939]), 120.
19. The *Mātṛki-Rukmiṇī- Svayaṃvar* is published with *Dhavaḷe* of Mahadaise, in *Ādya Marāṭhī Kavayitrī: Dhavaḷe-Purvārdha va Uttarārdha, Mātṛkī-Rukmiṇī-Svayaṃvar, Pāṭhabhed, Śabdakoś va Prastāvanā Yāṃsaha*, ed. V. N. Deshpande (Yavatamal: Sharada Ashram Press, 1935), 33–45. While *Dhavaḷe* is well-attested in the thirteenth century texts, the *Mātṛki-Rukmiṇi-Svayaṃvar* is not mentioned in the *Smṛtisthaḷ*; furthermore, there appears to be an almost identical poem, the *Rukmniṇī-Saiṃvaramālā*, attributed to another, unidentified poet by the name of Mukunda. See *Kāvyadīpika*, ed. Annasaheb Adsod (Pune: Snehavardhan Publishing, 2000), 53–60, for a print version of Mukunda's poem. The *Garbhakāṇḍa-ovyā* are also not attested in the early literature, and there is a work of the same name attributed to another woman named Pomaisa according to a commentarial work. Neither poem is available in its entirety. See the editorial note by Adsod in *Kāvyadīpika* (123). But this does not mean they were not first written by Mahadaise, and they should not be dismissed. It is only the need to focus that prevents me from including more on them here.
20. See Raeside, "A Bibliographic Index," 488.
21. For works attributed to Nagaise, see Raeside, "A Bibliographical Index," 470, 478, 486, 497, 503. Many of these works are not extant. According to the *Mahārāṣṭra Sārasvat*, this Nagaise is different from the granddaughter of Nagdev also named Nagaise and mentioned in the *Smṛtisthaḷ*. See V. L. Bhave, *Mahārāṣṭra Sārasvat*, vol. 1, ed. S. G. Tulpule (Mumbai: Popular Publishers, 1963 [1898]), 698. See Feldhaus and Tulpule, *In the Absence of God*, 137, 209, for more on the other Nagaise, also a very learned figure. The archival record of women's writing is especially vulnerable to slow attrition over time, likely due to the lesser value placed on women's writing. More research on these and other women Mahanubhava writers is needed.
22. *NG*, 963, *abhaṅga* 324.
23. J. R. Ajgaonkar, *Mahārāṣṭra Kavicaritra*, vol. 6 (Mumbai: 1924), 87–88.
24. Nandapurkar shows the verbatim overlap in over thirty lines between Janabai's and Mukteshvar's Harischandra stories. See N. G. Nandapurkar, *Mukta Mayūrāñcī Bhāratem̐* (Hyderabad: Marathwada Sahitya Parishad, 1956), 728–730. He also goes on to show the same overlap in their respective versions of *Thālipāk*, 733–736.
25. See Dauke's invaluable translations of poems attributed to over a dozen women, including lesser known figures from Namdev's family, Tukaram's

niece, and others: Daukes, "Female Voices," 310–394. On the poet Nagari, likely Namdev's niece, see R. C. Dhere, *Śrī Nāmdev, Janī āṇi Nāgarī* (Pune: Padmagandha Publishers, 2015).

26. Grundmann's formulation of a "strict division" between "Latin literature" and "nonliterary speech" has also come under scrutiny by scholars studying the influence of orality on early vernacular texts. See Mary Ellen Lamb and Karen Bamford, *Oral Traditions and Gender in Early Modern Literary Texts* (Burlington, VT: Ashgate Publishing, 2008); A. N. Doane and Carol Braun Pasternack, *Vox Intexta: Orality and Textuality in the Middle Ages* (Madison: University of Wisconsin Press, 1991); Mark C. Amodio, *Writing the Oral Tradition: Oral Poetics and Literate Culture in Medieval England* (Notre Dame: University of Notre Dame Press, 2004).
27. Andrew Ollett, *Language of Snakes: Prakrit, Sanskrit, and the Language Order of Premodern India*. South Asia Across the Disciplines (Berkeley: University of California Press, 2017), 119.
28. See Julie Bergljot Chiarucci, "Kavva and Kāvya: Hāla's Gāhākosa and Its Sanskrit Successors" (PhD diss., University of California, Berkeley, 2014), 219.
29. Anne Klinck, "Introduction," in *Medieval Woman's Song: Cross-Cultural Approaches*, ed. Anne L. Klinck and Ann Marie Rasmussen (Philadelphia: University of Pennsylvania Press, 2002), 3. See also Anne Klinck, "Lyric Voice and the Feminine in Some Ancient and Mediaeval *Frauenlieder*," *Florilegium* 13 (1994): 13–36.
30. Grundmann, "Women and Literature in the Middle Ages," 36. See also Klinck, "Introduction," 6; Klinck, "Sappho and Her Daughters," 25.
31. Anne L. Klinck, "Sappho and Her Daughters: Some Parallels Between Ancient and Medieval Woman's Song," in *Medieval Woman's Song: Cross-Cultural Approaches*, ed. Anne L. Klinck and Ann Marie Rasmussen (Philadelphia: University of Pennsylvania Press, 2002), 25.
32. On the Mahanubhava's understanding of Krishna, see Anne Feldhaus, "Kṛṣṇa and the Kṛṣṇas: Kṛṣṇa in the Mahānubhāva Pantheon," in *Bhakti in Current Research, 1979–1982*, ed. M. Thiel-Horstmann (Berlin: Dietrich Reimer, 1983), 133–142.
33. Janabai Thorat, Bhendegaon, recorded June 26, 2006. Personal collection.
34. Ruth Vanita reads the intimacy between Vitthal, figured as a female, and Janabai as romantic. It's true Vitthal is invoked by Janabai as a female friend, but there is never any explicitly erotic charge to their friendship. See Ruth Vanita, "God as Sakhi: Medieval Poet Janabai and her Friend Vitthabai," in *Gandhi's Tiger and Sita's Smile: Essays on Gender, Sexuality and Culture* (New Delhi: Yoda Press, 2005), 100.
35. *NLC*, U109; *KLC* U102. Kolte's edition says that Chakradhar was angry at Sarangpandit, but Nagpure's says he explained things to Sarangpandit.

36. Feldhaus, trans. *God at Play*, vol 1. Murty Classical Library (Cambridge, MA: Harvard University Press, 2024), 312–313, P105.
37. See Feldhaus, *God at Play*, 139–141, E74; 144–149, P1–2.
38. See, for example, *KLC* U536. Kolte's inclusion of a number of other *līḷās* describing Chakradhar's mistreatment and death are the reason that the Kolte edition, though meticulously edited and comprehensive, has been rejected by many Mahanubhavas and even banned in Maharashtra. See the translation and insightful analysis of this *līḷā* in Novetzke, *Quotidian Revolution*, 205–207.
39. In one *līḷā*, for example, Chakradhar refuses gold coins by the Yadava king. The various editions and manuscripts of the *Līḷācaritra* specify different kings involved in this episode. In Feldhaus, *God at Play*, 81, U39, it is the King Krishnadev (r. 1246–1260) and his grandfather Singhanadev (r. 1210–1246) who are referenced; in the Kolte edition Krishnadev and Mahadev are referenced. See *KLC* U61 and *NLC* U56. Novetzke discusses this *līḷā* and others as evidence that Chakradhar's "quotidian revolution" is "not financed by state or secular power, but buoyed by the slow accretions of everyday life," 97. See Novetzke, *Quotidian Revolution*, 193–201.
40. Feldhaus, *God at Play*, 313–314, P106.
41. Baise's death by suicide is narrated in *NLC,* U509; *KLC*, U535; in Feldhaus, *God at Play*, U452
42. Raeside, "A Bibliographic Index,"484.
43. *KLC*, AL58; *NLC*, AL66. Nagpure's gloss in modern Marathi was helpful in translating this *līḷā*.
44. For Mahadaise's family tree re-created from Mahanubhava sources, see V. N. Deshpande, introduction to *Ādya Marāṭhī Kavayitrī: Dhavaḷe-Purvārdha va Uttarārdha, Mātṛkī-Rukmiṇī-Svayaṃvar, Pāṭhabhed, Śabdakoś va Prastāvanā Yāṃsaha* (Yavatamal: Sharada Ashram Press, 1935), 3–4.
45. For examples, see *NLC,* U343, U377, U437, U438.
46. *NLC,* U436. This *līḷā* is included in *KLC,* U448 but is not in *God at Play* because it is not in the Nene edition. Kolte notes that this *līḷā* is referenced in an important commentarial work on the *Sūtrapāṭh*, the *Prakaraṇavaśa* (ca. 1325) attributed to Parasharambas, an early disciple. See *KLC,* 642; cf. Nagpure cites two manuscripts as his sources for this *līḷā*, as well as references to it in the "Vicār Mālikā," a section of the *Sūtrapāṭh*. For a brief description of the history of the "Vicār Mālikā" see Feldhaus, *The Religious System of the Mahānubhāva Sect: The Mahānubhāva Sūtrapāṭha* (New Delhi: Manohar, 1983), 10–11, 20. These references attest to the early date of the *līḷā* and show that it received attention within the tradition, so it is not entirely clear why Nene excluded it.
47. Mahadaise is translating and condensing the Bhagavad Gītā, 10.21, 10.22, and 10.26 in this embedded verse.

48. Feldhaus, *God at Play,* SP4.
new Feldhaus, *God at Play,* SP7.
49. Feldhaus, *God at Play,* SP7.
50. See *NLC,* U560 to U612. Many of these *līḷās* are not included in Feldhaus's translation because they were excluded by Nene. Many of the *līḷās* in which Mahadaise asks questions about her *purāṇa* readings are omitted by Nene.
51. *NLC* U571.
52. Feldhaus and Tulpule, *In the Absence of God,* 125, chap. 168.
53. Feldhaus and Tulpule, *In the Absence of God,* 73, chap. 15. See also the discussion of this same quote in Novetzke, *Quotidian Revolution,* 182–183.
54. *Smṛtisthaḷ,* 15. S. G. Tulpule and Anne Feldhaus, *A Dictionary of Old Marathi* (New York: Oxford University Press, 2000), 367.
55. *Smṛtisthaḷ,* 123; see also translation in Feldhaus and Tulpule, *In the Absence of God,* 109, chap. 123.
56. There are several manuscript recensions of *Śrīkṛṣṇacaritra,* including one longer version that appears to have been expanded at a later time. While some scholars attribute authorship to Bhaskar, most consider it part of Mhaimbhat's corpus of writings. See Priti Kishor Umathe, *Mhāīmbhaṭaviracit Tīn Caritragrantha* (Nagpur: Sahitya Prasār Kendra, 2021), 87–120, for a detailed history of this work. Kolte includes a short version of it appended at the end of *Līḷācaritra;* see *KLC,* 733–750. It is also published as an independent work; see S. G. Tulpule, ed., *Śrīkṛṣṇacaritra* (Pune: Venus Publishers, 1966).
57. Feldhaus and Tulpule, *In the Absence of God,* 126–127, chap. 174.
58. *Smṛtisthaḷ,* 174.
59. Irlekar, *Mahadaṃbece Dhavaḷe,* 21–32.
60. For an insightful comparison of the story of Rukmini's wedding in the *Bhagavata Purāṇa,* a fourteenth-century Braj version by the poet Nanddas, and a modern television version, see Heidi Pauwels, *The Goddess as Role Model: Sita and Radha in Scripture and on Screen* (New York: Oxford University Press, 2008). There are important parallels between Mahadaise's version and Nanddas's *Rukminī Maṅgal.* Nanddas, like Mahadaise, is not interested in battles or the "proper" wedding and wraps up his version soon after the abduction as well, according to Pauwels, and no one claimed it was unfinished or tried to write a new ending for him.
61. Although the *Smṛtisthaḷ* recounts that Narendra wrote a work of 1,800 *ovīs,* Kolte writes that all the manuscripts he could find on Narendra's *Rukmiṇī-Svayaṃvar,* except one, comprised approximately 871 to 900 *ovīs.* The one exception was a manuscript of almost 3,000 *ovīs* that he believes was likely extended by a later writer. Kolte made the decision to publish the version

that was attested in the most manuscripts with 871 *ovīs*, and it ends in the middle of descriptions of Krishna's palace when the messenger sent by Rukmini reaches it. See Kolte, introduction to *Rukmiṇī-Svayaṃvar* of Narendra, 11–12.

62. H. C. Bhayani, *Apabraṁśa Language and Literature: A Short Introduction* (Delhi: B. L. Institute of Indology, 1989), 26–27; see *Svayambhūchandas* of Svayambhu, ed. H. D. Velankar, Rājasthāna Purātana Granthamāla 37 (Jodhpur: Rajasthana Pracyavidya Pratisthana, 1962), 4.16–4.22. In Velankar's introduction to this text (xiv), he provides an English summary of the verses on the *dhavala*. Hemachandra gives examples of six varieties of *dhavala* in *Chandonuśāsana*, 5.32–40. See *Chandonuśāna* of Hemachandra, ed. H. D. Velankar, Singhi Jain Series 49 (Mumbai: Bharatiya Vidya Bhavan, 1961).
63. *Mānasollāsa* of Someshvara, vol. 3, ed. G. K. Shrigondekar (Baroda: Oriental Institute, 1961), 4.16.449, 552. See H. C. Bhayani, "The Dhavala Songs in Prakrit Apabraṁśa and Post-Apabraṁśa Traditions," in *Indological Studies: Prakrit and Performing Arts: Prakrit and Apabraṁśa Studies* (Ahmedabad: Parshva Publishers, 1993), 85–86.
64. The *dhavala* appears to be related to a Gujarati song type called *dhoḷ*, which continues to have an oral life in marriage ceremonies in that region. According to Bhayani, some early Gujarati poetry featuring the marriage of a hero might include *dhavalas* as songs within a larger work, as we see in the Marathi works of Narendra, Eknath, and Dasopant. Or the poetic work as a whole can be "synonymous" with the *dhavala*, as we see with Mahadaise's *Dhavaḷe*. See Bhayani, "The Dhavala Songs," 91–92. N. G. Joshi has an extensive discussion of the *dhavala* form with examples from Eknath, Dasopant and others, all related to their versions of the story of Rukmini's wedding. See Joshi, *Marāṭhī Chandoracanā* 184–194. A more careful study of Gujarati and Marathi vernacularization is needed but beyond the focus of this study.
65. Anne Feldhaus, trans., *Deeds of God in Ṛddhipur* (New York: Oxford University Press, 1984), 126, *līḷā* 224.
66. This line is *Dhavaḷe*, P31.4.
67. Feldhaus, *Deeds of God*, 126, *līḷā* 224.
68. Feldhaus and Tulpule, *In the Absence of God*, 105, chap. 113.
69. Feldhaus and Tulpule, *In the Absence of God*,125, chap. 167.
70. *Dhavaḷe*, P82.
71. Pauwels discusses Rukmini's abduction in the context of two types of weddings outlined in the *Dharmaśāstras*, the *svayaṃvara*, in which the bride ostensibly chooses her husband, and the *rākṣasa-vivāha* or "demonic wedding," in which a bride is kidnapped. The abduction is known as a *rākṣasī* or demonic wedding, but Pauwel notes that it actually seems to give much more agency to Rukmini than the famous *svayaṃvar* gave to Sita. See Pauwels, *Goddess as*

Role Model, 114–142. Interestingly, Marathi versions have primarily used the title *Rukmiṇī-Svayaṃvar* rather than *Rukmiṇī Haraṇa* (The abduction of Rukmini), downplaying the kidnapping, but for Mahadaise, the abduction is the wedding.

72. Kirin Narayan lists several songs by a woman in Kangra named Sita Devi to convey the "the vast knowledge that a person without written literacy can carry," one of which is a song about "Rukman's" wedding. See Kirin Narayan, *Everyday Creativity* (Chicago: University of Chicago Press, 2012), 70–72.
73. Bhagu Dive, Village Shrirampur (Ahmednagar District), GSP, https://ccrss.org/database/songs.php?song_id=40455.
74. See for example the 375 songs on the marriage of Rukmini to Vitthal, GSP, Semantic Class B:VI-2.11aiii (B06-02-11a03), "Paṅḍharpur pilgrimage / Viṭhṭhhal and Rukhmini / Māher of Rukhmini / Marriage of Viṭhṭhhal Rukhmini," https://ccrss.org/database/songs.php?song_id=40455.
75. Parvati Nikam, Village Nandgaon (Pune District), GSP, https://ccrss.org/database/songs.php?song_id=46697.
76. *Dhavaḷe*, P10.
77. *Dhavaḷe*, P21.
78. *Rukmiṇī-Svayaṃvar* of Narendra, 79.675–685.
79. Padmini Jadav, Village Jamkhed (Ahmednagar District), GSP, https://ccrss.org/database/songs.php?semantic_class_id=B06-02-11a03.
80. Gajara Jadav, Village Jamkhed (Ahmednagar District), GSP, https://ccrss.org/database/songs.php?song_id=44769.
81. Sathaye," Why Did Hariścandra Matter," 133.
82. *NG*, 1003 cfn1, 2; 1004 cfn1. For the dating of the Dhule manuscript, see the editorial preface to *NG*, 28. The Dhule manuscript has been lost since the publication of *NG*, so we have no way of knowing whether Janabai's *Hariścandra Ākhyāna* was included in it. I was unable to locate any manuscripts of Janabai's *Hariścandra Ākhyāna*, but I did find copies of Janabai's *Thālipāk* in both the Rajwade Samshodhan Mandal archives in Dhule and in the *Bharat Itīhās Saṃśodhan Manḍaḷ* in Pune (BISM II 1027).
83. Christian Lee Novetzke, *Religion and Public Memory: A Cultural History of Saint Namdev in India* (New York: Columbia, 2008), 139.
84. On the Portuguese translation of Vishnudas Nama, see A. K. Priolkar, "Junyā Marāṭhī Granthāñcī Portūgīj Bhāṣāntare," in *Marāṭhī Saṃśodhan*, vol. 1, ed. A. K. Priolkar (Mumbai: Marathi Samshodhan Mandal, 1966), 154–155.
85. S. B. Kulkarni, "Sant Janābāī," *Lokmat* (July 17, 1994): 2–4.
86. Sarojini Shende suggests the dates 1580 to 1633 for the writings of Vishnudas Nama based on a colophon of 1595 for his story the *Śukākhyāna* and of 1609

for a manuscript of his *Ādiparva*. She believes the *Hariścandrapurāṇakathā* was written circa 1580. She also points out that Mukteshvar refers derisively to Vishnudas Nama, critiquing him for his inclusion of local stories in his *Mahābhārata*, which shows that he knew of Vishnudas Nama's works (6). Indeed the overlaps between Mukteshvar's and Vishnudas Nama's Harischandra stories show that Mukteshvar quite liberally used his texts as source materials for his own. Sarojini Shende, "The *Mahābhārata* of Viśnudāsanāma: A Critical Study" (PhD diss., University of Mumbai, 1960), 6–8.

87. Shende, "The *Mahābhārata* of Viśnudāsanāma," 8.
88. See P. B Godbole, *Navanīt athavā Marāṭhī Kavitāñce Veñce* (Pune: Shubhada Sarasvat Publishers, 1990 [1854]), 222–250. An excerpt of Narendra's *Rukmiṇī-Svayaṃvar* is also included in this anthology, 40–42.
89. For a list of quotations showing the verbatim repetition of lines in Janabai's and Mukteshvar's Harischandra stories, see Nandapurkar, *Mukta Mayūrāñce Bhārateṃ*, 728–730. Nandapurkar also shows the same overlaps in Janabai's and Mukteshvar's versions of *Thālīpāk* and *Draupadīvastraharaṇ* (733–738). He does not, however, take up Vishnudas Nama's version.
90. *Hariścandra Ākhyāna* of Janabai, in *Śrī Nāmdev Gāthā [Sakaḷa Santa Gāthā]*, ed. N. Sakhare (Pune: Varada Books, 2002), 299.3–4.
91. *Hariścandrapurāṇakatha* of Vishnudas Nama, ed. J. S. Deshpande, in *Nāmdevāce Sphūṭ Ākhyāne*, vol. 4, *Prācīn Marāṭhī Kavitā* (Muṃbaī Marāṭhī Grantha Saṅgrahalaya, 1966), 13–53, 1.40
92. *Hariścandrākhyāna* of Mukteshvar, ed. Dada Gore and Sunetra Oak (Aurangabad: Goda Publishers, 1975), 1.27–1.28.
93. Nandapurkar, *Mukta Mayūrāñce Bhārateṃ*, 730. Though he makes no mention of the *Hariścandra Ākhyana*, Ajgaonkar noted the similarities in a version of *Draupadīvastraharaṇ* attributed to Janabai and Mukteshvar's version but dismisses Janabai's text as an interpolation since it is unthinkable to him that a learned poet of the status and caliber of Mukteshvar might have copied a work attributed to the lowly Janabai. See Ajgoankar, *Mahārāṣṭra Kavicaritra*, 88.
94. A. N. Deshpande, *Prāchin Marāthī Vaṅmayācā Itīhās*, vol. 4 (Pune: Venus Publishers,1966), 383.
95. Songs on Harischandra can be found at GSP, Semantic Class B:III-1.9a (B03-01-09a), "Rām cycle / Ancestors of Rām / Hariṣcaṅdra," https://ccrss.org/database/songs.php?semantic_class_id=B03-01-09a.
96. Bhima Gonate, Village Jadhavwadi (Pune District), https://ccrss.org/database/songs.php?song_id=47985.
97. Sita Pimple, Nashik City (Nashik District), GSP, https://ccrss.org/database/songs.php?song_id=88372.

98. Vishnudas Nama has a long section on what constitutes good kingship and good citizenry when Harischandra relinquishes his kingdom into Vishvamitra's hands, including the maintenance of hierarchies and caste duties. See *Hariścandrapurāṇakatha* of Vishnudas Nama, 1.90–100.
99. This story of the dancing girls takes up a whole chapter in Raghavanka's story. See Viswanatha, trans., *Life of Harishchandra*, chap. 7, 313–335. In that version Harischandra is described as viciously "skinning their backs, breaking their teeth, lacerating their mouths, dragging them by the hair, and beating their bodies to a pulp" (333, 7.25)." In the introduction Viswanatha writes that "Raghavanka moves the conflict between castes to center stage in his text by inventing the characters of the two dark and lovely *holati* maidens" (xx). Janabai does not include these caste insults, distinct from both Mukteshvar's and Vishnudas Nama's versions. For Janabai's verses on this, see *Hariścandra Ākhyana* by Janabai, 302.13–19.
100. *Hariścandrapurāṇakatha* of Vishnudas Nama, 4.44–54.
101. *Hariścandra Ākhyana* by Janabai, 317.10–11.
102. *Hariścandra Ākhyana* by Janabai, 319.11–12. This particular scene is also in Vishnudas Nama's story, *Hariścandrapurāṇakatha* of Vishnudas Nama, 4.373–374.
103. These were composed for the daughters of his patron. See A. K. Priolkar, ed., *Moropantañce Samagra Grantha, Vol. 12: Sphuṭ Kavyeṃ 3* (Mumbai: Marathi Samshodhan Mandal, 1964), 48–73, 190–202.
104. Kedar Kulkarni, *World Literature and the Question of Genre in Colonial India: Poetry, Drama, and Print Culture 1790-1890* (New Delhi: Bloomsbury, 2022), 72. See also his discussion of Chiplunkar's poetic valorization of simple, emotionally concentrated poetry (61). Vishnu Krishna Chiplunkar, *Viśṇupadī* (Pune: Suvichar Prakashan Mandal, 1974), 7.
105. Sane Guruji, "Two Words," in *Strījīvan* (Pune: Indrayani Sahitya Publishers, 1998 [1940]), 3.

Postscript

1. *Bhaktavijay* of Mahipati, ed. S. R. Devale (Pune: Sharada Sahitya, n.d.), 48.63.
2. *Bhaktavijay*, 48.70, 74.
3. Paul Rekret, *Take This Hammer: Work, Song, Crisis* (London: Goldsmiths Press, 2024), 6.
4. See Marek Korczynski, Michael Pickering, and Emma Robertson, *Rhythms of Labour: Music at Work in Britain* (Cambridge: Cambridge University Press, 2013), 62–86.

5. Franco Moretti, *Graphs, Maps, Trees: Abstract Models for Literary History* (New York: Verso, 2005), 67–92.
6. G. N. Devy, *"Of Many Heroes": An Indian Essay in Literary Historiography* (Hyderabad: Orient Longman, 1998), 168.
7. Anna Lowenhaupt Tsing, *The Mushroom at the End of the World: On the Possibility of Life in Capitalist Ruins* (Princeton, NJ: Princeton University Press, 2015), viii.

Bibliography

Abbreviations

AL	"Ajñāt Līḷās" (Līḷās of unknown place), appended to most editions of the *Līḷācaritra*
FH	"First Half" in Feldhaus, trans., *God at Play*
KLC	*Līḷācaritra* as edited by V. B. Kolte (see primary sources)
NG	*Śrī Nāmdev Gāthā,* ed. Dandekar et al. (see primary sources)
NLC	*Līḷācaritra* as edited by P. C. Nagpure (see primary sources)
P	"Purvārdha," the "First Half" in Marathi editions of the *Līḷācaritra*
SP	"Solitary Period," in Feldhaus, trans., *God at Play*

Primary Sources

Bhaktalīlāmṛta of Mahipati, ed. Damodar Savalaram et al. Mumbai: Induprakash Press, 1935.

Bhaktavijay of Mahipati, ed. S. R. Devale. Pune: Sharada Sahitya, n.d.

Brihat Kalpasutra and Original Niryukti of Sthavir Arya Bhadrabahu Swami and A Bhashya by Shri Sanghadas Gani Kshamashramana thereon with a Commentary Begun by Acharya Malayagiri and Completed by Acharya Shri Kshemakirti, vol. 3, ed. Guru

Shri Chaturvijaya and Punyavijaya. Bhavnagar, Gujarat: Shri Atmanand Jain Sabha, 1992.

Chandonuśāsana, of Hemachandra, ed. H. D. Velankar, Singhi Jain Series 49. Mumbai: Bharatiya Vidya Bhavan, 1961.

Darśanaprakāśa Grantha of Murarimalla. In *Matiratnākar Grantha 1 va Darśanaprakāśa Grantha 2*, ed. Shankar Narahara Joshi. Pune: Manager Chitrashala Press, n.d.

"Dāsopantanivedita Ekā Saṃskṛtaniṣṭhācī Kathā" [Excerpt of *Gitārṇavā*]. *Marāṭhī Saṃśodhan Patrikā* 23, no. 2 (January–March 1976): 1-60.

Dhavaḷe of Mahadaise. In *Ādya Marāṭhī Kavayitrī: Dhavaḷe-Purvārdha va Uttarārdha, Mātṛkī-Rukmiṇī-Svayaṃvar, Pāṭhabhed, Śabdakoś va Prastāvanā Yāṃsaha*, ed. V. N. Deshpande. Yavatamal: Sharada Ashram Press, 1935.

Hariścandra Ākhyana of Janabai. In *Śrī Nāmdev Gāthā [Sakaḷa Santa Gāthā]*, ed. N. Sakhare, Pune: Varada Books, 2002; also in *NG*, 989–1002, *abhaṅgas* 432–454.

Hariścandrākhyāna of Mukteshvar, ed. Dada Gore and Sunetra Oak. Aurangabad: Goda Publishers, 1975.

Hariścandrapurāṇakatha of Vishnudas Nama, ed. J. S. Deshpande. In *Nāmdevāce Sphūṭ Ākhyāne*, vol. 4, *Prācīn Marāṭhī Kavitā*, 13–53. Mumbai Marathi Granth Sangrahalay, 1966.

Jñāneśvarī of Jnaneshvar, ed. and with gloss by S. V. Dandekar. Pune: Svanand Publishers, 1976.

Kuvalayamālākahā of Uddyotanasuri. Vols. 1–2, ed. and trans., Prem S. Jain. Jaipur: Prakrit Bharati Akademy, 2016.

Līlācaritra of Mhaimbat, ed. V. B. Kolte. Mumbai: Maharashtra Rajya Sahitya Sanskrti Mandal, 1978. [Cited as *KLC*].

Līḷācaritra of Mhaimbhat, ed. P. C. Nagpure. Nagpur: Omkar Publishers, 2015. [Cited as *NLC*].

Mahārāṣṭra Kāvyadīpikā of Lakshadhira. In Adsod, Annasaheb, ed. *Kāvyadīpika*, 103–110. Pune: Snehavardhan Publishing House, 2000.

Mānasollāsa of Someshvara, vol. 3, ed. G. K. Shrigondekar. Baroda: Oriental Institute, 1961.

Rukmiṇī-Svayaṃvar of Narendra, ed. V. B. Kolte. Nagpur: Arun Publishers, 1966.

Saṅgīta-Ratnākara of Śārṅgadeva: Sanskrit Text and English Translation with Comments and Notes, Volume 2, Chapters 2–4, ed. and trans. R. K. Shringy under supervision of Prem Lata Sharma. New Delhi: Munshiram Manoharlal, 1989.

Smṛtisthaḷ, ed. V. N. Deshpande. Pune: Venus Publishers, 1960 [1939].

Śrī Eknāth Gāthā [Sakaḷa Santa Gāthā], ed. N. Sakhare. Pune: Varada Books, 2002.

Śrī Nāmdev Gāthā, ed. S. V. Dandekar et al. Mumbai: Central Government Press, 1970. [Cited as *NG*].

Śrī Nāmdev Gāthā: Visobā Khecar, Parasā Bhāgavat, Janābāī Yāñcyā Abhaṅgāsaha [Sakaḷa Santa Gāthā], ed. N. Sakhare. Pune: Varada Books, 2002.

Śrī Tukārām Gāthā [Sakaḷa Santa Gāthā], ed. N. Sakhare. Pune: Varada Books, 2002.

Śrījñāneśvarī, ed. V. K. Rajwade; 2nd edition, ed. S. W. Dandekar, B. M. Khuperkar, N. R. Phatak, A. K. Priolkar. Mumbai: Marathi Central Press, 1963.

Śrīkṛṣṇacaritra, ed. S. G. Tulpule. Pune: Venus Publishers, 1966.

Svayambhūchandas of Svaymbhu, ed. H. D. Velankar. Rājasthāna Purātana Granthamāla 37. Jodhpur: Rajasthana Pracyavidya Pratishthan, 1962.

Secondary Sources

Abbas, Shemeem Burney. *The Female Voice in Sufi Ritual.* Austin: University of Texas Press, 2002.

Abbott, Justin E., trans. *Bahiṇā Bāī: A Translation of Her Autobiography and Verses.* New Delhi: Motilal Barsidass, 1985 [1929].

——. *Tukaram: The Poet Saint of Maharashtra: Translation from Mahipati's Bhaktalīlāmṛta.* Delhi: Sri Satguru Publications: 1996 [1931].

Adsod, Annasaheb, ed. *Kāvyadīpika.* Pune: Snehavardhan Publishing House, 2000.

Ajgaonkar, J. R. *Mahārāṣṭra Kavicaritra.* Vol. 6. Mumbai, 1924.

Altekar, A. S. "The Yādavas of Seunadeśa." In *The Early History of the Deccan*, Parts 7 to 11, ed. G. Yazdani, 513–574. London: Oxford University Press, 1960.

Amodio, Mark C. *Writing the Oral Tradition: Oral Poetics and Literate Culture in Medieval England.* Notre Dame, IN: University of Notre Dame Press, 2004.

Aklujkar, Vidyut. "Between Pestle and Mortar: Women in the Marathi Sant Tradition." In *Goddesses and Women in Indic Religious Traditions*, ed. Arvind Sharma. 105–130. Leiden: E. J. Brill.

Apte, Vaman Shivaram. *Revised and Enlarged Edition of Prin. V. S. Apte's The Practical Sanskrit-English Dictionary.* 3 vols. Poona: Prasad Prakashan, 1957–1959.

Arondekar, Anjali. *Abundance: Sexuality's History.* Durham, NC: Duke University Press, 2023.

——. "What More Remains: Slavery, Sexuality, South Asia." *History of the Present* 6, no. 2 (2016): 146–154.

Asif, Manan Ahmed. *The Loss of Hindustan: The Invention of India.* Cambridge, MA: Harvard University Press, 2020.

Atre, P. K. "Preface." In Bahinabai Chaudhari, *Bahiṇāīcī Gāṇī*, 1st edition, 7–19. Mumbai: Popular Publishers, 1978 [1952].

Auerbach, Erich. "Figura." In *Scenes from the Drama of European Literature.* Manchester: Manchester University Press, 1984 [1959].

——. *Mimesis: The Representation of Reality in Western Literature*, trans. Willard Trask. Princeton, NJ: Princeton University Press, 2003.

Bakhtin, M. M. "The Problem of Speech Genres." In *Speech Genres and Other Late Essays*. Austin: University of Texas Press, 2002.

Babar, Sarojini. *Jā Mājhyā Māherā, Mahārāṣṭra Rājya Lokasāhitya Mālā* 8. Pune: The Maharashtra Government Council on Folk Literature, 1963.

——. *Folk Literature of Maharashtra*. New Delhi: Maharashtra Information Center, 1968.

——. *Lokasaṅgīta*. Mumbai: Prasiddhi Vibhaga, Maharashtra Shasan, 1962.

——. *Mahārāṣṭra Lokasāhitya Mālā* 2. Pune: The Maharashtra Government Council on Folk Literature, 1957.

——. *Mahārāṣṭra Lokasāhitya Mālā* 3. Pune: The Maharashtra Government Council on Folk Literature, 1959.

——. *Striyāmñce Kheḷ āṇi Gāṇī*. Pune: The Maharashtra Government Council on Folk Literature, 1977.

Baker, Houston A. *Blues, Ideology, and Afro-American Literature: A Vernacular Theory* Chicago: University of Chicago Press, 1987.

Bauman, Richard, and Charles L. Briggs. "Poetics and Peformance as Critical Perspectives on Language and Social Life." *Annual Review of Anthropology* 19 (1990): 59–88.

Beecroft, Alexander. *An Ecology of World Literature: From Antiquity to the Present Day*. London: Verso, 2015.

Bhagwat, A. R. "Maharashtrian Folksongs on the Grind Mill." *Journal of the University of Bombay* 10 (July 1941): 134–186.

——. "Maharashtrian Folksongs on the Grind Mill, Part II," *Journal of the University of Bombay* 10 (January 1942): 137–174.

Bhagwat, Durga. *Lokasāhityācī Rūparekhā*. Pune: Varada Books, 2017 [1956].

Bhagwat, Vidyut. "Heritage of *Bhakti*: *Sant* Women's Writings in Marathi." In *Culture and the Making of Identity in Contemporary India*, ed. Kamala Ganesh and Usha Thakkar, 164–183. New Delhi: Sage Publications, 2005.

Bhavalkar, Tara. *Loka Paramparā āṇi Strīpratibhā*. Mumbai: The House of Folk Literature, 2002.

——. *Sītāyan: Vedanā-Vidrohāce Rasāyan*. Pune: Manovikas Publishers, 2023.

Bhave, V. L. *Mahārāṣṭra Sārasvat*, vol. 1, ed. S. G. Tulpule. Mumbai: Popular Publishers, 1963 [1898].

Bhayani, H. C. *Apabraṁśa Language and Literature: A Short Introduction*. Delhi: B. L. Institute of Indology, 1989.

——. "The Dhavala Songs in Prakrit Apabraṁśa and Post-Apabraṁśa Traditions." In *Indological Studies: Prakrit and Performing Arts: Prakrit and Apabraṁśa Studies*, 85–94. Ahmedabad: Parshva Publishers, 1993.

——. "The Rise of Apabhraṃśa as a Literary Language." In *Indological Studies: Literary and Performing Arts, Vol. 2*. Ahmedabad: Parshva Publishers, 1993.

Bhingarkar, D. B. *Sant Kaviyitrī Janābāī: Caritra, Kāvya, Kāmagirī*. Mumbai: Majestic Publishers, 1981.

Biber, Douglas, and Edward Finegan. "Drift and the Evolution of English Style: A History of Three Genres." *Language* 65, no. 3 (September 1989): 487–517.

Bloch, Jules. *The Formation of the Marāṭhī Language*, trans. Dev Raj Chanana. New Delhi: Motilal Banarsidass, 1970 [1941].

Bose, Mandrakanta, and Priyadarshani Bose. *A Woman's Rāmāyana: Candrāvati's Bengali Epic*. New York: Routledge, 2013.

Bozzone, Chiara. "Weaving Songs for the Dead in Indo-European: Women Poets, Funerary Laments, and the Ecology of **ḱ léu̯os**." In *Proceedings of the 27th Annual UCLA Indo-European Conference*, ed. David M. Goldstein, Stephanie W. Jamison, and Brent Vine, 1–22. Bremen: Hempen, 2016.

Bradley, Adam. *The Poetry of Pop*. New Haven, CT: Yale University Press, 2017.

Campbell, Gwyn. "Introduction: Slavery and Other Forms of Unfree Labour in the Indian Ocean World." In *Structure of Slavery in Indian Ocean Africa and Asia*, ed. Gwyn Campbell, vi–xxxi. London: Frank Cass, 2004.

Chakravarti, Uma. "Whatever Happened to the Vedic Dasi? Orientalism, Nationalism, and a Script for the Past." In *Recasting Women: Essays in Colonial History*, ed. Kumkum Sangari and Suresh Vaid, 27–87. New Brunswick, NJ: Rutgers University Press, 1990

Chatterjee, Indrani. "Renewed and Connected Histories: Slavery and the Historiography of South Asia," in *Slavery and South Asian History*, ed. Indrani Chatterjee and Richard M. Eaton, 17–43. Bloomington: Indiana University Press, 2006.

Chattopadhyaya, Brajadulal. *The Making of Early Medieval India*. New Delhi: Oxford University Press, 2012.

Chaudhari, Bahinabai. *Bahiṇāīcī Gāṇī [Songs of Bahinabai]*. 1st edition, ed. Sopan Dev. Mumbai: Popular Publishers, 1978 [1952].

Chiarucci, Julie Bergljot. "Kavva and Kāvya: Hāla's Gāhākosa and Its Sanskrit Successors." PhD diss., University of California, Berkeley, 2014. ProQuest ID: Chiarucci_berkeley_0028E_14943. Merritt ID: ark:/13030/m5gj2nd7.

Chinitz, David. *T. S. Eliot and the Cultural Divide*. Chicago: University of Chicago Press, 2003.

Chiplunkar, Vishnu Krishna. *Viśṇupadī*. Pune: Suvichar Prakashan Mandal, 1974.

Chitgupi, B. B. "Vithal and Abhaṅga." *Journal of the University of Bombay* 27, no. 2 (July 1958): 1–24.

Chitre, Dilip, trans. *Says Tuka: Selected Poems of Tukaram*, vol. 1. Pune: Sontheimer Cultural Association, 2003.

Chorghade, Vimala. *Mahāvidharbātīl Lokagītāñceṃ Saṅgīt*. Pune: Manohar Granthamala Publishers, 1987.

Cornish, Alison. "A Lady Asks: The Gender of Vulgarization in Late Medieval Italy." *PMLA* 115, no. 2 (March 2000): 166–180.

Culler, Jonathan. *Theory of the Lyric.* Cambridge, MA: Harvard University Press, 2015.

Cutler, Norman. *Songs of Experience: The Poetics of Tamil Devotion.* Bloomington: Indiana University Press, 1987.

Dabre, Thomas. "Sasar-Maher Antithesis in the Abhaṅgas of Tukaram: From Alienation to Fulfillment." In *House and Home in Maharashtra*, ed. Irina Glushkova and Anne Feldhaus, 102–110. New York: Oxford University Press, 1998.

Dante Alighieri, *Vita Nuova* 16, Frisardi translation. *Digital Dante* (Columbia University), https://digitaldante.columbia.edu/text/library/la-vita-nuova-frisardi/.

Daukes, Jacqueline. "Female Voices in the Vārkarī Sampradāya: Gender Constructions in a Bhakti Tradition." PhD thesis. University of London, School of Oriental and African Studies, 2014.

de Bruijn, J. T. P. "The Name of the Poet in Classical Persian Poetry." In *Proceedings of the Third European Conference of Iranian Studies (held in Cambridge, 11th to 15th September 1995).* Part 2: Mediaeval and Modern Persian Studies, ed. Charles Melville. Wiesbaden: Dr. Ludwig Reichert Verlag, 1999.

Deak, Dusan. "Maharashtra Saints and the Sufi Tradition: Eknath, Chand Bodhale and the Datta Sampradaya." *Journal of Deccan Studies* 3, no. 2 (2005): 22–47.

Deshmukh, Bhagwant. *Dagaḍī Jātyācā Reśamī Gaḷā.* Pune: Pratima Publishers, 2000.

Deshmukh, M. "The Mothers and Daughters of *Bhakti*: Janābāī in Marathi Literature." *International Journal of Hindu Studies* 24 (2020): 33–59.

Deshpande, A. N. *Prāchin Marāthī Vaṅmayācā Itīhās*, vol. 4. Pune: Venus Publishers,1966.

Deshpande, Kamalabai. *apaurūṣeya Vāṅmaya Arthāt Strīgīteṃ.* Pune: Manohar Granthamala Publishers, 1948.

Deshpande, Prachi. *Scripts of Power: Writing, Language Practices, and Cultural History in Western India.* Ranikhet: Permanent Black, 2023.

———. "The Writerly Self: Literacy, Discipline and Codes of Conduct in Early Modern Western India." *The Indian Economic and Social History Review* 53, no. 4 (2016): 449–471.

Deshpande, V. N. *Ādya Marāṭhī Kavayitrī: Dhavaḷe-Purvārdha va Uttarārdha, Mātṛkī-Rukmiṇī-Svayaṃvar, Pāṭhabhed, Śabdakoś va Prastāvanā Yāṃsaha.* Yavatmal: Sharda Ashram, 1935.

Dev, Sopan. "Mājhī Āī." In Bahinabai Chaudhari, *Bahiṇāīcī Gāṇī*, 29–33. Mumbai: Popular Publishers, 1978 [1952].

Devy, G. N. *"Of Many Heroes": An Indian Essay in Literary Historiography.* Hyderabad: Orient Longman, 1998.

Dhere, R. C. *Lokasaṃskṛtīce Upāsak.* Pune: Padmagandha Publishers, 2007 [1996].

——. *Nāmayācī Janī*. Pune: Vohra and Company Publishers, 1960.
——. *The Rise of a Folk God: Viṭṭhal of Pandharpur*, trans. Anne Feldhaus. New York: Oxford University Press, 2011.
——. "Sāne Gurujiñce *Strījīvan*." In *Lokasāhitya: Śodha āṇi Samikṣā*. Pune: Padmagandha Publishers, 2015.
——. *Sant, Loka aṇī Abhijan*. Pune: Padmagandha Publishers, 2005 [1998].
——. *Śrī Nāmdev, Janī āṇi Nāgarī*. Pune: Padmagandha Publishers, 2015.
——. *Śrīviṭṭhal: Ek Mahāsamanvaya*. Pune: Padmagandha Publishers, 2004.
Doane, A. N., and Carol Braun Pasternack. *Vox Intexta: Orality and Textuality in the Middle Ages*. Madison: University of Wisconsin Press, 1991.
Doniger, Wendy. "Fluid and Fixed Texts." In *Boundaries of the Text: Epic Performances in South and Southeast Asia*, ed. Joyce Flueckiger and Laurie Sears. Ann Arbor: University of Michigan Press, 2020.
——. "The Zen Diagram of Hinduism." In *The Norton Anthology of World Religions, Vol. 1*, ed. Jack Miles, Wendy Doniger, Donald S. Lopez Jr., James Robson, 55–69. New York: Norton, 2015.
Du Bois, W. E. B. *The Souls of Black Folk*. New York: Dover, 1994 [1903].
Dundes, Alan. "Metafolklore and Oral Literary Criticism." *The Monist* 50, no. 4 (1966): 505–16.
Dylan, Bob. *The Lyrics: 1961–2012*, ed. Christopher Ricks, Lisa Nemrow, and Julie Nemrow. New York: Simon and Schuster, 2014.
——. "Nobel Lecture," *The Nobel Prize*. Nobel Foundation (June 5, 2017). Video and transcript. https://www.nobelprize.org/prizes/literature/2016/dylan/lecture/.
Eaton, Richard. Introduction to *Slavery and South Asian History*, ed. Indrani Chatterjee and Richard M. Eaton. Bloomington: Indiana University Press, 2006.
——. *India in the Persianate Age, 1000–1765*. Berkeley: University of California Press, 2019.
——. *Sufis of Bijapur, 1300–1700: Social Roles of Sufis in Medieval India*. New Delhi: Munshiram Manoharlal, 2011.
Eisner, Martin. "Bridge Essay: Vernacularization and World Literature: The Language of Women in the World of God." In *A Companion to World Literature*, ed. Ken Seigneurie. New York: John Wiley & Sons, 2020.
Eliot, T. S. "The Music of Poetry." In *On Poetry and Poets*. New York: Farrar, Straus and Giroux, 2009 [1943].
Elizarenkova, Tatyana. *Language and Style of the Vedic Ṛṣis*. New York: State University of New York Press, 1995.
Engblom, Philip. "The Marathi Sonnet: Origins of the Species: A Thesis." PhD diss., University of Minnesota, 1983.
Fanfani, Giovanni. "Weaving a Song. Convergences in Greek Poetic Imagery between Textile and Musical Terminology. An Overview on Archaic and Classical Literature." In *Textile Terminologies: From the Orient to the Mediterranean and*

Europe, 1000 BC to 1000 AD, ed. Salvatore Gaspa, Cécile Michel, and Marie-Louise Nosch, 421–436. Lincoln, NE: Zea Books, 2017.

Feldhaus, Anne. "The Art of the Ovīs." Introduction to *Say to the Sun, "Don't Rise" and to the Moon, "Don't Set:" Two Oral Narratives from the Countryside of Maharashtra.* ed. and trans. Anne Feldhaus with Ramdas Atkar and Rajaram Zagade, 25–57. New York: Oxford University Press, 2014.

——. "The Devatācakra of the Mahānubhāvas," *Bulletin of the School of Oriental and African Studies* 43, no. 1 (1980): 101–109.

——. "Gender and Women in the Ovīs." In *Say to the Sun, "Don't Rise" and to the Moon,"Don't Set:" Two Oral Narratives from the Countryside of Maharashtra*, ed. and trans. Anne Feldhaus with Ramdas Atkar and Rajaram Zagade, 108–126. New York: Oxford University Press, 2014.

——. "God and Madman: Guṇḍam Rāuḷ." *Bulletin of the School of Oriental and African Studies* 45, no. 1 (1982): 74–83.

——. "*Kṛṣṇa* and the *Kṛṣṇas: Kṛṣṇa* in the Mahānubhāva Pantheon." In *Bhakti in Current Research, 1979–1982*, ed. M. Thiel-Horstmann, 133–142. Berlin: Dietrich Reimer, 1983.

——. "The Mahānubhāvas and Scripture," in *Journal of Dharma* 3, no. 3 (1978): 295–308.

——. *The Religious System of the Mahānubhāva Sect: The Mahānubhāva Sūtrapāṭha.* New Delhi: Manohar, 1983.

Feldhaus, Anne, trans. *Deeds of God in Ṛddhipur.* New York: Oxford University Press, 1984.

——. trans. *God at Play.* Vol 1. Murty Classical Library. Cambridge, MA: Harvard University Press, 2024.

Feldhaus, Anne, and S. G. Tulpule, trans. *In the Absence of God: In the Early Years of an Indian Sect: A Translation of Smṛtisthaḷ with an Introduction.* Honolulu: University of Hawaiʻi Press, 1992.

Ferrante, Joan M. *To the Glory of Her Sex: Women's Roles in the Compositon of Medieval Texts.* Bloomington: Indiana University Press 1997.

Ferrante, Joan M., ed. and trans. *Epistolae: Medieval Women's Letters.* Columbia Center for Teaching and Learning, 2022. https://epistolae.ctl.columbia.edu/.

Finnegan, Ruth. *Oral Poetry: Its Nature, Significance and Social Context.* London: Cambridge University Press, 1979.

Fishkin, Shelley Fisher. *Was Huck Black? Mark Twain and African-American Voices.* New York: Oxford University Press, 1994.

Flueckiger, Joyce Burkhalter. *When the World Becomes Female: Guises of a South Indian Goddess.* Bloomington: Indiana University Press, 2013.

Flueckiger, Joyce, and Laurie Sears, eds. *Boundaries of the Text: Epic Performances in South and Southeast Asia.* Ann Arbor: University of Michigan Press, 2020.

Fuller, Mary. "Marathi Grinding Songs." *The New Review* 11 (June 1940): 382–392.

Galvez, Marisa. *Songbook: How Lyrics Became Poetry in Medieval Europe*. Chicago: University of Chicago Press, 2012.

Gates, Henry Louis. *The Signifying Monkey: A Theory of African-American Literary Criticism*. New York: Oxford University Press, 1988.

Gioia, Ted. *Work Songs*. Durham, NC: Duke University Press, 2006.

Glushkova, Irina. "Janabai and Gangakhed of Das Ganu: Towards Ethnic Unity and Religious Cohesion in a Time of Transition." *The Indian Economic & Social History Review* 58, no. 4 (2021): 505–532.

——. "The Tool of Domestic Labor in the Iconography of Janabai's Temples in Maharashtra." *Studia Religiosa Rossica: Russian Journal of Religion* (January 2023): 5-75.

Godbole, Parshuram B. *Navanīt athavā Marāṭhī Kavitāṃce Veṃce*. Pune: Shubhada Sarasvat Publishers, 1990 [1854].

——. *Vṛttadarpaṇa*, ed. V. V. Natekar and N. G. Joshi. Baroda: Good Companions Publishers, 1964 [1860].

Goehr, Lydia. *The Imaginary Museum of Musical Works*. Oxford: Oxford University Press, 1992.

Gogate, Sharad. "James Thomas Molesworth: A Biographical Sketch." In *Molesworth's Marathi-English Dictionary, Sixth Reprint with Corrections*. Pune: Shubhada-Saraswat Publishers, 1996 [1831].

Gokhale, Parvati. *Strīgītaratnākar athavā Ābāḷavṛddha Strīyānī Mhaṇaṇyās va Aikṇyās Yogya aśī Devādikāñcī Vagaire aśī Gāṇī*, vols. 1–3. Pune, 1915.

Gonda, Jan. *A History of Indian Literature: The Ritual Sūtras*. vol. 1. Wiesbaden: Otto Harrassowitz, 1977.

Gore, P. S. *Varhāḍī Lokagite*. Amravati: Seva Publishers, 1940.

Gosavi, R. R. *Śrīsakalasantagathā*, vol. 2. Pune: Sarathi Publishers, 2000.

Grundmann, Herbert. "Women and Literature in the Middle Ages: A Contribution on the Origins of Vernacular Writing." In *Herbert Grundmann (1902–1970), Essays on Heresy, Inquisition, and Literacy*, ed. Jennifer Kolpacoff Deane, trans. Steven Rowan, 30–55. Rochester, NY: York Medieval Press, 2019.

Guha, Sumit. "Serving the Barbarian to Preserve the Dharma: The Ideology and Training of a Clerical Elite in Peninsular India ca. 1300–1800." *The Indian Economic and Social History Review* 47, no. 4 (2010): 497–525.

——. "Slavery, Society, and the State in Western India, 1700–1800." In *Slavery and South Asian History*, ed. Indrani Chatterjee and Richard M. Eaton, 162–186. Bloomington: Indiana University Press, 2006.

Hallisey, Charles. "Devotion in the Buddhist Literature of Medieval Sri Lanka." PhD diss. University of Chicago, 1988.

Hallisey, Charles. trans. "Note on the Text and Translation." In *Therigatha: Poems of the First Buddhist Women*. Murthy Classical Library of India. Cambridge, MA: Harvard University Press, 2015.

——. *Therigatha: Poems of the First Buddhist Women*. Murthy Classical Library of India. Cambridge, MA: Harvard University Press, 2015.

Haraway, Donna. *Staying with the Trouble: Making Kin in the Chthulucene*. Durham, NC: Duke University Press, 2016.

Hawley, John Stratton. "Author and Authority in the Bhakti Poetry of North India." *The Journal of South Asian Studies* 47, no. 2 (1988): 269–290.

Hawley, John Stratton, Christian Lee Novetzke, and Swapna Sharma, eds. *Bhakti and Power*. Seattle: University of Washington Press, 2019.

Hess, Linda. *Bodies of Song: Kabir Oral Traditions and Performative Worlds in North India*. New York: Oxford University Press, 2015.

Holquist, Michael. "Answering as Authoring: Mikhail Bakhtin's Trans-Linguistics." *Critical Inquiry* 10, no 2 (December 1983): 307–319.

Ingalls, Daniel H., Jeffrey Moussaieff Masson, and M. V. Patwardhan, eds. and trans. *The Dhvanyaloka of Anandavardhana with the Locana of Abhinavagupta*. Cambridge, MA: Harvard University Press, 1990.

Ingole, Pratima. *Varhāḍī Lokagītāñcā Cikitsak Abhyās*. Pune: Sonal Publishers, 2013.

Irlekar, Suhasini. *Sant Janābāī*. Mumbai: Marathi Literature and Culture Association, 2002.

——. *Mahadambece Dhavaḷe: Samīkṣā āṇi Saṃhitā*. Pune: Snehavardhan Publishing House, 2012 [1977].

Jagdale, Kunta N. *Marāṭhī-Muslim Ovyā (Jātyāvarcyā): Tulanātmak Abhās*. Barshi, Maharashtra: Narayan Jagdale, 2004.

Jakobson, Roman. "Grammatical Parallelism and Its Russian Facet." *Language* 42, no. 2. (1966): 399–429.

Jamison, Stephanie W. *Sacrificed Wife, Sacrificer's Wife: Women, Ritual, and Hospitality*. New York: Oxford University Press, 1996.

Jamison, Stephanie W., and Joel P. Brereton, trans. *The Rigveda: The Earliest Religious Poetry of India, Vol. 1*. New York: Oxford University Press, 2014.

Janabai Education Foundation. *Sant Janābāī: Caritra va Kāvya*. Gangakhed: Diamond Publication, 2018.

Jassal, Smita Tewari. *Unearthing Gender: Folksongs of North India*. Durham, NC: Duke University Press, 2012.

Jones, Gayl. *Liberating Voices: Oral Tradition in African-American Literature*. Cambridge, MA: Harvard University Press, 1991.

Joshi, N. G. *Marāthī Chandoracanecā Vīkās: Layadṛṣṭyā Punarvicār*. Mumbai: Mauj Publishers, 1964.

Kalelkar, Dattatreya Balkrishna, and Vamana Krishna Chorghade. *Sāhityācem Mūladhana*. Mumbai: Karnataka Publishing House, 1938.

Karanika, Andromache. *Voices at Work: Women, Performance, and Labor in Ancient Greece.* Baltimore, MD: Johns Hopkins University Press, 2014.

Ketkar, Sachin. "Jnaneshwar's 'Duji Shrushti:' Poetics and Cultural Politics of Precolonial Translation of Dnaneshwari." In *India in Translation: Translation in India*, ed. G. J. V. Prasad, 1–27. New Delhi: Bloomsbury, 2019.

Keune, Jon. *Shared Devotion, Shared Food: Equality and the Bhakti-Caste Question in Western India.* New York: Oxford University Press, 2021.

Khaladkar, Varada. *The Protohistoric Village: Its Form and Economy in Chalcolithic North Western Deccan.* MPhil thesis. Jawaharalal Nehru University, 1998.

Khoroche, Peter, and Herman Tieken, trans. *Hāla's Sattasaī (Gāthā Saptaśatī in Prakrit), Life and Love in Ancient India.* Delhi: Motilal Banarsidass, 2014.

Kittel, Ferdinand. *Kittel's Kannada-English Dictionary,* rev. and enl. ed. Madras [Chennai]: University of Madras, 1968–1971.

Klinck, Anne. "Introduction," in *Medieval Woman's Song: Cross-Cultural Approaches.* Ed. Anne L. Klinck and Ann Marie Rasmussen, 1–14. Philadelphia: University of Pennsylvania Press, 2002.

——. "Lyric Voice and the Feminine in Some Ancient and Mediaeval *Frauenlieder.*" *Florilegium* 13 (1994): 13–36.

——. "Sappho and Her Daughters: Some Parallels Between Ancient and Medieval Woman's Song." In *Medieval Woman's Song: Cross-Cultural Approaches*, ed. Anne L. Klinck and Ann Marie Rasmussen, 5–28. Philadelphia: University of Pennsylvania Press, 2002.

Korczynski, Marek, Michael Pickering, and Emma Robertson. *Rhythms of Labour: Music at Work in Britain.* Cambridge: Cambridge University Press, 2013.

Kulkarni, Kedar. *World Literature and the Question of Genre in Colonial India: Poetry, Drama and Print Culture, 1790–1890.* New Delhi: Bloomsbury, 2022.

Kulkarni, S. B. "Sant Janābāī, " *Lokmat* (July 17, 1994): 2–4.

Kulkarni, S. R. *Ovī te Lāvaṇī: Prācin Marāṭhī Padabandhācī Saṅgīt-Preraṇā āṇi Paramparā.* Dhule: Vani Marathi Pragat Adhyayan Sanstha, 1994.

Lamb, Mary Ellen, and Karen Bamford. *Oral Traditions and Gender in Early Modern Literary Texts.* Burlington, VT: Ashgate Publishing, 2008.

Leslie, I. Julia, trans. *The Perfect Wife: (Stridharmapaddhati) by Tryambakayajvan.* New Delhi: Penguin, 1995.

Lord, Albert B. *The Singer of Tales*, ed. Stephen Mitchell and Gregory Nagy. Cambridge, MA: Harvard University Press, 2000.

——. *The Singer Resumes the Tale.* Ed. Mary Louise Lord. Ithaca, NY: Cornell University Press, 1995.

Lorde. Audre. "Poetry Is Not a Luxury." In *Sister Outsider: Essays and Speeches by Audre Lorde.* Berkeley: Crossing Press, 2007.

Macdonell, Arthur Anthony. *A Practical Sanskrit Dictionary with Transliteration, Accentuation, and Etymological Analysis Throughout.* London: Oxford University Press, 1929.

Mande, Prabhakar. *Lokagāyakāñcī Paramparā*. Aurangabad: Godavari Publishers, 2011.

——. *Lokasāhityāce Svarūp*. Aurangabad: Godavari Publishers, 2017.

Maslov, Boris. "Lyric Universality." In *The Cambridge Companion to World Literature*, edited by Ben Etherington and Jarad Zimbler, 133–148. Cambridge Companions to Literature. Cambridge: Cambridge University Press, 2018.

Masters, Alfred. "Gleanings from the Kuvalayamālā Kahā I: Three Fragments and Specimens of the Eighteen Desabhāsās." *Bulletin of the School of Oriental and African Studies, University of London* 13, no. 2 (1950): 410–415.

Māyavāṭecā Māgovā: Dr. Tara Bhavalkar, Video Series. Doordarshan, Sahyadri. Episode 1, https://www.youtube.com/watch?v=dNa_ZE3sfhk.

McCash, June Hall. *The Cultural Patronage of Medieval Women*. Athens: University of Georgia Press, 1996.

——. "The Role of Women in the Rise of the Vernacular." *Comparative Literature* 60, no. 1 (2008): 45–57.

Miller, Barbara Stoler. "The *Therīgāthā*: Women's Songs of Early Buddhism." *Journal of South Asian Literature* 19, no. 2 (Summer/Fall 1984): 129–135.

Moi, Toril. *Revolution of the Ordinary: Literary Theory after Wittgenstein, Austin, and Cavell*. Chicago: University of Chicago Press, 2017.

Molesworth, J. T. *A Dictionary, Marathi and English*, 2nd. ed. Bombay: Bombay Education Society Press, 1857.

Monier-Williams, M. *A Sanskrit English Dictionary*. Springfield, VA: Natraj Books, 2015.

More, Sadanand. *Trayodaśī: Śrī Jñānadev Sāhitya Saṃśodhan*. Pune: Sakal Publishers, 2014.

Moretti, Franco. *Graphs, Maps, Trees: Abstract Models for Literary History*. New York: Verso, 2005.

——. "The Slaughterhouse of Literature." *MLQ: Modern Language Quarterly* 61, no. 1 (March 2000): 207–227.

Nagaraj, D. R. "Critical Tensions in the History of Kannada Literary Culture." In *Literary Cultures in History: Reconstructions from South Asia*, ed. Sheldon Pollock, 323–382. Berkeley: University of California Press, 2003.

Nagy, Gregory. "Genre, Occasion, and Choral Mimesis Revisited, with Special Reference to the 'Newest Sappho.'" In *Genre in Archaic and Classical Greek Poetry: Theories and Models*. Studies in Archaic and Classical Greek Song, vol. 4, ed. Margaret, Leslie Kurke, and Naomi Weiss Foster, 31–54. Boston: Brill, 2019.

——. *Poetry as Performance: Homer and Beyond*. Cambridge: Cambridge University Press, 1996.

Nandapurkar, N. G. *Marāṭhīcā Mohor*. Hyderabad: Jayahind Printing Press, 1953.

——. *Mukta Mayūrāñcī Bhārateṃ*. Hyderabad: Marathwada Sahitya Parishad, 1956.

Narayan, Kirin. *Everyday Creativity*. Chicago: University of Chicago Press, 2012.

——. "The Practice of Oral Literary Criticism: Women's Songs in Kangra, India." *The Journal of American Folklore* 108, no. 429 (1995): 243–264.

Nilsson, Usha. "Grinding Millet But Singing of Sita: Power and Domination in Awadhi and Bhojpuri Women's Songs." In *Questioning Ramayanas: A South Asian Tradition*, ed. Paula Richman, 137–158. Berkeley: University of California Press, 2001.

Novetzke, Christian Lee. *The Quotidian Revolution: Vernacularization, Religion, and the Premodern Public Sphere.* New York: Columbia University Press, 2016.

——. *Religion and Public Memory: A Cultural History of Saint Namdev in India.* New York: Columbia, 2008.

O'Hanlon, Rosalind. "Social Worth of Scribes: Brahmins, Kayasthas and the Social Order in Early Modern India," *Indian Economic and Social History Review* 47, no. 4 (2010): 563–595.

Oliphant, Samuel. "The Vedic Press Stones," in *Studies in Honor of Maurice Bloomfield*, ed. A Group of His Pupils, 225–250. New Haven, CT: Yale University Press, 1920.

Ollett, Andrew. "Anuṣṭup (Ślōkaḥ)." *Chandorṇava: A Guide to Sanskrit and Prakrit Meters.* Website. http://prakrit.info/meter/anustubh.html.

——. Email to author, July 24, 2022.

——. *Language of the Snakes. Prakrit, Sanskrit, and the Language Order of Premodern India.* South Asia Across the Disciplines. Berkeley: University of California Press, 2017.

Orsini, Francesca, and Katherine Butler Schofield. *Tellings and Texts: Music, Literature and Performance in North India.* Open Book Publishers, 2015.

Paik, Shailaja. *The Vulgarity of Caste: Dalit, Sexuality, and Humanity in Modern India.* Stanford, CA: Stanford University Press, 2022.

Pandharipande, Rajeshwari. "Janabai: A Woman Saint of India." In *Women Saints in World Religions*, ed. Arvind Sharma, 145–180. Albany: State University of New York Press, 2000.

Pathade, Mangala P. "Sarvajña Srīcakradharaviṣayak Saṅkalit Ovīgītāñcā Ābhyās." MPhil thesis. Babasaheb Ambedkar Marathwada University, Aurangabad, 2014.

Pathare, Ranganath et al. *Submission for the Classical Status of Marathi Language to Ministory of Culture, Government of India, by Department of Marathi Language.* Mumbai: Government of Maharashtra, 2013.

Patil, Krisha. *Ahirāṇī Bolīcyā Itīhāsāsaha: Nātī Goṭī*, Ahirāṇī Lokasāhitya Darśan, vol. 2. Mumbai: The Maharashtra Government Council on Folk Literature, 1990.

Patil, Sharad. *Dāsa-Śūdra Slavery: Studies in the Origins of Indian Slavery and Feudalism and Their Philosophies.* Vols. 1 and 2. New Delhi: Allied Publishers, 1978.

Patwardhan, M. T. *Chandoracanā.* Mumbai: Karnatak Publishing House, 1937. https://archive.org/details/Chandorachana/mode/2up.

Paul, Meenakshi Faith. "Sita in Pahari Lok Ramain." In *In Search of Sita: Revisiting Mythology*, ed. Malashri Lal and Namita Gokhale, 147–154. New Delhi: Penguin, 2009.

Pauwels, Heidi. *The Goddess as Role Model: Sita and Radha in Scripture and on Screen.* New York: Oxford University Press, 2008.

——. "The Vernacular Pulse of Sanskrit: Metre and More in the Songs of the *Gītagovinda* and the *Bhāgavata Purāṇa.*" *The Journal of Hindu Studies* 13, no. 3 (November 2020): 294–319.

Pawar, Urmila. *The Weave of My Life: A Dalit Woman's Memoirs*, trans. Maya Pandit. New York: Columbia University Press, 2009, EPUB.

Petievich, Carla. *When Men Speak as Women: Vocal Masquerade in Indo-Muslim Poetry.* New Delhi: Oxford University Press, 2007.

Phukan, Shantanu. " 'Through Throats Where Many Rivers Meet:' The Ecology of Hindi in the World of Persian." *Indian Economic and Social History Review* 38, no.1 (March 2001): 33–58.

Phule, Jotirao. *Slavery*, trans. P. G. Patil. In *Collected Works of Jotirao Phule, Vol. 1.* Bombay: Government of Maharashtra Education Department, 1990.

Phule, Savitribai. *Sāvitrībāī Phule Samagra Vāṅmaya*, ed. M. G. Mali. Mumbai: Government of Maharashtra, 2011.

Poitevin, Guy. *The Voice and the Will: Subaltern Agency: Forms and Motives.* New Delhi: Manohar, 2002.

Poitevin, Guy, and Hema Rairkar. *Stonemill and Bhakti: From the Devotion of Peasant Women to the Philosophy of Swamis.* New Delhi: D. K. Printworld Private Limited, 1996.

Pollock, Sheldon. "Introduction: An Intellectual History of Rasa." In *A Rasa Reader: Classical Indian Aesthetics*, trans. and ed. Sheldon Pollock, 1–46. New York: Columbia University Press, 2016.

——. *Language of the Gods in the World of Men: Sanskrit, Culture, and Power in Premodern India.* Berkeley: University of California Press, 2006.

——. "Literary History, Indian History, World History." *Social Scientist* 23, no. 10/12 (October–December 1995): 112–142.

Pratt, Mary Louise. *Toward a Speech Act Theory of Literary Discourse.* Bloomington: Indiana University Press, 1977.

Preminger, Alex, and T. V. F. Brogan, eds., *The New Princeton Encyclopedia of Poetry and Poetics.* Princeton, NJ: Princeton University Press, 1993.

Prentiss, Karen Pechilis. *The Embodiment of Bhakti.* New York: Oxford University Press, 1999.

Priolkar, A. K., "Junyā Marāṭhī Granthāñcī Portūgīj Bhāṣāntare." In *Marāṭhī Saṃśodhan*, vol. 1, ed. A. K. Priolkar, 151–155. Mumbai: Marathi Samshodhan Mandal, 1966.

——. *Grānthika Marāṭhī Bhāshā āṇi Koṅkaṇī Bolī.* Pune: University of Pune, 1966.

——, ed. *Moropantañce Samagra Grantha, Vol. 12: Sphuṭ Kavyeṃ 3.* Mumbai: Marathi Samshodhan Mandal, 1964.

Proto-Indo-European Etyma, 6. Clothing & Adornment, 6.33 "to weave." Linguistics Research Center, The University of Texas at Austin, https://lrc.la.utexas.edu/lex/semantic/field/CA_WE.

Radhakrishnan, S., trans and ed. *The Bhagavadgita: With an Introductory Essay, Sanskrit Text, English Translation and Notes.* New Delhi: Harper Collins, 2002.

Raeside, Ian. "A Bibliographic Index of Mahānubhāva Works in Marathi." *Bulletin of the School of Oriental and African Studies* 23, no. 3 (1960): 464–507.

Rajwade, V. K. "*Marāṭhī Chanda.*" In *Itihāsācārya Vi. Kā. Rājavāḍe Samagra Sāhitya,* vol. 1, ed. M. B. Shah, 65–92. Dhule: Rajwade Samshodhan Mandal, 1994.

Ramanujan, A. K. "Three Hundred *Rāmāyaṇas*: Five Examples and Three Thoughts on Translation." In *Many Rāmāyaṇas: The Diversity of a Narrative Tradition in Sotuh Asia,* ed. Paul Richman, 22–49. Berkeley: University of California Press, 1991.

——. "Two Realms of Kannada Folklore." In *The Collected Essays of A. K. Ramanujan,* ed. Vinay Dharwadkar, 485–512. New Delhi: Oxford University Press, 2004.

——. *Speaking of Śiva.* London: Penguin, 1973.

Ramaswamy, Vijaya. "Aspects of Women and Work in Early South India." *The Indian Economic and Social History Review* 26, no. 1, 1989, 81–99.

——. "Women and Farm Work in Tamil Folk Songs." *Social Scientist* 21, nos. 9–11 (September--October 1993): 113–129.

Ramazani, Jahan. "Lyric Poetry: Intergeneric, Transnational, Translingual?" *Journal of Literary Terms* 11, no. 1 (2017): 91–107.

——. *Poetry and Its Others: News, Prayers, Song, and the Dialogue of Genres.* Chicago: University of Chicago Press, 2014.

Ramey, Lauri. *History of African-American Poetry.* New York: Cambridge University Press, 2021.

——. *Slave Songs and the Birth of African American Poetry.* New York: Palgrave MacMillan, 2008.

Ranade, Ashok D. *Keywords and Concepts in Hindustani Classical Music.* New Delhi: Promilla and Company Publishers, 1990.

——. *Lokasaṅgītaśāstra.* Mumbai: Dr. Ashok Da Ranade Memorial Trust, 2021 [1975].

Rao, Velcheru Narayana. "Epics and Ideologies: Six Telugu Folk Epics." In *Another Harmony: New Essays on the Folklore of India,* ed. Stuart H. Blackburn and A. K. Ramanujan. Berkeley: University of California Press, 1986.

——. "A *Rāmāyaṇa* of Their Own: Women's Oral Tradition in Telugu." In *Many Rāmāyaṇas: The Diversity of a Narrative Tradition in South Asia,* ed. Paul Richman. Berkeley: University of California Press, 1991.

Rekret, Paul. *Take This Hammer: Work, Song, Crisis.* London: Goldsmiths Press, 2024.

Rice, B. Lewi. *Epigraphia Carnatica* 8.2. Bangalore: Mysore Government Press, 1904. https://archive.org/details/epigraphiacarnat08myso/page/n23/mode/2up

Rigopoulos, Antonio. *Mahānubhāvs.* Firenze: Firenze University Press, 2005.

Roberts, Deborah. "Sphragis." *Oxford Classical Dictionary*, March 7, 2016. https://oxfordre.com/classics/view/10.1093/acrefore/9780199381135.001.0001/acrefore-9780199381135-e-6041.

Rocher, Ludo. "Orality and Textuality in the Indian Context." *Sino-Platonic Papers* 49, no. 1 (1994): 1–28.

Sandywell, Barry. "The Myth of Everyday Life: Toward a Heterology of the Ordinary." *Cultural Studies* 18, no. 2–3 (January 1, 2004): 160–180.

Sane Guruji (Sadashiv Pandurang Sane). "Two Words." In *Strījīvan.* Pune: Indrayani Sahitya Publishers,1998 [1940].

Sankalia, H. D., Shantaram B. Deo, Zainuddin D. Ansari, and Sophie Ehrhardt. *From History to Pre-history at Nevasa (1954–56).* Pune: Deccan College Postgraduate and Research Institute: 1960.

Sant, Indira, comp. *Mālanagāthā*, vols. 1–2. Pune: Mehta Publishing House, 2013 [1993].

Sapir, Edward. *Language: An Introduction to the Study of Speech.* New York: Harcourt, Brace and World, 1921. https://brocku.ca/MeadProject/Sapir/Sapir_1921/Sa pir_1921_07.html.

Sathaye, Adheesh. "The Scribal Life of Folktales in Medieval India," *South Asian History and Culture* 8, no. 4 (2017): 430–447.

———. "Why Did Hariścandra Matter in Early Medieval? Truth, Fact, and Folk Narrative in the Sanskrit *Purāṇas.*" *Journal of Hindu Studies* 2, no. 2 (November 2009): 131–159.

Shakespeare, William. *The Complete Works of Shakespeare, Third Edition*, ed. David Bevington. Glenview, IL: Scott, Foresman, and Co., 1980.

Shende, Sarojini. "The *Mahābhārata* of Viśṇudāsanāma: A Critical Study." PhD diss. University of Mumbai, 1960.

Schmidt, Hanns-Peter. "Ṛgveda 1.28 and the Alleged Domestic Soma-Pressing." *Electronic Journal of Vedic Studies* 16, no.1 (2009): 3–13.

Shukla, Rohini. "Authorship and Generative Embodiment in Bahiṇāī's Songs." *Transnational Literature* 10, no. 2 (May 2018): 1–15.

Schultz, Anna. *Singing the Hindu Nation: Marathi Devotional Performance and Nationalism.* New York: Oxford University Press, 2013.

Simard, Suzanne. *Finding the Mother Tree.* New York: Knopf, 2021.

Simard, Suzanne, and D. A. Perry, M. D. Jones, D. D. Myrold, D. M. Durall, and R. Molina. "Net Transfer of Carbon between Ectomycorrhizal Tree Species in the Field," *Nature* 388, no. 6642 (1997): 579–582.

Sohoni, Pushkar. "Vernacular As a Space: Writing in the Deccan." *South Asian History and Culture* 7, no. 3 (2016): 258–270. DOI: 10.1080/19472498.2016.1168101.

Tharu, Susie, and K. Lalita. "Literature of the Ancient and Medieval Periods: Reading Against the Orientalist Grain." In *Women Writing India: 600 BC to the Early Twentieth Century*, vol. 1. New York: The Feminist Press at CUNY, 1991.

Thurman, Howard. "The Negro Spiritual Speaks of Life and Death." In *African-American Religious Thought: An Anthology*, ed. Cornel West and Eddie Glaude Jr. Louisville, KY: Westminster Knox Press, 2003.

Tsing, Anna Lowenhaupt. *The Mushroom at the End of the World: On the Possibility of Life in Capitalist Ruins*. Princeton, NJ: Princeton University Press, 2015.

Tukdev, Rohini. *Ovī Chanda: Rūp aṇī Āviṣkār*. Pune: Pratibha Publishers, 2004.

Tulpule, Shankar. *Classical Marathi Literature: From the Beginning to A.D. 1818*. Vol. 9 of *A History of Indian Literature*, ed. Jan Gonda. Weisbaden: Harassowitz, 1979.

Tulpule, S. G., and Anne Feldhaus, *A Dictionary of Old Marathi*. New York: Oxford University Press, 2000.

Tuck, Anthony. "Singing the Rug: Patterned Textiles and the Origins of Indo-European Metrical Poetry." *American Journal of Archaeology* 110, no. 4 (October 2006): 539–550.

Umathe, Priti Kishor. *Mhāīmbhaṭaviracit Tīn Caritragrantha*. Nagpur: Sahitya Prasar Kendra, 2021.

Vanita, Ruth. "God as Sakhi: Medieval Poet Janabai and her Friend Vithabai." In *Gandhi's Tiger and Sita's Smile: Essays on Gender, Sexuality and Culture*. New Delhi: Yoda Press, 2005.

Velankar, H. D. "Apabhraṁśa and Marāṭhī Metres." *New Indian Antiquary* 1, no. 4 (July 1938).

Viswanatha, Vanamala, trans. *The Life of Harishchandra*. Murty Classical Library of India. Cambridge, MA: Harvard University Press, 2017.

Warder, A. K. *Indian Kāvya Literature: The Origin and Formation of Classical Kāvya*, vol. 2. Delhi: Motilal Banarsidass, 1990 [1974].

Watt, Diane. *Women, Writing and Religion in England and Beyond, 650–1100*. London: Bloomsbury, 2020.

Williams, Raymond. *Marxism and Literature*. New York: Oxford University Press, 1977.

Woolf, Virginia. *A Room of One's Own*. New York: Harcourt Brace, 1981 [1929].

Yardi, M. R. *The Jnaneshwari*. Pune: Bharati Vidya Bhavan, 2000.

Zelliot, Eleanor. "Chokhāmeḷā: Piety and Protest." In *Bhakti Religion in North India: Community, Identity and Political Action*, by David N. Lorenzen, 212–221. Albany: State University of New York Press, 1995.

——. "Eknath's *Bhāruḍs*: The Sant as Link Between Cultures." In *The Sants: Studies in the Devotional Tradition of India*, ed. Karine and W. H. McLeod Schomer, 91–110. New Delhi: Motilal Banarsidass, 1987.

———. "Women Saints in Medieval Maharashtra." In *Faces of the Feminine in Ancient, Medieval and Modern India*, ed. Mandakranta Bose, 192–200. New York: Oxford University Press, 2000.

Zumthor, Paul. *Oral Poetry: An Introduction*. Trans. Kathryn Murphy-Judy. Minneapolis: University of Minnesota Press, 1990.

———. *Toward a Medieval Poetics*. Trans. Philip Bennett. Minneapolis: University of Minnesota Press, 1992.

Index

Abbott, Justin E. (English translator), 26–27, 292n93
abhaṅga, 5, 8–9, 26, 101, 119, 138, 176–196, 199–202; *devadvāra,* 178, 186; *devīvara,* 178, 237; Janabai's, 9, 12, 76–77, 152, 201–202, 208, 234, 237–238; as *kavitva,* 31, 193; and motif of the blouse (*coḷī*), 85–86; Namdev's, 173, 247; oral and/or written, 18, 61, 89, 109–110, 118, 178–179; origins of, 178–180; poetics of, 101, 132–135, 178–179, 182–183; relationship to *ovī,* 17, 31, 35, 64, 70, 73, 76–77, 109, 119, 123–124, 147, 156, 160, 166, 179–180, 182–187, 189, 193, 195, 216; signature line in (*See* signature line); and Tukaram, 85, 156, 185–186; as vehicle of *bhakti* poetry, 5, 8–9, 17, 101, 109, 138, 166, 176–180, 182–186, 188–196, 199, 201, 208; and Vitthal, 26, 109, 177–178, 200; and women (*See* women, and *abhaṅga*)
Abhinavagupta (eleventh-century philosopher), 139, 282n54
acacia tree, 37, 71–72, 244
adivasi, 14, 23
aesthetics, 29, 273n19; of everyday life, 58; of the female voice, 25; of the grind mill, 35, 62, 72, 82, 223, 237, 240; of *kāvya,* 216; of Marathi literature, 204, 240–241; of orality, 33–34, 181, 234; of *ovī,* 34, 112; oral vs. written, 33–34, 65, 90–91, 94, 181, 223, 234, 237; and "the separability principle," 29–30; and theology, 140, 146; of writing, 57
African American spirituals ("sorrow songs" of enslaved Africans), 11, 35, 59, 74, 161–167, 257n21
Ajgaonkar, A. R., 208, 301n93
akṣaragaṇavṛtta (quantitative-syllabic meters), 133–135
alaṅkāra (ornament), 84, 139
Altekar, A. S., 277n77
Ambedkar, B. R., 69, 124, 159, 285n3
Anandavardhana (ninth-century poet and literary theorist), 55, 139, 282n54

anuṣṭubh (octosyllabic quatrain), 143–144
Apabhramsha: and colloquialization, 94–97; and Sankrit and Prakrit, 11, 34, 91, 95–97, 119, 136, 138, 180, 210, 227, 273n24, 273n29; and *ovī*, 136–137; song forms, 136–138, 227
Apabraṁśa. *See* Apabhramsha
apaurūṣeya, 53–54
apostrophe, 70, 77–79, 81, 149, 182; to the grind mill, 56, 70, 77–79, 161
Arondekar, Anjali, 12, 256n11
Asif, Manan Ahmed, 272n12
Atre, P. K., 53, 55–56, 72
Auerbach, Erich, 274–275n41, 277n76, 290n70
authorship: in *bhakti* poetry, 5–8, 12, 18, 38, 98, 178–183, 199, 234; figural (*See* figural authorship); idea of, 18, 57, 180, 223, 228, 234; Janabai, 233–235; of *Līḷācaritra*, 103–104, 216, 222–224; and Mahadaise, 98, 203, 207, 216, 223–226, 295n19; and oral poetry (*See* oral poetry, and authorship); and women, 98, 200, 205–206, 225, 295n16

Babar, Sarojini, 54, 265n16; 267n47
bāḍa (performance notebook), 181, 292n93
Bahinabai (seventeenth-century *bhakti* poet), 26–27, 194, 208
Bahiṇāīcī Gāṇī (Songs of Bahinabai), 54, 265n20
bāī (feminine address), 1, 75, 117, 173, 182, 220
Baise, 107, 112, 214–216, 297n41
Baker, Houston A., 11
Bakhtin, Mikhail M., 64–65, 75, 86, 98, 101, 155, 170–171, 176, 184
Banjara (tribe), 13–14
Bauman, Richard, 23, 26
Bel, Bernard, 13, 54
Bhagavad Gītā (Gītā), 8, 98, 100, 140–141, 143, 145, 153, 176, 183–184, 218–219, 261n58, 283n59, 283n66
Bhāgavata Purāṇa, 142, 211, 218, 225, 271n7, 298n60
Bhagwat, Vidyut, 261n63, 293n2
bhajan, 93, 157, 159, 171, 178, 181–182, 195
Bhaktalilāmṛta, 192
Bhaktavijay, 121–122, 155–156, 188, 191, 195, 212, 216, 246
bhakti, 30–31, 33, 58, 123, 146, 166–176, 246, 250–251, 262n65, 271n4, 285n3; and *abhaṅga, See abhanga,* as a vehicle of *bhakti* poetry; and authorship, *See* authorship, in/of *bhakti* poetry; and Bahinabai Chaudhari, 170, 287n23; and grind mill songs, 13, 17–18, 25, 69–70, 73, 158–161, 184, 188; and Janabai, 5–8, 10–11, 63–64, 89, 121, 152, 156, 157, 190, 196, 199, 201–203, 238, 242, 286n17; and Mahadaise, 108–111, 219, 241; in the Mahanubhava sect, 16, 104–105, 110, 159, 226, 296n32; and *mamāyana* (*See mamāyana*); oral archives of, 14–15, 18, 35, 159–160, 198; oral traditions of (*See* oral tradition, *bhakti*); and Pandharpur, 5, 7, 13, 63, 84, 159, 166, 194, 198; poetry/poetics, 5, 10, 12–17, 25–26, 35, 64, 73, 81, 94, 101, 104, 109, 111, 123, 138, 155–156, 158–160, 170, 172–174, 176, 178, 180–183, 188, 193, 201; and Tukaram, 192–195; and vernacularization, 17, 33, 35, 203–205, 242; and Vitthal, 5–7, 8, 81, 109, 155, 157, 159, 162, 166–167, 176–177, 188, 196, 200, 284n87, 286n17, 286n18; and women (*See* women, and *bhakti*)
bhāruḍ, 176–177, 288n42

Bhaskar (fourteenth-century Marathi poet), 102, 206–207, 298n56
Bhatobas. *See* Nagdev
Bhavalkar, Tara, 68, 74, 80, 125, 161–162, 258n25, 267n51
Bhayani, H. C., 32, 34, 91, 95–96, 210, 227, 262n67, 299n62, 299n63, 299n64
Biber, Douglas, 97
Bijapur: Sufis, 24, 93, 260n42, 260n43; sultanate, 191
Black expressivity, 11, 34, 59
Bozzone, Chiara, 275n24, 279–280n24
Bradley, Adam, 67
Brahmins, 8–9, 26, 33, 59, 102, 104, 116, 133, 163, 191–192, 194, 208, 215, 221–223, 239–240, 291n88; women (*See* women, Brahmin)
Brahmin Ecumene, 17, 31, 101, 114, 223, 242, 258n29
Bṛhatkalpasūtra, 41
Briggs, Charles, 23, 26

cakkī (grind mill), 25, 260n44
cakkī-nāmā (poems by Bijapur sufi poets), 24–26, 93, 159
caste, 28, 53, 56, 89, 116, 130, 191–192, 258n26; and *bhakti*, 5, 89, 160, 176, 208, 271n4; and gender, 9, 16, 116, 205–206, 223, 235, 239, 243, 245, 250; and grind mill tradition, 20–23, 28, 53, 56, 79, 81, 89, 123, 177, 245, 246, 265n21, 285n3; and Janabai, 1, 10, 89, 208, 291n86, 302n99; and Mahanubhavas, 16, 102, 116; and Marathi, 59–60; and Marathi vernacularization, 59, 134; patriarchy, 9, 11, 116, 162, 165, 193, 245, 249–250; and slavery, 9, 162, 165, 190–191, 239; and vernacularization, 92, 205; and women (*See* women, and caste); "women, low castes, and others" (*See śūdra,* "women, *śūdras,* and others"); and/in writing and textuality, 11, 59, 61, 92, 190–193, 203, 235, 239–240, 243, 261n58, 291n86, 302n98, 302n99
Chakradhar, 16, 90, 101–117, 121, 129, 159, 195, 200, 212–224, 232, 242, 249, 275n47, 276n57, 297n35, 297n38, 297n39; and Mahadaise (*See* Mahadaise, and Chakradhar); relationship to Baise (*See* Baise); and Vitthal (*See* Vitthal, and Chakradhar)
chanda (metrical class), 135
Chandonuśāsna (Hemachandra), 277, 299n62
Chandoracanā (Patwardhan), 65–67, 135
Chatterjee, Indrani, 10
Chattopadhyaya, Brajadulal, 272n12
Chaucer, *The Canterbury Tales,* 89
Chaudhari, Bahinabai (twentieth-century poet), 54–57, 60, 72, 97, 168, 170, 188, 217–219, 265n20, 287n23; son of (*See* Dev, Sopan)
Chawre, Gita (grind mill singer), 165
Chinitz, David, 273n27
Chiplunkar, Vishnu Krishna, 242, 262n64, 302n104
Chokhamela, 168, 190–191, 195, 208
coḷī (blouse), 58, 82–86, 149, 153–154, 177, 188, 232, 244
colloquial, 151, 169, 226; English, 11, 59, 97; language, 61, 77, 95–96, 117; Marathi (*See* Marathi, colloquial); style, 97–98, 101; turn, 60, 97–99, 106–107, 134, 138, 147, 240, 242
colloquialization, 34–35, 55, 59–60, 91, 94–99, 116, 119, 123, 137, 142, 144, 147, 154, 210, 223, 237, 243, 274n41
Culler, Jonathan, 73, 75, 77, 79
Cutler, Norman, 152, 170, 174

Dalit (caste), 9, 19–20, 22, 60, 74, 76, 124, 159, 165, 172, 195, 285n3; women, 11, 19–20, 62, 110, 143, 148, 155, 230
Dandekar, S. V., 261n58, 282n57, 283n59
Dante, Alighieri, 205, 294n10
Darśanaprakāśa (Mahanubhava work), 138
dāsī, 1, 7–12, 64, 189, 191, 196, 198–199, 202, 237–238, 242; definition, 9
Dasopant, 98–100, 201, 293n3, 299n64
Daukes, Jacqueline, 255–256n1, 286n18, 292n1, 293n2, 296n25
death: as poetic theme, 165
Demati, 112–113
Deshmukh, Bhagwant, 283n62
Deshpande, A. N., 237
Deshpande, Kamalabai, 53–54
Deshpande, Prachi, 191, 281
deśī (regional), 91, 95, 125, 131–132, 138–139, 145, 178, 281n43
Dev, Sopan, 55–57, 59, 97, 168–170, 188, 217–218, 220, 265n20, 265n21; mother of (*See* Chaudhari, Bahinabai)
Devy, G. N., 192, 244, 250
dhangars, 24, 94, 176; *ovī* of (*See ovī, dhangar*)
dhavala (poetic form), 98, 138, 201, 226–228, 231, 299n62, 299n64
Dhavaḷe (narrative poem by Mahadaise), 98, 102, 138, 155, 201–203, 207, 216, 218, 224–234, 240, 293n3, 295n19, 299n64; authorship of, 98, 218, 224–226
Dhere, R. C., 15, 31, 40, 53, 124, 128, 153–155, 262n65, 264n5, 273n17, 284n87, 296n25
Dhule Manuscripts, 234, 289n50, 300n82
Dhurandar, M. V., 42, 204
dhvanī (implicature), 55, 58
Doniger, Wendy, 36
drone (musical instrument), 39, 60, 67–68; *see also tamborā*
Du Bois, W. E. B., 257n21
Dundes, Alan, 79
dung, 62–64, 71, 84, 116, 124, 189
Dylan, Bob, 66–67

Eaton, Richard, 10, 24–25, 93, 257n12, 257n14, 260n42, 260n43, 272n12
ecological metaphors, 18, 36–38, 259n30
Eknath (sixteenth-century poet), 82, 122, 149, 176, 194, 201, 208; grandson of (*See* Mukteshvar)
Eliot, T. S. (English writer), 96–97
embodiment, 168, 203, 240, 287n23; and Mahanubhava theology, 110, 232, 212, 223, 226
embroidery: as metaphor for literary writing, 82–84, 86, 149
enslavement. *See* slavery
erotic, 41–42, 53, 83–84; poetry, 29, 105–106, 212–213, 297n34; *rasa,* 58, 140, 155, 216, 222, 282n52
everyday: metonyms of, 62, 63, 116, 149; orality, 59, 61, 64–65, 68, 79, 88, 91, 93–95, 98–101, 112, 131, 137, 163, 167, 189, 211, 242; poetics of, 10, 28–31, 34, 35, 41–42, 52–53, 57–65, 68, 76, 82, 84, 110, 146, 166, 175, 184, 258n29, 259n31, 274n41, 297n39; poiesis, 35, 203; as topos, 60, 175
everyday creativity (Kirin Narayan), 18, 26, 69

familiarization, 98
Feldhaus, Anne, 24, 101, 103–104, 106, 114–116, 144, 154, 180, 220–221, 258n26, 259n40, 262n66, 272n11, 274n38, 274n39, 275n47, 275n48,

275n53, 276n58, 276n62, 289n60, 295n21, 296n32, 297n39, 297n46, 297n50
feminine, 23, 53–54, 57, 76, 80, 258n24; performativity, 23–25, 75–76, 155; structures of address/addressivity, 70, 75, 108, 117, 119, 155, 220
feminist, 23, 26–27, 205, 256–257n11, 293n2
Ferrante, Joan M., 205, 294n9
figural authorship, 7, 38, 57, 182, 188, 199–200, 203, 216–225, 234–235, 242, 251, 295n19
figural poet, 5, 12
Finegan, Edward, 97
Finnegan, Ruth, 82, 180
Flueckiger, Joyce B., 24
folk, 4, 32, 38, 52, 92, 237, 271n7; literature, 25, 28, 31, 54, 106, 132, 265n16, 267n51; and *loka,* 31–32, 262n65; music, 19, 24, 26, 54, 61–62, 68, 88, 106, 111, 264n13, 269n79; studies, 28, 32, 54, 94; theater, 171, 233
folklore, 2, 31, 53, 259n34, 271n7, 280n31
folk song(s), 28, 31–32, 35, 52, 54, 64, 88, 93, 111, 160, 210, 261–262n63, 264–265n13, 269n79
Frankfurt School, 14
Fuller, Mary, 20

Gajāṣṭaka, 131
Galvez, Marisa, 181
Ganesh, 146–147
Gangakhed, 6, 12, 255n1
Garbhakāṇḍa Ovyā (by Mahadaise), 207, 295n19
gāthā: as collection/anthology, 18, 58, 192–193; compared to *ovī,* 59, 71, 137, 141–142; etymology of, 141; and Indira Sant, 59; and literarity, 181, 210, 223; Prakrit verse form, 41, 58–59, 71, 77, 141–142, 210, 223; by Sanghadas, 40–42, 52, 59, 69, 77, 163
gaulaṇa (song form), 112, 176–177, 288n42
Gavale, Lakshmibai (grind mill singer), 126
gender, 23, 235, 239, 250, 255n1, 281n43, 286n18, 292n1, 294n8, 294n9, 296n26; and femininity, 23–24, 76, 84; fluidity, 23–24; and labor, 9, 90, 116; in literary traditions, 13, 27, 130, 211, 223, 243; and the Mahanubhavas, 16, 102, 206; segregation, 11, 245; and vernacularization, 204–205. *See also* vernacularization, women
Gioia, Ted, 67
Gītā. *See* Bhagavad Gītā
Gītārnṇva (Dasopant), 98
Glushkova, Irina, 255n1
Godavari River Valley, 12, 23, 41, 104, 107, 264n11
Godbole, Parashuram B., 132–133, 178, 186, 235, 237, 280n35, 280n36
Goehr, Lydia, 28–29
Gonda, Jan, 129
Gopalpur, 63, 158, 163–164
Greek literature, 73, 77, 129–130, 181
grind mill: archeology of, 2, 88; electric, 2, 4, 88; embodied poetics of, 56–57, 61–62, 75; figuration of, 39–42, 79–81, 161; mortar and pestle, *See* mortar and pestle; *ovī* (*See ovī*); poetics of (*See* poetics, of the grind mill); rotary quern, 88; and *saṃsār,* 163–166; as site of *sāsar* and/or *māher,* 165–166, 184, 286n17; song traditions, 90, 247; stone hand mill, description of, 2–3; as symbol, 81, 166, 183–184; musicality of, 60, 67–69, 128

grind mill songs, 36, 56, 77, 122, 124–125, 128, 136, 150, 154, 181, 220, 241, 244, 247–250; and *abhaṅga,* 76, 109, 176, 181, 183, 186, 188; as an archive, 2, 12, 14–15, 18, 22–23, 33, 35, 37, 54, 78–79, 108, 159–160, 211, 229–230; and *bhakti,* 13, 17–18, 69, 108–109, 152, 156–161, 166, 176, 183, 188; and the everyday, 60, 175; in Greek literature, 77; history of, 90; and literarity, 11, 13, 16, 52, 54, 156, 264n13; of the Mahanubavhas, 16, 276n59; in Maharashtra, 4, 15, 260n43, 260n44, 265n17; in Marathi, 16–17, 27, 32, 77, 201; musicality, 68–69; orality, 52, 64, 82, 170–171; oral-formulaic refrains in, 128, 220; and Vitthal, 15, 195, 212–213, 252–253; and women, 13, 19, 37, 83, 152, 232–233. *See also ovī*, grind mill
Grindmill Songs Project, The, 13, 22, 56, 159, 165, 244, 248, 284n2, 285n8
Grundmann, Herbert, 205–206, 210, 294n9, 294n13, 296n26
Guha, Sumit, 9, 257n12, 291n88
Gujarati literature/poetics, 119–220, 227, 299n64
Gurav (caste), 58, 164

Hala (Satavahana king), 41
Hallisey, Charles, 167, 180
Haraway, Donna, 38
Hari, 168. *See* Vitthal
Hariścandra Ākhyāna (Janabai), 201, 203, 207–208, 232–234, 300n82, 302n99; authorship, 203
Hariścandrākhyāna (Mukteshvar), 235–237, 302n99
Hariścandrapurāṇakathā (Vishnudas Nama), 235, 301n86, 302n98, 302n102
Harischandra (legendary king of Ayodhya), 201, 211, 232–241, 302n99
Hawley, John Stratton, 179
Hemachandra (Jain scholar-poet), 227, 299n62
Hess, Linda, 17, 262n65
Hingoli district, 3, 14–15, 19–20, 23, 25, 85, 126, 198
Hiraise (Mahanubhava writer), 104, 207, 275n53
Homer, 67, 78, 269n78
huruda (heart), 17, 33, 62, 80, 82, 154, 242
hypocorism, 168, 171, 172, 173, 222
hypotaxis, 34, 114, 147–150, 186, 226, 236–237, 241

incarnation, 218; Cangdev Raul, 115, 220; Chakradhar, 16, 105, 115, 220; Gundam Raul, 102, 105, 115, 228; Krishna, 218, 228; Mahanubhava dieties, 110; Vishnu, 187
inscriptions: Humcha, 131–132; Marathi, 7
intertext/intertextuality, 2, 12, 15, 17, 31, 35, 81–82, 150–151, 168, 170, 181, 188, 195, 204, 211, 228, 262n65
interweb, 35, 206, 211
Irlekar, Suhasini, 225
Itīhās (undated account of Mahanubhava history), 103

Jakobson, Roman, 267n57
Jamison, Stephanie, 78, 268n75, 279n24
Janabai, 1–18, 23, 27, 70, 76–77, 83, 89, 152–153, 156, 159, 173, 182, 192, 195–199, 233–241, 246–247, 249, 251–252, 255n1n 291n85, 291n86, 296n24, 300n82, 301n89, 301n93, 302n99; as *dāsī*, 10–12; compared to Mahadaise, 35, 201–204, 211, 232, 241–243; historicity, 203; name

etymology, 7, 75; poetic style of, 4, 189, 236–238, 240; and textuality and literacy, 16, 62–64, 158, 207–209; and Vitthal, 121, 157, 163, 167, 188–190, 195, 197, 212–213, 216, 232, 297n34
Jassal, Smita Tiwari, 18, 259n34
jāta (grind mill), 18–19, 56, 68, 71–72, 265–266n21
jātī (morae counting meters), 133–135, 189, 227
Jnaneshvar, 8, 30, 35, 85, 100–101, 119, 121, 123, 138–156, 176, 180, 188–189, 194, 202–203, 216, 218, 261n58, 262n66, 275n43, 278n8, 282n52, 282n54, 283n60, 283n66
Jñāneśvarī, 8, 98, 145, 176–177, 188, 202, 218, 243, 261n58, 275n43, 278n8, 282n57, 283n59; and the everyday, 100–101, 117–119; and grind mill songs, 26, 42; and *ovī*, 80, 85, 112, 123, 128, 138–139, 141, 147–149, 151–155; signature line in, 180
Jogdand, Chandrakalabai (grind mill singer), 19
Joshi, N. G., 136, 178, 283n60, 293n3, 299n64
Julian, Madhav. *See* M. T. Patwardhan

Kamble, Tulasa (grind mill singer), 74
Kannada: language, 25, 131; literature, 92, 105, 119, 127, 191, 201, 205, 234, 241
Karanika, Andromache, 77–78
Karve, C. G., 54
Kavirājamārga, 92
Kaviśvar. *See* Bhaskar
kavitva, 30–31, 141, 189–190, 193, 262
kāvya, 30, 32–33, 55, 94, 105, 113, 119, 141–142, 146–147, 216; *dhvanikāvya*, 58; *gadya kāvya*, 66; *kāvyanaye*, 282n54; *paṇḍit kāvya*, 134
Ketkar, Sachin, 273n19, 275n43
Khaladkar, Varada, 270n1
Khandesh/Khandeshi (region in Maharashtra), 60, 169, 265n21
kīrtan, 8, 155, 157, 159, 168–174, 178, 181–183, 189–190, 192, 194–195, 203, 208, 218, 233–234, 275n43, 287n24
Klinck, Anne, 211
Kolte, V. B., 275–276n53, 276n58, 276n61, 276n63, 297n35, 297n38, 297n39, 298n56, 299n61
Korczynski, Marek, 267n53
Krishna (deity), 94, 98, 100, 102, 105, 108, 110–112, 149–150, 153–154, 176, 184, 201, 208, 212, 218–220, 224, 226–229, 231–232, 240–241, 296n32, 299n61
Krishnayagnavalki (late sixteenth-century poet), 201
Kulkarni, Kedar, 32, 242, 262n64, 262n66, 262n67, 281n40, 302n104
Kulkarni, S. R., 113
Kunte, Keshavchaitanya, 178
Kuvalayamālā (eighth-century Prakrit work), 88

labor, 10, 74, 78, 238, 244; and gender (*See* gender, and labor); and *ovī* (*See ovī*, labor); as analogy for poetic composition, 5, 35, 82, 91, 117, 129–130, 137–138, 144, 149, 223, 225; everyday, 13, 25, 32, 40–42, 55, 63–64, 94, 115–116, 124, 157, 166–167, 170, 189, 196, 199, 215, 239, 242; of grinding, 2–4, 17, 34–35, 40, 62, 68, 72, 79, 82, 107, 119, 125–127, 130, 136, 147, 160–163, 166, 174–175, 191, 246–247; women's, 7–8, 57, 68–69, 89–90, 106, 119, 130, 155, 184, 200, 212, 214–215, 245, 264n5
Lakshadhira (Mahanubhava poet), 134–135, 281n43

Lakshmidharbhat (Mahanubhava poet): and Mahadaise (*See* Mahadaise, and Lakshmidharbhat); and Mhaimbhat (*See* Mhaimbhat, and Lakshmidharbhat)
lāvaṇī, 134, 195
Leslie, Julia, 270n3
līḷā (Mahanubhava prose form), 34, 101, 109–110, 122, 147, 214–221, 224, 227, 242, 275n47, 276n58, 276n61, 276n63, 276n72, 297n38, 297n39, 297n43, 297n46, 298n50; as counter-form, 104–107; influence of *ovī* on, 113–117
Līḷācaritra, 16, 34, 90, 97, 102–123, 127, 147, 155, 191, 202–204, 211–225, 232, 275n48, 276n57, 277n63, 297n39, 298n56; authorial role of Mahadaise in, 215–224; authorship of, 103–105, 222–224; influence of women's *ovīs* on, 113–117, 119–220, 223; Mahadaise's *ovīs* in, 107–111, 276n58, 276n6; reconstruction of, 104, 207; scatalogical references in, 101, 275n47; women and, 102, 106–107, 213–216, 223; women's songs in, 107–110, 222
listener: role of, 37, 41, 52, 72–73, 94, 150, 152, 170–171, 182–184, 251
literacy, 97, 179, 258n29, 300n72; among Black Americans, 11, 162; among women, 170, 206–208, 222
literarity, 5, 11, 16, 52, 59, 90, 95–96, 119, 142, 147, 176, 234, 241, 243; and Janabai, 11, 35; and women, 5, 41, 55, 79, 86, 200, 204, 206, 223; in the West, 28, 59, 67
literarization, 34–35, 90, 94–95, 117, 119, 123, 137, 147, 237, 243
literature: concept and definition, 26–34, 54, 59, 65, 67; vernacular, 59, 90–94, 175, 205, 241
literization, 94
loka. *See* folk and loka
lokagīta/e (folk song), 28, 31, 32, 54, 160
lokasāhitya (folk literature), 28, 31
Lord, Albert, 74, 269n78
lullabies, 25, 68, 75, 125, 244, 278n8
lyric, 58, 84, 161, 182–184, 197–198, 201, 206, 210–211, 229, 232, 237, 241–242, 250–251; apostrophe in, 77–81; and European Romanticism, 73–74, 242; and Greek literature, 70, 73, 77–78; and grind mill songs, 70–78; and orality, 40; and *ovī*, 20, 33, 40, 64, 80, 84, 86, 110, 137–138, 151, 154–155; poetic features of, 70–78, 182–183; ritual and, 78–79; in South Asian poetics, 70–71; universality of, 71

Mahābhārata, 74, 139–140, 142, 159, 170, 183–184, 208, 235, 282n54, 301n86
Mahadaise, 17–18, 98, 102, 121–122, 127, 138, 155, 226–234, 275n57, 276n58, 277n72, 293n3, 295n19, 298n47, 298n50, 298n60, 299n64, 300n71; *abhaṅga* of, 288n46; and Chakradhar, 107–113, 117, 212, 216, 219–223, 232, 249, 276n61, 277n72, 297n47; compared to Janabai (*See* Janabai, compared to Mahadaise); family background, 217–218; as figural poet, 203, 224–225, 242; and Gundam Raul, 106–107, 110–112, 216; and Lakshmidharbhat, 225; and the *Līḷācaritra*, 16, 34, 106–107, 110, 112–113, 122, 127, 202–204, 216–225, 232, 276n58, 276n61; and Mhaimbhat, 216, 222–224; and Nagdev, 221–222; origin of name, 216–217; as Rupai, 217
Mahadev. *See* Yadavas, kings, Mahadev
Mahanubhavas, 16, 30, 90, 101–104, 110, 166, 200, 215, 224, 297n38; literature

of, 16, 26, 34, 92, 94, 104–106, 109, 119, 129, 131, 133–134, 138, 156, 159, 188, 201–202, 207, 211, 217, 222, 226, 229, 242–243, 248, 258n27, 276n59, 276n62, 288n46, 293n3, 295n21, 296n32; origins of, 16, 103; sect, 101, 215; secret codes of, 234, 281n43; theology, 115, 212, 224, 226, 276–277n62
Mahar (caste), 19, 191, 208
Maharashtra, 1–6, 8–10, 15–16, 19, 23, 25, 28, 30–32, 59, 68, 85, 88, 124, 128, 134, 152, 159, 160, 162, 166, 174, 200, 204–207, 212, 214, 242, 257n15, 260n43, 260n44, 260n47, 262n65, 265n17, 267n51, 273n29, 297n38; struggle for linguistic statehood of, 54
Maharashtra Government Council on Folk Literature, 54, 265n16
Mahārāṣtra Kāvyadīpika (Lakshadhira), 134, 142
māher (natal home), 84, 166–167, 173, 175, 184–185, 286n17
Mahipati (eighteenth-century poet-scribe, author of *Bhaktavijay*), 121–122, 133, 156–158, 189–190, 192–193, 195–196, 246
Mālanagāthā, 39, 57, 157
mamāyana, 167–168, 171–172, 177, 197
Mānasollāsa, 32, 124–125, 128, 133, 227, 278n12
Mande, Prabhakar, 24, 262n63
Maratha (seventeenth-nineteenth-century ruling dynasty), 93, 191, 234, 270n3, 272n12
Marathas (caste), 22, 165
Marathi: *bhakti* traditions in, 8, 15–16; as classical language, 274n29; colloquial, 32, 90, 99–101, 141; figuration of, 97, 144, 294n8; and folk, 24; language, 2, 24–25, 58–59, 98–100, 139, 187, 189, 191, 200, 260, 265n21, 269n86; literarity in, 16, 18, 26, 31, 32, 35; literature, 7–9, 16–18, 26–27, 35, 42, 55, 65, 72, 77, 80, 86–87, 97–98, 105, 107, 114, 119–120, 121–127, 132–137, 140–142, 144–150, 153–155, 160, 163, 170, 176, 177, 178, 180, 188, 195, 200–202, 204, 216, 218, 225–227, 233–237, 239–241, 244, 255n1, 258n29, 260n42, 260n44, x–xi; and oral, 31–32; origins of, 273–274n29; and other languages, 25; and poetics, 17, 30, 32, 34, 35, 92, 132, 141–145; and Prakrit, 97–100, 133, 144, 273–274n29; vernacular turn, 30, 34, 120, 206, 211, 240, 243; vernacularization of, 30–32, 34, 52–54, 90–94, 97, 101–103, 117, 138, 153, 205–206, 211, 219, 242; words for slave in, 9, 247n12; writing, 57, 129, 207
Marathwada (region of Maharashtra), 13, 247
Marcuse, Herbert, 245
marhāṭa, 100, 274n39
Maslov, Boris, 71, 73, 267n57
maternal: imagery and figuration, 153–155, 172, 276n61, 284n87
Māṭṛki-Rukmiṇī-Svayaṃvar (Mahadaise), 295n19
McCash, June, 294n9, 295n16
metafolkloristics, 33, 79
metaphor, 58, 70–72, 144, 147, 190–192, 235, 286n17; in *bhakti,* 8, 171–172; ecological, 18, 82; embroidery (*See* emboidery); maternal, 152, 276n61; vs. simile, 150; of unraveling (*See* unraveling); of weaving (*See* weaving, as metaphor)
metapoetics, 79–80, 123, 140
metonymy, 62–64, 70, 103, 116, 144, 149–150, 165, 181

Mhaimbhat, 103–104, 106, 191, 216, 222–225, 229, 241, 298n56; and Mahadaise (*See* Mahadaise, and Mhaimbhat)
mimesis, 8, 172
Molesworth, James Thomas, 63, 132–133, 137, 262n66, 281n38
More, Sadanand, 139, 154–155
Moretti, Franco, 250, 263n73
Moropant, 134, 201, 241–242, 302n103
mortar and pestle, 2, 22, 78–79, 81, 88, 106, 256n3, 270
Mukteshvar, 201, 208, 235–237, 239–241, 296n24, 301n86, 301n89, 301n93, 302n99
Mulgaonkar, Raghuvir, 6
music: grind mill songs and, 69, 125; and poetry, 7, 57–58, 65–68, 135–136, 141–142, 245, 253; South Asian, 25, 178, 210; Western classical, 28–29; "work concept" in, 28
Muslim women's songs, 14, 25, 53, 159, 260n44, 284n2
mycorrhizae, 171; mycorrhizal, 18, 35–36, 251

Nagaise (woman Mahanubhava writer), 207, 295n21
Nagaraj, D. R., 91–92, 105–106, 132, 138, 188, 205
Nagdev, 103–104, 215, 221–222
Nagpure, P. C. (editor, Hiraise edition of *Līḷācaritra*), 275n53, 276n58, 276n61, 277n72, 297–298n46, 297n35, 297n43
Nagubai. *See* Baise
Nagy, Gregory, 7–8
Nama, Vishnudas, 201, 208, 235–241, 301n84, 301n86, 302n98, 302n99, 302n102
Namdev, 8–10, 85, 121, 156, 173–174, 178–179, 182–184, 186, 189, 194, 198, 202–203, 208, 233–235, 246, 286n18, 291n85, 293n2, 296n25; figural, 5
Nandapurkar, N. G., 208, 237, 296n24, 301n89, 301n93
Nanddas (Braj poet), 298–299n60
Narayan, Kirin, 33, 259n30, 267n54, 280n31, 300n72
Narendra, 102, 128, 138–140, 155, 180, 226, 228, 231, 241, 299n61
nāṭya saṅgīt, 134, 195
Nevasa (central Maharashtrian town), 88
nomen loquens (speaking name), 7–8, 12, 64, 84, 182, 200, 203
nostalgia, 42, 245–246
Novetzke, Christian Lee, 7–8, 31, 92, 103, 175, 202, 205, 234, 256n7, 257n15, 258n29, 261n58, 262n65, 275n43, 277n77, 282n52, 283n66, 286n17, 291n85, 291n86, 294n8, 296n39, 297n38, 297n39, 298n53

Ollett, Andrew, 91, 95, 97, 141, 144, 210, 269n79, 280n28
oral: aesthetics, 234; archive, 2, 14, 35, 37, 78; composition, 55, 180; forms/genres, 12, 19, 24, 32, 73, 92, 138, 223, 227; hagiography, 121; and/or literary, 25, 32, 34, 35, 59, 64, 80, 87, 96, 113, 192–193; *ovī* (*See ovī,* oral); performers/performance, 23, 36, 54, 57, 78, 94, 95, 129, 162, 169, 181, 206; recitation, 145, 151, 218; in Romanticism, 34; style, 97, 98, 119, 225, 232; and sung, 65, 138, 142, 145; vs. spoken, 65; and/or written, 2, 16–18, 23, 31, 33, 37–38, 52, 57, 70–71, 73–75, 107–113, 124, 132, 135, 142, 154, 160, 171, 181–182, 188–193, 201

oral literacy, 170
oral literary criticism, 33
oral poetics, 35, 90, 92, 94, 106, 113, 122, 175–176, 201, 211, 241–243, 266n26, 269n78, 289n60
oral poetry, 17, 33, 52, 65, 74, 82, 90–92, 95, 106, 113, 122, 147, 168, 175–176, 189, 201, 211, 224, 241–243, 266n26; and authorship, 56–57, 179–180; *bhakti,* 35, 160, 162, 176; *ovī* as, 56–57, 70, 182; signature line and, 179, 181, 289n60; and vernacularization, 91–94, 175, 242–243; and women, 25, 40, 94, 136, 243
oral tradition, 36, 74, 124, 272n16, 289n60; authorship, 179, 181; Black American, 257n21; contrasted with written, 33, 38, 175, 183, 194; Greek literature, 130; grind mill songs (*See* grind mill, song traditions); in Maharashtra, 23, 93, 202, 265n16; and/of women, 25, 201–202, 211, 218, 237
orality, 5, 32–34, 42, 57, 60–61, 69, 90–91, 94, 98, 104, 131, 136–137, 181, 190, 195, 223, 276n58, 296n26; and writing, 12, 17, 52, 59, 65, 92, 151, 170, 175, 248–249, 262n65, 275n43
ordinary language philosophy, 60, 266n26
ōvanige, 131, 280n31
oveṇaka, 131
ovī: alternate spellings of: *vahī* (*See vahī*); *vaī,* 24, 120; *vavī,* 24; *vovi/vovī,* 24; and *abhaṅga, See abhaṅga,* and *ovī*; categorized as folk song, 31–32, 64, 160; *dhangar,* 24, 289n60; etymology of, 17, 24, 82, 128–131, 137; formal definition, 125–136, 186; grind mill, 2–7, 24, 31–33, 57, 64, 67–87, 124, 147, 150, 178–283n62; history of, 31–32, 124–137; hypotaxis in (*See* hypotaxis); and Janabai, 62–64, 76, 121–122; and labor, 2, 4, 7, 17, 33–34, 62, 63–64, 68, 82, 119, 124–130, 137, 147, 149, 189; lyric form of, 70–79; Mahadaise's, 108–110, 222; in Mahanubhav texts, 107–112, 122, 222; influence on Marathi writing, 117–120, 122, 188; maternal figuration and, 124, 153–155; meter, 71–72, 99, 113–115, 122; musical characteristics of, 68–69; oral, 18–23, 34, 53–61, 64, 70–71, 86, 94, 97, 132–133, 160, 169–174, 178–179, 183, 190, 192–202, 216, 225, 230–232, 238–239, 245, 252, 269n82, 276n58, 276n59, 280n34, 283n60; relationship of oral/literary, 59, 107–124, 137, 146–154, 292n94; parataxis in (*See* parataxis); poetics/metapoetics of, 56–59, 61, 64, 68, 70–71, 79–87, 138–147; prosody of, 123, 132–137, 142; rhyme schemes in, 71–72, 122; in Sanskrit texts, 124–125, 128; sequence structure in, 71–73; written (textual/literary), 24–25, 59, 66, 122–124, 132–133, 136, 138–156, 182, 207–209, 222, 226–227, 236–237, 242, 248, 264n12, 276n61, 278n12, 283n59, 299n61

Paik, Shailaja, 9, 165
Pandharpur (city in western Maharashtra), 13, 19, 62–64, 71, 84, 149, 166–168, 185, 198, 212; pilgrimage to, 19, 173, 252; Vitthal's temple in, 5, 7, 159, 194, 197
parallelism, 70–72, 113, 115, 150–151, 239, 267n57
parataxis, 70, 72, 113–115, 119, 147, 149, 185–186, 241

Parry, Milman, 268n57
Pathade, Mangala, 276n59
Patwardhan, Madhav T., 65–66, 69, 135–136, 280n36, 282n54
Pauwels, Heidi, 271n7, 298–299n60, 300n71
Pawar, Urmila, 124, 159
pestle. *See* mortar and pestle
pestle songs, 2, 22, 78–79, 131
Phukan, Shantanu, 38
Phule, Jotirao (non-Brahmin thinker), 9, 59
Phule, Savitribai, 9, 60, 200
Phulwadkar, Deenanath, 6
Plutarch, 77
poetics: *bhakti*, 10, 12, 17, 35, 104, 109–111, 155, 158–160, 170, 174–175, 182–184, 191, 193; of the everyday (*See* everyday, poetics of); figural, 57; of the grind mill, 13, 17, 33–34, 72, 79–87, 90, 175, 184, 199, 240–243; Kannada, 91–92; Marathi, 17, 30, 92–93, 132–135 142, 202; oral (*See* oral poetics); of the *ovī* (*See ovī*, poetics/metapoetics of); superposed/Sanskrit, 52, 137, 139, 140, 145, 237, 282n54; and religion/theology, 30, 110, 146; vernacular, 11, 17, 30, 145; of work, 17, 19, 34, 68, 117–119, 137, 145–151, 199, 202, 240–242
poetry: accessibility of, 63, 123, 135, 142–144, 151, 210, 261n58; concept and definition of, 5, 10, 28, 39, 52, 55, 57–59, 61, 65–67; lineation and, 56–57; and orality (*See* oral poetry); and song, 13, 37, 52, 64–70, 136, 141, 154–156, 175, 242–243, 252
poiesis, 5, 17, 28, 35, 60, 64, 75, 82, 84, 86–87, 104, 147, 149–150, 155, 161, 165, 170, 203, 243, 247, 252–253; *bhakti* as, 64, 157, 166, 168, 171–172, 183, 196, 198, 203, 287n24; etymology, 28; *see also sympoiesis*
Poitevin, Guy, 13, 23, 54, 60, 80, 82, 175–176, 258n24, 258n25
Pollock, Sheldon, 11, 29, 34, 42, 90–92, 94–95, 105, 141, 204–205, 258n29, 273n19, 291n85
potarāj (devotee of the goddess), 23–24, 26, 94
pothī (book), 62–63, 116, 167–168, 172–174, 181, 206
povāḍa, 134, 195
prabandha (song form), 32, 91, 124, 138
Prabhu, Govind. *See* Raul, Gundam
Prakrit: and colloquialization, 95–97; *gāthā,* 41, 52, 58, 71, 141; poetics/poetry, 71, 92, 133–137, 141–142, 180, 227; and Apabhramsha, 11, 34, 91, 95–97, 119, 133, 138, 180, 210, 227; and Marathi, 17, 97–99, 125, 132–138, 141–142, 180, 273–274n29; and Sanskrit, 11, 17, 34, 41, 91, 95, 99, 119, 132, 137–138, 141, 176, 210, 265–266n21, 273–274n29; and women, 210; figuration of, 51, 91, 97, 100, 144, 210; in Sanghadas, 40–41, 52
Pratt, Mary Louise, 62
Prentiss, Karen Pechilis, 167–168
Priolkar, A. K., 180, 282n–283n57
Pune, 12, 60
purāṇa(s), 74, 93, 114, 142, 146, 159, 170, 217–218, 221, 298n50
puranic: figures, 169, 225; stories/texts, 206, 211, 224, 230; traditions, 143

Raeside, Ian, 101, 201, 216, 281n43, 288n46, 293n3, 295n21
ragaḷe, 92
Raghavanka (thirteenth-century Kannada poet), 201, 302n99

Rairkar, Hema, 12–13, 23, 54, 60, 250, 255n1, 258n24
Rajwade, V. K., 135–136, 282–283n57, 300n82
Ramanujan, A. K., 36–37, 194
Rāmāyaṇa, 13, 36–37, 73, 159, 175, 211, 233
Ramazani, Jahan, 70, 268n69
Ramdas (seventeenth-century scribe and philosopher-poet), 191–192, 195
Ramdev. *See* Yadavas, kings, Ramdev
Ranade, Ashok D., 67
rarification, 52, 95–96, 223, 243
rasa, 30, 55, 139–140, 144, 189, 282n54; erotic (*śṛṅgārarasa*), 58, 140, 155, 216, 222, 282n52; of peace. *See śāntarasa*
Raul, Cangdev, 115, 220
Raul, Gundam, 102–103, 105–107, 111–112, 115, 216, 221, 224, 227–230
Ṛddhipurcaritra (1287 text), 102–107, 111–113, 127, 202, 211, 216, 222, 227–230
Rekret, Paul, 165, 247
Rohidas (son of Harischandra), 238–240
Romantic: concept of the "folk," 4, 38, 82; poetry, 34, 38, 73, 97, 134, 242
Romanticism, 4, 97, 134, 242
Rukmini (wife of Vitthal), 13, 76, 83–86, 98, 102, 159, 174, 177, 201, 207, 211–213, 226–233, 238, 240–241, 252–253, 299n61, 300n71, 300n74
Rukmiṇī Svayaṃvar: and Mahadaise, 127, 201, 226; in Marathi literature, 201, 224; by Narendra, 102, 128, 138–139, 180, 226
Rupai. *See* Mahadaise

Sadhe (Mahanubhava woman disciple), 111–112, 127
śāhirī poetry, 262n64
sāhitya (rhetoric/poetics), 32, 146, 262n66
saṃsār (Marathi term for married life, domesticity), 100, 163–167, 184, 188
saṃsāra (Sanskrit theological term), 99, 163, 166, 183–186
Sane, Guruji (Sadashiv Pandurang Sane), 53–54, 56–57, 124, 242, 245
Sanghadas (Jain poet). *See gāthā*, by Sanghadas
Saṅgīta Ratnākara, 7, 125, 129, 131, 135, 138, 139, 178, 278–279n12
Sankalia, H. D., 88–89
Sanskrit: accessibility of, 143; and the cosmopolitan, 11, 92, 101; and *deśī*, 132; 258–259n29, 281n43, 294n28; and folk, 32, 91–92, 271n7; and *Jñāneśvarī*, 138–153, 282n57; literarity, 29, 41, 55, 58, 147, 176, 206–207, 210, 218–219, 221–222, 242, 262n65, 271n7, 280n36, 293n4; Mahadaise and, 207, 218–219; and orality, 206–207; poetry/poetics, 58, 84, 113, 125, 129, 131–133, 135, 137, 139–145, 226, 237, 242, 280–281n36 (*See also kāvya*); in relation to Marathi, 97–100, 137–138, 142, 147, 221–222, 280n36, 281n42, 281n43, 282-283n57, 294n8; in relation to Prakrit and Apabramsha, 11, 17, 34, 41, 91, 95–100, 132, 144, 176, 210; and vernacularization, 91–92, 175–176, 210, 233, 258n29, 273n19; weaving analogies in, 129–130; word for grind mill in, 265n21; words for slave/devotee in, 9, 256n11, 257n12
Sant, Indira (poet), 39, 57–59, 80, 97, 157–158
śāntarasa (*rasa* of peace), 139–140, 155, 282n52, 282n54
Sapir, Edward, 96

Sappho, 7, 78
Sarangpandit, 114, 213–214, 277n68, 297n35
Sarasvati (goddess), 246
sāsar (conjugal home), 166, 286n17
Sathaye, Adheesh, 233, 262n65, 271n7, 293n4
Sattasaī, 41–42, 210, 216, 223
Savitri (epic and puranic figure), 169, 220
scribes/scribal communities, 18, 57, 181, 189–192, 195, 205, 234, 278n12, 281n36, 291n86; Vitthal/God as scribe, 188–192, 195, 207, 216
separability principle, 26, 28–30, 34–35, 84, 87, 102, 116, 132, 140, 146, 175, 211
separation of styles, 101, 274–275n41
sewing, 97, 215; as metaphor for poetic composition, 33, 34, 82, 84– 86, 91, 99, 119, 129–130, 136, 147, 149
Shakespeare, William, 26–28, 67, 181, 290n67
Sharangadeva, 125, 127–128, 131, 178
Shende, Sarojini, 301n86
Shirad Shahapur (village), 19, 126, 260n44
Shridhar (eighteenth-century Marathi poet), 201
Shukla, Rohini, 287n23
signature line/verse: in *abhaṅgas,* 179–180, 182; and *bhakti* poetry, 180–182, 186–188, 199, 229, 242, 251; in *dhangar ovī*, 289n60; in early European vernacular poetry, 181; and figural authorship, 5–9, 12, 182–183, 187–188, 218, 234, 237–238, 251; history of, 180–182; of Janabai, 5, 7–9, 12, 180, 199, 218, 234, 237, 238; of Mahadaise, 242; Marathi words for, 180, 193; in South Asia, 180, 193; of Tukaram, 186–188, 193. *See also sphragis, takhallus*
Simard, Suzanne, 35–36
simile, 70, 82, 143–144, 150, 236
Singhana. *See* Yadavas, kings, Singhana
Sita, 13, 22, 36–37, 69, 72–73, 124, 128, 172, 211, 244, 250, 258n25, 259n34, 263n77, 300n71
Sitāyan (women's songs on Sita) 13, 37, 175, 232–233, 259n34
slavery: American, 11, 35, 59, 74, 162; South Asian, 1, 8–12, 86, 165, 189–190, 201, 203, 233, 238–239, 240
ślōkaḥ. *See anuṣṭubh*
Smṛtisthaḷ (Mahanubhava text), 103, 107, 127, 180, 206, 211, 221–222, 224–226, 228, 295n19, 295n21, 299n61
Sohoni, Pushkar, 93
song. *See* poetry, and song
song lyrics, 66–67
sorrow songs. *See* African American spirituals
sphragis (signature verse, Greek and English poetry), 181, 193
Śrīkṛṣṇacaritra, 224, 298n56
Strīdharmapaddhatī, 270n3
śṛṅgārarasa, See rasa, erotic
śudra, 192. *See also* "women, *śudras,* and others"
Sufi: and *bhakti* modes, 75, 225; poets, 25, 25, 159; poetry, 24–25, 75, 181; *pirs*, 75; teachings, 25
sultanates, 93, 234; Bijapur, 191; Delhi, 92, 104
sūtra, 129
Sūtrapāṭh (Mahanubhava text), 103, 116, 129, 221, 275n48, 297–298n46
svagata, 74–75, 80, 161–162, 165, 184, 199, 245

Svayambhūchandas, 227, 299n62
sympoiesis, 60, 76, 87, 104, 152, 166, 183, 203, 252–253; definition, 38

takhalluṣ (signature line in Persian/Urdu poetry), 187
tāla (rhythmic pattern), 131, 178
tamborā (drone), 60, 68. *See also* drone
Tamil work songs, 128, 264n5
Taramati (Queen and wife of Harischandra), 203, 211, 233, 238–241
Thālipāk (work by Janabai), 208–209, 234, 296n24, 300n82, 301n89
Therīgāthā (Poems of the First Buddhist Women), 79, 106, 180, 222, 269
Thorat, Janabai, 3, 19–22, 62, 64, 76, 118, 196, 198, 249, 252, 270n1
Thurman, Howard (Black theologian), 74, 162, 165, 167, 172
Tīrthāvaḷī (foundational text of Vitthal *bhakti*), 8
tripadi (Kannada verse form), 127
Tsing, Anna Lowenhaupt, 251
Tukaram, 85, 168, 185–188, 192–195, 286n17
Tulpule, S. G., 93–94, 144, 180, 262n66, 272n11, 272n12, 272n16, 273n29, 274n38, 274n39, 275n48, 295n21
Twain, Mark, 59

Uddyotanasuri (Jain poet), 10
Ughade, Rama (grind mill singer), 176
Ujgare, Mahananda (grind mill singer), 172
ukalaṇeṃ (to unravel), 80, 82
underview, 35, 37, 87, 171, 195, 202, 223, 230, 232, 241, 243, 246, 249, 251, 253
unraveling, 17, 33–34, 80–82, 86, 91, 96, 100–101, 106, 110, 130–131, 146–147, 151, 154–155, 160, 184, 186, 188, 223, 241–243, 247–250
untouchable castes, 22, 79, 102, 116, 167, 191, 239, *See also* Dalit

vacana (Kannada poetic form), 92, 105–106, 194, 234
vahī, 24, 129
vaī. *See ovī*
Vaman Pandit (seventeenth-century Marathi poet), 66
Vanita, Ruth, 255–256n1, 297n34
vāṅmaya, 32, 54, 262n66
Varkaris, 5, 16–17, 30, 85, 153, 178, 192, 195, 200, 202, 208, 212, 255n1, 260n47, 286n17, 286n18, 292n1, 293n2
vavī. *See ovī*
Vedas, 2, 53, 74, 78, 81, 129, 142, 146, 174, 217, 256n3, 261n58, 283n66
Velankar, H. D., 136, 178–179, 283n60, 299n62
verbal art, 79, 98
verna (Latin: household slave), 10–11
vernacular: aesthetics/poetics, 11, 17, 30, 34–35, 94–95, 132, 141–145, 202, 299n64; audience, 175, 176, 203, 218, 219, 221, 225, 230, 233, 261n58; and *bhakti,* 33, 35, 188, 242–243; and the Bijapur sultanate, 93, 191; Black American, 11, 59, 257n21; and colloquial turn, 33–35, 96–120, 132; as concealment, 188; cosmopolitan vs., 20, 52, 92, 96, 98–100; definitions of, 10–11, 91; European, 181, 204–206, 210–211, 274n41, 277n76, 295n16, 294n9, 294n11, 294n13, 295n16, 296n26; and the everyday, 76, 93–95, 98–100, 175; as language of the household, 11, 86, 106; literarity/

vernacular (*continued*)
literature, 91–92, 95–98, 116–120, 175–176, 201–205; Marathi, 17, 25, 30, 97, 99, 103, 138, 200–207, 211, 219, 234, 240–243, 291n85; orality and, 90, 91–94, 138, 175; in other regional languages, 25, 91–92, 119, 201; revolution, 91, 234; era, 90–91, 103, 200, 211; and Sanskrit, 98–100, 271n7; spaces, 93, 99, 101, 191; and women, 86, 98, 102, 106, 120, 176
vernacular turn: in America, 59; in Europe, 205; Marathi, 30, 34, 120, 206, 211, 240, 243
vernacularity, 91, 105, 116–117, 205–206, 258–259n21, 299n64
vernacularization: colloquialization and, 34, 94–96, 97–98, 103, 107, 119, 137, 142, 210, 274n41; definitions and paradigms of, 91–103, 175, 258n29, 258n29, 273n19; in Europe, 204–206, 210–211, 294n9, 294n11, 294n13; and the everyday, 175–176; and familiarization, 98; Kannada, 91–92, 105–106, 205, 234; Marathi, 31, 90–98, 100, 103–107, 116–120, 211, 219, 234, 242; oral poetics in, 90–94, 211, 223; scribal communities and, 191–192, 234; and women (*See* women, and vernacularization)
Viswanatha, Vanamala, 302n99
Vitthal, 85–86, 111, 153, 161, 167–168, 172, 174, 188–191, 206, 229–230, 246, 252–253; *abhaṅga* (*See abhaṅga,* and Vitthal); *bhakti* (*See bhakti,* and Vitthal); and Chakradhar, 195, 212–216; and Janabai (*See* Janabai, and Vitthal); as a mother, 185; and Rukmini, 13, 84–85, 252–253; temple in Pandharpur, 7
vovi/ī. *See ovī*
vṛtta (quantitative-syllabic class of meters). *See akṣaragaṇavṛtta*
Vṛttadarpaṇa (Godbole), 132–133, 178, 280, 280n36

Warder, A. K., 264n11
weaving: and women, 130, 279–280n24; as metaphor for writing and composition, 17, 32–34, 56, 68, 70, 74, 78, 82, 84, 91, 96, 106, 119, 129–131, 137, 143–150, 154, 184, 186, 188, 221, 223, 237, 243, 248, 250, 279–280n24; etymology of, 34, 130, 279–280n24; and Penelope, 86; as poiesis, 86
Williams, Raymond, 28, 253
"woman's song" (European female-voiced vernacular lyrics), 210–211, 260n44
women: and *abhaṅga,* 166, 208; and *bhakti,* 26, 33, 35, 75, 80, 84, 94, 149, 152–153, 159–160, 163, 193, 205–208, 255n1, 286n18, 292n1, 292n96, 293n2; Brahmin, 14, 22, 53, 200, 206, 207, 214, 270n3; and caste, 13, 20, 22–23, 75, 79, 81, 89, 123, 130, 160, 176–177, 240, 245–246, 261n58, 265n16, 265n21, 283n66, 285n3; Dalit, 9, 19, 74, 22, 124, 159, 165, 172, 250, 285n3; and vernacularization, 94, 102, 106- 107, 200–242, 294n9, 294n11, 294n13, 295n16
"women, *śudras,* and others," 31, 64, 120, 142–144, 151, 155, 176, 199, 218, 243, 261n58
women's songs, 52, 75, 124–125; ambivalence toward/denigration of, 40–41, 122, 188–195; circulation of/in, 25–26, 31, 233; in Europe, 210–211; influence on, 137; injunctions against, 210–211; literary depictions of, 40–44;

Serbo-Croatian and Latvian, 74; on Sita (*See Sītāyan*); and spirituals, 161–163, 164; textual concealment of, 35, 86, 120, 188; tropes, structures and motifs of, 25, 75, 120, 121 147, 151; and weaving, 129; and/in writing/texts, 17, 25, 35–36, 40–42, 75–76, 78, 86–87, 90, 119–120, 155, 183–184, 188, 210–211, 269n79
Woolf, Virginia, 26–27
work songs, 11, 68, 76, 130–131, 165, 176, 247; ancient Greek, 77–78; Black American, 11, 59, 74, 162; women's, 107, 124–125
Yadav, Anand, 39–42, 52, 57, 60–61, 97, 245; mother of, 41, 62, 68–69, 74–75, 77, 80, 82, 97
Yadavas, 92–93, 258n29, 272n16; and Chakradhar, 214–215, 217, 297n39; kings, 297n39; local chieftain, 278–279n12; Mahadev, 214, 217, 297n39; Ramdev, 92; Singhana, 7, 125

Zelliot, Eleanor, 200, 260n47, 288n43, 292–293n1
Zumthor, Paul, 33, 65, 119, 130–131, 179, 182

GPSR Authorized Representative: Easy Access System Europe, Mustamäe tee 50, 10621 Tallinn, Estonia, gpsr.requests@easproject.com

www.ingramcontent.com/pod-product-compliance
Lightning Source LLC
Chambersburg PA
CBHW022028290426
44109CB00014B/793

* 9 7 8 0 2 3 1 2 1 7 9 2 7 *